"Michael Vlach ably defends the view that New Testament writers read the Old Testament contextually. He surveys and critiques various views and then illustrates his own understanding by considering many biblical texts. My conclusions would differ from Vlach's in some respects, but he helpfully charts the landscape of views and charitably sets forth his own."

**Thomas R. Schreiner**
Associate Dean & James Buchanan Harrison Professor of
New Testament Interpretation
The Southern Baptist Theological Seminary

"Evangelical scholarship has had over fifty years of extensive (and at times, heated) discussion over the usage of the Old Testament in the New Testament. However, now with the appearance of Professor Vlach's book, *The Old in the New: Understanding How the New Testament Authors Quoted the Old Testament*, perhaps we have now come to a grand summary of that extensive dialogue. Michael J. Vlach has carefully summarized seven key positions held by various evangelicals (including my own view) and has given a legitimate critique of each view. But more than that, he has also taken up a wide sample of most, if not all, of the passages usually raised on this subject and has given a reasonable solution in Scripture text after Scripture text—in a succinct, but credible manner. I cannot endorse Vlach's work too highly, for I found that he had hit the nail on the head in case after case. In years to come, theological students and pastors will turn to this excellent treatment of this subject and they will find it is exactly what they had been looking for. Thank you, Professor, for carrying out this task so successfully."

**Walter C. Kaiser, Jr.**
President Emeritus
Gordon-Conwell Theological Seminary

# THE OLD IN THE NEW

*Understanding How the New Testament*
*Authors Quoted the Old Testament*

MICHAEL J. VLACH

Cover Design: Danielle Reeves
Interior Design: Anastasia Prinzing

ISBN: 978-1-934952-67-2

Kress Biblical Resources
The Woodlands, TX
www.kressbiblical.com

The Master's Seminary Press
13248 Roscoe Blvd.
Sun Valley, CA 91352
www.tms.edu

Printed in the United States of America

*To the students at The Master's Seminary*
*who took the class, "New Testament Use of the Old Testament."*

*Much in this book is the result of our study together.*

# CONTENTS

# PART THREE
## Case Studies

# PREFACE

The idea for this book began with a paper I presented at the 2011 Annual Meeting of the Evangelical Theological Society in San Francisco. My paper surveyed the major views concerning how the New Testament (hereafter "NT") quotes and uses the Old Testament (hereafter "OT"). The interest stemming from this presentation encouraged me to pursue further how the NT uses the OT. I also regularly teach a NT use of the OT seminar for Master of Theology students at The Master's Seminary. Presenting and examining my findings while interacting with the research of others in an academic context has been a rewarding and sharpening endeavor.

How the NT uses the OT is an essential, yet often overlooked topic. About ten percent of the NT consists of quotations and allusions to the OT. But if you were to ask a group of Christians to articulate their view as to how the NT uses the OT, you would likely receive blank or puzzled stares. Most simply have not considered this issue. In my four decades as a Christian, I cannot recall a single sermon or message devoted specifically to the NT writers' use of the OT and how this shapes our understanding of the Bible. My experience probably is not unique. This lack of attention is not intentional or nefarious. After all, this topic is complex and challenging. Good scholars often disagree on this issue. Concerning the discussion about this topic, Walter Kaiser rightly observed, "This whole debate has been no small tempest in a teapot."[1] Hopefully, this book can contribute to a richer understanding of the NT's use of the OT.

This topic and its implications are important. If the NT writers quoted the OT in accord with the meanings of the OT texts, this would reveal significant continuity

---

[1] Walter C. Kaiser, Jr., "Single Meaning, Unified Referents," in *Three Views on the New Testament Use of the Old Testament*, eds. Kenneth Berding and Jonathan Lunde (Grand Rapids: Zondervan, 2007), 45.

between the OT and the NT. However, if the NT writers often quoted the OT non-contextually, then major discontinuity likely exists. Perhaps the Bible's storyline has been transcended or reinterpreted. Thus, comprehending how the NT quotes and alludes to the OT is important for grasping the Bible's storyline and message.

*Based on an inductive study of the biblical evidence, this book will argue that the NT uses the OT in an overwhelmingly contextual manner. The NT is not reinterpreting or transforming the texts or overall message of the OT.*

An accurate understanding of this topic must ultimately begin with an inductive study of the many quotations of the OT in the NT, both individually and collectively. We should not come to this study with a predetermined theory of how the NT uses the OT and then manipulate the Bible into that theory. Nor should we pick out only a few examples and then adopt a theory based simply on these. All the evidence must be considered. To develop a view I could enthusiastically grasp, I sought to study all quotations of the OT in the NT. Of course, such a study must be done with an ear to what scholars past and present have discovered. So in addition to offering my own findings in this book, I also interact with the scholarship of many others.

This is a complex topic, and in no way do I intend to communicate that I have a perfect grasp on every use of the OT in the NT. I also do not expect my readers to agree with everything in this book. But based on my research, I do wish to offer four main contributions. This book:

1. Introduces key terms and statistics concerning NT use of the OT.
2. Presents the seven major views of NT use of the OT, with analysis of each.
3. Reveals the major ways the NT writers used and quoted the OT.
4. Interprets most cases where the NT quotes the OT, including the most difficult examples to understand.

My goal is to pursue these four matters in an understandable and accurate way.

The study of NT use of the OT is not limited to formally trained Bible scholars. Any Christian should be able to interact with this issue. I write this book to all who are interested in this topic. Also, this work covers much ground, examining many views, examples, and issues. Of course, the danger of covering much ground is, at times, depth. I am one person surveying a broad and complicated issue. In any particular case, one likely could find another book or article that addresses that example in more depth. But this book attempts to give a big-picture presentation without becoming bogged down in any one issue or example.

In sum, I hope this book introduces the reader to the main issues involved with NT use of the OT as a basis for better understanding this subject. And most importantly, I hope this book stirs the reader to further personal study on this topic. If this book stimulates greater interest and study in this topic, my efforts will be rewarded.

One final note. I want to thank all students at The Master's Seminary who took "BI829: New Testament Use of the Old Testament." I also want to thank Yadid Del Rey and Trey Meester for their help with reviewing initial drafts of this book.

Mike Vlach
Good Friday
April 10, 2020

# INTRODUCTION

The use of the Old Testament (hereafter "OT") in the New Testament (hereafter "NT") is a vast topic. So where should we begin? We begin with an explanation of key concepts related to how the NT writers and persons quoted and used the OT. Below are strategic definitions and statistics.

## Quotations

There are approximately 350 quotations of the OT in the NT.[1] But what is a quotation in this context? G. K. Beale explains: "A quotation is a direct citation of an OT passage that is easily recognizable by its clear and unique verbal parallelism."[2] In other words, *a quotation is an obvious direct citation of the wording of an OT verse or passage by a NT person or author*. This does not always mean a verbatim, word-for-word citation, but the wording is so similar that an obvious reliance on an OT passage is evident. Most of this book will be devoted to cases where a clear quotation exists.

Why say "approximately 350 quotations"? Isn't there an exact number? There is no undisputed, exact number of OT quotations upon which everyone agrees. In my research, I found one source that listed 266 quotations, while another noted 278. Roger Nicole counted at least 295 unquestionable references to the OT in the NT. He observed that these occupy 352 verses in the NT, or 4.4 percent of the entire NT. If

---

[1] Louis M. Sweet found approximately three hundred direct citations. "Quotations: New Testament," in *International Standard Bible Encyclopedia*, 5 vols. (Grand Rapids: Eerdmans, 1939), 4:1516.

[2] G. K. Beale, *Handbook on the New Testament Use of the Old Testament* (Grand Rapids: Baker, 2012), 29.

correct, this means one out of every twenty-two-and-a-half verses in the NT is a quotation of the OT.[3] The fourth edition of the UBS Greek New Testament (1993) lists 343 direct quotations. I personally identified approximately 350 quotations. If pushed for specificity, I estimate 355 to 360, which is higher than most scholars would agree. Most agree that there are approximately 300 to 360 quotations of the OT in the NT.

Offering an exact number of quotations is difficult because it can be challenging to differentiate between a quotation and an allusion. The issue may be determined by how one differentiates quotations from allusions. Yet, in my opinion, determining the exact number of quotations and allusions is not critical for understanding this issue.

It is interesting also to consider how often individual books of the OT are quoted in the NT. The numbers below are my estimates after my research and consultation of other works, but these numbers too may vary.

The most quoted OT book in the NT is Psalms (seventy-nine times). This is followed by Isaiah (seventy), Deuteronomy (fifty-one), Genesis (forty-six), and Exodus (thirty-nine).[4] A big drop in usage occurs after these five books. Altogether, at least twenty-six OT books are quoted in the NT. The most cited OT verse is Psalm 110:1: "The LORD says to my Lord, 'Sit at my right hand until I make your enemies a footstool for your feet'" (eight times). OT books that do not appear to be directly quoted in the NT are Joshua, Judges, 2 Kings, 1 and 2 Chronicles, Ezra, Nehemiah, Esther, Ecclesiastes, Song of Solomon, Lamentations, Obadiah, and Zephaniah.[5] While not directly quoted, some scholars believe these books are alluded to in the NT. When allusions are included, the number of OT books represented in the NT grows.

At least nineteen of the twenty-seven NT books explicitly quote the OT. The only NT books that might not explicitly quote the OT are Colossians; Philemon; Titus;[6] 1, 2, 3 John; and Jude. Even then, the OT is alluded to in several of these books. Some claim Revelation has no OT quotations, but a quotation might exist in Revelation 2:26–27 (Ps. 2:9) and perhaps Revelation 1:7 (Dan. 7:13 and Zech. 12:10). Revelation does, however, contain many allusions to the OT.

The NT books with the highest number of OT quotations are Romans (sixty-six) and Matthew (sixty-five). Since these two are so close in OT usage, it is difficult to declare either the clear frontrunner in OT quotations cited. Other NT books with a high number of OT quotations include Acts (forty-three), Hebrews (thirty-eight),

---

[3] Roger Nicole, "New Testament Use of the Old Testament," in *Rightly Divided: Readings in Biblical Hermeneutics*, ed. Roy B. Zuck (Grand Rapids: Kregel, 1996), 183.

[4] This is according to my own count.

[5] Ruth is often viewed as an OT book not quoted in the NT, but Ruth 4:18–22 is heavily alluded to, if not quoted, in the genealogy of Matthew 1:3–6.

[6] Some have noted similar wording between Psalm 130:8 and Titus 2:14b, but this does not appear to be a quotation.

Mark (thirty-one), Luke (twenty-seven), 1 Corinthians (seventeen), John (sixteen), 1 Peter (thirteen),[7] 2 Corinthians (eleven), and Galatians (eleven).[8] Significantly, in his explanation concerning Israelites and Gentiles in Romans 9–11, Paul quoted the OT thirty-two times. The largest use of the OT in a single passage is found in Romans 3:10–18 where Paul quoted a cluster of verses from Psalms and Isaiah to establish the sinfulness of humanity. The largest quotation of one specific passage is found in Hebrews 8:8–12, where the author cites the New covenant passage of Jeremiah 31:31–34.

Sometimes, quotations are preceded by an introductory formula. For example:

"It is written" (Mark 7:6)
"Is it not written" (Mark 11:17)
"Haven't you read this Scripture" (Mark 12:10)
"This is what the prophet has written" (Matt. 2:5)
"To fulfill what was said" (Matt. 4:14)
"For Moses said" (Mark 7:10)
"For David himself says in the book of Psalms" (Luke 20:42)
"It is written in the prophets" (John 6:45)
"The word that is written in their Law" (John 15:25)
"The Holy Spirit rightly spoke through Isaiah the prophet to your fathers, saying" (Acts 28:25b–26a)
"But what does the Scripture say?" (Gal. 4:30)

# Allusions

In addition to quotations, there are "allusions" to the OT in the NT. Compared to quotations, allusions are shorter and more indirect, but the cluster of words used are recognizably linked with an OT text. Beale offers a definition of allusion:

An "allusion" may simply be defined as a brief expression consciously intended by an author to be dependent on an OT passage. In contrast to a quotation of the OT, which is a direct reference, allusions are indirect references (the OT wording is not reproduced directly as in a quotation).[9]

---

[7] For its size, 1 Peter is second only to Matthew and Romans for its density of OT quotations. See Steve Moyise, *The Old Testament in the New* (London and New York, 2001), 109.

[8] One source that comes close to these numbers in this list is Felix Just, S.J., "Quotations from the Old Testament in the New Testament," http://catholic-resources.org/Bible/Quotations-NT-OT.htm. Updated February 19, 2014. (accessed February 16, 2019).

[9] G. K. Beale, *Handbook on the New Testament Use of the Old Testament* (Grand Rapids: Baker, 2012), 31.

Beale also notes, "The telltale key to discerning an allusion is that of recognizing an *incomparable or unique parallel in wording, syntax, concept, or cluster of motifs in the same order or structure.*"[10]

If quotations are difficult to quantify, allusions are even more challenging. Some lists count anywhere from 400 to 4,100 allusions. The book of Revelation is particularly interesting since it has few to no quotations of the OT, yet it possesses over three hundred allusions to the OT. Ironically, this book with few to no quotations could be the NT book most saturated with the OT.

Likewise, Jude has no quotations of the OT, but there are several clear allusions to OT events such as Israel's exodus from Egypt (v. 5), angels who disobeyed in the time of Noah (v. 6), the immorality at Sodom and Gomorrah (v. 7), the death of Moses (v. 9), Cain's sin (v. 11), Korah's rebellion (v. 11), Enoch (vv. 14–15), and Adam (v. 14). Thus, while not having any direct OT quotations, Jude is filled with OT content.

Sometimes it is difficult to determine whether a quotation or allusion occurs. For example, Peter refers to "new heavens and a new earth," and John says he saw "a new heaven and a new earth" (2 Pet. 3:13; Rev. 21:1). Both Isaiah 65:17 and 66:22 predict a coming "new heavens" and "new earth." So are Peter and John quoting or alluding to these verses in Isaiah? It is hard to say, although the latter is more likely. I do not believe much is at stake concerning whether the examples should be explicitly identified as quotations or allusions.

While the exact number of allusions is difficult to pinpoint, the existence of allusions along with quotations reveals a large presence of the OT in the NT. Nicole observes, "It can therefore be asserted, without exaggeration, that more than 10 percent of the New Testament text is made up of citations or direct allusions to the Old Testament."[11] On average, for every ten verses in the NT, one is reliant on OT wording.

# Similar Wording Without a Quotation or Allusion

Are there times where OT wording is used in the NT without the occurrence of an intentional quotation or allusion? If so, this could relate to the concept of "echoes" in which "an allusion is so slight that conscious intention is unlikely."[12] Since the NT writers and persons were saturated with the OT, it is possible, at times, that they used OT language naturally without intending to formally quote or allude to a specific OT text. Just as an English-speaker might naturally use wording from English literature or popular culture without making an intentional connection with those sources, it is possible that NT writers, deeply immersed in the Hebrew Scriptures, sometimes used

---

[10] Beale, ibid. Emphasis in original.

[11] Nicole, "New Testament Use of the Old Testament," 183.

[12] Steve Moyise, *The Old Testament in the New: An Introduction* (New York: Continuum, 2001), 6.

OT language naturally without making a deep theological connection. As Roger Nicole observes, "It was quite natural that people nurtured and steeped in the oracles of God should instinctively use forms of language and turns of thought reminiscent of Old Testament Scripture."[13]

For example, in Psalm 22:21 David stated, "Save me from the lion's mouth." Yet in 2 Timothy 4:17, Paul said, "But the Lord stood with me…I was rescued out of the lion's mouth." Was Paul quoting or alluding to Psalm 22:21 to make a strategic connection here? Perhaps, but more likely Paul was simply using similar wording to Psalm 22:21. In Psalm 6:8, David offered a psalm of prayer during distress when he said, "Depart from me, all you who do iniquity, for the LORD has heard the voice of my weeping." But in a judgment context Jesus said, "DEPART FROM ME, ALL YOU EVILDOERS" (Luke 13:27). Jesus' wording is very similar to Psalm 6:8, but He does not appear to be quoting that verse. Another possible example is Peter's statement in 1 Peter 3:14 concerning avoiding fear—"AND DO NOT FEAR THEIR INTIMIDATION, AND DO NOT BE TROUBLED." The wording is similar to Isaiah 8:12, but it does not appear to be a direct quotation or allusion to this verse.

Thus, it is possible that the NT writers and persons sometimes alluded to OT language without making a conscious connection. Whether this means there is a third category of OT usage called "echoes" is a debate for another time.[14] But it is possible that similar wording from the OT has been used without an intentional quotation or allusion. Since this book is mostly about OT quotations in the NT, we will not focus on echoes.

# OT Quotations in the NT Are Not Always Exact

The NT writers did not always quote the OT exactly.[15] This might seem surprising or alarming to modern readers who are used to quotations being cited verbatim with documentation. But for the NT writers, alterations in wording were acceptable as long as the general idea of an OT passage was maintained.

One such alteration involves *substituting a pronoun for a noun*. For example, Isaiah 40:3 tells of making smooth a highway for "God," but Matthew 3:3 substitutes "His" for God: "MAKE HIS PATHS STRAIGHT!" Isaiah 54:13 refers to "all your sons" being taught by God, but John 6:45 substitutes "all your sons" with "they": "AND THEY SHALL ALL BE TAUGHT OF GOD."

---

[13] Nicole, "New Testament Use of the Old Testament," 192.

[14] Moyise says, "Some regard 'echoes' as too tenuous and would prefer the more neutral term, 'literary parallels.'" *The Old Testament in the New*, 6.

[15] This section acknowledges the categories and examples of Roy B. Zuck in *Basic Bible Interpretation: A Practical Guide to Discovering Biblical Truth* (Colorado Springs, CO: Victor Books, 1991), 254–59.

Sometimes, however, NT authors do just the opposite: *sometimes a pronoun in the OT is replaced with a specific noun*. Psalm 118:26a says, "Blessed is the *one* who comes in the name of the LORD" (emphasis mine). But Luke 19:38a states, "BLESSED IS THE KING WHO COMES IN THE NAME OF THE LORD." A change from "one" to "King" occurs. Then there are times when a NT writer *changes a pronoun*. Zechariah 12:10 says, "They will look on *Me*…" (emphasis mine). But John 19:37 says, "THEY SHALL LOOK ON HIM WHOM THEY PIERCED." John substitutes "Him" for "Me."

There are also times when *a singular noun is replaced by a plural noun*. For example, Psalm 78:2a states, "I will open my mouth in a *parable*" (emphasis mine). But Matthew 13:35a says, "I WILL OPEN MY MOUTH IN *PARABLES*" (emphasis mine). Using the potter-clay analogy, Isaiah 29:16 states, "*He* did not make me" (emphasis mine), while Romans 9:20 says, "Why did *you* make me like this?" (emphasis mine). Paul uses "you" instead of "He." Also notice that Isaiah makes his statement in the indicative, while Paul puts it in the form of a question.

Sometimes *a general reference is made more specific*. Amos referred to "the star of your gods" (Amos 5:26), while Stephen makes this more specific: "THE STAR OF THE GOD ROMPHA" (Acts 7:43). The *extent of a reference can be changed* as well. Amos 5:27 refers to an "exile beyond Damascus," but Stephen says "beyond Babylon" (Acts 7:43).

At times, a NT author will combine words from two different OT authors but only cite one, usually the more prominent writer. In Mark 1:2–3, both Malachi 3:1 and Isaiah 40:3 are quoted, but Mark only mentions Isaiah:

As it is written in Isaiah the prophet:
"BEHOLD, I SEND MY MESSENGER AHEAD OF YOU,
WHO WILL PREPARE YOUR WAY (Mal. 3:1)

THE VOICE OF ONE CRYING IN THE WILDERNESS,
'MAKE READY THE WAY OF THE LORD,
MAKE HIS PATHS STRAIGHT.'" (Isa. 40:3)

Sometimes a paraphrase of an OT section takes place. Psalm 78:2b says: "I will utter dark sayings of old." But Matthew 13:35b states, "I WILL UTTER THINGS HIDDEN SINCE THE FOUNDATION OF THE WORLD."

Also, the *order of material can be altered*. Jesus quoted five of the ten commandments in Luke 18:20, but this order differs from the original list found in Exodus 20:12–16. Also, the NT writers can use synonyms for OT words. The term "highway" in Isaiah 40:3 is changed to "paths" in Matthew 3:3. Psalm 40:6 uses "ear" while Hebrews 10:5 uses "body."

# Sources for OT Quotations

The OT was primarily written in Hebrew, while the NT was written in Greek. The NT writers often quoted the Septuagint (or LXX)—that is, the Greek translation of the OT. At times, NT authors quoted the Hebrew text. But over half of Paul's quotations agree entirely or mostly with the LXX (Septuagint). Gloer notes, "Of Paul's 93 quotes, 51 are in absolute or virtual agreement with the LXX, while only 4 agree with the Hebrew text."[16] Gloer also observes, "This means that 38 diverge from all known Greek or Hebrew OT texts."[17]

At times, the NT writers might quote the OT from memory or use a version of the OT not known to us. On two occasions, a NT writer quoted a non-canonical book or source. Jude quoted from 1 Enoch in Jude 14 and 15. Paul referred to non-canonical material with his reference to Jannes and Jambres in 2 Timothy 3:8. Paul quoted pagan poets in Acts 17:28: "for in Him we live and move and exist, as even some of your own poets have said, 'For we also are His children.'"

With these introductory definitions and statistics in mind, we now shift to a survey of the various scholarly views of NT use of the OT. If we are going to adopt a view of NT use of the OT, it is helpful to know what options exist so we can consider and weigh their merits. So we turn now to present and examine the seven major approaches to NT use of the OT.

---

[16] Hulitt Gloer, "Old Testament Quotations in the New Testament," in *Holman Illustrated Bible Dictionary*, ed. Chad Brand, Charles Draper, and Archie England (Nashville, TN: Holman Bible Publishers, 2003), 1217.

[17] Ibid.

# PART ONE

## SEVEN VIEWS OF
## NEW TESTAMENT USE OF THE
## OLD TESTAMENT

# CHAPTER ONE

# HISTORY OF THE STUDY OF THE VARIOUS VIEWS

How have Christians throughout history dealt with this issue of NT use of the OT? Several articles and books have addressed this issue. Yet the complexity of this topic and the wide range of solutions to the problem have led to some frustration and confusion. The task is formidable, and there is no consensus on the proper approach. In the last few decades, some works have summarized the differing views on NT use of the OT. These have allowed students to compare the differing approaches in a side-by-side manner.

With this chapter, I highlight seven major approaches to how the NT uses the OT, and I have included key adherents of each view. The following chapters in this section then provide an explanation for each view, and I also point out some potential problems for each position. I then offer a chapter on "test cases" where I compare the various views in their understandings of certain biblical passages.

In 1985, Darrell Bock offered a helpful two-part article, "Evangelicals and the Use of the Old Testament in the New," in the journal, *Bibliotheca Sacra*.[1] Here, Bock categorized four approaches concerning NT use of the OT along with main representatives of each approach:

1. Full Human Intent School (Walter C. Kaiser, Jr.)
2. Divine Intent—Human Words School (S. Lewis Johnson, J. I. Packer, Elliott Johnson)

---

[1] Darrell L. Bock, "Part 1: Evangelicals and the Use of the Old Testament in the New," *Bibliotheca Sacra* 142, no. 567 (July 1985): 209–20; "Part 2: Evangelicals and the Use of the Old Testament in the New," *Bibliotheca Sacra* 142, no. 568 (October 1985): 306–16.

3.   Historical Progress of Revelation and Jewish Hermeneutic School (Earl Ellis, Richard Longenecker, Walter Dunnett)
4.   Canonical Approach and New Testament Priority School (Bruce Waltke)

In 1986, Douglas Moo examined issues such as Jewish exegetical methods, *sensus plenior*, and the canonical approach in his article, "The Problem of Sensus Plenior."[2] With his 2002 book, *Evangelical Hermeneutics: The New Versus the Old*,[3] Robert Thomas compared differing views on NT use of the OT while also offering his own approach called Inspired *Sensus Plenior* Application. Here he documented how his view differed from other evangelical options. In 2008, editors Kenneth Berding and Jonathan Lunde contributed to this topic via the Zondervan Counterpoint Series with their book, *Three Views on the New Testament Use of the Old Testament*.[4] This informative work presented three differing perspectives with accompanying representatives of each view:

1.   **Single Meaning, Unified Referents:** Accurate and Authoritative Citations of the Old Testament by the New Testament (Walter C. Kaiser, Jr.)
2.   **Single Meaning, Multiple Contexts and Referents:** The New Testament's Legitimate, Accurate, and Multifaceted Use of the Old (Darrell L. Bock)
3.   **Fuller Meaning, Single Goal:** A Christotelic Approach to the New Testament Use of the Old in Its First-Century Interpretive Environment (Peter Enns)[5]

This book marked the first time differing positions on NT use of the OT were placed next to each other with scholars presenting and defending their views in the same work. In the attempt to keep an 'apples to apples' comparison, the editors asked the three main contributors—Kaiser, Bock, and Enns—to address five key issues surrounding the NT use of the OT debate:

1.   The legitimacy of *sensus plenior*.
2.   How typology is best understood.
3.   Do NT writers take into account the context of the OT passages they cite?
4.   The significance of Jewish exegetical methods for explaining NT use of the OT.
5.   Whether we can replicate the exegetical and hermeneutical approaches of the NT writers.[6]

---

[2] Douglas J. Moo, "The Problem of Sensus Plenior," in *Hermeneutics, Authority, and Canon*, ed. D. A. Carson and John D. Woodbridge (Grand Rapids: Zondervan, 1986), 179–211.

[3] Robert L. Thomas, "The New Testament Use of the Old Testament," in *Evangelical Hermeneutics: The New Versus the Old* (Grand Rapids: Kregel, 2002), 241–69.

[4] Kenneth Berding and Jonathan Lunde, eds. *Three Views on the New Testament Use of the Old Testament* (Grand Rapids: Zondervan, 2007).

[5] This book did not directly address two schools discussed by Bock—the *sensus plenior* and the canonical approaches. These concepts were certainly treated but they were not discussed as their own categories.

[6] Jonathan Lunde, "Introduction," in *Three Views on the New Testament Use of the Old Testament*, 12.

In 2009, Rynold Dean published, *Evangelical Hermeneutics and the New Testament Use of the Old Testament*.[7] Dean interacted with the four approaches mentioned in Bock's 1985 articles and Robert Thomas's Inspired Sensus Plenior Application view. Dean then offered his own critique of each.

While not a summary of the differing approaches, editors G. K. Beale and D. A. Carson presented a comprehensive commentary on NT uses of the OT with their book, *Commentary on the New Testament Use of the Old Testament*.[8] This large and substantial work, with many contributors, offered specific attention to most quotations of and allusions to the OT in the NT. It avoided promoting a specific methodology or theory. But it did offer the most detailed treatment of OT uses in the NT to date. Beale later published his *Handbook on the New Testament Use of the Old Testament: Exegesis and Interpretation* in 2012.[9] This work addressed several topics related to NT use of the OT and included Beale's thoughtful approach and theory to understanding this issue.

In 2018, Abner Chou published, *The Hermeneutics of the Biblical Writers: Learning to Interpret Scripture from the Prophets and Apostles*. Focusing on intertextual connections in Scripture, Chou argued that the NT writers used the OT in a contextual manner. As the sources above show, the last few decades, and the last fifteen years in particular, have brought several summaries and discussions on the various approaches to understanding NT use of the OT.

# Approaches to NT Use of the OT

What follows is a listing of the various Christian approaches to understanding NT use of the OT. These will be explained more specifically in the following chapters. These seven views are:

1. Single Meaning—Multiple Implications (or Consistent Contextual Use of the OT by the NT Writers Approach)
2. Human Meaning Plus Hidden Divine Meaning (or *Sensus Plenior* Approach)
3. Contemporary Judaism/Second Temple Judaism (or NT Writers Used Jewish Interpretive Principles of the Day Approach)

---

[7] Rynold D. Dean, *Evangelical Hermeneutics and the New Testament Use of the Old Testament* (Iron River, WI: Veritypath Publications, 2009).

[8] G. K. Beale and D. A. Carson, eds. *Commentary on the New Testament Use of the Old Testament* (Grand Rapids: Baker, 2007).

[9] Published by Baker Academic.

4. Canonical Interpretation (or Broader Canon as Basis for Understanding the OT Approach)
5. Inspired *Sensus Plenior* Application (or Inspired Subjectivity Approach)
6. Historical-Exegetical and Theological-Canonical (or Eclectic Approach)
7. **7.** New Testament Reinterpretation of the Old Testament (or NT Priority Over the OT Approach)

# CHAPTER TWO

# SINGLE MEANING / MULTIPLE IMPLICATIONS

## (OR "CONSISTENT CONTEXTUAL USE OF THE OT BY THE NT WRITERS" APPROACH)

The "single meaning/multiple implications" or "consistent contextual" view asserts that the NT writers quoted the OT contextually in the vast majority of cases. There is no broad pattern of non-contextual or non-literal uses of the OT in the NT.

According to this approach, each OT passage has a single meaning, which is the human author's meaning under inspiration of the Holy Spirit. And when a NT writer quotes an OT text, he does so contextually—in accord with the intended meaning of the OT author. This could take place through explaining the *meaning* of an OT passage or offering an *implication* consistent with the meaning.

First, the NT author could explain the OT author's *meaning* by explicating what the OT author meant by what the OT author wrote. Or second, the NT author could give an *implication* of a text. This implication could be a significance or application of an OT text, perhaps applying or drawing upon a moral principle or theological truth. Yet if implication occurs, the implication is consistent with the spirit of the OT author's meaning. The implication is not entirely disconnected from what the OT author meant. With this perspective, the NT writer respected the original meaning of the OT writer and did not use the OT text or passage out of context.

According to this view, contextual uses of the OT are so common and dominant we can rightly concur that contextual use of the OT is the norm. If there are non-contextual uses of the OT, these are rare and do not overturn the reality that the NT writers overwhelmingly used the OT contextually.

The chief scholarly representative and defender of this view has been Walter C. Kaiser.[1] His views are found in the book, *The Uses of the Old Testament in the New*, published in 1985.[2] In the more recent book, *Three Views on the New Testament Use of the Old Testament*, Kaiser's view is identified as "Single Meaning, Unified Referents." Abner Chou also fits into the contextual-use camp. His book, *The Hermeneutics of the Biblical Writers*, argues for a contextual interpretation of the OT by the NT writers. I (Michael Vlach) also consider myself an advocate of the single-meaning/multiple implications perspective. Let us now examine the components of this position in greater detail.

# Single Meaning

The belief that a text only has one meaning is foundational for the single-meaning/multiple implications view. Kaiser mentions the strong influence of Bishop J. C. Ryle (1818–1900) on him concerning the belief that there is only one sense for a Scripture passage. Ryle declared:

> I hold it to be a most dangerous mode of interpreting Scripture, to regard everything which its words may be tortured into meaning, as a lawful interpretation of the words. I hold undoubtedly that there is a mighty depth in all Scripture, and that in this respect it stands alone. But I also hold that the words of Scripture were intended to have one definite sense, and that our first object should be to discover that sense, and adhere rigidly to it. I believe that, as a general rule, the words of Scripture are intended to have, like all other language, one plain, definite meaning, and that to say that words do mean a thing, merely because they can be tortured into meaning it, is a most dishonorable and dangerous way of handling Scripture.[3]

In affirmation of Ryle's quote, Kaiser states, "I could not agree more heartily; for this has become the standard by which I not only interpret the text as a biblical teacher,

---

[1] "The most notable champion of the single intent or meaning of biblical texts is Walter C. Kaiser. He has written not only to defend the position, but also to show that it works in practice." Paul D. Feinberg, "Hermeneutics of Discontinuity," in *Continuity and Discontinuity: Perspectives on the Relationship Between the Old and New Testaments*, ed. John S. Feinberg (Wheaton, IL: Crossway, 1988), 115. I am not saying Kaiser would say everything exactly like I just have in this chapter.

[2] Walter C. Kaiser, *The Uses of the Old Testament in the New* (Chicago: Moody Press, 1985).

[3] J. C. Ryle, *Expository Thoughts on the Gospels* (Grand Rapids: Zondervan, 1953), 2:383.

but it is the same view I urgently press other evangelicals to adopt."[4] This quote was the basis for Kaiser's defense of the single meaning position in the *Three Views* book.

In sum, the "contextual use" view believes the meaning of any passage of Scripture is one—not several or many. This view also holds that there are no hidden meanings in passages.

# OT Authors Understood What They Wrote

Also important to the single-meaning/multiple implications view is the belief that the OT authors consciously understood what they wrote. Commenting on this view, Darrell Bock explains:

> The basic premise of this school is that if hermeneutics is to have validity then all that is asserted in the Old Testament passage must have been a part of the human author's intended meaning. Thus the Old Testament prophets are portrayed as having a fairly comprehensive understanding of what it is they are declaring about the ultimate consummation of God's promise.[5]

This belief that the OT authors understood what they wrote applies to meaning, but it does not mean the authors always grasped all the *implications, applications,* and *significances* of their texts. While meaning is singular—implications, applications, and significances can be multiple. For example, when David wrote Psalm 2 he meant that one day a coming Davidic King would rule over the nations. But David likely did not envision that the Messiah would use this psalm as a source of motivation for the church at Thyatira in the 90s AD (see Rev. 2:26–27; Ps. 2:9). While David did not foresee this application of his psalm to the church, Jesus used Psalm 2:9 in a way consistent with David's meaning. Jesus' followers will share in Messiah's reign as foretold in Psalm 2.

Likewise, when an OT author wrote about moral commands and theological truths, he did not foresee how the NT authors would apply these to their audiences. For example, Moses commanded the children of Israel to obey their parents, and then Paul applied this principle to his readers in the church in Ephesians 6:1–3. Moses did not foresee this application, but it was consistent with what Moses meant.

---

[4] Kaiser, "Single Meaning, Unified Referents," in *Three Views on the New Testament Use of the Old Testament*, 46.

[5] Bock, "Part 1: Evangelicals and the Use of the Old Testament in the New," 210–11. Bock himself does not hold to this view that he is commenting on.

Also, affirming that the OT authors understood what they wrote does not mean the OT authors always knew the specific *referents* of their prophecies or the *timing* of fulfillment. This is Peter's point when he stated that the OT prophets "made careful searches and inquiries, seeking to know what person or time the Spirit of Christ within them was indicating as He predicted the sufferings of Christ and the glories to follow" (1 Pet. 1:10–11). According to Peter, the prophets understood what they wrote. They wrote of a coming Messiah, knowing that He would suffer and then enter glory. But the OT prophets did not know *who* the Messiah would be or *when* the events concerning His suffering and glory would occur.

Likewise, predictions of a coming antichrist in the prophets (see Dan. 9:27; 11:36–45) do not mean the prophets comprehended the specific identity of this person or when he would arrive. Even today, we do not know those matters. In short, the OT prophets knowingly predicted the coming of specific persons along with details concerning them. But they did not always know the identities of the people they wrote about or the timing of fulfillment.

# NT Authors Quoted the OT Contextually

A third belief of the single-meaning/contextual perspective is that the NT writers overwhelmingly used the OT contextually. A connecting link exists between OT meaning and NT use of that OT passage. But seeing a connection often means recognizing certain biblical concepts such as (1) previous theology, (2) the concept of "the one and the many," (3) a specific messianic hope, and (4) typological connections. All of these can be grasped through the use of consistent grammatical-historical hermeneutics. If one grasps the presence of these concepts, then many of the alleged non-contextual uses of the OT will be shown to be contextual after all.

First, a contextual view recognizes *informing* or *previous* theology in which NT writers rely not only on the meaning of specific OT verses quoted, but also upon the theology and ideas associated with these verses, i.e. the surrounding context. When a NT writer quoted an OT verse, he sometimes assumed and carried over the theology from that OT passage. For example, when Paul mentioned "seed" in Galatians 3, a biblical theology of "seed" from Genesis preceded his statement. Paul brought over the individual and corporate senses of "seed" found in Genesis (see Gen. 3:15; 22:17–18) as he discussed Jesus' connection to seed (Gal. 3:16) and all believers to seed (Gal. 3:29). Thus, understanding the contexts of OT passages quoted in the NT is important for understanding how NT writers used OT passages.

Second, this view accounts for the concept of "the one and the many," in which a leader or head represents a group. This is linked with the idea of corporate headship. Not only is this found with the "seed" concept mentioned above, but it is also true of Jesus and Israel. Israel is a corporate entity ("many") in the OT, but Jesus is the ultimate individual Servant of Israel ("one") in Isaiah 49:1–6 who restores national Israel and blesses the Gentiles. This "one and the many" connection is found in Matthew 2:15 where Matthew links corporate Israel's coming out of Egypt at the time of the exodus with Jesus' coming out of Egypt after fleeing Herod's persecution (see Hos. 11:1). Matthew links Jesus ("the one"), the corporate head of Israel, with corporate Israel ("the many") to show that Jesus is Israel's Savior.

Third, this perspective affirms a specific messianic hope in which OT saints expected a coming Deliverer who would bring salvation and remove the curse (see Gen. 4:1; 5:28–29; Acts 3:21–22). Jesus is the coming "Shiloh" to whom will be the obedience of the peoples (see Gen. 49:8–12). Psalms 2 and 110 reveal an explicit messianic expectation and demonstrate that David himself wrote about the coming Messiah. So when Peter says David was a "prophet" who foresaw the resurrection of the Messiah, we know that David actually predicted events concerning the Messiah (see Acts 2:25–31; cf. Ps. 16:8–11). When NT passages connect Jesus with OT verses, this often reveals a literal fulfillment of messianic expectation in the OT.

Fourth, the contextual perspective also acknowledges the presence of typology in which OT persons, events, and institutions correspond to greater NT persons, events, and institutions. Hebrews 7–10, for example, highlights that the Mosaic covenant with its priesthood and sacrifices was a "shadow" (Heb. 10:1) of Jesus' New covenant with its superior priesthood and sacrifice. The presence of typology, however, does not mean the NT reinterprets or transcends the OT.[6] Instead, the presence of types can be discovered by grammatical-historical hermeneutics.

Adherents of the contextual view realize that not all NT uses of the OT will immediately make sense to twenty-first century readers. There are time and culture gaps between first-century writers and modern readers that must be considered. But these gaps can be overcome with proper study. The writers of the Bible understood the intertextual connections between passages and the deep theology behind them. Readers from different eras and cultures might not grasp all of these connections at first glance, so a superficial evaluation might lead to the conclusion that the NT writers quoted the OT out of context. But this is not correct. As Chou asserts, "In fact, the problem is not that the apostles had a revolutionary interpretative approach but rather our lack of understanding of the Old Testament."[7] When the OT and its informing theology are taken into account, and intertextual connections are considered, it will become evident that the NT writers were using the OT contextually.

---

[6] Beale says, "Typology by nature does not necessitate a non-contextual approach." G. K. Beale, *Handbook on the New Testament Use of the Old Testament: Exegesis and Interpretation* (Grand Rapids: Baker, 2012), 23.

[7] Abner Chou, "A Hermeneutical Evaluation of the Christocentric Hermeneutic," *The Master's Seminary Journal* 27, no. 2 (Fall 2016): 131.

# Meaning and Significance

As mentioned earlier, the concepts of *meaning* and *significance* are important for understanding how the NT writers and persons quoted and used the OT. These two ideas are different but related.[8] *Meaning* refers to the specific intended idea of an author expressed in a text. It is single and linked with an author's intent. But "significance," as Chou explains, "denotes the various valid repercussions...or implications stemming from the author's meaning."[9] Significance involves the *consequences* of a text's meaning and "the ramifications of a text's meaning on our lives today or its bearing on a theological topic."[10] Significance, therefore, involves the sum total of all the various consequences of an author's meaning.[11] Succinctly, Paul Feinberg states, "'Meaning' has to do with the interpretation of a text, while 'significance' is concerned with its application."[12] While meaning is one, there can be several or multiple implications. These two ideas are compatible.

Single meaning advocates often point to E. D. Hirsch's distinctions between meaning and significance in his book, *Validity in Interpretation*. Hirsch writes, "Meaning is that which is represented by a text; it is what the author meant by his use of a particular sign sequence; it is what the signs represent."[13] But, "Significance, on the other hand, names a relationship between that meaning and a person, or a conception, or a situation, or indeed anything imaginable."[14]

Robert Stein links significance with a "willed pattern of meaning" in which the *implications* of a text are consistent with the *meaning* of an author.[15] According to Stein, "Implications are those meanings in a text of which the author was unaware but nevertheless legitimately fall within the pattern of meaning he willed."[16] These implications are related to the spirit of what the author meant and seem to be a natural extension of the author's meaning.

Put together, this view asserts that an OT author had a specific, conscious meaning in what he wrote. But he might not foresee all the implications and

---

[8] Some English dictionaries view "meaning" and "significance" as synonymous terms or use one to describe the other. Our view, though, is that there is a real difference. They are related but different concepts.

[9] Abner Chou, *The Hermeneutics of the Biblical Writers* (Grand Rapids: Kregel, 2018), 32.

[10] Ibid.

[11] Chou, "A Hermeneutical Evaluation of the Christocentric Hermeneutic," 114.

[12] Paul D. Feinberg, "Hermeneutics of Discontinuity," in *Continuity and Discontinuity: Perspectives on the Relationship Between the Old and New Testaments*, ed. John S. Feinberg (Wheaton, IL: Crossway, 1988), 113–14.

[13] E. D. Hirsch, *Validity in Interpretation* (Yale University Press, 1967), 8.

[14] Ibid.

[15] Robert H. Stein, *A Basic Guide to Interpreting the Bible* (Grand Rapids: Baker Academic, 1994), 39–44. I am not claiming Stein is an open advocate of the single meaning approach explained in this chapter.

[16] Ibid., 39.

applications of his text as they relate to later audiences, including those in the NT era. Yet, these ramifications are consistent with what he meant. Significance, although different from meaning, operates on the same plane as meaning. In fact, an author's meaning establishes the parameters of significance. While the OT author does not see all the applications or significances that a NT writer might make, these applications are consistent with what the OT author meant. They are tied to the intent of the author.

For example, scriptural commands to avoid being drunk with wine could also apply to being under the influence of other alcoholic beverages, narcotics, or drugs taken intravenously, even if the biblical author did not consider these other examples.[17] To use another example, imagine a father who tells his oldest son, "Take care of the house and your brother and sister while your mother and I are at a movie." The father's meaning is that the son should take care of both the house and his younger siblings. If an hour later the son detects an intruder in the backyard and the son calls the police, this would be an application of the father's meaning. The father did not say anything concerning an intruder or calling the police, but the son's action was entirely consistent with the father's meaning. The son took care of the house and kids by calling the police when an intruder arrived. The father would probably affirm that the son acted consistently with his meaning, although he had neither thought nor said anything about calling the police. The son acted in accord with the spirit of the father's meaning. On the other hand, if, upon detecting the intruder, the son left the house to go bowling because the father had said nothing about calling the police, that would not be consistent with the father's meaning. In that case, the son would probably get an earful from his father.

But how do meaning and significance relate to how the NT writers and persons quoted the OT? According to the contextual perspective, they relate in that *quotations of the OT in the NT do not always explain the meaning of an OT passage. Sometimes a NT writer is drawing significance from an OT text.* Thus, the reader must take into account both meaning and significance in order to discern the connection that is being made. For example, in Acts 2:25–33 Peter says that when David wrote Psalm 16:8–11, David foresaw the resurrection of the Messiah. Thus, Peter is telling us the meaning of Psalm 16: David foresaw the resurrection of the Messiah. But when Matthew connects the Babylonian captivity of Jerusalem to the slaughter of infants at the time of Jesus' birth (Matt. 2:16–18/Jer. 31:15), Matthew is not explaining the meaning of Jeremiah 31:15, he is offering significance. Matthew certainly knew that the deportation of young men to Ramah with the Babylonian Captivity was not the murder of infants in Bethlehem centuries later, but these events correspond to

---

[17] Stein, *Interpreting the Bible*, 39–40.

each other. Matthew reveals significance here. A tragic event in Israel's history corresponds to another tragic event in the days of Jesus the Messiah. Both Jeremiah 31 and Matthew 2 speak of tragedy for Israel in the context of hope, and that is the significance to be grasped.

Addressing the difference between meaning and significance, Chou cites Jesus' use of Exodus 3:6 in Luke 20:37 as support that there will be a resurrection to the Sadducees who did not believe in resurrection. In Exodus 3:6, God declared to Moses that He was the God of Abraham, Isaac, and Jacob to show Moses who He was. Some have questioned why Jesus would use Exodus 3:6 in Luke 20:37 since Exodus 3:6 is not discussing resurrection. Chou, however, asserts that in this passage, "Jesus deals with significance and not meaning."[18] Yes, Exodus 3:6 is not primarily about resurrection, but implications for resurrection do exist. With the background theology of Genesis, the fact that God is the God of Abraham, Isaac, and Jacob means more than identity; it also involves God's covenant faithfulness to His promises. And these promises involve the patriarchs. Since the patriarchs did not see the fulfillment of the covenant promises, they must be resurrected to experience them. As Chou states, "for God to keep his promises to them requires a resurrection. If there is no resurrection, then God's covenant faithfulness is nullified."[19] Thus, Jesus used Exodus 3:6 "to prove those who deny the resurrection, deny God's faithfulness to his covenant."[20] So while Jesus did not explain the meaning of Exodus 3:6 in Luke 20, He offered significance from this text consistent with the meaning of Exodus 3:6.

In sum, adherents of a contextual approach believe the NT writers quoted the OT both for meaning and significance. Context will determine which is being emphasized. *Not every quotation of the OT in the NT is intended to give the meaning of an OT passage. Sometimes significance is offered.*[21] Error occurs when we assume that every use of the OT concerns meaning. Meaning and significance must be considered and distinguished, or wrong conclusions can arise. Contextual advocate, Walter Kaiser, refers favorably to E. D. Hirsch's work, *Validity in Interpretation* (1967) to support this point. Kaiser says, "Hirsch's distinction between the unchangeable *meaning* of the original audience and the various applications of this meaning's *significance* is important."[22]

---

[18] Chou, *The Hermeneutics of the Biblical Writers*, 41.

[19] Ibid., 42–43.

[20] Ibid., 43.

[21] Kevin DeYoung states, "The NT may press home the *significance* of a passage without trying to explain its original *meaning*." "Can That Be Right? The Use of Old Testament Prophecy in the New Testament," https://www.thegospelcoalition.org/blogs/kevin-deyoung/new-testaments-use-of-old-testament-prophesy/ December 8, 2015. Accessed December 18, 2018. I am not claiming that DeYoung identifies with the position discussed in this chapter.

[22] Kaiser, "Single Meaning, Unified Referents," 52.

# Human and Divine Authors

Similar to other views, those who hold to a contextual view acknowledge the dual authorship of Scripture—human and divine. But unlike some other views, contextual advocates deny that dual authorship demands embedded or hidden/fuller divine meanings beyond what the human OT authors intended in their texts. Dual authorship does not necessarily mean a separation or gap between human meaning and divine meaning.[23] Instead, the inspired human meaning in a text exactly represented what God wanted conveyed at that time. So there is no *sensus plenior* (i.e. "fuller meaning") that goes beyond the human intent. What the human author intended is what God intended to communicate at the time.

There is no need to postulate divine meaning beyond human meaning because what God intended to communicate can be found in the inspired human author's intent. To argue for fuller or hidden divine meanings can add unneeded subjectivity to the interpretive process, since now we must account for meanings that go beyond what an author intended in his text. More will be said on this in the chapter addressing *sensus plenior*.

Adherents of a consistent contextual view believe that when God wanted to give more information, He did so with later inspired Scripture that harmonized with earlier revelation. He did not have to embed fuller or hidden meanings in passages to be discovered later. Progress of revelation makes the need for hidden meaning unnecessary.

Also, the fact that God perfectly knows all implications and significances of an OT passage does not mean the OT passages have hidden or multiple meanings. This is so because meaning and significance are different. The contextual view claims that authors understood their meanings, not that they understood all the implications and significances of their writings. To compare:

**OT authors** understood the meaning of what they wrote, but not all the implications and significances.

**God** understands the meaning of what the OT authors wrote *and* all the implications and significances.

The next paragraph will discuss criticisms of this single-meaning/multiple implications view, but some critics have noted that this perspective has been helpful. Concerning Kaiser's single meaning view, Douglas Moo says, "Once sufficient account is taken of this theological context, and the New Testament context is similarly understood in all its theological richness, apparent discrepancies between the

---

[23] This view acknowledges that God also knew all further applications and significances of these passages.

meaning of an Old Testament text and the meaning given that text in the New Testament disappear."[24] Commenting on one potential benefit of this outlook, Kenneth Berding declares, "It is the approach that most directly satisfies the inclination of many readers that there *should* be a direct connection between a 'prophecy' and its 'fulfillment.'"[25]

# Questions and Criticisms of the
# Single Meaning / Multiple Implications Approach

Not all are convinced by the "single meaning/multiple implications" view. Some say this approach works in many cases but falls short at times and does not account for all NT uses of the OT. Bock states, "This view has too many hurdles to climb to be the most likely solution to the use of the OT in the NT."[26] Moo also says, "While remaining extremely sympathetic to Kaiser's general approach, and, in fact, strongly supporting much of what he says, I am not convinced that his approach offers an ultimately satisfactory answer to all the problems raised by the use of the Old Testament in the New."[27] Commenting on criticism of Kaiser's approach, Paul Feinberg notes, "It has been argued that his view does not take adequate account of the divine authorial intent, and that his position does not accord with the practice of apostolic exegesis in the NT."[28] Thus, some believe this contextual view does not deliver on what it promises and fails to adequately explain all uses of the OT in the NT.

Another criticism of the single-meaning approach is that it has the OT authors understanding more than what is likely. In his criticism of Kaiser, Berding points out that "interpreters may find themselves presuming upon the conscious intention of an OT author ideas that cannot readily be shown from the immediate context to be in his mind."[29]

Still another criticism is that this approach ignores the first-century Jewish hermeneutical milieu in which *pesher* and *midrash* approaches were common. No one is denying that the NT authors used contextual understandings of the OT, but

---

[24] Douglas J. Moo, "The Problem of Sensus Plenior," in *Hermeneutics, Authority, and Canon*, ed. D. A. Carson and John D. Woodbridge (Grand Rapids: Zondervan, 1986), 199.

[25] Berding, "Conclusion," in *Three Views*, 241.

[26] Bock, "Response to Kaiser," in *Three Views*, 95. Bock is responding to Kaiser's "Single Meaning, Unified Referents" view.

[27] Moo, "The Problem of Sensus Plenior," 201.

[28] Feinberg, "Hermeneutics of Discontinuity," 115.

[29] Berding, "Conclusion," in *Three Views*, 241–42.

allegedly there are several cases where this is not the case, and the contextual approach struggles to fit these non-contextual uses into a contextual mold.

In recent years an emotional argument also has been introduced against those like Kaiser who do not affirm a *sensus plenior* approach. Allegedly, those who argue for a grammatical-historical hermeneutic that does not utilize *sensus plenior* have been charged with missing Christ in Scripture or preaching a bare moralism that misses Christ and the gospel.[30] Also, sometimes this approach is seen as contrary to the doctrine of inspiration and as being more in line with Rationalism and Deism. These charges are false. Believing in a consistent grammatical-hermeneutic and being skeptical of *sensus plenior* is consistent with a robust belief in the inspiration of Scripture and a high view of Christ in Scripture. Adherents of this view believe all writers of Scripture were inspired by the Holy Spirit. Belief that the Bible writers understood what God inspired them to write in their texts is entirely consistent with the doctrine of inspiration and Christian orthodoxy. Also, adherents of this view are often strong and clear in emphasizing a messianic hope in the Old Testament and the centrality of Jesus' person and work in God's plans. Whether this approach is best must be evaluated on its merits, but the idea of it being sub-Christian should be rejected.

As mentioned earlier, the single-meaning/multiple implications view is the one we adopt in this book. Yet we must explain the other views, and that is where we now turn. The other positions that will be examined argue that there are many non-contextual uses of the OT.

---

[30] See David E. Prince, "The Danger of Preaching Biblical Truth but Missing Christ," https://equip.sbts.edu/article/danger-preaching-biblical-truth-yet-missing-christ/; November 6, 2018. Accessed June 3, 2020.

# CHAPTER THREE

# HUMAN MEANING PLUS FULLER DIVINE MEANING

## (OR *SENSUS PLENIOR* APPROACH)

Proponents of the "human meaning plus fuller divine meaning" position hold that there are two levels of meaning in some OT passages. First, there is the *human authorial intent*. This involves what the human OT author consciously understood. But since Scripture is a divine book as well, there also is a God-intended *fuller and/or hidden meaning* that goes beyond what the human Bible author intended or knew. As Paul Feinberg notes about this view, "The human authors at times spoke better than they knew."[1] So there is a divine hidden, fuller meaning beyond or in addition to what the human author understood. This introduces the issue of *sensus plenior*. The Latin phrase *sensus plenior* means "fuller meaning" or "fuller sense." Raymond Brown offered the classic definition of *sensus plenior*:

> That additional, deeper meaning, intended by God but not clearly intended by the human author, which is seen to exist in the words of a biblical text (or group of texts, or even a whole book) when they are studied in the light of further revelation or development in the understanding of revelation.[2]

Brown also contrasts the literal meaning the human author understood and God's meaning to be discovered later:

---

[1] Feinberg, "Hermeneutics of Discontinuity," 113. Feinberg is not an advocate of *sensus plenior*.

[2] Raymond E. Brown, *The Sensus Plenior of Sacred Scripture* (Baltimore: St. Mary's University, 1955), 92.

The literal sense answers the question of what this text meant according to its author's intention as that author was inspired to compose it in his particular stage in the history of God's plan of salvation. The SP [*sensus plenior*] answers the question of what the text means in the whole context of God's plan, a meaning which God, who knew the whole plan from the start, intended from the moment He inspired the composition of the text.[3]

Graeme Goldsworthy, in his support of *sensus plenior*, gives a succinct definition of the concept:

The *sensus plenior* of an OT text, or indeed of the whole OT, cannot be found by exegesis of the texts themselves. Exegesis aims at understanding what was intended by the author, the *sensus literalis*. But there is a deeper meaning in the mind of the divine author which emerges in further revelation, usually the NT.[4]

Klein, Blomberg, and Hubbard support a hidden meaning view: "Along with the literal sense intended by the human author, the Holy Spirit may encode a hidden meaning not known or devised at all by the human author."[5] Moo and Naselli link *sensus plenior* with "a meaning that traditional grammatical-historical exegesis cannot demonstrate."[6]

As these authors argue, because the Bible is both a human and divine book, at times it seems likely that God intended deeper and fuller meanings in a text that were not comprehended by the original biblical writer. These hidden, fuller meanings are discovered "in the light of further revelation or development in the understanding of revelation."[7] It is often NT revelation that allows the student to unearth these hidden, fuller meanings that already existed in the OT passages. In some OT passages therefore, human meaning + divine meaning = full meaning of an OT passage. But the NT is needed to grasp the full meaning. It was not known to the original writer and readers of the OT passage.

Adherents of a classic *sensus plenior* view do not deny that many OT passages can be understood contextually. They are not claiming *sensus plenior* exists everywhere in the OT. Nor do they deny the importance of human authorial intent in a text discovered

---

[3] Raymond E. Brown, "The *Sensus Plenior* in the Last Ten Years," *Catholic Biblical Quarterly*, vol. 25 (July 1963): 278.

[4] Graeme Goldsworthy, "The Relationship of the Old Testament and New Testament," in *New Dictionary of Biblical Theology*, ed. T. Desmond Alexander, et al. (Downers Grove, IL: InterVarsity Press, 2000), 88.

[5] William W. Klein, Craig L. Blomberg, and Robert L. Hubbard, Jr., *Introduction to Biblical Interpretation* (Nashville, TN: Thomas Nelson, 1993), 178.

[6] Douglas J. Moo and Andrew David Naselli, "The Problem of the New Testament's Use of the Old Testament," in *The Enduring Authority of the Christian Scriptures*, ed. D. A. Carson (Grand Rapids: Eerdmans, 2016), 731.

[7] Brown, *The Sensus Plenior of Sacred Scripture*, 92.

through grammatical-historical hermeneutics. In fact, some see the human intent as the anchor of meaning. Nor do they see God's hidden meaning as contradicting the human meaning. As J. I. Packer stated:

> The point here is that the *sensus plenior* which texts acquire in their wider biblical context remains an extrapolation on the grammatico-historical plane, not a new projection on to the plane of allegory. And, though God may have more to say to us from each text than its human writer had in mind, God's meaning is never less than his. What he means, God means.[8]

Packer uses "extrapolation" which means to infer an unknown from something that is known. Since Packer ties *sensus plenior* with "the grammatico-historical plane," he believes hidden meaning is related to the contextual meaning of an OT passage. The meaning is not based on "the plane of allegory." Also important is Packer's mention that God could intend more than what the human author meant, but "God's meaning is never less than [the human author's meaning]." For Packer, this excludes the idea that later NT revelation reinterprets or transcends previous revelation in the OT.

Paul Feinberg noted that two passages are sometimes used as support for the *sensus plenior* view: 1 Peter 1:10–12 and Daniel 12:6–9.[9] With the former, Peter says the OT prophets did not know the person or time involved with their prophecies. With the latter, Daniel is told about events to come but then says, "As for me, I heard but could not understand" (v. 8). So Daniel admits he had revelation he could not understand.

# Questions and Criticisms of the *Sensus Plenior* Approach

Many embrace the *sensus plenior* idea or approach because it appears to explain how the NT writers can appeal to the OT in ways that seem to go beyond the OT authors' intentions. It also seems logical that if the Bible is a confluence of human and divine authorship, that there could be divine meanings beyond human meanings. The Chicago Statement on Biblical Hermeneutics affirms the possibility of a *sensus plenior* idea in which the meaning of a writer's words is not restricted to his own understanding: "The single meaning of a prophet's words includes, but is not

---

[8] J. I. Packer, "Biblical Authority, Hermeneutics, and Inerrancy," in *Jerusalem and Athens: Critical Discussions on the Philosophy and Apologetics of Cornelius Van Til*, ed. E. R. Geehan (Nutley, N.J.: Presbyterian and Reformed, 1977), 147–48.

[9] Feinberg, *Continuity and Discontinuity*, 113.

restricted to, the understanding of those words by the prophet and necessarily involves the intention of God evidenced in the fulfillment of those words" (Article XVIII).

Yet several criticisms of the *sensus plenior* approach have been voiced. First, Paul Feinberg challenges the idea that God's involvement in a text must mean there are hidden meanings:

All of this [*sensus plenior*] has an initial attraction, rooted as it seems in our piety. However, in the end I think that it must be rejected. God has committed his will and truth to a written text, and what is true for the human authors' intentions will be true for God's. If, as has been argued, human authors are able to express their intentions in a text, why should we not expect similar things to be true of God?[10]

Second, some have argued that if a deeper and fuller meaning behind OT texts exists, this relegates the human OT authors to a secondary level, or perhaps, as Kaiser argues, "a nuisance for getting at the really deep things of God."[11]

A third objection is that these alleged "deeper meanings" are not really Scripture. Bruce Vawter stated, "If, as in scholastic definitions, Scripture is the *conscriptio* [writing together] of God and man, does not the acceptance of a *sensus plenior* deprive this alleged scriptural sense of one of its essential elements, to the extent that logically it cannot be called scriptural at all?"[12] Adding to this point, Kaiser asks, "If the deeper meaning was one that was not located in the words, sentences, and paragraphs of the text, then it was not 'Scripture,' which in the Greek is called *graphe*, 'writing' (i.e. that which stands written in the text)!"[13]

A fourth problem concerns the original OT writers and audiences. Were they deprived of the true meaning of the messages addressed to them? Were they deprived of the "deeper" meanings? Did they possess a lesser revelation? The original audiences seem to be stepping stones to the fuller meanings that come centuries later. But is that fair to the original readers? Promises to an audience contain an ethical expectation that these promises will be fulfilled with that audience.

A fifth objection is the charge of *eisegesis*—reading backwards from the NT to the OT and giving new meanings to the OT that are not discoverable by exegesis.[14]

A sixth objection is that *sensus plenior* removes apologetic value from the Bible. How could early Christians defend the unity of the testaments if the alleged connections between the two appeared arbitrary and contrived by the NT writers? Didn't Paul say, "I stand to this day testifying both to small and great, stating nothing

---

[10] Feinberg, "Hermeneutics of Discontinuity," 117.

[11] Kaiser, "Single Meaning, Unified Referents," in *Three Views on the New Testament Use of the Old Testament*, 49.

[12] Bruce Vawter, *Biblical Inspiration* (Theological Resources; Philadelphia: Westminster, 1972), 115.

[13] Kaiser, "Single Meaning, Unified Referents," 49.

[14] Ibid., 51.

but what the Prophets and Moses said was going to take place" (Acts 26:22)? Paul says he was explaining the OT at face value, not offering hidden meanings.

A seventh concern involves the close connection between *sensus plenior* and Roman Catholic hermeneutics. Jonathan Lunde observes, "Protestants often respond negatively to the concept [of *sensus plenior*] because of their perception of its use by Catholic theologians to develop doctrines that go beyond the bounds of scripturally intended meanings."[15] Kaiser notes that Roman Catholics "can fall back on the magisterium of the church, to the ecclesial tradition," but "to what can Protestants appeal that matches such additional grounds of appeal?"[16] Perhaps one response to Kaiser would be that the authority is the NT which reveals the *sensus plenior* meaning.

A final criticism is that the case for *sensus plenior* meanings has not been adequately proven. Specific cases are lacking in which the *sensus plenior* idea seems best or probable. The claim that 1 Peter 1:10–12 affirms *sensus plenior* is not persuasive. The fact that the OT prophets did not know the identity of the Messiah or the timing of the fulfillment of prophetic matters does not mean the OT writers were ignorant about what they wrote. They knew *what* they wrote, but they were trying to figure out *who* the Messiah was and *when* fulfillment would happen. This text actually affirms OT prophets knew what they wrote.

Daniel 12:6–9 also is not support for *sensus plenior*. Daniel received many complex prophetic details in symbols which covered future events. Since the majority of prophecies concerned the distant future, it is understandable why Daniel did not understand some things. Perhaps Daniel's lack of understanding related to what Peter referred to—the identity of referents and the timing of these prophecies. Or perhaps it concerned how all these many details tied together. But to make a case for hidden meanings in OT passages from Daniel seems dubious.

# Is Galatians 4:21–31 an Example?

Does *sensus plenior* exist with Paul's use of allegory wording in Galatians 4:21–31? Here Paul appeals to the Genesis account concerning Sarah/Isaac and Hagar/Ishmael to make a point about the superiority of the Abrahamic covenant over the Mosaic covenant. The contrast between these covenants does not seem natural in Genesis since Sarah/Isaac and Hagar/Ishmael predate the Mosaic covenant by several

---

[15] Jonathan Lunde, "Introduction," in *Three Views*, 16.

[16] Kaiser, "Single Meaning, Unified Referents," 48.

hundred years. But in introducing this contrast Paul states, "Tell me, you who want to be under law, do you not listen to the law?"

Paul tells his readers to "listen to the law," yet the law's account of Sarah/Isaac and Hagar/Ishmael does not seem to support Paul's point. In addition, Paul says the Genesis account "is allegorically speaking" (Gal. 4:24). Significantly, Paul is not saying he is speaking or interpreting allegorically. Instead, the Genesis account "is allegorically speaking," thus pointing to the text. So is Paul appealing to a hidden meaning in Genesis? Is there a *sensus plenior* meaning here? While I do not advocate *sensus plenior*, I realize that a reasonable person might conclude so from this example. I think Paul is using the Sarah/Isaac and Hagar/Ishmael example as an illustration to support a theological point previously stated. More will be said on this example in a later chapter.

# CHAPTER FOUR

# SECOND TEMPLE JUDAISM

## (OR "NT WRITERS USED JEWISH INTERPRETIVE PRINCIPLES OF THEIR DAY" APPROACH)

Another approach to understanding NT use of the OT involves the hermeneutics of Second Temple Judaism (ca. 515 BC–AD 70). Allegedly, the Jews of the second temple period often used non-contextual methods of interpretation such as *midrash*, *pesher*, and allegory. And since Jesus and the NT writers lived in this era, their hermeneutics probably resembled the hermeneutical assumptions common in that period. As Richard Longenecker stated, "The Jewish roots of Christianity make it *a priori* likely that the exegetical procedures of the New Testament would resemble, at least to some extent, those of Judaism of the time."[1] Peter Enns argues, "The interpretive methods of Christ and the NT writers were quite at home in the Second Temple world."[2]

For some, this hermeneutical influence should be embraced, not resisted. Addressing the issue of Jewish interpretation, G. K. Beale noted, "One widely held position is that Jesus and the writers of the NT used non-contextual hermeneutical

---

[1] Richard N. Longenecker, *Biblical Exegesis in the Apostolic Period* (Grand Rapids: Eerdmans, 1975, 1999), 186. For a helpful summary and discussion of the views of both Richard N. Longenecker and Peter Enns, see Rynold D. Dean, *Evangelical Hermeneutics and The New Testament Use of the Old Testament* (Iron River, WI: Veritypath Publications, 2009), 67–85.

[2] Peter Enns, "Apostolic Hermeneutics and an Evangelical Doctrine of Scripture: Moving Beyond a Modernist Impasse," *Westminster Theological Journal* 65/2 (Fall 2003): 270.

methods that caused them to miss the original meaning of the OT texts that they were trying to interpret."[3]

With the "Second Temple Judaism" perspective, much attention is given to the historical environment of the second temple period in order to understand the interpretive approaches of the NT persons and writers. While not disregarding grammatical-historical hermeneutics altogether, adherents of a contemporary Judaism approach claim that the NT persons were not driven by grammatical-historical hermeneutics because the hermeneutical environment of their day was not. Thus, modern students should try to understand the OT like they did, which means accepting non-contextual uses of the OT. The apostles were not operating according to Enlightenment/Modern Era standards of interpretation that often obsess over grammatical-historical hermeneutics for understanding meaning. They were not driven by faithfulness to literal hermeneutics like modern Christians expect, instead, they often relied upon the interpretive methods of their day.

Peter Enns says a study of NT writers "shows that the NT authors' engagement of their Scripture was not directed by grammatical-historical principles." Thus, "there is often a 'disconnect' between what an OT passage means in its context and how it is employed by NT writers."[4] Enns' use of "disconnect" emphasizes belief in non-contextual uses of the OT by NT persons.

In addition to operating in their cultural context, it is claimed that the NT writers also wrote according to their belief that Jesus of Nazareth brought a dramatic and climactic fulfillment of God's plans. Jesus changes everything. So the NT writers interpreted the relationship between the testaments in light of the coming of Jesus and used Jesus to read meaning back into the OT. Thus, all that came before Christ must be interpreted with a Christotelic lens in which Christ is the goal of the OT. NT writers could use the *pesher* approach of "this is that" to apply OT words to a NT setting, regardless of the context of the OT message.

According to Enns, a unique "apostolic hermeneutic" was the merger between the apostles' "cultural moment" and "eschatological moment." The "cultural moment" is the interpretive traditions of Second Temple Judaism. The "eschatological moment" involves "their belief that Jesus of Nazareth was God with us and that he had been raised from the dead."[5] Or to put it another way: the cultural context of Second Temple hermeneutics + eschatological fulfillment in Jesus = the apostles' hermeneutic.

What does this mean for modern students of the Bible trying to understand how the NT persons used the OT? The Bible student must grasp that the NT writers were

---

[3] G. K. Beale, *Handbook on the New Testament Use of the Old Testament* (Grand Rapids: Baker, 2012), 291. Beale himself does not adopt this approach.

[4] Peter Enns, "Fuller Meaning, Single Goal," in *Three Views on the New Testament Use of the Old Testament*, eds. Kenneth Berding and Jonathan Lunde (Grand Rapids: Zondervan, 2007), 174.

[5] Enns, "Apostolic Hermeneutics," 275. See also Dean, 71.

not bound by modern conceptions of how the OT should be used. Instead, they used the OT to support their understanding that Jesus the Messiah was the fulfillment of the OT. If this involves non-contextual uses of the OT, so be it. Strict faithfulness to the literal meaning of the OT was not their concern, and we should not force literal meanings upon their writings. Modern interpreters often miss what the NT writers were doing because they expect the NT authors to operate according to the same interpretive principles that moderns use. Moderns expect precise connections with quotations, but the NT authors did not think like that. Enns believes this presents a serious problem:

> A problem arises, however, when we observe how the Apostles handled the OT. Despite protestations to the contrary, grammatical-historical hermeneutics does not account for the New Testament's use of the Old. However self-evident grammatical historical hermeneutics may be to us, and whatever very important contributions it has made and continues to make to the field of biblical studies, it must be stated clearly that the Apostles did not seem overly concerned to put this principle into practice.[6]

Alleged examples where a grammatical-historical hermeneutic alone is insufficient include Matthew's use of Hosea 11:1 in Matthew 2:15; Paul's use of Isaiah 49:8 in 2 Corinthians 6:2; Paul's universal sense of "seed" in Galatians 3:29; and Paul's use of Psalm 69:9 in Romans 15:1–4.[7]

The contemporary Judaism approach is not mutually exclusive to the idea of *sensus plenior*, although it emphasizes Second Temple hermeneutics as the main reason for non-contextual uses of the OT. Longenecker says, "In actual fact, there appear to be numerous cases of *sensus plenior* in the New Testament—that is, of instances where Scripture is cited in a manner that goes beyond a literal sense, or beyond what can be determined by the rules of historical-critical exegesis to have been the Old Testament author's message for his time."[8] He also says, "I believe any normal reading of the data supports some type of *sensus plenior* understanding."[9]

---

[6] Enns, "Apostolic Hermeneutics," 268. He also says, "But when the smoke clears, the overall picture remains: apostolic hermeneutics apart from the expenditure of significant mental energy and denial of plain fact, cannot be categorized as being 'essentially' grammatical-historical" (269).

[7] See Enns, "Apostolic Hermeneutics," 276–78.

[8] Longenecker, *Biblical Exegesis in the Apostolic Period*, xxxiii.

[9] Ibid.

# Questions and Criticisms of the Contemporary Judaism Approach

One objection against this view asks why such emphasis is given to the Jewish interpretive practices of the day. Did not Jesus often correct the false understandings of the Jewish religious leaders? Did he not rebuke the Jewish leaders for adding traditions of men to their understanding of the Law?

Second, G. K. Beale has challenged the claim that the NT writers often used the OT non-contextually with midrashic exegesis. He says, "Our starting point is to observe that it is not at all clear that non-contextual midrashic exegesis was as central to earlier Pharisaic and Qumran exegesis as is suggested by scholars."[10] He then offers two reasons:

> First, it may not be appropriate to speak of a non-contextual *rabbinic* method in the pre-A.D. 70 setting, since most examples come from after A.D. 70 and those which can be dated with probability that do not appear to reflect such an atomistic approach. Second, concern for contextual exegesis is found not uncharacteristically both in Qumran and in Jewish apocalyptic.[11]

Concerning his first point, Beale challenges the belief that pre-AD 70 rabbinic methods were non-contextual in nature. He appeals to the work of D. Instone Brewer[12] who identified the exegetical examples of purported pre-AD 70 proto-rabbinic exegesis. According to Beale, Brewer concluded that "while these Jewish exegetes may not have always succeeded, they attempted to interpret the Old Testament according to its context, and they never supplanted the primary meaning by a secondary or allegorical one."[13] This shows "an early concern for context to varying significant degrees which previously has not been sufficiently acknowledged."[14]

If Beale is correct, this "has far-reaching implications for the argument of those who believe that early Christian exegetes were influenced by a prevalent atomistic

---

[10] G. K. Beale, "Did Jesus and His Followers Preach the Right Doctrine from the Wrong Texts? An Examination of the Presuppositions of Jesus' and The Apostles' Exegetical Method," in *The Right Doctrine from the Wrong Texts?: Essays on the Use of the Old Testament in the New*, ed. G. K. Beale (Grand Rapids: Baker, 1994), 388.

[11] Ibid.

[12] D. Instone Brewer, "The Hermeneutical Method of Early Judaism and Paul," [published as *Techniques and Assumptions in Jewish Exegesis before 70 C.E.* (Tübingen: Mohr [Paul Siebeck], 1992.].

[13] Beale, "Right Doctrine," 388, n. 2.

[14] Ibid.

Jewish hermeneutic."[15] In fact, this analysis may put the validity of the contemporary Judaism approach into jeopardy.

Another concern with the contemporary Judaism approach concerns whether the case for non-contextual uses of the OT is overstated. Beale makes this point:

> It is often claimed that an inductive study of the New Testament reveals a predominately non-contextual exegetical method. But, in fact, of all the many Old Testament citations and allusions found in the New Testament, only a very few plausible examples of non-contextual usage have been noted by critics.[16]

Beale lists various examples where non-contextual uses of the OT allegedly occur but then notes, "It is by no means certain that even these examples are actually non-contextual. A number of scholars have offered viable and even persuasive explanations of how they could well be cases of contextual exegesis."[17] He further explains that even if it could be established that there are examples of non-contextual hermeneutics, "it does not necessarily follow that they are truly representative of a wider hermeneutical pattern in the New Testament. They may be exceptional rather than typical."[18] In fact, to claim that the NT writers used the OT in mostly non-contextual ways is "a substantial overstatement."[19] Douglas Moo appears to agree when he writes:

> We should recognize that the degree of influence of Jewish exegetical methods on New Testament procedure has often been considerably exaggerated. A vast gulf separates the often fantastic, purely verbal exegeses of the rabbis from the generally sober and clearly contextually oriented interpretations found in the New Testament.[20]

Who is right on this issue of non-contextual uses of the OT by NT persons is debated and subject to case-by-case studies. But the claim of contemporary Judaism adherents that non-contextual uses of the OT are many and undeniable is seriously challenged by other scholars. Scholars like Kaiser and Beale have asserted that when the OT contexts are properly understood, the "clear" cases of non-contextual uses of the OT are not so "clear" anymore. In fact, good explanations from a contextual

---

[15] Beale, "Right Doctrine," 388.

[16] Ibid., 388–89.

[17] Ibid., 389.

[18] Ibid.

[19] Ibid., 398.

[20] Douglas J. Moo, "The Problem of Sensus Plenior," in *Hermeneutics, Authority, and Canon*, eds. D. A. Carson and John D. Woodbridge (Grand Rapids: Zondervan, 1986), 193.

approach exist. Paul Feinberg observes that solid exegesis removes the need for the Second Temple hypothesis: "If one is careful in the exegesis of the prediction and its fulfillment, paying particular attention to antecedent Scripture and theology, *pesher* and *pesher midrash*, or any similar hermeneutical approach will not be needed."[21]

Still another criticism concerns apologetics and the early defense of the Christian faith against unbelieving Jews. Paul and the early Christians were involved in debates with unbelieving Jews concerning Jesus being the resurrected Messiah who is now at the right hand of God. In doing so, they often appealed to OT passages as support for this conviction. What value would there be if the early Christians adopted non-literal understandings of OT passages as they interacted with their Jewish opponents? How would this convince their Jewish audiences, who certainly would scoff at the apostles for tinkering with OT passages? As Kaiser writes, "One would be hard-pressed to find any apologetic value in appealing to such procedures as *midrash, pesher*, allegory, or the like to validate the claims of what was regarded as an intrusion of an outside force."[22] In his defense before Agrippa concerning accusations from the Jews (Acts 26:2), Paul argued that he was only stating what the OT prophets had predicted:

> So, having obtained help from God, I stand to this day testifying both to small and great, *stating nothing but what the Prophets and Moses said was going to take place*; that the Christ was to suffer, and that by reason of His resurrection from the dead He would be the first to proclaim light both to the Jewish people and to the Gentiles. (Acts 26:22–23, emphasis mine)

Paul said he relied upon the straight-forward meaning of the OT passages.

This author is not convinced of the Second Temple Judaism view for the reasons stated above. Plus, the case for many non-contextual uses of the OT has not been proven. As this book will attempt to demonstrate, contextual advocates have offered adequate, even convincing explanations for the passages that Second Temple Judaism advocates claim as support for their view. This includes the examples of Matthew 2:15/Hosea 11:1 and Galatians 3:29, which are discussed later in this book.

---

[21] Paul D. Feinberg, "Hermeneutics of Discontinuity," in *Continuity and Discontinuity: Perspectives on the Relationship Between the Old and New Testaments*, ed. John S. Feinberg (Wheaton, IL: Crossway, 1988), 116.

[22] Walter C. Kaiser, *The Uses of the Old Testament in the New* (Chicago: Moody, 1985), 14.

# CHAPTER FIVE

# CANONICAL INTERPRETATION

## (OR "BROADER CANON AS BASIS FOR UNDERSTANDING THE OT" APPROACH)

One popular approach to understanding NT use of the OT is "canonical interpretation." This position asserts that the broader canon of the Bible should be the starting point and lens for understanding earlier parts of Scripture, particularly the OT. Thus, when it comes to understanding the OT, the completed canon and the clearer revelation of the NT is the place to start. The meanings of OT texts allegedly become deeper and clearer as the parameters of the biblical canon expand. With this view, OT texts undergo a progressive perception of meaning as they are examined from the finished canon of Scripture. This occurs because God is the divine author behind all Scripture. As Douglas Moo comments when defining this view, "Any specific biblical text can legitimately be interpreted in light of its ultimate literary context—the whole canon, which receives its unity from the single divine author of the whole."[1] Bruce Waltke also states, "The Christian doctrine of the plenary inspiration of Scripture demands that we allow the Author to tell us at a later time more precisely what he meant in his earlier statements."[2]

For Waltke, the canonical approach is linked with the concept of NT priority in interpretation in which the NT unpacks and explains the meaning of the OT. The classical rule, "the New interprets the Old—should be accepted by all Christian

---

[1] Douglas J. Moo, "The Problem of Sensus Plenior," 205.

[2] Bruce K. Waltke, "Is It Right to Read the New Testament into the Old?," *Christianity Today* (September 2, 1983), 77.

theologians."[3] This perspective emphasizes the meaning of Scripture as a whole and the *analogia fidei*—that is, the "analogy of faith"—in which Scripture interprets Scripture.

Does this approach affirm *sensus plenior* or the reinterpretation of the OT? Waltke says it does not:

> This approach is similar to *sensus plenior* in that both methods depend on further revelation to find the full meaning of an earlier text. But the distinction from it lies in this: whereas the supposed *sensus plenior* depends exclusively on further revelation and may allow a reinterpretation of the prophecy, the canonical process approach combines further revelation with the sharpening focus of history itself and disallows the possibility of reinterpretation.[4]

In a similar way, Moo further explains that the canonical approach is not about "hidden meaning":

> Appeal is made not to a meaning of the divine author that somehow is deliberately concealed from the human author in the process of inspiration—a "*sensus occultus*"—but to the meaning of the text itself that takes on deeper significance as God's plan unfolds—a "*sensus praegnans*." To be sure, God knows, as He inspires the human authors to write, what the ultimate meaning of their words will be; but it is not as if He has deliberately created a *double entendre* or hidden meaning in the words that can only be uncovered through special revelation. The "added meaning" that the text takes on is the product of the ultimate canonical shape—though, to be sure, often clearly perceived only on a revelatory basis.[5]

With the canonical interpretation approach, the meaning of OT texts is not found only in grammatical-historical contexts of the OT passages themselves. Instead, the meaning of a passage develops in the growing canon that informs previous revelation. Supposedly, there can be an *organic relationship* with what came before, much like a seed to a flower or an acorn to an oak. As God inspired the OT authors to write what they did, God knew the full meaning of their words, even if they did not. As Moo notes: "The original human author may often have had an inkling that his words were

---

[3] Bruce K. Waltke, "Kingdom Promises as Spiritual," in *Continuity and Discontinuity: Perspectives on the Relationship Between the Old and New Testaments*, ed. John S. Feinberg (Wheaton, IL: Crossway, 1988), 264.

[4] Ibid., 284.

[5] Moo, "The Problem of Sensus Plenior," 206.

pregnant with meaning he himself did not yet understand, but he would not have been in a position to see the entire context of his word."[6]

But supposedly this does not mean "hidden meaning." Instead, "added meaning" to earlier texts occurs as the canon takes shape.[7] The end result, though, is that the canon as a whole is needed to understand earlier portions of Scripture.

G. K. Beale, as discussed above, argues often for consistent contextual uses of the OT by NT writers. While expressing caution in which passages can be labeled as contextual or non-contextual, he says, "On the other hand, my position lies on the side of those who affirm that the NT uses the OT in line with its original contextual meaning."[8] Yet he also promotes a canonical approach that involves "organic expansion" and "development of meaning" of the OT:

> Accordingly, this means that in light of progressive revelation, OT passages do not receive brand-new or contradictory meanings but undergo an organic expansion or development of meaning, such as the growth of an "acorn to an oak tree, a bud to a flower, or a seed to an apple." Another way to say this is that OT passages contain thick descriptive meanings that are unraveled layer after layer by subsequent stages of canonical revelation. This means that OT passages can be understood more deeply in light of the developing revelation of later parts of the OT and especially of the NT. The OT authors had a true understanding of what they wrote but not an exhaustive understanding. This means that a NT text's contextual understanding of an OT text will involve some essential identity of meaning between the two, but often the meaning is expanded and unfolded, growing out of the earlier meaning.[9]

According to Beale, there is both a connection with the original meaning of an OT passage, but also an "expanded" meaning in light of the canon. Beale also says that later history and revelation must function as the contexts for understanding earlier revelation:

> It may be deduced that the later parts of biblical history function as the broader context to interpret earlier parts because they all have the same, ultimate divine author, who inspires the various human authors. One deduction from this premise is that Christ and his glory as the end-time center and goal of

---

[6] Moo, "The Problem of Sensus Plenior," 205.

[7] Ibid., 206.

[8] G. K. Beale, *Handbook on the New Testament Use of the Old Testament* (Grand Rapids: Baker, 2012), 13.

[9] Ibid., 26–27.

redemptive history are the *key to interpreting the earlier portions of the OT and its promises.*[10]

For him, OT passages "contain thick descriptive meanings that are unraveled layer after layer to subsequent stages of canonical revelation."[11] OT passages can be understood more deeply in light of later OT and NT revelation. This also means that OT writers had a true, but not exhaustive understanding of what they wrote.[12] Beale believes contextual and canonical approaches can be harmonized with what he calls "canonical contextual exegesis."[13]

Another advocate of the canonical interpretation approach is Douglas Oss, who says: "The progress of revelation dictates that the meaning of scriptural texts became deeper and clearer as the canon unfolded. The exegete, by considering the Bible as an integrated whole, reaches a fuller understanding of individual texts of Scripture."[14]

Is a canonical approach something that can be modeled today? Moo believes there is a sense in which it can:

> On the one hand, we do not have the same revelatory authority to make the specific identifications made in the New Testament. But, on the other hand, we can usually see the theological structure and hermeneutical principles on which the New Testament interpretation of the Old rests; and we can follow the New Testament in applying similar criteria in our own interpretation.[15]

# Questions and Criticisms of the Canonical Interpretation Approach

The canonical approach is favored by many today. For some it seems right that later passages of the canon should inform what earlier passages meant. Formal critiques of this view are lacking at this point. But one criticism is similar to that posed to the *sensus plenior* approach, namely, that it introduces meanings not known to the original writers and leaves the original writers and readers of the OT passages largely unaware of their true meanings. If there are "thick meanings" that the OT

---

[10] Beale, *New Testament Use of the Old Testament*, 53. Emphases in original.

[11] Ibid., 27.

[12] Ibid.

[13] Ibid., 25.

[14] Douglas A. Oss, "Canon as Context: The Function of Sensus Plenior in Evangelical Hermeneutics," *Grace Theological Journal* 9/1 (Spring 1988): 105.

[15] Moo, "The Problem of Sensus Plenior," 206.

authors did not know about that require unraveling with later revelation, then we are back to the *sensus plenior* problem—namely, the presence of meanings unknown to the original writers and readers.

Can OT passages contain meanings the human OT authors did not mean? Perhaps God put the "extra meanings" there, but then again we are back to the problems inherent to the *sensus plenior* view. While some canonical interpretation advocates claim their view is different from *sensus plenior*, the two seem closely related. Both affirm meanings of which the OT authors were unaware. The claim that this is not *hidden meaning* but some "organic" connection, seems to commit the fallacy of "distinction without difference" in which a difference is claimed when there really is none.

Also, the claim that there are "thick" meanings of OT passages that need to be unraveled in layers like an onion might sound convincing to some, but proof needs to be offered. Other than simply asserting that meanings must be peeled away layer by layer, what evidence is there that this actually occurs? The evidence will need to come with inductive study of how the NT uses the OT. But actual examples of this sort are lacking in my opinion. In my own inductive studies, I have not found this paradigm to be helpful. I am not aware of any OT passage in which its meaning is unraveled throughout the OT and into the NT, and then ends up being something other than what the OT author understood.

Another objection to the canonical view concerns the possibility that the parameters of the canon are not expanding and transcending the meanings found in OT passages, but instead are affirming them quite literally. For example, Jesus and the apostles seem to affirm the future of national Israel (see Matt. 19:28; 23:37–39; Acts 1:6; Rom. 11:26). The earth and Jerusalem still have prophetic significance (see Matt. 5:5; Luke 21:24; Rom. 8:19–24). Temples still have a place in NT prophetic sections (see Matt. 24:15; Rom. 9:4; 2 Thess. 2:4; Rev. 11:1–2). Those who affirm a canonical interpretation approach often assume that matters concerning Israel—physical blessings, temple, David's throne, and land in the OT—are transcended or redefined by the NT. When one reads Waltke's writings, for instance, much is made of national and physical promises of the OT being transcended by "spiritual" realities. Waltke claims that in the NT, "the kingdom's character is 'heavenly' and 'spiritual,' not 'earthly' and 'political.'"[16] This assertion has a Platonist, anti-material taint to it. Waltke also asserts a replacement theology concerning Israel and the church when he says the NT imprints "the hard fact that national Israel and its law have been permanently replaced by the church and the New Covenant."[17] A canonical approach

[16] Waltke, "Kingdom Promises as Spiritual," 270.
[17] Ibid., 274.

allows him to have a replacement theology position that does not see a literal fulfillment of the promises to Israel. Is this where a canonical approach leads?

Beale's canonical approach appears to lead him to a view that the NT transforms the storyline begun in the OT. He states, "Thus, the NT storyline will be a *transformation* of the OT one in the light of how the NT is seen to be an unfolding of the OT."[18] Beale also says, "Perhaps one of the most striking features of Jesus' kingdom is that it appears not to be the kind of kingdom prophesied in the OT and expected by Judaism."[19] This is strong *discontinuity* language. So while Beale commendably argues for much contextual use of the OT by the NT writers, he believes the NT writers are transforming the storyline offered by the OT writers. The canonical interpretation can be a vehicle for legitimizing major discontinuities in the Bible's storyline.

While I cannot say with certainty that a canonical interpretation approach is inherent to the idea that the NT changes, transforms, and transcends the Bible's storyline, key adherents of the canonical interpretation approach assert this idea. It seems that a face-value reading of the OT suggests that national Israel and land promises to Israel are significant aspects of the Bible's storyline. But supposedly, with the canonical interpretation approach, the unfolding and developing canon in light of Christ will reveal these to be types and shadows that prefigure greater NT realities. Yet while appealing to the "broader canon" seems right to some, the broader canon is still made of specific parts of the canon that together make up the whole. So specific texts at some point would need to show the alleged transformation of the OT storyline. Have canonical approach advocates shown this? Some certainly would say yes, but others like myself do not think so. It is not enough to appeal to the "broader canon" when there are no specific texts that clearly support the claim that the ideas of the OT have been transcended. Certainly, adherents of the canonical approach think there are texts that do this (Matt. 5:5; Rom. 4:13; Gal. 3:29; 6:16), but these are highly disputed. Many NT texts seem to reaffirm the expectations of the OT authors, including those related to Israel, Israel's land, Jerusalem, the temple, etc. (Matt. 19:28; 23:39; Luke 21:24; Acts 1:6; Rom. 11:11–32; Rev. 7:4–8). The more that the NT makes a connection with the storyline of the OT, the less likely it is that the canonical approach is accurate.

The soundness of the canonical approach comes down to whether there are specific NT texts that transcend the literal meaning of the OT prophets. If there are no texts that do this, then we cannot appeal to a broader canon in general since the canon is made up of individual parts. If the *parts* do not teach something, then we cannot say the *whole* does.

[18] G. K. Beale, *A New Testament Biblical Theology: The Unfolding of the Old Testament in the New* (Grand Rapids: Baker Academic, 2011), 6. Emphasis mine.

[19] Ibid., 431.

# CHAPTER SIX

# INSPIRED *SENSUS PLENIOR* APPLICATION

## (OR "INSPIRED SUBJECTIVITY" APPROACH)

Robert L. Thomas offered an approach to NT use of the OT called Inspired Sensus Plenior Application (or ISPA). This ISPA position, according to Thomas, accounts for "two kinds of New Testament uses of the Old Testament." The first occurs when "the New Testament writer observes the grammatical-historical sense of the Old Testament passage." The second happens when "the New Testament writer goes beyond the grammatical-historical sense in using a [OT] passage."[1] In short, there are two uses of the OT in the NT—contextual and non-contextual. Thomas says the latter are "nonliteral uses of the Old Testament."[2] ISPA is the designation for these non-literal examples. But he says these non-literal uses of the OT do not cancel the literal meaning of OT passages as determined by grammatical-historical hermeneutics:

> Clearly the New Testament sometimes applies Old Testament passages in a way that gives an additional dimension beyond their grammatical-historical meaning. This does not cancel the grammatical-historical meaning of the Old Testament; it is simply an application of the Old Testament passage beyond its original meaning, the authority for which application is the New Testament passage.[3]

---

[1] Robert L. Thomas, "The New Testament Use of the Old Testament," in *Evangelical Hermeneutics: The New Versus the Old* (Grand Rapids: Kregel, 2002), 241.

[2] Ibid., 242.

[3] Ibid., 251.

According to Thomas, examples of nonliteral uses of the OT include (but are not limited to):

Hebrews 2:13a with Isaiah 8:17
Matthew 4:12–16 with Isaiah 9:1–2
1 Corinthians 15:54 with Isaiah 25:8
Matthew 11:5 with Isaiah 29:18 and 35:5
Acts 13:47 with Isaiah 49:6
Matthew 8:16–17 with Isaiah 53:4
Romans 10:20 with Isaiah 65:1
Matthew 2:15 with Hosea 11:1[4]

Concerning these examples and more, Thomas says, "In such uses, New Testament writers applied Old Testament texts to situations entirely different from what was envisioned in the corresponding Old Testament contexts."[5] The words "entirely different" highlight the strong discontinuity Thomas sees at times between the OT and the NT. Belief in strong discontinuity is also found in the following statement: "The New Testament writers *disregarded* the main thrust of grammatical-historical meaning of the Old Testament passages and applied those passages in different ways to suit different points they were making."[6]

After using such strong discontinuity language, Thomas does say the NT writers "usually maintained some connecting link in thought to the Old Testament passages, but the literal Old Testament meanings are absent from the quotation."[7] The use of "some connecting link" is not explained.

Thomas says the ISPA meanings of certain OT passages did not exist "until the time of the New Testament citation, being occasioned by Israel's rejection of her Messiah at His first advent."[8] Two points are noteworthy here. The first is that ISPA meanings did not exist until NT writers employed them. This means that Thomas' understanding of *sensus plenior* differs from the traditional, Raymond Brown understanding of *sensus plenior* that views the hidden or fuller meanings of OT texts to be embedded in the original OT passages. There is a difference between saying a *sensus plenior* meaning exists in the original words of the OT writers and saying that it began to exist when the NT writers used the OT passage.

Second, according to Thomas, the reason for the non-contextual uses of the OT is twofold: "The new meaning given to an Old Testament passage relates to Israel's

---

[4] Thomas, "New Testament Use of the Old Testament," 247–51.

[5] Ibid., 247.

[6] Ibid. Emphases mine.

[7] Ibid.

[8] Ibid.

rejection of her Messiah at His first advent and the consequent opening of the door to a new people, the Gentiles, for God to bless (see Rom. 9–11)."[9] Thus, the nonliteral uses of the OT are not random, but instead are connected with Israel's rejection of the Messiah and a new blessing for the Gentiles.

Also significant to Thomas's ISPA view is that the subjectivity of the apostles is not transferable to others because the apostles operated under inspiration, whereas we do not:

> First, can today's interpreter imitate what New Testament writers did in assigning additional and different meanings in applying Old Testament passages? No, they cannot, because that would depart from grammatical-historical interpretation and violate the principle of single meaning. Current interpreters and preachers may apply the Old Testament passages to different situations, but their applications are not inspired, as are those of New Testament writers.[10]

In short, non-literal uses of the OT are limited to the apostles only. This is not transferable to other Christians because of inspiration.

# Questions and Criticisms of ISPA

Questions have been raised about the ISPA view. Rynold Dean claims that Thomas injected some confusion into the debate by using the title, "*sensus plenior*" in a different way from how most scholars understand the designation. Dean says, "The problem stems from the fact that Thomas has chosen to use words that have a relatively established meaning in hermeneutical circles, but in ways that differ from their normally accepted use in the field."[11]

Most scholars operate under Raymond Brown's definition of *sensus plenior* which involves the idea that God embedded "hidden meanings" in the OT passages.[12] Even though the OT writers did not understand these hidden meanings, they were there, nonetheless, waiting to be unearthed by later NT revelation. But Thomas denies hidden meanings in OT passages since, according to him, this would violate the

---

[9] Thomas, "The New Testament Use of the Old Testament," 253.

[10] Ibid., 252.

[11] Rynold D. Dean, *Evangelical Hermeneutics and the New Testament Use of the Old Testament* (Iron River, WI: Veritypath Publications, 2009), 173.

[12] Raymond E. Brown, *The Sensus Plenior of Sacred Scripture* (Baltimore, MD: St. Mary's Univ. Press, 1955), 92. Brown's definition: "The *sensus plenior* is that additional, deeper meaning, intended by God, but not clearly intended by the human author, which is seen to exist in the words of a biblical text (or group of texts, or even a whole book) when they are studied in the light of further revelation or development in the understanding of revelation."

principle of single meaning. For Thomas, God knows that in NT times these OT passages will be used in different ways from the intents of the OT authors, but there is no *sensus plenior,* or hidden meaning, contained in OT passages.

Thomas's use of *sensus plenior* in a non-traditional sense does not necessitate the rejection of his ISPA view. A position can be correct even if its title is confusing. Perhaps a better title for Thomas's position could be *Inspired Application* since Thomas does not believe in embedded hidden meaning in OT passages, but sees the NT writers *applying* OT passages in non-contextual ways. Dean seems to affirm a similar point: "One could argue that the issue is really about the meaning generated through the NT's *employment* or *utilization* of the OT passage, not about the OT passage receiving an additional meaning."[13] Dean's point is well-taken.

Second, Thomas asserts that "New Testament writers applied Old Testament texts to situations entirely different from what was envisioned in the corresponding Old Testament contexts."[14] In doing so, he claims NT writers were using the OT to make points significantly divorced from the intents of the OT authors. A question could be raised, though, concerning why the NT authors would appeal to OT texts to make points unrelated to the meanings of the original OT passages. *Does not the appeal to something previous (in this case the OT) mean that some real connection exists with what is appealed to?* If not, why is an appeal to the OT even made? Usually an appeal to a text is made because some connection exists. Since the apostles were inspired, they could simply give new revelation in the form of mysteries not revealed in the OT, which they do on other occasions (see Eph. 3:4–5). But when they quote the OT, they seem to be making some sort of connection with the intent of the OT passages and expect their readers to see these connections. In addition, there is no teaching from the NT writers that their readers should expect non-contextual uses of the OT.

Third, some could argue that the passages Thomas believes are examples of non-contextual uses of the OT actually could be contextual uses, or at least that the claimed number of non-contextual uses of the OT is overstated. As noted earlier, Beale believes the claims of non-contextual uses of the OT has largely been exaggerated. Who is right on this issue involves close scrutiny of many passages. But our view is that the case for many non-contextual uses of the OT is largely an exaggeration.

---

[13] Dean, *Evangelical Hermeneutics*, 175.

[14] Thomas, "New Testament Use of the Old Testament," 247.

# CHAPTER SEVEN

# HISTORICAL-EXEGETICAL AND THEOLOGICAL-CANONICAL

## (OR "ECLECTIC" APPROACH)

As one could guess, whenever there are multiple views to a complicated issue, one solution is to take an eclectic or "all of the above" or "some of the above" approach. Darrell Bock indicated an affinity to this way of thinking when he stated: "The author [Bock] also hopes that in being rather eclectic with the various approaches, the wheat has been successfully retained from each view while the chaff has been left behind."[1] Bock said this in regard to the four positions he explained in his two articles from 1985.

In the more recent *Three Views* book, Bock argues that much of the debate on the NT use of the OT issue has been historical/exegetical vs. theological/canonical. In other words, there are some who emphasize the grammatical-historical meanings of OT passages, while others emphasize broader canonical and theological considerations for understanding the OT. Also, in the *Three Views* book, Kaiser leans to the "historical/exegetical" side, whereas Peter Enns leans to the "theological/canonical." But for Bock, an either/or approach is "unnecessary" when perhaps a both/and paradigm is better.[2] And in the *Three Views* book, Bock's approach seems to be a mediatory position. Bock has identified his approach as "Single Meaning, Multiple

---

[1] Darrell L. Bock, "Evangelicals and the Use of the Old Testament in the New, Part 2," *Bibliotheca Sacra* 142 (Oct. 1985): 302–19.

[2] Darrell L. Bock, "Single Meaning, Multiple Contexts and Referents," in *Three Views on the New Testament Use of the Old Testament*, ed. Kenneth Berding and Jonathan Lunde (Grand Rapids: Zondervan, 2008), 115.

Contexts and Referents."[3] Bock's explanation is quite complicated, but for Bock the original context of an OT passage plays a key role for setting the parameters of how a text is used, but it is not always the only factor.[4] It appears for Bock that there is a stable meaning found in the OT context that is the foundation of meaning for that passage, but earlier passages become clearer as later revelation arrives. There can also be "new referents" as new contexts and revelation unfold.[5] He argues, then, that there can be two ways of reading the Bible—"historical-exegetical and theological-canonical."[6] Thus, there should be a "both/and" and not an "either/or" approach to the NT use of the OT issue. The "exegetical" should not be pitted against the "theological-canonical" since both can be harmonized.[7]

This mediating approach is viewed by some as a strength. Commenting on Bock's chapter in comparison with those of Kaiser and Peter Enns, Craig Blomberg stated, "As is often the case with theologically mediating viewpoints, Bock appears to have the best of this 'debate.'"[8] Enns on the other hand says Bock's approach "shows marks of an inconsistent analysis."[9]

Douglas Moo, in his chapter "The Problem of Sensus Plenior," seems at times to take an eclectic approach. He admittedly says he is "extremely supportive" in general to the single-meaning approach of Kaiser.[10] Moo thinks Kaiser has done a good job in showing how some disputed texts actually are contextual. Then, in regard to Second Temple Judaism principles, Moo also asserts that "there can be no doubt that the New Testament often utilizes citation techniques that are quite similar to practices amply illustrated in first-century Jewish sources."[11] Concerning *sensus plenior*, Moo writes,

> It is not clear, then, that the usual objections brought against the idea of *sensus plenior* are cogent. There does not appear to be any compelling reason for rejecting the hypothesis. On the other hand, there are reasons to hesitate before embracing it as a comprehensive explanation of the 'problem' uses of the Old Testament in the New.[12]

---

[3] This is the title of his view given in *Three Views on the New Testament Use of the Old Testament*, 105–51.

[4] Bock, "Single Meaning, Multiple Contexts and Referents," 106.

[5] Ibid., 114.

[6] Ibid.

[7] Ibid., 115.

[8] Craig Blomberg, "Three Views on the NT Use of the OT—A Review," http://www.bethinking.org/resources/three-views-on-the-nt-use-of-the-ot---a-review.htm. Accessed Nov 10, 2011.

[9] Enns, "Response to Bock," in *Three Views*, 160.

[10] Douglas J. Moo, "The Problem of Sensus Plenior," in *Hermeneutics, Authority, and Canon.* ed. D. A. Carson and John D. Woodbridge (Grand Rapids: Zondervan, 1986), 201.

[11] Ibid., 192. Yet even as Moo does this, he expresses concerns that adherents of this view exaggerate the issue of non-contextual uses of the OT.

[12] Ibid., 204.

Moo also says, "It may be that some citations are best explained according to the traditional *sensus plenior* model: by direct, inspired apprehension, the New Testament authors perceive the meaning in a text put there by God but unknown to the human author."[13] Yet even this meaning is "compatible with the meaning intended by the human author."[14]

These comments seem consistent with an eclectic view. Yet, Moo seems comfortable with a canonical approach.[15] After stating that not all NT uses of the OT can be explained by grammatical-historical hermeneutics, he notes:

> When this happens, it is best to think that the New Testament authors have read the text against the background of the whole scope of revelation, preserved in the developing canon. The meaning intended by the human author of a particular text can take on a "fuller" meaning, legitimately developed from his meaning in the light of the text's ultimate canonical context.[16]

With his chapter concerning, "The Problem of the New Testament's Use of the Old Testament" (2016), Moo, along with Andrew Naselli, argue that there are three approaches that help provide a rationale for the NT's use of the OT: (1) the canonical approach; (2) typology; and (3) *sensus plenior*.[17] This seems to reaffirm Moo's leanings to a more eclectic approach.

My intention is not to pin down certain scholars as clear and open representatives of an eclectic approach, but to demonstrate that it is a real position. Whether this view is helpful or a confusing concoction of mutually exclusive perspectives depends on a study of the evidence.

---

[13] Moo, "The Problem of Sensus Plenior," 210.

[14] Ibid.

[15] I am not claiming that Moo openly identifies with the title, "canonical approach."

[16] Moo, "The Problem of Sensus Plenior," 210.

[17] Douglas J. Moo and Andrew David Naselli, "The Problem of the New Testament's Use of the Old Testament," in *The Enduring Authority of the Christian Scriptures*, ed. D. A. Carson (Grand Rapids: Eerdmans, 2016), 736.

# CHAPTER EIGHT

# NEW TESTAMENT REINTERPRETATION OF THE OLD TESTAMENT

## (OR "NT PRIORITY OVER OT" APPROACH)

This last approach is not as clearly identifiable as the other views discussed, and I am not aware of anyone who openly identifies with it. So mentioning this as a distinct approach is somewhat tenuous. It is also possible that this view could be linked with another approach.[1] Yet some have used "reinterpretation" language to describe how the NT writers used the OT, so this reality should be noted. It is necessary, therefore, to discuss a view that we call, "New Testament Reinterpretation of the Old Testament."

Some believe the Christ-event means that OT passages and themes about physical and national matters have been "reinterpreted" to refer to greater spiritual realities and truths in the NT. Thus, the NT is perceived as the divine interpreter and reinterpreter of the OT and the lens through which the OT must be viewed. One should not start with the OT to understand the OT; one must start with the NT to understand the OT. For example, George Ladd stated:

---

[1] The two most likely candidates would be the *sensus plenior* and canonical approaches. Bruce Waltke, though, explicitly denies that "reinterpretation" is part of the canonical approach although it seems from my perspective that reinterpretation could be taking place within the canonical view.

The Old Testament must be interpreted by the New Testament. In principle it is quite possible that the prophecies addressed originally to literal Israel describing physical blessings have their fulfillment exclusively in the spiritual blessings enjoyed by the church. It is also possible that the Old Testament expectation of a kingdom on earth could be *reinterpreted* by the New Testament altogether of blessings in the spiritual realm.[2]

Ladd escalates the concept of "reinterpretation" of the OT to "radical reinterpretation." Concerning Peter's understanding of Jesus' ascension in Acts 2, Ladd writes: "This involves a rather radical reinterpretation of the Old Testament prophecies, but no more so than the entire reinterpretation of God's redemptive plan by the early church."[3]

"Reinterpretation" language is also used by Kim Riddlebarger, who states: "But eschatological themes are *reinterpreted* in the New Testament, where we are told these Old Testament images are types and shadows of the glorious realities that are fulfilled in Jesus Christ."[4] Stephen Sizer also says, "Jesus and the apostles *reinterpreted* the Old Testament."[5] It should be noted that these "reinterpret" quotes above are stated in the context of eschatology discussions and not hermeneutical theory, but it does show that some claim God reinterprets His previous revelation.

# Questions and Criticisms of the Reinterpretation of OT Approach

This emphasis on starting with the NT to understand the OT is not unique to the reinterpretation view; it also exists with the *sensus plenior*, contemporary Judaism, and canonical approaches as well. But notable of the quotes mentioned above is the open embracement of the idea that the NT, at times, *reinterpreted* the OT.

Yet this perspective, too, has faced strong criticism. Some have argued that if the NT reinterprets the OT, one could rightly wonder in what sense the OT revelations were actually revelations in good faith to the original writers and readers. In response to George Ladd's declaration that the NT reinterprets the OT, Paul Feinberg asked, "If Ladd is correct that the NT reinterprets the OT, his hermeneutic

---

[2] George E. Ladd, "Revelation 20 and the Millennium," *Review and Expositor* 57 (1960): 167. Emphasis mine.

[3] George E. Ladd, *A Theology of the New Testament* (Grand Rapids: Eerdmans, 1993), 373.

[4] Kim Riddlebarger, *A Case for Amillennialism: Understanding the End Times* (Grand Rapids: Baker, 2003), 37. Emphasis mine.

[5] Stephen Sizer, *Zion's Christian Soldiers: The Bible, Israel and the Church* (Nottingham, England: InterVarsity, 2008), 36. Emphasis mine.

does raise some serious questions. How can the integrity of the OT text be maintained? In what sense can the OT really be called a *revelation* in its original meaning?"[6] David L. Turner says, "If NT reinterpretation reverses, cancels, or seriously modifies OT promises to Israel, one wonders how to define the word 'progressive.' God's faithfulness to His promises to Israel must also be explained."[7] Turner also points out that this approach comes close to violating NT statements that uphold the truth claims of the OT: "It appears exceedingly doubtful that the NT reinterprets the OT...This comes perilously close to conflicting with such NT passages as Matt 5:18 and John 10:35b."[8]

Thus, the reinterpretation understanding has much to account for. Why does God need to reinterpret His previously inspired revelation? Does He ever say anything that has to be reinterpreted? And how do we view the nature of Scripture if later parts reinterpret earlier parts? In addition, as stated earlier concerning previous positions, the case for the NT changing the storyline started in the OT is hard to sustain.

---

### Seven Approaches to NT Use of the OT

1. Single Meaning-Multiple Implications
2. Human Meaning Plus Hidden Divine Meaning (*Sensus Plenior*)
3. Second Temple Judaism
4. Canonical Interpretation
5. Inspired *Sensus Plenior* Application
6. Historical-Exegetical and Theological-Canonical (Eclectic)
7. New Testament Reinterpretation of the Old Testament

---

[6] Feinberg, "Hermeneutics of Discontinuity," 116. Emphasis in original.

[7] David L. Turner, "The Continuity of Scripture and Eschatology: Key Hermeneutical Issues," *Grace Theological Journal* 6, no. 2 (1985): 281.

[8] Ibid., 282.

# CHAPTER NINE

# TEST CASES

It is one thing to discuss theories of NT use of the OT, it is quite another to see how these theories compare when addressing actual texts of Scripture alongside one another. This chapter compares the various positions with four specific test cases—Acts 2:25–28; Galatians 3:16; Matthew 2:15; and 1 Corinthians 9:9–10. Not every position is represented equally in these test cases, but it is my intention to include enough to demonstrate how the various positions compare.

## Case One
### Acts 2:25–28/Psalm 16:8–11

Peter's use of Psalm 16:8–11 in Acts 2:25–28 offers significant challenges. Acts 2:25–28 reads:

For David says of Him,
"I SAW THE LORD ALWAYS IN MY PRESENCE;
FOR HE IS AT MY RIGHT HAND, SO THAT I WILL NOT BE SHAKEN.
"THEREFORE MY HEART WAS GLAD AND MY TONGUE EXULTED;
MOREOVER MY FLESH ALSO WILL LIVE IN HOPE;
BECAUSE YOU WILL NOT ABANDON MY SOUL TO HADES,
NOR ALLOW YOUR HOLY ONE TO UNDERGO DECAY.
"YOU HAVE MADE KNOWN TO ME THE WAYS OF LIFE;
YOU WILL MAKE ME FULL OF GLADNESS WITH YOUR PRESENCE."

The issue is whether Peter's statement that David intentionally spoke of the Messiah aligns with David's intention in Psalm 16.

As Peter speaks to the "men of Israel" (Acts 2:22), he tries to convince them of Jesus' resurrection from the dead. Verse 24 states that God raised Jesus up since it was impossible for death to keep Him in its power. Also significant is that Peter again explicitly declares that David, the author of Psalm 16, explicitly wrote about the Messiah's resurrection:

> Brethren, I may confidently say to you regarding the patriarch David that he both died and was buried, and his tomb is with us to this day. And so, because he was a prophet and knew that GOD HAD SWORN TO HIM WITH AN OATH TO SEAT ONE OF HIS DESCENDANTS ON HIS THRONE, he looked ahead and spoke of the resurrection of the Christ, that HE WAS NEITHER ABANDONED TO HADES, NOR DID His flesh SUFFER DECAY. This Jesus God raised up again, to which we are all witnesses. (Acts 2:29–32)

However, several have argued that a plain reading of Psalm 16 reveals that David was only referring to himself—not the Messiah. So what do we do here? Peter says David wrote about the Messiah, yet some hold that Psalm 16 shows that David only referred to himself. How do the various views approach this passage?

In reference to Acts 2, the advocate for reinterpretation, George Ladd, said: "This involves a rather radical reinterpretation of the Old Testament prophecies, but no more so than the entire reinterpretation of God's redemptive plan by the early church."[1] This language of "radical reinterpretation" reveals a strong disconnect between the OT and what is occurring in Acts 2.

Longenecker, a proponent of the contemporary Judaism approach, says that the use of Psalm 16:8–11 in Acts 2:25–28 is an "obvious" example of *sensus plenior*.[2] He also ties it to a *pesher* understanding:

> The application of Pss 16:8–11 and 110:1 to the resurrection and ascension of Jesus in Acts 2:25–36. While a midrashic understanding has brought these two passages together, it is a pesher understanding that evokes such an introduction as "David said concerning him.[3]

Kaiser, as a single-meaning proponent, strongly disagrees with *sensus plenior* and *pesher* understandings. He argues that "Psalm 16 is best understood as being

---

[1] George E. Ladd, *A Theology of the New Testament*, 373.

[2] Richard N. Longenecker, *Biblical Exegesis in the Apostolic Period* (Grand Rapids: Eerdmans, 1975, 1999), xxxiii.

[3] Ibid., 84.

messianic in its own OT context, justifying the fulfillment affirmations of both Peter and Paul, without accusing them of 'reading' these into the OT text in a *pesher*-like manner."[4] Kaiser argues that both Peter and Paul "attribute to Psalm 16 a conscious prediction of the resurrection of Jesus the Messiah from the dead. Why is it, then, that so few contemporary commentators and readers of Psalm 16 concur with the apostles?"[5] Kaiser also believes that the first David had a messianic hope of the last David, so that when David uses "Holy One" he had the coming Messiah we now know as Jesus in mind. Kaiser writes, "The identity of God's 'Holy One' (*Hasid*) is a technical term as were the terms 'Seed,' 'Servant of the Lord,' and 'Messiah' in the OT."[6] Kaiser applies 'holy one' (*Hasid*) to the concept of corporate solidarity "in which the One (the Messiah) and the many (the Davidic line and those who believe in the Messiah) are embraced in a single meaning usually indicated by a collective singular, instead of it being either a simple singular or plural noun."[7] Thus, for Kaiser, Psalm 16 in its context refers to the coming Messiah and has implications for David too: "If Messiah could be resurrected, then David's hope of being raised from the dead was just as good and just as sure."[8] In sum, since David wrote with a messianic hope in mind, Peter can rightly say in Acts 2:25–28 that David spoke of the Messiah in Psalm 16.

In addition, this consistent contextual view says that we could have a case of inspired commentary here. As an inspired apostle, Peter is telling his audience (and us) that David was actually thinking of the Messiah when he wrote Psalm 16.

Bock, though, takes a different approach. In response to Kaiser's view of Psalm 16, Bock says, "The first person references throughout this psalm make a more natural reading to refer to the psalmist himself, who is the subject throughout."[9] Thus, Bock believes David was referring to himself. Bock also says, "A better way to read Psalm 16 is as a typological text" which later "can ultimately be about Jesus."[10] So Psalm 16 is a case of "TYPOLOGICAL-prophetic" (emphasis in original) in which "the pattern is not anticipated by the language, but is seen once the decisive pattern (or fulfillment pattern) occurs."[11] Bock seems to be saying that Psalm 16 is about David with no explicit reference to Jesus the Messiah. But events in David's life have a correspondence to Jesus, and the NT highlights these correspondences. Roy Zuck

---

[4] Walter C. Kaiser, Jr., "Single Meaning, Unified Referents," in *Three Views on the New Testament Use of the Old Testament*, eds. Kenneth Berding and Jonathan Lunde (Grand Rapids: Zondervan, 2008), 75.

[5] Ibid., 74–75.

[6] Ibid., 77–78.

[7] Ibid., 78–79.

[8] Ibid., 79.

[9] Bock, "Response to Kaiser," in *Three Views*, 95.

[10] Ibid.

[11] Bock, "Single Meaning, Multiple Contexts," in *Three Views*, 119–20.

takes a similar view when he says, "Though David had himself in mind, Peter and Paul pointed out that from the New Testament perspective the psalm refers to Christ." Zuck says Psalm 16 has one meaning but "two referents"—"namely, David and ultimately, in the fullest sense, Christ."[12]

ISPA advocate Robert Thomas agrees with Zuck that the NT is bringing "additional meaning" to Psalm 16. In reference to Zuck's understanding of that text, Thomas says, "The source and authority for that additional meaning is the New Testament, not the Old Testament."[13] Thus, along with Longenecker, Bock, and Zuck, but contra Kaiser, Thomas seems to believe that David, in Psalm 16, is not consciously referencing Jesus. However, Thomas disagrees with Zuck's belief that single meaning is compatible with the idea of multiple referents. Thomas says, "The psalms themselves cannot have more than one referent, hermeneutically speaking. Such would assign them more than one meaning."[14] For Thomas, belief in multiple referents means a violation of single meaning.[15]

# Case Two
## Galatians 3:16 / "Seed" in Genesis

Paul states in Galatians 3:16: "Now the promises were spoken to Abraham and to his seed. He does not say, "And to seeds," as referring to many, but rather to one, "And to your seed," that is, Christ." At first glance, it seems that Paul's hermeneutic is off. He takes a collective or multiple sense of "seed" from Genesis and turns it into a single reference to Jesus. Yet most Genesis references to "seed" or "offspring" refer to Abraham's descendants collectively. Does Paul change or reinterpret the collective meaning in Genesis to an individual reference to Jesus? If so, is Paul using the OT non-contextually? Second Temple Judaism advocates think so. Using David Daube as support, Longenecker says Paul is using "a midrashic mode of interpretation" that goes beyond normal historical-grammatical hermeneutics.[16] Peter Enns also promotes a contemporary Judaism approach concerning this verse:

[12] Roy B. Zuck, *Basic Bible Interpretation* (Colorado Springs, CO: Chariot Victor Publishing, 1991), 276.

[13] Robert L. Thomas, "The New Testament Use of the Old Testament," in *Evangelical Hermeneutics: The New Versus the Old* (Grand Rapids: Kregel, 2002), 157.

[14] Ibid.

[15] Ibid.

[16] Richard Longenecker, "Can We Produce the Exegesis of the New Testament," *Tyndale Bulletin* 21 (1970): 37.

Paul's handling of the OT promises betrays an exegetical approach that would be deemed inappropriate by contemporary conventions, but hardly so for ancient, Second Temple standards.[17]

Paul's argument in Galatians 3 can be described as an example of *sensus plenior* and typology, but the hermeneutical practices that formed the exegetical 'logic' by which those terms are articulated are a function of the historical Second Temple context and must figure into the discussion.[18]

I do not think the ancient author or reader of Genesis thought that the seed promise referred to one person.[19]

Darrell Bock, who takes an eclectic approach, seems sympathetic to Second Temple Judaism principles here:

The many come through the one. So just as the children of Abraham became the nation of Israel, so now the children of God's new eschatological people come through the chosen seed of Abraham, the Christ, to become the eschatological people of God, and in a way that includes Gentiles who are incorporated in that seed. I suspect that this kind of theological underpinning and synthesis is at the core of Paul's argument in Galatians 3. It is such theologizing that belongs to methods so common in the Second Temple period.[20]

How would single meaning, consistent contextual use advocates understand Galatians 3:16? Kaiser appeals to the "one and the many" background for the seed concept going back to Genesis 3:15 where "seed" in this context appears to have both a collective and singular aspect to it. He uses this to say, "But Paul and the writer of Genesis knew that 'seed' was a collective word that had a singular focus in the one who would crush the head of 'the Serpent' (Gen. 3:15), yet with a plural reference that embraced all who would believe as Abraham did—Jew or Gentile!"[21] Thus, if the "seed" concept from the beginning was meant to encompass the one and the many, then a reference to Jesus as "seed" in Galatians 3:16 is not non-contextual since He is the ultimate Seed who arises from the collective seed. The "one and the many" concept is essential for Kaiser's understanding of Galatians 3:16.

---

[17] Peter Enns, "Fuller Meaning, Single Goal," in *Three Views*, 183.

[18] Ibid., 208.

[19] Ibid.

[20] Bock, "Response to Enns," in *Three Views*, 228–29.

[21] Kaiser, "Response to Enns," in *Three Views*, 220–21.

Yet there is another approach that could be used by single meaning adherents: *Paul may be relying literally on the grammar of the Genesis verse he is referring to.* Unanimity is lacking concerning which passage Paul is quoting in Galatians 3:16. Some believe he is referring to either Genesis 13:15, 17:8, or 22:18. But in his extensive study of what verse Paul was referring to, Collins opts for Genesis 22:18:

> Genesis 22:18 seems to be the best candidate for Paul's source here, because, of the Genesis "blessing" texts that might lie behind the composite quotation of Galatians 3:8, it is the one that has the dative of σπέρμα. This, then, allows us to make sense of Paul's argument in Galatians 3:16.[22]

If Collins is correct, this is significant. For if Paul is quoting Genesis 22:18, he could be relying on a straightforward understanding of this text in Galatians 3:16. As a result of researching all references to *zera* ("offspring"/"seed") in the Hebrew Bible, Collins concluded that a unitary single sense of *zera* ("seed") concerning one person can be discerned when the term is connected with singular verb inflections, adjectives, and pronouns. This applies to Genesis 3:15. Building upon the work of Collins, T. Desmond Alexander applies this criteria for a singular understanding of *zera* to Genesis 22:17–18a and 24:60.[23]

If this is accurate, the last reference to "seed" [*zera*] in Genesis 22:17 and the reference to "seed" in 22:18 should be understood in a singular way—"his." The ESV translates 22:17 as, "And your offspring shall possess the gate of *his* enemies" (emphasis mine). This is in contrast to other versions that opt for "*their* enemies" (emphasis mine). And if this singular sense is accurate in 22:17, it is likely that the "offspring" reference in 22:18 (which Paul may be quoting in Galatians 3:16) also refers to a single individual. Alexander explains:

> If the immediately preceding reference to "seed" in 22:17 denotes an individual, this must also be the case in 22:18a, for there is nothing here to indicate a change in number. The blessing of "all the nations of the earth" is thus associated with a particular descendant of Abraham, rather than all those descended from him.[24]

This unitary, individual understanding of "seed" is bolstered by the allusion to Genesis 22:17b–18a in Psalm 72:17: "May people be blessed in *him*" (ESV). Psalm 72 is likely a messianic passage that speaks of Messiah's coming kingdom. It connects the Messiah, an individual, with the fulfillment of the "seed" of

---

[22] C. John Collins, "Galatians 3:16: What Kind of Exegete Was Paul?," *Tyndale Bulletin* 54, no.1 (2003): 86.

[23] T. Desmond Alexander, "Further Observations of the Term 'Seed' in Genesis," *Tyndale Bulletin* 48, no. 1 (1997): 363.

[24] Ibid., 365.

Genesis 22:17–18. Thus, Psalm 72 heightens the possibility Paul could be literal when he uses "seed" in a singular sense in Galatians 3:16.

What does this all mean? *If Paul's reference to "seed" in Galatians 3:16 is a reference to Genesis 22:18, then Paul is being literal with his understanding.* Limiting the seed concept to a singular person (Jesus) is consistent with the literal meaning of Genesis 22:18. Concerning Galatians 3:16, Peter Gentry argues, "So Paul's argument in Galatians 3:16 that the text speaks of 'seed' and not 'seeds' appears to be based upon solid exegesis of the Hebrew Scriptures."[25]

# Case Three
## Matthew 2:15 / Hosea 11:1

The use of Hosea 11:1 in Matthew 2:15 could be the most debated case of NT use of the OT in the Bible. Concerning the context, Matthew 2:13–14 states that Mary and Joseph took Jesus to Egypt to escape Herod's attempt to kill the child. Then verse 15 relates Jesus' coming to Egypt with Israel's exodus journey centuries earlier: "'He [Jesus] remained there until the death of Herod. This was to fulfill what had been spoken by the Lord through the prophet: "OUT OF EGYPT I CALLED MY SON."'"

Jesus' connection with Egypt is said to "fulfill" Israel's journey from Egypt at the time of the exodus as explained in Hosea 11:1. The natural question is, "How can Jesus' going to Egypt be a fulfilment of an historical event that happened centuries earlier?" Hosea 11:1 refers to the past event of the exodus from Egypt. So how can Hosea's reference to a historical event hundreds of years earlier be fulfilled in Jesus? Some claim this is an example where a NT writer uses the OT out of context. Second Temple Judaism hermeneutic advocate, Peter Enns, believes Matthew is not being contextual with Hosea 11:1. He states: "What drives Matthew to handle Hosea's words is, in my view, something other than a commitment to how Hosea's words functioned in their original setting."[26] He also says, "Matthew's use of Hosea reflects a deep clarity of theological conviction, but one that can only come in light of the reality of Pentecost."[27]

Reinterpretation adherent, George Ladd, took a strong non-contextual approach when he argued that Matthew's use of Hosea 11:1 should be understood from the perspective of *reinterpretation*:

---

[25] Peter J. Gentry and Stephen J. Wellum, *Kingdom through Covenant: A Biblical-Theological Understanding of the Covenants* (Wheaton, IL: Crossway, 2012), 289.

[26] Enns, "Fuller Meaning, Single Goal," 199.

[27] Ibid., 200.

In Hosea [11:1] this is not a prophecy at all but a historical affirmation that God had called Israel out of Egypt in the Exodus. However, Matthew recognizes Jesus to be God's greater son and deliberately turns a historical statement into a prophecy. This is a principle which runs throughout biblical prophecy. *The Old Testament is reinterpreted* in light of the Christ event.[28]

That Ladd highlights "The Old Testament is reinterpreted" demonstrates how intentional he is with the reinterpretation principle.

Inspired Sensus Plenior Application promoter, Robert Thomas, lists Matthew 2:15 and its use of Hosea 11:1 in the category of "nonliteral uses of the Old Testament in the New Testament."[29] He writes, "Sometimes the New Testament treats a nonprophetic Old Testament passage, such as Hosea 11:1, as though it predicted a New Testament occurrence. Hosea wrote about the historical exodus of the people of Israel from Egypt, but Matthew applies the same words to Jesus' departure from Egypt with His family after their flight to escape Herod the Great. This furnishes another instance of ISPA."[30]

In response to Enns, Darrell Bock (eclectic approach) says that Matthew 2:15 fits with Jewish beliefs and hermeneutics. But he also sees a contextual link that is not far removed from the context of Hosea 11:1:

Yet there is an eschatological element in the near context, as Hosea 11:8–9 holds out the promise that Israel will not be destroyed by God's judgment. Now if we combine this future hope with the idea that salvation at the end is like the way it was at the start (theological pattern), then Matthew's reading becomes theologically comprehensible, using themes that made sense at the time. Enns's conclusion here—"What drives Matthew to handle Hosea's words is, in my view, something other than a commitment to how Hosea's words functioned in their original setting"—becomes an overstatement because something from Hosea's context (as well as something that fits basic Jewish beliefs and hermeneutical concerns) can be seen to be at play.[31]

Bock also says, "In sum, there is more at work here in the development of NT readings than merely a Christological principle."[32]

---

[28] George Eldon Ladd, "Historic Premillennialism," in *The Meaning of the Millennium: Four Views* (IVP, 1977), 21.

[29] Thomas, "The New Testament Use of the Old Testament," 247.

[30] Ibid., 251.

[31] Bock, "Response to Enns," 230–31.

[32] Ibid., 231.

Contextual-use advocate, Kaiser, sees the concepts of messianic hope and corporate solidarity ("one and the many") as evidence for a contextual connection. He says the focus in Hosea 11:1 and Matthew 2:15 should be "I called *my son*" (emphasis mine). Thus the emphasis in this passage is on God's calling of His son. This applies to Israel corporately and Jesus individually—both as God's sons in Scripture. Kaiser writes:

> It is in this sense that the divinely inspired Hosea deliberately chose to use two singular nouns to represent the whole nation, while also realizing from antecedent Scripture that there was a coming Man of Promise who would appear under the similar reference, "my son" (e.g. 2 Sam. 7:14; Pss. 2:7; 89:27; Prov. 30:4). Thus, when Israel was delivered by God as they crossed the Red Sea, there was in that crowd one who was the next installment in that promised line of messianic progenitors…"My son" is the key technical term for understanding this passage.[33]

According to Kaiser, if one understands the concepts of corporate solidarity, antecedent theology, and Messianic hope, one should see the connection between Israel corporately as God's son, and Jesus, the corporate head of Israel, who also is God's Son.

Some contextual advocates claim Matthew is using Hosea 11:1 in a contextual manner. Matthew knows what Hosea meant and is not overturning or reinterpreting the meaning of Hosea 11:1. Instead, Matthew connects a significant event in Israel's history with an event in Jesus' life to show that Jesus is connected with Israel. Jesus is the true representative of Israel who can save and restore national Israel (Isa. 49:6).

With the single-meaning view, a difference exists between interpreting a passage and showing how two events in the Bible correspond to each other. Matthew is not so much explaining the words of Hosea 11:1 as he is showing a correspondence between Israel and Jesus. The Jews understood the concept of corporate solidarity in which "one" can represent "many," and the experience of the one can relate to the many. Such a connection is not very familiar to a modern audience, but it was to ancient Jewish readers of Matthew's Gospel. As Craig Blomberg notes, "For believing Jews, merely to discern striking parallels between God's actions in history, especially in decisive moments of revelation and redemption, could convince them of divinely intended 'coincidence.'"[34]

Also, the corporate connection between Israel and Israel's coming King in relation to Egypt is taught in the OT. Compare the following oracles of Balaam in Numbers 23 and 24:

[33] Kaiser, "Response to Enns," in *Three Views*, 223.

[34] Craig L. Blomberg, "Matthew," in *Commentary on the New Testament Use of the Old Testament*, ed. G. K. Beale and D. A. Carson (Grand Rapids: Baker, 2007), 8. I am not claiming Blomberg is an advocate of single-meaning use of the OT.

- God brings them [Israel] out of Egypt, He [God] is for them like the horns of the wild ox. (Num. 23:22)
- God brings him [Israel's king (see Num. 24:7)] out of Egypt, He is for him like the horns of the wild ox. (Num. 24:8)

Numbers 23:22 refers to Israel while Numbers 24:8 refers to Israel's king. Note that God brought both Israel and Israel's king out of Egypt, showing a corporate and typological connection between Israel and Israel's coming king. As he had access to these texts, perhaps Hosea had this connection in mind when he wrote Hosea 11:1. If he did, then Hosea had more in mind than just the actual exodus of Israel centuries earlier. He may have been thinking of Israel's coming King in relation to Israel as well. When Matthew quotes Hosea 11:1, he could be drawing on a recognized OT type between Israel and Israel's king. To make such a connection is contextual since this connection was already made in Numbers.

# Case Four
## 1 Corinthians 9:9–10 / Deuteronomy 25:4

Another challenging example of NT use of the OT is 1 Corinthians 9:9–10. Not a few scholars have deemed this text as a clear case of non-contextual use of the OT. Some even say that in this passage Paul is allegorizing the OT. First Corinthians 9:8–11 reads:

> I am not speaking these things according to human judgment, am I? Or does not the Law also say these things? For it is written in the Law of Moses, "You shall not muzzle the ox while he is threshing." God is not concerned about oxen, is He? Or is He speaking altogether for our sake? Yes, for our sake it was written, because the plowman ought to plow in hope, and the thresher to thresh in hope of sharing the crops. If we sowed spiritual things in you, is it too much if we reap material things from you?

The preceding context of this passage shows that Paul is asserting his rights and those of others to be paid for their efforts in the cause of the gospel. Just as soldiers have a right to be supported and vineyard planters have a right to eat from vineyards (see 1 Cor. 9:7), so too, those who "sowed spiritual things" have a right to "reap material things" (9:11). In other words, ministers of the gospel are worthy of material support.

What has puzzled some interpreters, though, is how Paul supports his point from the OT. He refers to the OT by saying, "For it is written in the Law of Moses." He then appeals to Deuteronomy 25:4: "You shall not muzzle the ox while he is threshing." What makes some conclude that Paul is speaking allegorically is his statement, "God is not concerned about oxen, is He? [implied answer: "No"] Or is He speaking altogether for our sake? Yes, for our sake it was written" (1 Cor. 9:9b–10a).

Potentially baffling is that Deuteronomy 25:4 speaks about literal oxen, but Paul appears to be saying that God is not concerned about oxen and is only ("altogether" or "entirely") speaking about human workers. Is Paul using allegory? Richard Longenecker thinks so, saying that Paul "seems to leave the primary meaning of the injunction in Deut. 25:4" and "interprets the Old Testament allegorically."[35] Longenecker is emphatic that "1 Cor. 9:9–10 is certainly allegorical."[36]

Consistent with a *sensus plenior* approach, S. Lewis Johnson argues for a "spiritual or moral sense" that goes beyond the literal sense:

> Thus the apostle acknowledges that the Old Testament text, while not exclusively for men, does have an application to them. The literal meaning is not excluded, but the text is given a further spiritual or moral sense. In one sense, the passage is seen as referring to God, not as the Creator who cares for His creation (cf. Ps. 104:14, 21, 27; 145:9, 15; Matt. 6:26; 10:30), but as the Law-giver. As such it had a significance beyond the oxen, namely, that of moral justice to men. This viewpoint is in harmony with the apostle's words in 1 Corinthians 10:6, 11:15.[37]

On the other side, Walter Kaiser and G. K. Beale argue for a more contextual approach to this passage. The Greek term *pantos* in 1 Corinthians 9:10 is sometimes translated "altogether" or "entirely." And if this translation is correct, then the proper understanding would be that Deuteronomy 25:4 is *only* about human beings, and not at all about oxen. In this case, Paul would not be using Deuteronomy 25:4 contextually.

But Kaiser says a better rendering of the term is "mainly" or "especially."[38] Beale says *pantos* could be admirably understood in this context as "surely," "above all," or "doubtless."[39] According to Kaiser and Beale, Paul is not denying that Deuteronomy 25:4 is about animals, but the verse has implications beyond animals.

---

[35] Richard N. Longenecker, *Biblical Exegesis in the Apostolic Period* (Grand Rapids: Eerdmans, 1975, 1999), 109–10.

[36] Ibid., 109.

[37] S. Lewis Johnson, Jr., *The Old Testament in the New: An Argument for Biblical Inspiration* (Grand Rapids, MI: Zondervan, 1980), 48.

[38] Kaiser, "Single Meaning, Unified Referents," 85.

[39] Beale, *New Testament Use of the Old Testament*, 68.

The language could point to a "lesser to the greater" argument—what is true of the lesser (oxen) is also true of the greater (human gospel workers).[40]

If Kaiser and Beale are correct, Paul is not allegorizing Deuteronomy 25:4. Nor is he denying that Deuteronomy 25:4 refers to oxen. Instead, Paul's point is that what was true of oxen also applies to workers for the gospel. Thus, this could be an *application of a moral principle*. Just as it is compassionate and just to take care of an ox that is threshing, so too is it compassionate and just for Paul and other gospel ministers to benefit materially from their efforts. Paul worked hard to establish the church at Corinth, and he had a right to benefit from his efforts. Whether he chose to accept these benefits was another matter, but his right to such compensation existed nonetheless. Deuteronomy 25:4 expressed this principle. Summarizing a more contextual understanding, Beale states, "If such a latter rendering [of *pantos* as discussed above] is viable, then Paul is saying that while this text of Deuteronomy has meaning for animals, how much more so does it have application to human laborers."[41]

---

[40] Beale, *New Testament Use of the Old Testament*, 67.

[41] Ibid., 68.

# PART TWO

## HOW THE NEW TESTAMENT USES THE OLD TESTAMENT

# CHAPTER TEN

# THE VIEW OF THIS BOOK

I have strived to be objective in presenting the various views of NT use of the OT. Yet I also have my own ideas and perspectives. So with this chapter, I explicitly state my views on NT use of the OT.

After looking at many cases of NT use of the OT and evaluating the various views, I identify with the first position we surveyed— "Single Meaning-Multiple Significances," or, "Consistent Contextual Use of the OT by the NT Writers" approach. My view is similar to that of Walter Kaiser and Abner Chou. *In sum, I believe the NT writers and persons consistently quoted and used the OT in a contextual manner. Whether by explaining the meaning of an OT passage, or drawing implications or significances from an OT text, the NT persons and authors quoted the OT in ways consistent with the original meanings of the OT authors.* These meanings and significances can be discerned by applying grammatical-historical hermeneutics consistently to all Bible passages.

My reasons for adopting a consistent contextual position largely can be summed up in the following three assertions:

1. The vast majority of NT quotations of the OT are contextual uses of the OT.
2. Of the fourteen or so hard cases in which doubt exists about contextual usage, most of these can satisfactorily be explained as contextual uses of the OT.
3. Even if there are a few cases of non-contextual uses of the OT, these would be rare exceptions, and far from the norm.

While the issues are complex, there are not enough (or, arguably, any) clear cases of non-contextual uses of the OT to justify adopting a non-contextual approach. All, or nearly all cases, can be explained reasonably from a contextual perspective.

My view is not contingent on my one-hundred percent accuracy on every use of the OT in the NT. Nor is it reliant on convincing every critic that each use of the OT in the NT is contextual. That is an unrealistic standard. Instead, I assert that contextual uses of the OT in the NT are so dominant and pervasive that the consistent, contextual position rightly can be deemed the preferred and accurate view. For this position to be proven wrong, more than a few "non-contextual" uses of the OT would need to be proven. A pattern would have to be shown, and I do not think that can be demonstrated.

Thus, I believe the NT writers and persons overwhelmingly used the OT in a contextual manner. By "contextual," I mean that when a NT person or writer uses the OT there is some point of correspondence or connection with the OT author's intent (as inspired by the Holy Spirit) either in meaning or significance/implication. Concerning "meaning," there is a connecting point with the authorial intent of the OT writer. Concerning "significance," there is an implication or application that is consistent with the intent, spirit, or trajectory of the OT writer. This does not mean the OT author necessarily foresaw all the implications of his text, but the implications are consistent with his intent. This is related to the concept of "willed type" discussed earlier in this book.

I will cover many uses of the OT in the NT as we proceed in the coming chapters. But before doing so, I offer a list of ideas that summarize my understanding of NT use of the OT:

1. The writers of the Bible, both in the OT and NT, wrote under inspiration of the Holy Spirit; there is a human and divine author for each passage of Scripture.

2. For each passage in the Bible, including those in the OT, there is one, and only one, meaning. I affirm Article VII of the "Chicago Statement on Hermeneutics" which says: "We affirm that the meaning expressed in each biblical text is single, definite and fixed. We deny that the recognition of this single meaning eliminates the variety of its application."

3. Meaning is linked with authorial intent; thus, meaning is located in what an author meant.

4. A text with its symbols is the vehicle for the transmission of authorial intent; a text does not mean anything apart from the intent of its author.

5. Under inspiration, the meaning of an OT passage from the human author is God's meaning—there are no hidden or additional divine meanings in a text beyond what the human author intended (i.e. no *sensus plenior*).

6. The confluence of human and divine authorship does not necessitate double and hidden meanings; instead, what the human author intended is what God intended at that point in a text.

7. Progress of revelation makes the theory of fuller or hidden meaning or *sensus plenior* unnecessary; when God desired to add additional revelation, He did so through inspiring later authors of Scripture to write that revelation.

8. In addition to meaning, a Bible passage can have implications which include significances and applications that stem from the meaning an author intended in a text.

9. The fact that God understands all implications and applications of an OT passage that the OT author did not foresee does not mean there are hidden meanings in an OT text.

10. When the NT writers quote or allude to the OT writings, they are not just concerned with meaning; at times they also are drawing upon implications and applications; context will determine whether a NT writer is emphasizing OT meaning or significance.

11. When there is implication or significance drawn from an OT passage in the NT, this is consistent with the meaning of the OT author and follows the trajectory of an OT author's meaning.

12. The NT quotations and allusions of the OT are overwhelmingly done in a contextual manner.

13. The case for contextual use of the OT by the NT writers is not dependent on proving that every single quotation and allusion is contextual. The overwhelming contextual use of the OT by the NT writers establishes that the contextual view is accurate.

With these points established, we now transition to looking at how the NT writers used the OT.

# CHAPTER ELEVEN

# WHAT THE OT AND NT AUTHORS UNDERSTOOD

This chapter examines what the OT authors understood when it came to future events concerning the Messiah. It also considers certain assumptions the NT writers had when they quoted the OT writings.

## What the OT Prophets Were Looking For (1 Peter 1:10–12)

First Peter 1:10–12 is an important passage for hermeneutics. In it, Peter offers inspired commentary on what the OT prophets were looking for when they penned their prophecies:

> As to this salvation, the prophets who prophesied of the grace that would come to you made careful searches and inquiries, seeking to know what person or time the Spirit of Christ within them was indicating as He predicted the sufferings of Christ and the glories to follow. It was revealed to them that they were not serving themselves, but you, in these things which now have been announced to you through those who preached the gospel to you by the Holy Spirit sent from heaven—things into which angels long to look.

Peter says the OT prophets wrote concerning the "salvation" and "grace" that would come to followers of Jesus. Their words were forward-looking to a time beyond theirs. Concerning what they wrote, they made "careful searches" and "inquiries." They were inquisitive and searched intently. But what were they searching for? Verse 11 tells us. According to the NASB, they, "were seeking to know what person or time the Spirit of Christ [i.e. Holy Spirit] within them was indicating" concerning "the sufferings of Christ and the glories to follow." The NIV translates this: "what time or circumstances." Scholars disagree concerning which translation is most accurate—either "what person or time" or "what time or circumstances." Good grammatical arguments can be made for either side. If the first view is correct ("person or time"), then the apostles were searching intently to know (1) *which specific person* would be the referent who fulfilled their prophecies, and (2) *when* their prophecies would occur. With this view, the prophets wrote specifically about the coming Messiah, but they did not know exactly *who* this Messiah would be and *when* He would arrive.

If the latter understanding is correct ("time or circumstances"), then their search focused on the *timing* and *events* related to their prophecies. Yet even if this latter interpretation is correct, the person of the Messiah is still in view since they wrote about both the sufferings and glories of the Messiah. Either way, a significant person was on their minds. If one is writing about a person's sufferings and glory, that assumes the existence of a person who will experience these matters. So with either view, *the OT prophets wrote with a specific messianic hope in mind*. This passage is inspired affirmation that the OT prophets wrote with a hope about a personal Messiah and Savior. Peter, the writer of 1 Peter, said in Acts 2:30–31 that David was a "prophet" who "looked ahead and spoke of the resurrection of the Christ." So Peter believed David had a specific messianic hope and could write concerning the experiences of this coming Messiah.

Sometimes 1 Peter 1:10–12 is used to support the idea that the OT writers did not always understand the meaning of the prophecies they wrote. But this passage does not teach this. The OT prophets were not confused about the meaning of what they wrote. What they diligently sought was the *referent* for their prophecies and the *timing* for when the Christ would appear. To search for the person, timing, and circumstances of their prophecies is consistent with knowing what they wrote.

Verse 12 then reveals that the OT prophets knew they were writing for the benefit of others and not themselves—"they were not serving themselves, but you." They considered people who would live to see the days of the Messiah. In sum, we know five truths about the OT prophets and their writings from 1 Peter 1:10–12:

1. They had a specific messianic hope.
2. They wrote about the sufferings of the Messiah.
3. They wrote about the glories of the Messiah.
4. They knew that glory would follow suffering.
5. They knew that what they wrote would be fulfilled beyond their times.[1]

These specific insights from Peter help us understand what the OT prophets understood.

---

[1] This list is similar to that by Walter C. Kaiser, Jr. in *Three Views on the New Testament Use of the Old Testament*, ed. Kenneth Berding and Jonathan Lunde (Grand Rapids: Zondervan, 2008), 56.

# NT Expectations for Understanding the OT

On at least two occasions, NT persons stated that the OT message concerning Jesus could be understood. These involve Jesus and Paul. First, according to Luke 24, Jesus approached two men walking to the village of Emmaus after His resurrection. Jesus addressed them about the Scriptures and the Christ:

And He said to them, "O foolish men and slow of heart to believe in all that the prophets have spoken! Was it not necessary for the Christ to suffer these things and to enter into His glory?" Then beginning with Moses and with all the prophets, He explained to them the things concerning Himself in all the Scriptures. (24:25–27)

This mild rebuke from Jesus reveals certain truths. First, Jesus expected His traveling companions to understand and believe "all that the prophets" had already "spoken" concerning Him. The needed information about Jesus already was contained in the OT Scriptures. Second, not comprehending what the OT prophets predicted was considered "foolish" and being "slow of heart to believe." This could only be true if knowledge about Jesus was available to be understood. Third, Jesus took it upon himself to explain "the things concerning Himself in all the Scriptures." So by using Moses and all the prophets (i.e. the entire OT corpus), Jesus explained what already was there "concerning Himself." Jesus was not saying every single OT text was directly about Him, but the verses that did reference Himself He explained.

Of course, connecting all the "theological dots" about Jesus from the OT was challenging, and we are fooling ourselves if we think we would have done better. But the information was there. Later in the chapter after again saying that everything written about Him in the OT was fulfilled, we are told, "He [Jesus] opened their minds to understand the Scriptures" (Luke 24:44–45). Jesus did not give them new revelation or reveal hidden information, but He opened their minds to understand what was already written. Thus, Luke 24 demonstrates that information concerning Jesus' suffering and glory was available to be known.

The second example involves Paul. In Acts 26, Paul was on trial before King Agrippa concerning accusations from the Jews (Acts 26:1–2). Paul stated that his message should not be surprising since all he stated was already in the Hebrew Scriptures:

So, having obtained help from God, I stand to this day testifying both to small and great, *stating nothing but what the Prophets and Moses said was going to take place*; that the Christ was to suffer, and that by reason of His resurrection from the dead He would be the first to proclaim light both to the Jewish people and to the Gentiles. (Acts 26:22–23, emphasis mine)

Like Jesus, Paul stated that the Christ's suffering and resurrection were predicted in "the Prophets and Moses." Also, it was predicted that the Christ would proclaim light to both Jews and Gentiles (see Isaiah 42 and 49). Again, these key pieces of information concerning Jesus were revealed in the OT. Significant, too, is that Paul viewed himself as teaching what was already revealed in the OT. There is no reinterpretation of the OT; instead, there is a straightforward mention of what had already been known.

These two examples show that Jesus and His sufferings and glory were already revealed and could be known from the OT. Certainly, grasping these matters was easier after the fact, but no secret key was needed to grasp these truths.

# Presuppositions of the NT Writers

The NT writers were carried along by the Holy Spirit (2 Pet. 1:21), but they did not write in a vacuum apart from any context. There were certain assumptions or presuppositions behind their writings. The seven presuppositions mentioned below influenced how the NT writers quoted and alluded to the OT. All of these operate behind the ultimate presupposition—namely that the God who exists has revealed Himself in the Scriptures, and that what He says is true.

***First, the long-awaited Messiah appeared in Jesus of Nazareth.*** This is the most important and foundational of their beliefs. Jesus of Nazareth broke into history. This Jesus is not only Son and Messiah, He is the Last Adam (1 Cor. 15:45), the ultimate David (Matt. 9:27), the ultimate seed of Abraham (Gal. 3:16), and the Suffering Servant (Mark 10:45). Jesus' appearance means a transition from the era of the Mosaic covenant to the New covenant. Jesus is the culmination of the prophets' predictions (see 2 Cor. 1:20), and the One who brings to fulfillment all OT prophecies and covenants (see Matt. 5:17–19). With Jesus' coming, everything must be understood in light of Him.

***Second, Jesus' arrival is the realization of a specific messianic hope.*** Jesus is more than some ideal person who showed up in history to fulfill God's purposes. The OT prophets predicted Him, as a person. The OT Scriptures spoke of a specific Savior and Messiah. Passages like Genesis 3:15; 4:1; and 5:28–29 reveal from earliest times that there would be a particular Savior from the seed of the woman (Eve) who would reverse the curse and save humanity. A specific child would rule the world (see Isa. 9:6–7) and the people groups of the world (see Gen. 49:8–12). He is the prophet to whom the people would listen (Deut. 18:15; Acts 3:22). This specific messianic hope is realized in the person of Jesus, and the NT writers wrote in light of this fact. The importance of this point cannot be overstated. We do not have to force our interpretation to see Jesus in every passage of the OT. If we use proper hermeneutics, we will discover many passages predicting Jesus and what He would accomplish.

*Third, both verbal prophecies and historical events in Israel's history point to Jesus and New covenant realities.* The NT writers believed that OT persons and events anticipated other realities. The OT writers offered verbal prophecies concerning the Messiah's coming, kingdom, and other events. Certain prophecies were fulfilled directly in Jesus and events in His life (Micah 5:2 with Matt. 2:5–6). Yet in addition to these, certain events in Israel's history correspond to events in Jesus' life. For example, the exodus of God's son, Israel, from Egypt anticipated the coming out of Egypt of God's son, Jesus (Hos. 11:1 with Matt. 2:15). Also, the captivity of Israel's young men during the Babylonian Captivity corresponded to the slaughter of infants at the time of Jesus' birth (Jer. 31:15 with Matt. 2:17–18). These highlight the relationship of corporate Israel with the ideal, individual Israelite—Jesus. Thus, both prophecy and history point to Jesus.

*Fourth, corporate solidarity exists between "the one and the many."* With corporate solidarity or corporate representation, a key leader or representative ("the one") represents and acts on behalf of the "many." For example, in Romans 5:12–19 both Adam and Jesus are presented as representative heads of humanity who perform specific acts that impact the rest of humanity. In Galatians 3:16, Jesus is the ultimate seed of Abraham who allows others in Him to become the seed of Abraham (Gal. 3:29). In Matthew 2, Jesus is the ultimate representative of Israel who can restore national Israel. This understanding of corporate representation was strategic to the NT writers who viewed Jesus as being the ideal Man, Israel, David, seed of Abraham, Servant, etc. This allows sinful human beings in Jesus to participate in God's blessings by being in union with Him.

*Fifth, the last days were inaugurated in the first coming of Jesus.* This point and the next point are closely related. The arrival of Jesus meant the last days began. As Hebrews 1:1–2a states: "God, after He spoke long ago to the fathers in the prophets in many portions and in many ways, in these last days has spoken to us in His Son." This means certain promises and predictions from the OT came to fruition. In Acts 3:18, Peter said prophecies concerning the suffering of the Messiah were fulfilled. New covenant forgiveness of sins and the indwelling ministry of the Holy Spirit have occurred (see Matt. 26:28; Acts 2:4). Also, Gentiles today receive messianic salvation without having to be a member of Israel (see Acts 15:14–18; Amos 9:11–12). But this truth does not mean everything promised in the OT was fulfilled with Jesus' first coming. This leads to the sixth point below.

*Sixth, whatever was not fulfilled in Jesus' first coming will be fulfilled in events involving Jesus' second coming.* Some prophecies and predictions await fulfillment with events surrounding Jesus' return. In Acts 3:21, Peter said that the second coming of Jesus and the "restoration of all things" still needed to occur. In Matthew 19:28, Jesus placed in the future the renewal of planet earth, His assumption of the Davidic throne, and the apostles' judging of the twelve tribes of Israel. In addition, Paul said the salvation and restoration of Israel would occur someday (see Rom. 11:26–27). Thus, the NT persons and writers often refer to OT prophecies that await future fulfillment (see Matt. 24:15, 29–31). So while rightly grasping first-coming fulfillments, we must also note that many prophecies will be fulfilled in Jesus' second coming.

*Seventh, Jesus, the ultimate Israelite, came to save and restore the nation Israel and bring salvation to the Gentiles as Gentiles.* The covenants of promise in the OT (Abrahamic, Davidic, New) were given to and mediated through Israel for the ultimate purpose of blessing the Gentile nations (see Gen. 12:2–3; 22:18; 2 Sam. 7:19; Isa. 52:15). So there is a both/and scenario—the covenants relate to Israel and Gentiles. Jesus, the ultimate representative of Israel, came to save and restore Israel and save the Gentiles (see Isa. 49:3–6). Luke 2:32 says Jesus would be "A LIGHT OF REVELATION TO THE GENTILES, and the glory of Your people Israel." With Romans 15:8–9a, Paul declared, "For I say that Christ has become a servant to the circumcision [i.e. Israel] on behalf of the truth of God to confirm the promises given to the fathers, and for the Gentiles to glorify God for His mercy." Many theologians today miss this point, but Jesus did not come to make Gentiles "Israel" or replace Israel with the church. He came to bring salvation both to Israel and the Gentiles. The church Jesus founded is the New covenant community of saved Israelites and Gentiles in this age. When Jesus returns, "all Israel will be saved" (Rom. 11:26) and the nation Israel will be restored (see Matt. 19:26; Acts 1:6; 3:20–21). Blessings to Gentile peoples also will increase when Israel is saved and restored (see Rom. 11:12, 15).

Each of these seven points above are relevant concerning how the NT persons and writers used the OT. Being familiar with these helps us understand how the NT writers and persons used the OT.

# What Others Say

Two other books have also offered lists concerning assumptions and presuppositions of the NT authors. In his introduction to the book, *Three Views on the New Testament Use of the Old Testament*, Jonathan Lunde listed five interpretive assumptions of New Testament authors: (1) Jesus is the One in whom the Scriptures find fulfillment; (2) the days of fulfillment have come; (3) corporate solidarity ("the one in the many"); (4) pattern (correspondence) in history; and (5) the inaugurated fulfillment of the Scriptures.[2]

Also, G. K. Beale in his book, *Handbook on the New Testament Use of the Old Testament*, lists "Presuppositions of NT Writers in Interpreting the OT." These are:

1. There is the apparent assumption of *corporate solidarity* or *representation*.
2. In the light of corporate solidarity or representation, Christ as the Messiah is viewed as representing the *true Israel* of the OT *and* the true Israel—the church—in the NT.
3. *History is unified* by a wise and sovereign plan so that the earlier parts are designed to correspond and point to the latter parts. (cf., e.g., Matt 5:17; 11:13; 13:16–17)
4. The age of *eschatological fulfillment* has come in Christ.
5. As a consequence of the preceding presupposition, it follows that the latter parts of biblical history function as the broader context for interpreting earlier parts because they all have the same, ultimate divine author who inspires the various human authors. One deduction from this premise is that Christ is the goal toward which the OT pointed and is the end-time center of redemptive history, which is the *key to interpreting the earlier portions of the OT and its promises*.[3]

I agree with Lunde's list, but I would also add the categories of a specific messianic hope, the expectation that unfulfilled prophecy will be fulfilled, and the meaning of Jesus for Israel and the Gentiles. Concerning Beale, I agree with his points 1, 3, and 4. Regarding point 2, I agree that Jesus is "true Israel," if understood correctly, but I disagree with the assumption that the true Israel is the church. The church is the New covenant community of believing Israelites and Gentiles in this age, but the NT does not teach or imply that the church is the "true Israel." Jesus' role as the "true Israel" means the eventual salvation and restoration of national Israel and messianic salvation extending to Gentiles (see Isa. 49:3–6). I also disagree with his point 5. I think the basis for understanding any Bible passage is consistent grammatical-historical hermeneutics applied to that passage in its context. While later revelation harmonizes with and builds upon earlier revelation, I do not think that later revelation is the "key" to interpreting the earlier OT revelation. The meaning of a passage is found in that passage, even in OT passages. Later revelation harmonizes with earlier revelation, but it does not reinterpret or transcend earlier revelation.

---

[2] Kenneth Berding and Jonathan Lunde, eds., *Three Views on New Testament Use of the Old Testament* (Grand Rapids: Zondervan, 2008), 35–39.

[3] Beale, *New Testament Use of the Old Testament*, 96–97.

# Has the Case for Non-Contextual
# Use of the OT Been Exaggerated?

Many treatments of the NT use of the OT issue focus on hard cases or examples where a non-contextual use of the OT seems to occur (Matt. 2:15/Hos. 11:1; Matt. 2:17–18/Jer. 31:15; Gal. 3:16/"seed"; Acts 2:25–28/Ps. 16:8–11, etc.). In one sense, this is understandable since attention often is given to more debated or difficult examples. But by devoting so much time to hard cases, an impression can be given that difficult cases are numerous, even normative. But difficult and possibly non-contextual uses of the OT are not many nor normative. At most, there are a few, and they certainly are not the norm.

Of the approximately 350 quotations of the OT in the NT, most can be understood contextually. Beale rightly notes that non-contextual uses of the OT are actually quite rare:

> It is often claimed that an inductive study of the New Testament reveals a predominately non-contextual exegetical method. But, in fact, of all the many Old Testament citations and allusions found in the New Testament, only a very few plausible examples of non-contextual usage have been noted by critics.[4]

Beale lists approximately a dozen cases where alleged non-contextual uses of the OT may occur, but then rightly observes, "It is by no means certain that even these examples are actually non-contextual. A number of scholars have offered viable and even persuasive explanations of how they could well be cases of contextual exegesis."[5] In addition, Beale notes that even if examples of non-contextual hermeneutics are established, "it does not necessarily follow that they are truly representative of a wider hermeneutical pattern in the New Testament. They may be exceptional rather than typical."[6] So to claim that the NT writers used the OT in mostly non-contextual ways is "a substantial overstatement." [7]

My own inductive study affirms Beale's observations. Of the 357 quotations of the OT in the NT I have identified, fourteen cases exist where a non-contextual understanding could be plausible. Note that I am not saying these fourteen are clear

---

[4] G. K. Beale, "Did Jesus and His Followers Preach the Right Doctrine from the Wrong Texts? An Examination of the Presuppositions of Jesus' and The Apostles' Exegetical Method," in *The Right Doctrine from the Wrong Texts?: Essays on the Use of the Old Testament in the New*, ed. G. K. Beale (Grand Rapids: Baker, 1994), 388–89.

[5] Ibid., 389.

[6] Ibid.

[7] Ibid., 398.

cases of a non-contextual use of the OT, but they are possible at first glance. These fourteen are:

1. Matthew's use of Zechariah 11:12–13 in Matthew 27:9–10
2. Matthew's use of Hosea 11:1 in Matthew 2:15
3. Matthew's use of Jeremiah 31:15 in Matthew 2:17–18
4. Peter's use of Joel 2:28–32 in Acts 2:16–21
5. Peter's use of Psalm 16:8–11 in Acts 2:25–32
6. Peter's use of Psalm 132:11 in Acts 2:30
7. James's use of Amos 9:11–12 in Acts 15:16–17
8. Paul's use of Deuteronomy 30:11–14 in Romans 10:6–8
9. Paul's use of Deuteronomy 25:4 in 1 Corinthians 9:9–10
10. Paul's use of Leviticus 18:5 in Romans 10:5 and Galatians 3:12
11. Paul's use of "seed" in Galatians 3:16
12. Paul's use of Genesis in Galatians 4:21–31
13. Paul's use of Psalm 68:18 in Ephesians 4:8
14. Paul's use of Genesis 2:24 in Ephesians 5:31–32

Of these fourteen, I believe a satisfactory contextual explanation exists for numbers 2, 3, 4, 5, 6, 7, and 9. So in my estimation, these are not actually cases of non-contextual uses of the OT. This leaves seven where a real possibility of non-contextual uses of the OT could be occurring—1, 8, 10, 11, 12, 13, and 14. Again, I am not saying this group of seven definitively offers clear cases of non-contextual uses of the OT. But I see how a reasonable person could conclude them to be non-contextual uses. Yet of this latter group of seven, I believe only three truly could be examples of non-contextual usage—12, 13, and 14. In Galatians 4:21–31, Paul says "the law" is saying that the accounts of Sarah/Isaac and Hagar/Ishmael reveal truths about the Abrahamic and Mosaic covenants even though the Mosaic covenant was hundreds of years from being established. This is challenging to understand contextually. Then in Ephesians 4:8, it is challenging to connect Jesus' ascension and the giving of gifts to the church with what Psalm 68 describes. Finally, in Ephesians 5:31–32, Paul says that the man-woman marriage of Genesis 2:24 is connected with Christ's relationship with the church. But one could argue that Genesis 2:24 does not speak of Christ and the church. As will be shown later, I do not argue that these are non-contextual uses of the OT, but these offer the greatest challenge to the idea that the NT always quotes the OT contextually.

In sum, however, the vast majority of NT uses of the OT are contextual and have connecting points with the original meaning of OT passages. If it can be shown that most cases of NT use of the OT are contextual, should not this truth impact the significance we give to the harder cases? If non-contextual uses of the OT exist, perhaps these are exceptions to the rule and are not normative. So instead of focusing on the hard cases, what if one examined the vast majority of contextual uses of the OT first? This method establishes the harder cases in a different light.

The case for the primacy of a contextual approach for understanding the OT is not reliant on proving every single example as clearly contextual. Instead, if it can be shown that the strong majority of OT uses in the NT are contextual, this is enough to establish this as the primary and best view. An exception to a rule does not overturn the rule.

One more thing. I often find scholars saying that Kaiser's single meaning/consistent-contextual approach is admirable and works in most cases, but it does not account for all NT uses of the OT. But as I read their examples describing where a contextual approach allegedly breaks down, I am not convinced those are really non-contextual examples. For example, Moo cites Peter's use of Psalm 16:8–11 in Acts 2:25–28 and says that Peter's statement that David spoke of the Messiah "cannot be demonstrated from exegesis of the psalm."[8] But I am convinced that Psalm 16:10b actually is messianic in its own context. Only Jesus fits the criteria of One who will not experience bodily decay. Plus, Peter explicitly stated that David was a "prophet" who wrote about the Messiah. Can we say Peter was wrong? Also, passages like Psalm 110 indicate that David had a specific messianic hope. Why could this not be the case in Psalm 16? Is it not possible that David had the Messiah in mind as a referent when he referred to "the Holy One" in Psalm 16:10?

At this point, we shift to examining the ways in which the NT persons and writers quoted and used the OT.

---

[8] Moo, "The Problem of Sensus Plenior," 210–11.

# CHAPTER TWELVE

# LITERAL PROPHETIC FULFILLMENT

At this point, we begin a survey of the various ways the NT writers used the OT. The categories that follow are not exhaustive, but I believe they cover the majority of ways the NT writers used the OT. Before looking at these, however, I want to explain how I discovered these categories.

In studying the ways the NT writers used and quoted the OT, I studied others who put together their own lists.[1] I found these lists to be helpful. Yet to be original and as inductive as possible, I started with a blank slate. This meant studying each example of a NT quotation of the OT on my own. I also compiled a list of all the quotations of the OT in the NT and then sought to categorize each one. I studied each individually to see what

---

[1] G. K. Beale lists the following "primary ways the New Testament uses the Old Testament": (1) to indicate direct fulfillment of Old Testament prophecy; (2) to indicate indirect fulfillment of Old Testament typological prophecy; (3) to indicate an analogical or illustrative use of the Old Testament; (4) to indicate the symbolic use of the Old Testament; (5) to indicate an abiding authority carried over from the Old Testament; (6) to indicate a proverbial use of the Old Testament; (7) to indicate a rhetorical use of the Old Testament; (8) to indicate the use of an Old Testament segment as a blueprint or prototype for a New Testament segment; (9) to indicate an alternate textual use of the Old Testament; (10) to indicate an assimilated use of the Old Testament; and (11) to indicate an ironic or inverted use of the Old Testament. See *Handbook on the New Testament Use of the Old Testament: Exegesis and Interpretation* (Grand Rapids: Baker Academic, 2012), 55–93. Roy B. Zuck offers the following "purposes": (1) to point up the accomplishment or realization of an Old Testament prediction; (2) to confirm that a New Testament incident is in agreement with an Old Testament principle; (3) to explain a point given in the Old Testament; (4) to support a point being made in the New Testament; (5) to illustrate a New Testament truth; (6) to apply the Old Testament to a New Testament incident or truth; (7) to summarize an Old Testament concept; (8) to use Old Testament terminology; (9) to draw a parallel with an Old Testament incident; (10) to relate an Old Testament situation to Christ. *Basic Bible Interpretation: A Practical Guide to Discovering Biblical Truth* (Colorado Springs, CO: Victor Books, 1991), 260–70.

categories emerged and where each use of the OT in the NT fit. I focused mostly on explicit quotations. In this process, I discovered the following seven categories:

1. Literal Prophetic Fulfillment
2. Affirmation that an Old Testament Prophetic Text Not Yet Fulfilled Will Be in the Future
3. Literal Application of Timeless Moral or Theological Point
4. Literal Reliance on an Old Testament Event or Statement
5. Divine Correspondence between Israel and Jesus
6. Divine Correspondence between David and Jesus
7. Generational Fulfillment

Not every NT quote of the OT fits neatly somewhere in the above seven categories, but the vast majority do. In order for a category to exist, there had to be at least several examples that fit. Some of these categories I found matched well with what others had discovered, like numbers 1, 2, and 3 above.

Also note that listing several "ways" the NT quotes the OT does not mean there are different hermeneutical principles for understanding the OT. I believe these seven categories can be discovered by a consistent use of grammatical-historical hermeneutics.

As the title of this chapter indicates, one major category of NT use of the OT is "Literal Prophetic Fulfillment." This occurs when the NT uses an OT text to indicate an OT prophecy has been fulfilled in a direct and literal way. A one-to-one connection occurs between OT expectation and NT realization. There are many examples of this in the NT.

# Examples of Literal Prophetic Fulfillment

## Matthew 2:5–6 / Micah 5:2

When Jesus was born, the Magi from the East came to Jerusalem looking for this newborn king of the Jews. Herod inquired of the chief priests and scribes of Israel concerning Jesus' whereabouts (Matt. 2:1–4). Their response was:

> They said to him, "In Bethlehem of Judea; for this is what has been written by the prophet:
>
> > 'AND YOU, BETHLEHEM, LAND OF JUDAH,
> > ARE BY NO MEANS LEAST AMONG THE LEADERS OF JUDAH;
> > FOR OUT OF YOU SHALL COME FORTH A RULER
> > WHO WILL SHEPHERD MY PEOPLE ISRAEL.'" (Matt. 2:5–6)

This is a direct prophetic fulfillment of Micah 5:2. Micah 5:2 predicted that the Messiah would be born in Bethlehem, and this prophecy was literally fulfilled with Jesus' birth in Bethlehem. The chief priests and scribes understood Micah 5:2 literally, which explains why they could declare to Herod that the Ruler would come from the actual geographical town of Bethlehem. Thus, Jesus being born in Bethlehem is a clear example of literal prophetic fulfillment.

## Matthew 3:3; John 1:23 / Isaiah 40:3

Isaiah 40 speaks of the Lord's comfort coming to Israel and Jerusalem. This chapter also tells of a "voice" who would clear the way for the Lord (Isa. 40:3). Matthew 3:3 states that Isaiah 40:3 was fulfilled in the ministry of John the Baptist:

> For this is the one referred to by Isaiah the prophet when he said,
>
> > "THE VOICE OF ONE CRYING IN THE WILDERNESS,
> > 'MAKE READY THE WAY OF THE LORD,
> > MAKE HIS PATHS STRAIGHT!'"

According to John 1:23, when the priests and Levites came to John the Baptist asking who he was, John the Baptist quoted Isaiah 40:3 to show he was not the Christ, but the one who prepared the way for the Christ: "He [John the Baptist] said, 'I am A VOICE OF ONE CRYING IN THE WILDERNESS, 'MAKE STRAIGHT THE WAY OF THE LORD,' as Isaiah the prophet said." Köstenberger rightly notes that "several elements of the original context of Isa. 40:3 resonate with the passage's use in John 1:23."[2] These include:

> (1) the wilderness as the site of prophetic activity…(2) the focus away from the messenger and onto the message; (3) the coming revelation of God's glory through his visible coming and bringing of salvation, not merely to Israel, but to all of humanity; (4) the need for repentance to prepare the way.[3]

Thus, John the Baptist was the literal fulfillment of Isaiah 40:3.

## Mark 1:2–3 / Malachi 3:1; Isaiah 40:3

Malachi 3:1a states: "Behold, I am going to send My messenger, and he will clear the way before Me. And the Lord, whom you seek, will suddenly come to His temple." This speaks of a forerunner who will prepare the way for the Lord. Malachi

---

[2] Andreas J. Köstenberger, "John," in *Commentary on the New Testament Use of the Old Testament*, ed. G. K. Beale and D. A Carson (Grand Rapids: Baker Academic, 2007), 427.

[3] Ibid.

4:5 indicated this forerunner will be Elijah: "Behold, I am going to send you Elijah the prophet before the coming of the great and terrible day of the LORD."

Mark combined Malachi 3:1 and Isaiah 40:3 in Mark 1:2–3 to show that John the Baptist was the direct prophetic fulfillment of OT prophecy in which a "messenger" and a "voice" would come to "make ready the way of the Lord." While John the Baptist himself was not Elijah (see John 1:21), John was "a forerunner before Him [Jesus] in the spirit and power of Elijah" (Luke 1:17). Not only was the Messiah explicitly predicted in the OT, so too was the forerunner of the Messiah— John the Baptist.

## Luke 3:4–6 / Isaiah 40:3–5

Like the two examples immediately above, Luke also links John the Baptist and his ministry with Isaiah 40. Luke 3:4 states, "as it is written in the book of the words of Isaiah the prophet," and then Luke quotes most of Isaiah 40:3–5. All four Gospel writers see John the Baptist's ministry as a fulfillment of Isaiah 40.

## Luke 1:17 / Malachi 4:6

Malachi 4:6 is the last verse of the OT, and its message is found in Luke 1:17. In Malachi 4:5, God declared that He was going to send Elijah the Prophet before the Day of the Lord. Verse 6 then states that Elijah "will restore the hearts of the fathers to their children and the hearts of the children to their fathers, so that I will not come and smite the land with a curse." In Luke 1, an angel of the Lord announced to Zacharias that Zacharias would have a boy who would be named John (Luke 1:13). The angel also told him that John would be a forerunner who would operate "in the spirit and power of Elijah, 'TO TURN THE HEARTS OF THE FATHERS BACK TO THE CHILDREN, and the disobedient to the attitude of the righteous'" (1:17). Malachi 4:6 is a prophecy, and Luke 1:17 reveals that John the Baptist is the fulfillment of the Malachi 4:6 prophecy. This is a clear case of literal prophetic fulfillment of an OT prophetic passage. While John is not actually Elijah, he fulfills the Elijah role in his ministry to Israel.

## Matthew 4:13–16 / Isaiah 9:1–2

Immediately after overcoming Satan's temptation (see Matt. 4:1–11), Jesus launched His public ministry by making a strategic forty-mile trek from Nazareth to Capernaum by the sea of Galilee in the region of Zebulun and Naphtali (Matt. 4:12–13). Zebulun and Naphtali comprised the northern part of Israel and were the first tribes of the northern kingdom to be exiled by the

Assyrians around 722 BC. From here, Jesus would begin His ministry to Israel proclaiming, "Repent, for the kingdom of heaven is at hand" (Matt. 4:17).

That Jesus would go to the northern region of Israel to preach the nearness of the kingdom of heaven indicates His desire to first preach the restoration of the kingdom to Israel in the location first conquered by a Gentile power (Assyria). Joel Willetts notes the strategic significance of this for the land and tribes of Israel:

> Significantly, then, the geographical structure of the narrative suggests that bound up in Matthew's portrayal of Jesus' ministry in Galilee may be a concern for the restoration of Eretz ["land"] Israel and the twelve-tribe league of national-political Israel consonant with his Jewish contemporaries.[4]

That Gentiles were associated with this area both in Isaiah's day and in the first century AD seems significant, as the Messiah's ministry involved both Israel and the Gentiles.

Matthew viewed Jesus' geographical move to be the fulfillment of Isaiah 9, which not only discussed the coming of the Messiah (see 9:6–7), but also good news for Zebulun, Naphtali, and nearby Gentiles. Isaiah 9:1a says gloom would be removed from Israel, and "the land of Zebulun and the land of Naphtali," which experienced "contempt," would be made "glorious." Matthew then quoted Isaiah 9:1–2:

> This was to fulfill what was spoken through Isaiah the prophet:
> "THE LAND OF ZEBULUN AND THE LAND OF NAPHTALI, BY THE WAY OF THE SEA, BEYOND THE JORDAN, GALILEE OF THE GENTILES—
> "THE PEOPLE WHO WERE SITTING IN DARKNESS SAW A GREAT LIGHT, AND THOSE WHO WERE SITTING IN THE LAND AND SHADOW OF DEATH, UPON THEM A LIGHT DAWNED." (Matt. 4:14–16)

Thus, Jesus' coming to Zebulun and Naphtali in connection with a message of kingdom hope to Israel with implications for Gentiles is a direct, literal fulfillment of Isaiah 9:1–2.

# Luke 4:18–19 / Isaiah 61:1–2a

Isaiah 61 describes the message of a special person on whom the Spirit of the Lord will reside. He will be anointed of God and bring blessings to Israel and the nations (61:11). Verses 1–2 lay out the mission of this anointed One:

---

[4] Joel Willetts, "Zionism in the Gospel of Matthew," in *The New Christian Zionism: Fresh Perspectives on Israel & the Land*, ed. Gerald R. McDermott (Downers Grove, IL: InterVarsity Press, 2016), 121.

> The Spirit of the Lord GOD is upon me,
> Because the LORD has anointed me
> To bring good news to the afflicted;
> He has sent me to bind up the brokenhearted,
> To proclaim liberty to captives
> And freedom to prisoners;
> To proclaim the favorable year of the LORD
> And the day of vengeance of our God;
> To comfort all who mourn.

This special person does not arrive without context. As Pao and Schnabel observe, "This individual has parallels in the servant figure of Isa. 40–55."[5] This is the same Servant of Isaiah 42:1:

> Behold, My Servant, whom I uphold;
> My chosen one in whom My soul delights.
> I have put My Spirit upon Him;
> He will bring forth justice to the nations.

This is the same Servant of Isaiah 49 who will restore Israel and bring light to the nations (vv. 3–6), and the Servant who will atone for the sins of Israel and the Gentiles (Isaiah 52–53).

Since this person will be a righteous Servant who restores Israel and blesses the Gentiles, this Servant is not Israel as a corporate entity. Israel as a people is sinful and cannot save itself or others. Instead, this is a special representative from Israel who can save Israel and the Gentiles. Thus, these Servant texts, including Isaiah 61, concern the Messiah we now know as Jesus.

Jesus explicitly said that He fulfilled the message of Isaiah 61:1–2a. Jesus quoted this text in Luke 4:17–21, when He read from the Book of Isaiah in a synagogue in Nazareth:

> And the book of the prophet Isaiah was handed to Him. And He opened the book and found the place where it was written,
>
> > "THE SPIRIT OF THE LORD IS UPON ME,
> > BECAUSE HE ANOINTED ME TO PREACH THE GOSPEL TO THE POOR.
> > HE HAS SENT ME TO PROCLAIM RELEASE TO THE CAPTIVES,
> > AND RECOVERY OF SIGHT TO THE BLIND,

---

[5] David W. Pao and Eckhard J. Schnabel, "Luke," in *Commentary on the New Testament Use of the Old Testament*, ed. G. K. Beale and D. A. Carson (Grand Rapids: Baker, 2007), 288.

> To set free those who are oppressed,
> To proclaim the favorable year of the Lord."

And He closed the book, gave it back to the attendant and sat down; and the eyes of all in the synagogue were fixed on Him. And He began to say to them, "Today this Scripture has been fulfilled in your hearing."

This is a contextual use of the OT since Isaiah 61, along with other Servant passages in Isaiah, is messianic in nature. Isaiah 61 predicted that a coming anointed person on whom God's Spirit resided would bring good news and blessings to Israel and the nations. This is the mission of the Messiah. And that is the message Jesus proclaimed as described in Luke 4. Jesus preached good news to the poor; He proclaimed liberty to captives; He restored sight to the blind; He set free the oppressed; He proclaimed the favorable year of the Lord.

Note that Jesus did not quote Isaiah 61:2b, which foretells "the day of vengeance of our God." Such Day of the Lord vengeance awaits Jesus' second coming, not His first coming. Nevertheless, the use of Isaiah 61:1–2a in Luke 4:18–19 is a case of literal prophetic fulfillment. What Isaiah 61 predicted was fulfilled with Jesus and His ministry.

# Matthew 8:16–17 / Isaiah 53:4

According to Matthew 8:16-17, Jesus cast out demons and performed physical healings, restoring "all who were ill." Matthew viewed Jesus' healings as a fulfillment of Isaiah 53:4 which says, "This was to fulfill what was spoken through Isaiah the prophet: 'He Himself took our infirmities and carried away our diseases.'" Thus, Matthew connected Jesus' healing ministry with the Suffering Servant's ministry of Isaiah 53.

The healings of Matthew 8:16-17 undeniably refer to physical healings. But does this fit with the message of Isaiah 53:4? Some think Isaiah 53:4 refers only to spiritual healing, not physical healing. But Isaiah 53:4 seems to include the idea of physical healings. The two terms Isaiah used in 53:4 are *choli* and *makob*. The *choli* term often carries the idea of physical sickness (see Deut. 7:15; 28:59, 61; 1 Kings 17:17; 2 Kings 8:8; Isa. 38:9). *Makob* also is used of physical pain (see Job 33:19; Jer. 51:8). While the Suffering Servant of Isaiah 53 will certainly heal more than physical sickness and pain, the Servant's ministry includes holistic restoration in the physical realm. The ministry of Jesus, over the course of His two comings, ultimately brings both spiritual and physical healing. And physical restoration and resurrection are related to Jesus' atoning work (see Col. 1:20). Jesus' physical healings are part of His proclamation of the nearness of the kingdom at this time (see Matt. 10:5–8).

These miracles offered samples of kingdom blessings, including physical healings. Matthew, therefore, sees a literal fulfillment of Isaiah 53:4 in Matthew 8:16–17. Blomberg is correct when he says, "At the very least, Matthew is showing that Jesus' ministry of healing was prophesied as part of his messianic role."[6]

## Matthew 11:2–5 (and Luke 7:22) / Isaiah 35:5; 61:1

Seeking answers after his imprisonment, John the Baptist sought verification through his followers that Jesus truly was the Messiah. Jesus responded in Matthew 11:2–5 by quoting Isaiah 35:5–6, which speaks of the blind again seeing, the deaf hearing, and the lame leaping:

> Now when John, while imprisoned, heard of the works of Christ, he sent word by his disciples and said to Him, "Are You the Expected One, or shall we look for someone else?" Jesus answered and said to them, "Go and report to John what you hear and see: the BLIND RECEIVE SIGHT and the lame walk, the lepers are cleansed and the deaf hear, the dead are raised up, and the POOR HAVE THE GOSPEL PREACHED TO THEM."

Isaiah 35 foretold kingdom conditions involving physical restoration for both people and nature. While not explicitly mentioning the Messiah, the conditions described in Isaiah 35 fit the messianic kingdom upon the earth (see Isaiah 11). Thus, Jesus' miracles of restoration connect with what Isaiah 35 predicted so John could be reassured about Jesus. Also, Matthew's mention of the poor having the gospel preached to them is a quotation of Isaiah 61:1, which speaks of an anointed person with God's Spirit upon Him preaching the gospel to the poor. In sum, Jesus' acts of healing and preaching of the gospel were direct fulfillments of OT prophecy.

Luke 7:22 parallels Matthew 11:2–5. Both Isaiah 35:5–6 and Isaiah 61:1 are quoted in the same way.

## Matthew 11:10 (and Luke 7:27) / Malachi 3:1

Malachi 3:1 predicted that a "messenger" will appear who will clear the way for the Lord as He comes to His temple. Jesus says this was directly fulfilled with John the Baptist in Matthew 11:10: "This is the one about whom it is written, 'BEHOLD, I SEND MY MESSENGER AHEAD OF YOU, WHO WILL PREPARE YOUR WAY BEFORE

---

[6] Craig L. Blomberg, "Matthew," in *Commentary on the New Testament Use of the Old Testament*, ed. G. K. Beale and D. A. Carson (Grand Rapids: Baker, 2007), 33.

YOU.'" This also occurs in Luke 7:27 where Jesus quoted Malachi 3:1 to show that John the Baptist was the fulfillment of the messenger who preceded the Messiah.

## Matthew 12:15–21 / Isaiah 42:1–4

Matthew's citation of Isaiah 42:1–4 is the longest OT passage cited in Matthew's Gospel. Matthew declared that Jesus fulfilled Isaiah 42:1–4, which concerns who the Servant of the Lord is and what He will do. First, this "Servant" is God's "Beloved" who will have God's Spirit placed upon Him. Second, the Servant will perform His ministry in gentleness, in contrast to the hostile Jewish religious leaders who conspired against Jesus to destroy Him (see Matt. 12:14). Third, the Servant's ministry will bring hope to the Gentiles, thus anticipating a positive response from Gentiles to His ministry. Jesus literally fulfilled the three expectations of Isaiah 42:1–4.

## Matthew 21:4–5; John 12:14–15 / Zechariah 9:9

Zechariah 9:9 prophesied of the Messiah coming to Zion (i.e. Jerusalem) with salvation. He will do so humbly, on a donkey. Both Matthew (21:4–5) and John (12:14–15) present Jesus' "triumphal entry" into Jerusalem, just days before His death, as the literal fulfillment of Zechariah 9:9. As John 12:14–15 states, "Jesus, finding a young donkey, sat on it; as it is written, 'FEAR NOT, DAUGHTER OF ZION; BEHOLD, YOUR KING IS COMING, SEATED ON A DONKEY'S COLT.'"

Matthew and John do not quote the next verse, Zechariah 9:10, which speaks of the King's "dominion…from sea to sea" and to "the ends of the earth." Zechariah 9:10 will be fulfilled in the future with Jesus' second coming. But the use of Zechariah 9:9 in Matthew and John is a case of literal prophetic fulfillment.

## Matthew 26:31; Mark 14:27 / Zechariah 13:7

Zechariah 12–14 is a strategic OT prophetic section that foretells a final siege of Jerusalem and the rescue of Israel both politically and for salvation by the Messiah. Zechariah 12 described the return of the Messiah and the repentance of Israel as the Jewish people looked upon the One they pierced (see Zech. 12:10). Zechariah 14 tells of a final siege of Jerusalem when the Lord returns to the Mount of Olives to deliver Jerusalem and establish His kingdom upon the earth (see Zech. 14:1–9). The final fulfillment of Zechariah 12 and 14 concerns events associated with Jesus' second coming.

In the middle of Zechariah 12–14 is Zechariah 13, which describes how God will remove false prophets from Israel as a result of His rescue and salvation of Israel (Zech. 13:1–6). Zechariah contrasts the false prophets of 13:1–6 with God's true Shepherd depicted in Zechariah 13:7–9. Zechariah 13:7–9 is a poetic section that draws upon the messianic section of Zechariah 11:4–14 that described God's true Shepherd—the Messiah, and His rejection. Zechariah 13:7 states:

> "Awake, O sword, against My Shepherd,
> And against the man, My Associate,"
> Declares the LORD of hosts.
> "Strike the Shepherd that the sheep may be scattered;
> And I will turn My hand against the little ones."

This is a messianic verse. In contrast to the false prophets and shepherds of Israel described in 13:1–6, this is God's "man" who is God's "Shepherd" and "Associate." As Kaiser notes, "This messianic prophecy is speaking about a human being ('the man') who is also divine ('he is close to me,' or is 'my associate')."[7] Also, this Shepherd will be struck, which connects with the pierced Messiah of Zechariah 12:10 and the rejected Shepherd of Zechariah 11. This striking is salvific and done by God.

Also, the striking of this "Shepherd" results in the sheep of Israel being scattered—a reference to Israel's coming dispersion. Rydelnik observes that the scattering described in Zechariah 13:7 "is a prediction of the dispersion of the Jewish people around the world for nearly two thousand years. The gospels view the scattering of the disciples on the night of Jesus' betrayal as the inauguration of the dispersion."[8] In its own context, Zechariah 13:7 is messianic in nature and refers to events associated with the Messiah.

This message was picked up by Jesus as recorded in both Matthew 26:31 and Mark 14:27. After the Last Supper at the Mount of Olives, Jesus applied Zechariah 13:7 to His passion and the scattering of His disciples:

> Then Jesus said to them, "You will all fall away because of Me this night, for it is written, 'I WILL STRIKE DOWN THE SHEPHERD, AND THE SHEEP OF THE FLOCK SHALL BE SCATTERED.'" (Matt. 26:31)

Since Zechariah 13:7 is messianic in its own context, Jesus' application of this verse to Himself and His disciples is a case of direct literal fulfillment of an OT prophecy. That Jesus is the Shepherd of Zechariah 13:7 is obvious. As mentioned above, the

---

[7] Walter C. Kaiser, Jr., *The Messiah in the Old Testament* (Grand Rapids: Zondervan, 1995), 227.

[8] Michael Rydelnik, "Zechariah," in *The Moody Bible Commentary*, ed. Michael Rydelnik and Michael Vanlaningham (Chicago: Moody Publishers, 2014), 1434.

scattering of Jesus' Jewish disciples relates to the dispersion of Israel connected with the events of Acts 8 and the destruction of Jerusalem and the temple in AD 70 as described in Luke 21:20–24.

## Luke 2:32 / Isaiah 42:6; 49:6

Simeon was a righteous man. The Holy Spirit revealed that Simeon would not die until he had seen the Messiah. Quoting Isaiah 42:6/49:6, Simeon referred to the infant Jesus as "A LIGHT OF REVELATION TO THE GENTILES." Jesus fulfilled this prophecy since His first coming brought light to Gentiles as predicted in Isaiah 42 and 49.

## Luke 4:17–19 / Isaiah 61:1–2

Isaiah 61 foretells an anointed person with God's Spirit upon Him who will bring salvation and restoration to Israel, including rebuilt cities and "an everlasting covenant" (i.e. New covenant). According to verses 1–2a, this person will preach the gospel to the poor, release captives, give sight to the blind, free the oppressed, and proclaim the favorable year of the Lord. Centuries later at a synagogue in Nazareth, Jesus stood up and read Isaiah 61:1–2a and declared: "Today this Scripture has been fulfilled in your hearing" (Luke 4:21). Isaiah 61 is a messianic passage about what the Messiah would do for Israel, and Jesus viewed Isaiah 61:1–2a as being fulfilled by Him. Jesus did not quote verse 2b, which speaks of the day of God's vengeance. That will be fulfilled with Jesus' second coming. Nevertheless, Jesus' first coming brought fulfillment of parts of Isaiah 6:1–2.

## Acts 2:16–21 / Joel 2:28–32

Peter's quotation of Joel 2:28–32 in Acts 2:16–21 has several theological implications. Joel 2 concerns judgment (2:1–17) and deliverance for Israel (2:18–32). This is associated with a coming "day of the Lord" (2:31). This day of the Lord coincides with a judgment of the nations and kingdom blessings for Israel in the land (Joel 3). A messianic hope also could exist in Joel 2:23. Some believe there is mention here of a "teacher of righteousness" who brings the conditions described in Joel 2.[9]

The stimulus for Peter's first speech in Jerusalem after Jesus' ascension involved Jesus' followers being filled with the Holy Spirit (see Acts 2:4) and

---

[9] For a defense of this view see Michael A. Rydelnik, "Joel 2:23: The Teacher of Righteousness," in *The Moody Handbook of Messianic Prophecy: Studies and Expositions of the Messiah in the Old Testament*, ed. Michael Rydelnik and Edwin Blum (Chicago: Moody Publishers, 2019), 1167–75.

speaking various languages (see Acts 2:5–12). Many in the crowd were amazed, but others mocked the apostles, claiming they were drunk with sweet wine (Acts 2:13). Peter explained that they were not drunk; instead, what occurred was predicted by the prophet Joel: "but this is what was spoken of through the prophet Joel" (Acts 2:16).

Peter then quoted Joel 2:28–32 which predicted: (1) in the last days God would pour forth His Spirit on all mankind; (2) Israel's sons and daughters would prophesy; (3) young men would see visions; (4) old men would dream dreams; (5) great wonders would occur in the sky; (6) signs would appear on earth; and (7) the sun will be turned to darkness and the moon into blood (Joel 2:28–31). This is all in connection with the "day of the Lord" (Acts 2:20) and the reality that every person who calls on the Lord's name will be saved (see Joel 2:32a; Acts 2:21).

There are various views of what is happening in this connection. Some think there is no fulfillment of Joel 2 in Acts 2. Others think the NT is reinterpreting Joel 2 and transferring Israel's promises to the church. Better, though, is the view that there is a *partial fulfillment* of the Joel 2:28–32 prophecy. By "partial," this means that parts of Joel 2:28–32 were fulfilled with the events of Acts 2, yet some aspects await future fulfillment.

The Lord's pouring out of His Holy Spirit upon His people was fulfilled with the events of Acts 2. So, too, all who called on the Lord were saved. Thus, what began and ended Peter's quotation of Joel was fulfilled. Not fulfilled, though, were great signs in the sky and earth, and the cosmic signs involving the sun and the moon. These Day of the Lord events await future fulfillment. In 2 Thessalonians 2, Paul said the Day of the Lord had not started yet since the apostasy and the revealing of the man of lawlessness had not yet happened (2:1–4). Peter, himself, argued that the Day of the Lord is a future event: "But the day of the Lord will come like a thief" (2 Pet. 3:10a). This is significant since Peter quoted Joel 2 in Acts 2. If decades later Peter viewed the Day of the Lord as future, this reveals he did not believe the Day of the Lord was fulfilled with the events of Acts 2.

Also, in Acts 1:7 Jesus stated, "It is not for you to know times or epochs which the Father has fixed by His own authority." Since Jesus said the timing of future events could not be known at this time, perhaps Peter believed the Day of the Lord events could be unfolding soon. But Jesus' words did not demand that the Day of the Lord was already occurring. So while the Holy Spirit had been poured out, the Day of the Lord would await another time.

## Acts 2:34–35 / Psalm 110:1

In Acts 2, Peter argued that the crucified and risen Jesus is both Lord and Messiah (Acts 2:36). Part of his argument is that Jesus is at the right hand of God as David predicted in Psalm 110:1. Acts 2:34–35 reads:

For it was not David who ascended into heaven, but he himself says:
'THE LORD SAID TO MY LORD,
"SIT AT MY RIGHT HAND,
UNTIL I MAKE YOUR ENEMIES A FOOTSTOOL FOR YOUR FEET.'"

Psalm 110 is a messianic psalm in which David said that the coming Messiah, who is David's Lord, would have a session at the right hand of God for a time until the Messiah reigns from Jerusalem (Ps. 110:2). Peter viewed Jesus' current session at God's right hand as being fulfilled by the risen Jesus who now is in heaven at God's right hand. This is an example of direct literal prophetic fulfillment of an OT prophetic and messianic passage.

*The following four cases are examples of direct literal fulfillment concerning Isaiah 53—a passage that predicts the substitutionary atoning work of the Suffering Servant.*

# John 12:38 / Isaiah 53:1

Isaiah 53:1–2 presents the Servant of the Lord as One not accepted by His people, Israel. John 12 also presents a sad situation. Even though Jesus performed many incredible signs, the people of Israel "were not believing in Him" (12:37). John saw Israel's rejection of Jesus as a fulfillment of Isaiah 53:1: "This was to fulfill the word of Isaiah the prophet which he spoke: 'LORD, WHO HAS BELIEVED OUR REPORT? AND TO WHOM HAS THE ARM OF THE LORD BEEN REVEALED?'" Isaiah 53 is a prophecy about the Suffering Servant being rejected by His people, and what occurs in John 12 is a fulfillment of Isaiah's prophecy since Israel rejected Jesus.

# Acts 8:32–33 / Isaiah 53:7–8

Acts 8:26–40 describes an encounter between the apostle Philip and an Ethiopian eunuch who was sitting in a chariot reading the book of Isaiah while returning from Jerusalem. The Ethiopian's attention was drawn to Isaiah 53:7–8, which tells of a man of God being led like a sheep to slaughter, yet like a lamb He faces His execution without saying a word. The Ethiopian then asked Philip of whom Isaiah was speaking, and Philip explained it was Jesus (Acts 8:34–35). This is a case where someone read an OT prophetic passage seeking knowledge about its meaning. This is followed by an explanation that fulfillment of this passage occurs with Jesus. Isaiah 53 predicted a coming, righteous Suffering Servant who dies on behalf of others, and Jesus is the direct literal fulfillment of this passage.

# 1 Peter 2:22 / Isaiah 53:9

In 1 Peter 2:21, Peter argued that Jesus gave us a pattern for suffering. Then in 2:22, he quoted Isaiah 53:9b: "WHO COMMITTED NO SIN, NOR WAS ANY DECEIT FOUND IN HIS MOUTH." Jesus is the literal fulfillment of the Servant of Isaiah 53:9b who suffered while being righteous. This should be a pattern for Jesus' followers who also will suffer. So Peter quoted Isaiah 53:9b to show that Jesus is the fulfillment of Isaiah 53 and to reveal that Jesus serves as an example to His followers of how to suffer.

# Luke 22:37 / Isaiah 53:12

Isaiah 53:12 predicted that the Suffering Servant would be "numbered with the transgressors" as He bore the sin of many. Concerning this verse, Jesus said, "For I tell you that this which is written must be fulfilled in Me, 'AND HE WAS NUMBERED WITH TRANSGRESSORS'; for that which refers to Me has its fulfillment." Jesus explicitly said Isaiah 53:12 was fulfilled with Him. This is direct literal fulfillment of Isaiah 53:12.

# Romans 15:12 / Isaiah 11:1, 10

In Romans 15:8–12, Paul explained how Jesus brought blessings to the Gentiles in addition to confirming God's promises to Israel (15:8). In 15:12, Paul combined parts of Isaiah 11:1 and 11:10 which speak of a root springing from the stem of Jesse (11:1) who will help and bless the Gentile nations (11:10). Isaiah 11 is a passage about the coming Messiah and what this Messiah will mean for the nations. Paul viewed Jesus as the fulfillment of Isaiah 11.

# Hebrews 8:8–12 / Jeremiah 31:31–34

The quotation of Jeremiah 31:31–34 in Hebrews 8:8–12 is the longest verbatim quotation of a single OT passage in the NT. In Jeremiah 31, the prophet predicted a day when God would give Israel a New covenant that replaced the Mosaic covenant that Israel broke. In Hebrews, the writer extols the superiority of Jesus, including Jesus' superior New covenant that He established with His blood. This superiority of the New covenant over the Mosaic covenant is the focus of Hebrews 7–10.

Since Jesus inaugurated the New covenant, the quotation of Jeremiah 31:31–34 is a case of literal prophetic fulfillment. Jeremiah predicted a New covenant, and Hebrews 8 informs us that Jesus brought this covenant. This does not mean all aspects of the New covenant have already been fulfilled. Physical and national aspects of the covenant still need to be fulfilled in the future, and national Israel's incorporation into the New covenant is future as well (see Rom. 11:26–27). But Jesus has ended the era of the Mosaic covenant and ushered in the New covenant with His superior sacrifice.

# CHAPTER THIRTEEN

# AFFIRMATION THAT AN OLD TESTAMENT PROPHETIC TEXT NOT YET FULFILLED WILL BE IN THE FUTURE

On several occasions, NT persons quoted OT prophetic texts that still needed to be fulfilled. Some of these prophetic texts involve reward for the righteous, the abomination of desolation, cosmic signs, the Messiah's coming on the clouds, the Messiah's rule over the earth, the salvation of Israel, and the reign of the saints. We call this category of NT usage of the OT: "Affirmation that an Old Testament Prophetic Text Not Yet Fulfilled Will Be in the Future." Such uses of the OT reveal a strong continuity between the original meanings of OT eschatological passages and the expectations of the NT writers and persons.

## Examples

### Matthew 13:41–43 / Daniel 12:3

In His parable of the wheat and the tares, Jesus explained that His followers (the wheat) would coexist in the world with those who belong to the devil (tares). This situation would remain until Jesus returns with His angels to separate the two groups. In making this point, Jesus quotes Daniel 12:3:

The Son of Man will send forth His angels, and they will gather out of His kingdom all stumbling blocks, and those who commit lawlessness, and will throw them into the furnace of fire; in that place there will be weeping and gnashing of teeth. Then THE RIGHTEOUS WILL SHINE FORTH AS THE SUN in the kingdom of their Father. He who has ears, let him hear. (Matt. 13:41–43)

Daniel 12 predicted a time of unparalleled distress for Israel, but afterwards the righteous will be rescued and there will be a resurrection from the dead (Dan. 12:1–2). Daniel 12:3 then states, "Those who have insight will shine brightly like the brightness of the expanse of heaven." So after tribulation, the saints will shine brightly in the kingdom of God.

When speaking of the future, Jesus referenced the wording of Daniel 12:3 to show that fulfillment of this verse awaits His future return. When Jesus returns, believers will "shine brightly" in the kingdom of God.

# Matthew 24:15 (and Mark 13:14) / Daniel 9:27

On three occasions, the prophet Daniel predicted an event called the "abomination of desolation":

**Daniel 9:27a**
And he will make a firm covenant with the many for one week, but in the middle of the week he will put a stop to sacrifice and grain offering; and on the wing of *abominations* will come *one who makes desolate*, even until a complete destruction.

**Daniel 11:31**
Forces from him will arise, desecrate the sanctuary fortress, and do away with the regular sacrifice. And they will set up the *abomination of desolation.*

**Daniel 12:11**
From the time that the regular sacrifice is abolished and the *abomination of desolation* is set up, there will be 1,290 days.[1]

This "abomination of desolation" refers to a coming, horrible event when the Jerusalem temple will experience desolation. Stephen Miller rightly defines the abomination of desolation as "an idolatrous, object, or person that makes the temple

---

[1] Emphases in original.

desolate of worshippers."[2] The one who does the abomination of desolation in the temple is an evil figure.

The abomination mentioned in Daniel 11:31 probably was fulfilled by the Seleucid king, Antiochus Epiphanes IV. In 167 BC Antiochus halted the worship system in the Jewish temple, set up an altar or idol of Zeus, and then offered a swine as a sacrifice. This horrible abomination of idolatry caused the holy temple to be desolated.

Yet this "abomination of desolation" concept is not exhausted with Daniel 11:31. In the early 30s AD, Jesus referred to a coming "abomination of desolation" in Matthew 24:15:

> Therefore when you see the ABOMINATION OF DESOLATION which was spoken of through Daniel the prophet, standing in the holy place (let the reader understand).

Jesus said the "abomination of desolation" is what Daniel wrote about, thus drawing attention to what Daniel meant. The parallel passage in Mark 13:14 states:

> But when you see the ABOMINATION OF DESOLATION standing where it should not be (let the reader understand), then those who are in Judea must flee to the mountains.

Since Jesus predicted a coming "abomination of desolation" event many years after what Antiochus Epiphanes did, this shows that the "abomination of desolation" Daniel predicted also has a future aspect to it. This future aspect is tied to the meaning of Daniel 9:27 and 12:11.

In Matthew 24:15 and Mark 13:14, Jesus said that the abomination of desolation event will be tragic for the people in Judea, causing them to flee for their lives with no thought of returning for their possessions. So just days before His death, Jesus viewed the Daniel prophecies concerning the abomination of desolation as awaiting future fulfillment. Scholars debate whether this prophecy was fulfilled with the Roman destruction of Jerusalem and the temple in AD 70, or whether it will be fulfilled in the future with an eschatological antichrist. The evidence lies heavily with the latter view since what is described in Matthew 24:4–31 culminates in the personal, bodily return of Jesus and the rescue of Israel (see Matt. 24:27–31)—two events that did not occur in AD 70.

---

[2] Stephen R. Miller, "Abomination, Abomination of Desolation," in *Holman Illustrated Bible Dictionary*, ed. Chad Brand, Charles Draper, and Archie England (Nashville, TN: 2003), 10.

Jesus understood the abomination of desolation of Daniel 9:27 and 12:11 as awaiting future fulfillment. Thus, Matthew 24:15 is a case where a NT person (Jesus) viewed an OT prophecy as still needing literal fulfillment.

# Matthew 24:21 / Daniel 12:1

As Jesus explains the coming abomination of desolation and its devastation upon the people of Israel (see Matt. 24:15–20), He says this time period will be the worst in history: "For then there will be a great tribulation, such as has not occurred since the beginning of the world until now, nor ever will." This is a quotation or strong allusion to Daniel 12:1b: "And there will be a time of distress such as never occurred since there was a nation until that time." Daniel 12:1b is placed within the context of Daniel 11:36–12:7 which discusses a coming time of distress and rescue of Israel, a period that has not yet occurred. Jesus' use of Daniel 12:1b shows a contextual reliance on an OT verse whose fulfillment is still future.

# Matthew 24:29 / Isaiah 13:10

In his discussion of events concerning a future tribulation period in His Olivet Discourse, Jesus stated:

But immediately after the tribulation of those days THE SUN WILL BE DARKENED, AND THE MOON WILL NOT GIVE ITS LIGHT, AND THE STARS WILL FALL from the sky, and the powers of the heavens will be shaken.

Jesus' words fit closely with those found Isaiah 13:10 concerning the sun being darkened, the moon not giving light, and the stars not shining their light. There also could be a slight reliance on Isaiah 34:4 which speaks of the "host of heaven" wearing away and falling like a leaf from a vine.

In Isaiah 13:6–16, the prophet foretold a coming "day of the LORD" when God "will punish the world for its evil" (Isa. 13:11). The chapter begins with a message "concerning Babylon" (13:1), but the message soon goes global. The thrust of Isaiah 13–23 concerns nations and cities of the earth that will experience the judgment of God. Isaiah 13:10 declares:

For the stars of heaven and their constellations will not flash forth their light; The sun will be dark when it rises and the moon will not shed its light.

Isaiah says cosmic signs will coincide with the coming worldwide "day of the Lord." Most references to cosmic signs in the Bible refer to the actual sun, moon, and stars, and no good reason exists to avoid this understanding in Isaiah 13. The cosmic bodies were created "for signs" (Gen. 1:14), and God often used them for major events such as the exodus (see Ex. 10:21), Jesus' birth (Matt. 2:2, 7, 9) and Jesus' death (Luke 23:45). The book of Revelation mentions cosmic signs in connection with the return of Jesus (see Rev. 6:12–14; 8:12). It seems reasonable that the most dramatic moment in human history still to come—the second coming of Jesus—would be accompanied with great cosmic signs. Lack of stability concerning the sun, moon, and stars in the day of the Lord shows an unbelieving world that God's judgment is upon them and is intended to shake them from their lethargy.

The "tribulation" Jesus speaks of (Matt. 24:29) is related to the day of the Lord concept when God's judgment is being poured out on the world. Thus, Jesus relies upon the contextual meaning of Isaiah 13:10 concerning cosmic signs during the day of the Lord. This is a case where Jesus asserts that eschatological events predicted in the OT are still future from His standpoint. What Jesus declared in Matthew 24:29 also parallels Mark 13:24–25.

# Mark 13:26; Matthew 24:30, 26:64; Luke 21:27; Revelation 1:7 / Daniel 7:13

Daniel 7 describes a "dream" and "vision" where Daniel saw four great beasts coming from the sea (7:1–3). These four beasts represent four powerful Gentile kingdoms. Verses 4–7 describe the character of these four kingdoms, which probably represent Babylon, Medo-Persia, Greece, and Rome. Verse 8 then speaks of a "little horn" who appears to be an evil man, an antichrist figure, who makes great boasts. Verse 21 states that the "horn was waging war with the saints and overpowering them."

But while matters looked bleak for Israel on earth, Daniel 7:9–10 describes a heavenly scene where God, the "Ancient of Days," is pictured as seated on His glorious, heavenly throne. Then Daniel 7:13–14 tells of the Son of Man coming "with the clouds of heaven" before the Ancient of Days. Here, kingdom authority over the nations is given to this Son of Man by the Ancient of Days. But while kingdom authority is granted to the Son of Man in heaven, the focus of the Son of Man's kingdom is on earth. Daniel 7 shifts back to earth where the nations and the little horn persecute and wear down God's people (7:21). God then intervenes on behalf of the saints and gives them the kingdom—"the Ancient of Days came and judgment was passed in favor of the saints of the Highest One, and the time arrived when the saints took possession of the kingdom" (7:22). So the Son of Man's coming on the clouds of heaven is closely linked with kingdom authority and a reign upon the earth.

Jesus often referred to himself as the "Son of Man," yet on four occasions He quoted Daniel 7:13 in connection with His return to earth in glory.

### Mark 13:24–26

But in those days, after that tribulation, THE SUN WILL BE DARKENED AND THE MOON WILL NOT GIVE ITS LIGHT, AND THE STARS WILL BE FALLING from heaven, and the powers that are in the heavens will be shaken. Then they will see THE SON OF MAN COMING IN CLOUDS with great power and glory.

### Matthew 24:30

And then the sign of the Son of Man will appear in the sky, and then all the tribes of the earth will mourn, and they will see the SON OF MAN COMING ON THE CLOUDS OF THE SKY with power and great glory.

### Matthew 26:64

Jesus said to him, "You have said it yourself; nevertheless I tell you, hereafter you will see THE SON OF MAN SITTING AT THE RIGHT HAND OF POWER, and COMING ON THE CLOUDS OF HEAVEN."

### Luke 21:27

Then they will see THE SON OF MAN COMING IN A CLOUD with power and great glory.

In Mark 13:24–26, Jesus combined Isaiah 13:10 with Daniel 7:13. Then in Matthew 24:30, Jesus used Daniel 7:13 with Zechariah 12:10 concerning the mourning of the tribes of Israel. And in Matthew 26:64, Jesus referred to both Psalm 110:1 and Daniel 7:13 as He spoke to the high priest, Caiaphas. Psalm 110:1 predicted a session of the Messiah at the right hand of God in heaven before the Messiah returns to Jerusalem to rule (Ps. 110:2). Isaiah 13:10; Zechariah 12:10; Psalm 110:1; and Daniel 7:13 are all tied to eschatological events associated with the kingdom of God coming to earth. The Day of the Lord events of Isaiah 13 lead to an earthly kingdom described in Isaiah 14. Zechariah 12:10 is tied to the Lord being "king over all the earth" in Zechariah 14:9. The session of the Messiah at God's right hand in Psalm 110:1 leads to an earthly kingdom rule starting in Psalm 110:2. Also, the Son of Man being granted kingdom authority in heaven in Daniel 7:13–14 leads to an earthly kingdom for previously persecuted Israel as described in Daniel 7:22.

Another passage where Daniel 7:13 is quoted is Revelation 1:7: "BEHOLD, HE IS COMING WITH THE CLOUDS, and every eye will see Him, even those who pierced Him; and all the tribes of the earth will mourn over Him. So it is to be. Amen." Again, Jesus' coming in the clouds, as described in Daniel 7:13, is linked with His future return to earth. This is evidenced by the fact that His coming in the clouds is a visible event to those who pierced Jesus (the Jews) and to all the tribes of the earth who will mourn over Him. Zechariah 12:10 also is referred to in Revelation 1:7. Zechariah 12:10 states:

I will pour out on the house of David and on the inhabitants of Jerusalem, the Spirit of grace and of supplication, so that they will look on Me whom they have pierced; and they will mourn for Him, as one mourns for an only son, and they will weep bitterly over Him like the bitter weeping over a firstborn.

Thus, the Messiah who comes on the clouds of heaven is also the One who will save Israel and bring His Holy Spirit to them. This coincides with national Israel's deep mourning over the Messiah whom the people pierced.

The point is this: in the five passages mentioned above—Mark 13:24–26; Matthew 24:30; Matthew 26:64; Luke 21:27; and Revelation 1:7—Jesus and the apostle John appealed to Daniel 7:13 in a future context concerning Jesus' return to earth in glory. These are four examples of NT persons (Jesus and John) viewing an OT prophetic passage as still needing to be fulfilled in the future.

# Romans 11:26b–27 / Isaiah 59:20–21

In Romans 11:26b–27, Paul quoted Isaiah 59:20–21 and Isaiah 27:9 in a straightforward manner as support for a coming salvation of the nation Israel and Israel's entrance into the New covenant. More on this example can be found in chapter twenty-four.

# Hebrews 10:27 / Isaiah 26:11

Isaiah 24–27 often is known as Isaiah's Little Apocalypse since its contents are similar to what is discussed in Revelation 6–22. Isaiah 24–27 details a coming, global day of the Lord with terrifying judgment for the world that is followed by the return of the Lord and the kingdom of God. Isaiah 26:11c foretells coming wrath for God's enemies: "Indeed, fire will devour your enemies." In Hebrews 10:26–29, the writer explains that rejecting Jesus and His New covenant means no forgiveness of sins and brings an expectation of God's wrath. In 10:27, the writer quotes Isaiah 26:11 to warn his readers: "but a terrifying expectation of judgment and THE FURY OF A FIRE WHICH WILL CONSUME THE ADVERSARIES." The coming judgment of Isaiah 26:11 is used in Hebrews 10:27 to refer to a future judgment. As George Guthrie puts it, "In perhaps the harshest warning in the book (10:26–31), the writer of Hebrews, alluding to Isa. 26:11, notes that those who reject the truth concerning Christ face terrifying judgment, and that judgment probably should be understood as in the future, on the day of the Lord."[3]

---

[3] George H. Guthrie, "Hebrews," in *Commentary on the New Testament Use of the Old Testament*, ed. G. K. Beale and D. A. Carson (Grand Rapids: Baker, 2007), 979.

The use of Isaiah 26:11 in Hebrews 10:27 is a contextual use of the OT and reveals a case where a NT writer uses an OT prophetic text to refer to an event still future from his standpoint. In this case, it is God's fury upon His enemies.

# Hebrews 12:26 / Haggai 2:6

In Hebrews 11, the writer presented a list of people who exemplified faith in God. In Hebrews 12:1–17, the writer explained the importance of God's discipline in the lives of Christians and the need to persevere in pursuing sanctification. Then in 12:18–24, the writer contrasted the inferior Mosaic covenant associated with Mount Sinai and the superior New covenant associated with the heavenly Jerusalem and Jesus' superior sacrifice. This led to a warning in 12:25 that the audience in Hebrews should not refuse God who is warning them from heaven. If those who disobeyed Moses' earthly warning could not escape judgment, then certainly those who do not obey now cannot escape God who warns them from heaven. At Mount Sinai, God shook the earth in judgment, but a time is coming when God will shake not only the earth, but heaven as well. Quoting Haggai 2:6, the writer of Hebrews declared:

And His voice shook the earth then, but now He has promised, saying, "YET ONCE MORE I WILL SHAKE NOT ONLY THE EARTH, BUT ALSO THE HEAVEN." (Heb. 12:26)

This shaking, in the context of judgment, will remove temporary things so only that which is eternal will remain (12:27). Therefore, since we are receiving a kingdom that is coming, we should not be shaken, and we should serve God with gratitude (12:28).

The writer, probably writing in the 60s AD, is appealing to the future (i.e. eschatology) to stimulate his readers to faith and obedience in the present. God is going to shake heaven and earth in judgment and will establish His kingdom—so be ready!

So how does the writer of Hebrews quote Haggai 2:6 and its message of a coming shaking of heaven and earth? The short message of Haggai (sixth century BC) was about rebuilding the temple (1:1–2:9) and then cleansing and future restoration (2:10–23). In 2:6–9, there is the prediction of a great shaking of the heavens and earth in connection with the glory of God filling the temple at a time when all the nations will bring their wealth to the temple:

For thus says the LORD of hosts, "Once more in a little while, I am going to shake the heavens and the earth, the sea also and the dry land. I will shake all the nations; and they will come with the wealth of all nations, and I will fill this house with glory," says the LORD of hosts. "The silver is Mine and the gold is Mine," declares the LORD of hosts. "The latter glory of this house will be greater than the former," says the LORD of hosts, "and in this place I will give peace," declares the LORD of hosts. (Hag. 2:6–9)

Haggai foretold a great shaking in connection with Israel's restoration, an event that will be just as tangible as the shaking at Mount Sinai during Moses' day. While Jesus' coming to the temple at His first coming was significant (see John 2), that event did not fulfill all that Haggai 2:6 predicted. The writer of Hebrews viewed the shaking of Haggai 2:6 as remaining in the future. This is consistent with the futuristic sections of Matthew 24 and Revelation 6 which foretell earthquakes and cosmic signs in connection with Jesus' return and the restoration of national Israel. *Thus, the quotation of Haggai 2:6 in Hebrews 12:26 is an example of a NT writer viewing an OT prophecy as still needing to be fulfilled literally in the future.* Haggai 2:6 was not fulfilled at the time of the writing of Hebrews, but it will come to pass.

# Revelation 2:26–27 / Psalm 2:8–9

Psalm 2 is a messianic psalm that tells of kings and rulers on earth who take counsel together against the Lord and His anointed (i.e. the Messiah) (Ps. 2:1–3). But the Lord in heaven scoffs at them and warns them that He will "terrify them in His fury" by establishing His King (i.e. the Messiah) upon Mount Zion (Ps. 2:4–6). The Lord will give His Messiah the nations as His inheritance and the ends of the earth as His possession (2:7–8). And He will "shatter them like earthenware" (2:9). The nations should take heed and "do homage to the Son" to escape His wrath (2:10–12).

In the 90s AD, Jesus offered messages to the seven churches of Asia Minor (Rev. 2–3). As Lord of the church, Jesus told these churches what they were doing well and where they needed to improve. In Revelation 2:26–27, Jesus referenced Psalm 2:8–9 (and perhaps Isa. 30:14) with the church at Thyatira:

> He who overcomes, and he who keeps My deeds until the end, TO HIM I WILL GIVE AUTHORITY OVER THE NATIONS; AND HE SHALL RULE THEM WITH A ROD OF IRON, AS THE VESSELS OF THE POTTER ARE BROKEN TO PIECES, as I also have received authority from My Father.

Here Jesus says the overcomer will participate in Jesus' future reign upon the earth in fulfillment of Psalm 2. As mentioned, Psalm 2 is about the Messiah's coming reign, but here Jesus says He will share His messianic reign with overcomers in this age. The churches in Revelation 2–3 were not reigning at the time. They were suffering persecution from unbelieving Jews, the world, and from Satan. But if they overcome, they will rule the nations with Jesus when He returns (see Rev. 19:15). Through union with Jesus, Psalm 2:9 also applies to Christians. Jesus is being quite literal with Psalm 2:9, but He emphasizes a point of application, namely that His followers will share in His kingdom reign over the nations when that event occurs.

Both Messiah's reign and the reign of the saints are future. Jesus viewed Psalm 2:8–9 as needing to be fulfilled in the future. Thus, we again have an example of a NT person (Jesus) viewing an OT prophetic passage as needing to be fulfilled in the future.

## 2 Peter 3:13; Revelation 21:1 / Isaiah 65:17; 66:22

Peter said that Christians "are looking for new heavens and a new earth, in which righteousness dwells" (2 Pet. 3:13). The apostle John noted, "Then I saw a new heaven and a new earth" (Rev. 21:1). This anticipation of a coming new heaven(s) and earth, which replaces the current heavens and earth, was rooted in the OT. Both Isaiah 65:17 and 66:22 predicted a coming "new heavens" and "new earth." The language of these Isaiah passages was used by Peter and John to describe coming conditions associated with the return of Jesus. Since the new heaven and new earth have not occurred yet, this is an example of Peter and John referring to Isaiah's words to explain a future event.

## 1 Corinthians 15:54; Revelation 21:4 / Isaiah 25:8

Isaiah 25 describes God's coming kingdom on earth after a time of global tribulation and the return of the Lord to Jerusalem (see Isa. 24). This kingdom will involve a time of celebration for all nations and peoples (Isa. 25:6). It will also mean the removal of death and sorrow, as 25:8a reveals: "He will swallow up death for all time, And the Lord GOD will wipe tears away from all faces." Isaiah 25:8a notes the marvelous truth that God's kingdom and the return of the Messiah (see Isa. 24:21–22) will be associated with the removal of death and its ugly consequences.

Isaiah 25:8a is quoted or alluded to in 1 Corinthians 15:54 and Revelation 21:4.[4] First Corinthians 15 addresses God's resurrection program and the implications of Jesus' resurrection for Christians. In 1 Corinthians 15:52, Paul stated that "in a moment…the trumpet will sound, and the dead will be raised, and we will be changed." When this happens, Paul declared, "DEATH IS SWALLOWED UP in victory," a reference to Isaiah 25:8a. This resurrection of Christians, with the ensuing swallowing-up of death, refers to the second stage of God's resurrection program Paul explained in 1 Corinthians 15:23 when he said: "But each in his own order: Christ the first fruits, after that those who are Christ's at His coming."

While Isaiah 25:8 refers specifically to the removal of death for the nations after a coming global tribulation, Paul applies the truth of death being removed to the Corinthian readers in light of their coming resurrection. Thus, the truth from Isaiah

---

[4] An allusion to Isaiah 25:8a is also found in Revelation 7:17.

25:8 that God's people will have death removed from their lives is applied to the Corinthians. Paul's readers were headed for victory over physical death. Paul does not state when this resurrection and removal of death will happen for the Corinthians (and all Christians), but it will occur in the future with the return of Jesus.

Next, in reference to the coming New Jerusalem, Revelation 21:4 states: "And He will wipe away every tear from their eyes; and there will no longer be any death." This verse, written by John the Apostle, uses the wording of Isaiah 25:8a and picks up on both ideas from Isaiah 25:8a, that God will remove tears of sorrow from His people and that He will extinguish death. So like 1 Corinthians 15:54, Revelation 21:4 uses the wording of Isaiah 25:8a to describe a coming experience for God's people.

Both Paul and John view the fulfillment of Isaiah 25:8 as a future occurrence. This is a case where NT writers quoted the wording of an OT verse (Isa. 25:8a) for an event to come. Both the OT and NT taught that death and its consequences will be removed.

# CHAPTER FOURTEEN

# LITERAL APPLICATION
# OF A TIMELESS MORAL OR
# THEOLOGICAL POINT

On many occasions, a NT person or writer quoted an OT passage to apply a timeless moral or theological point. In fact, this is the largest category of NT uses of the OT. Below is a sampling of this type of usage:

## Examples

### Luke 1:50 / Psalm 103:17

In Psalm 103, David praised the Lord for His mercies. In verse 17, he declared the great truth that "the lovingkindness of the LORD is from everlasting to everlasting on those who fear Him." Then with her famous Magnificat of Luke 1:46–55, Mary drew upon the great truth of Psalm 103:17 by stating, "AND HIS MERCY IS UPON GENERATION AFTER GENERATION TOWARD THOSE WHO FEAR HIM." This is a literal application of a timeless theological truth that God shows mercy to those who fear Him.

### Luke 2:23 / Exodus 13:2, 12

Exodus 13:2, 12 stated that every firstborn in Israel belonged to the Lord. Mary and Joseph brought the infant Jesus to Jerusalem to present Him to the Lord in fulfillment of this requirement. Luke 2:23 states, "As it is written in the Law of the Lord, 'EVERY firstborn MALE THAT OPENS THE WOMB SHALL BE CALLED HOLY TO THE LORD.'" Mary and Joseph accomplished what Exodus 13 required concerning their firstborn, Jesus.

## Matthew 4:4–10 / Deuteronomy 8:3; 6:16; 6:13 (Luke 4:4–12 / Deuteronomy 8:3; 6:13; 10:20; 6:16)

Matthew 4:4–10 describes Jesus' responses to the temptations from Satan while Jesus was in the wilderness:

> But He [Jesus] answered and said, "It is written, 'MAN SHALL NOT LIVE ON BREAD ALONE, BUT ON EVERY WORD THAT PROCEEDS OUT OF THE MOUTH OF GOD.'" Then the devil took Him into the holy city and had Him stand on the pinnacle of the temple, and said to Him, "If You are the Son of God, throw Yourself down; for it is written, 'HE WILL COMMAND HIS ANGELS CONCERNING YOU'; and 'ON their HANDS THEY WILL BEAR YOU UP, SO THAT YOU WILL NOT STRIKE YOUR FOOT AGAINST A STONE.'"

> Jesus said to him, "On the other hand, it is written, 'YOU SHALL NOT PUT THE LORD YOUR GOD TO THE TEST.'" Again, the devil took Him to a very high mountain and showed Him all the kingdoms of the world and their glory; and he said to Him, "All these things I will give You, if You fall down and worship me." Then Jesus said to him, "Go, Satan! For it is written, 'YOU SHALL WORSHIP THE LORD YOUR GOD, AND SERVE HIM ONLY.'"

Jesus quoted the OT three times to refute Satan's temptations. Satan himself quoted Psalm 91:11–12. But Jesus then referenced Deuteronomy 8:3 to show the principle that man shall not live by bread alone. Jesus then cited Deuteronomy 6:16 to indicate God should not be tested. After that Jesus quoted Deuteronomy 6:13 and/or Deuteronomy 10:20 to show the principle that only God should be worshiped.

So on three occasions, Jesus quoted Deuteronomy and its timeless principles to resist and overcome temptations from Satan. In so doing, He succeeded where the first Adam failed.

## Matthew 9:13 / Hosea 6:6

Matthew 9:9–13 reveals that Jesus' ministry involved interaction with tax collectors and other sinners, including Matthew. The self-righteous Pharisees were upset with Jesus for His associations, and they asked Jesus' disciples why He met with sinners (Matt. 9:11). After comparing Himself to a physician who attends to the sick and not the healthy (9:12), Jesus said, "But go and learn what this means: 'I DESIRE COMPASSION, AND NOT SACRIFICE,' for I did not come to call the righteous, but sinners." Jesus drew upon a principle from Hosea 6:6 that God is more interested in matters of the heart than with ritual. This is a literal application of a timeless principle.

## Matthew 11:29 / Jeremiah 6:16

Jesus rebuked the cities of Israel for their unbelief (Matt. 11:20–24). Then He thanked the Father for those whom the Father entrusted to Him (11:25–27). After that, Jesus offered rest to all who come to Him (11:28). To support this call, Jesus quoted Jeremiah 6:16: "Take My yoke upon you and learn from Me, for I am gentle and humble in heart, and YOU WILL FIND REST FOR YOUR SOULS" (Matt. 11:29).

Jeremiah 6 discussed the impending destruction of Jerusalem for covenant disobedience. The Lord called on His people to "ask for the ancient paths," and in doing so they will find rest for their souls. Likewise, Jesus told His hearers that they can find rest for their souls if they come to Him. Just as Jeremiah 6 promised rest for those who seek God in the midst of judgment, Jesus' followers can find rest if they seek Him. This is application of a moral truth or principle from Jeremiah 6.

## Matthew 13:32; Mark 4:32; Luke 13:19 / Ezekiel 17:23

Ezekiel 17 rebukes Israel for resisting God's judgment by looking to Egypt for help against Babylon. This plan would turn on them, since Israel was rejecting God's plans at this time. Yet the chapter ends with a section in which lowly Israel will become a great kingdom in which the Gentile nations will take refuge (Ezek. 17:22–24). Verse 23 states:

> On the high mountain of Israel I will plant it [the "sprig"], that it may bring forth boughs and bear fruit and become a stately cedar. And birds of every kind will nest under it; they will nest in the shade of its branches.

God can take Israel under judgment and make it a great kingdom in which the nations, represented by "birds of every kind," can be blessed (see Gen. 12:3).

The words of Ezekiel 17:23 appear in Jesus' parable of the mustard seed as explained in Matthew 13:32; Mark 4:32; and Luke 13:19. In this parable, Jesus likens the kingdom of God to a mustard plant—likely the black mustard which grows from a tiny seed to approximately nine-feet tall. Birds then nest within its branches:

> He presented another parable to them, saying, "The kingdom of heaven is like
> a mustard seed, which a man took and sowed in his field; and this is smaller
> than all other seeds, but when it is full grown, it is larger than the garden plants
> and becomes a tree, so that THE BIRDS OF THE AIR come and NEST IN ITS
> BRANCHES." (Matt. 13:31–32)

Most agree that Jesus' point is that the kingdom will start very small, yet will grow
to be large in worldwide scope and influence. One point of discontinuity is that
Ezekiel 17 speaks of a mighty cedar tree, while Matthew 13; Mark 4; and Luke 13
refer to a much smaller mustard plant. While Jesus certainly could have chosen a tree
for this parable, His use of the tiny mustard seed best fits His point that the kingdom
of God will start small before it grows into something large.

But does Jesus quote Ezekiel 17:23 contextually? The main point is that the
kingdom of God grows from being tiny to large. Jesus does not seem to be making
the explicit point that Gentile nations will take refuge in a restored national Israel,
although nothing here nor in Matthew 13 refutes that idea. At the very least, Jesus'
parable suggests that the full blossom of the kingdom will bless many people.

## Matthew 15:4 / Exodus 20:12; 21:17

In Matthew 15:1–6, Jesus rebuked some Pharisees and scribes for putting their
own traditions above the commandments of God (15:2). Jesus said, "For God said,
'HONOR YOUR FATHER AND MOTHER,' and, 'HE WHO SPEAKS EVIL OF FATHER OR
MOTHER IS TO BE PUT TO DEATH.'" Yet the Pharisees and scribes invented their own
traditions to escape these commands (15:5–6). So Jesus quoted Exodus 20:12 and
21:17, which mandates honoring parents and not speaking evil of them. Jesus quoted
these two passages to highlight the timeless moral principle of honoring parents.

## Mark 10:7–8 / Genesis 2:24

Concerning God's intent for marriage, Genesis 2:24 states, "For this reason a
man shall leave his father and his mother, and be joined to his wife; and they shall
become one flesh." While discussing marriage and divorce in Mark 10:1–9, Jesus
said that the Mosaic Law allowance for divorce (see Mark 10:4) was no longer in
force. Jesus then appealed to Genesis 2:24 in Mark 10:7–8: "For this reason a man
shall leave his father and his mother, and be joined to his wife; and they shall become
one flesh." Here Jesus appeals to the Genesis account of marriage to show the
principle that God intends marriage to be forever, and that divorce is not part of God's
plan. This is how things must be in the New covenant era that the Messiah brings.

# Mark 11:17; Matthew 21:13; Luke 19:46 / Isaiah 56:7; Jeremiah 7:11

Upon entering Jerusalem before His death, Jesus went to the Court of the Gentiles in the temple and drove out the money changers. With quotes from Isaiah 56:7 and Jeremiah 7:11, Mark 11:17 states:

> And He began to teach and say to them, "Is it not written, 'MY HOUSE SHALL BE CALLED A HOUSE OF PRAYER FOR ALL THE NATIONS'? But you have made it a ROBBERS' DEN."

Isaiah 56 concerns future times when Gentiles would be invited to worship with Israel at the temple. By quoting Isaiah 56:7 in the Court of the Gentiles, Jesus revealed that the temple section for Gentiles should be treated with reverence, not as a venue for making money. His quotation of Jeremiah 7:11 drew upon Jeremiah's message at the temple gate. In Jeremiah's day, Israel thought the temple would protect them from judgment (see Jer. 7:4) but Jeremiah told them they had turned it into "a den of robbers" (Jer. 7:11).

By quoting Isaiah 56:7, Jesus used the theological principle from Isaiah that the temple was a holy place destined to be a place of prayer for all Gentile nations. Next, Jesus' reference to Jeremiah 7:11 shows that Israel once again turned God's holy temple into a place of wrongdoing. There also could be an element of generational fulfillment as the current generation of Israel is repeating the error of Jeremiah's generation hundreds of years earlier. What is stated here is true also for the parallel sections of Matthew 21:13 and Luke 19:46.[1]

# Matthew 22:37–39, Mark 12:29–31 / Deuteronomy 6:5; Leviticus 19:18

In Matthew 22:36, the Pharisees asked Jesus, "Which is the great commandment in the Law?" Jesus responded:

> And He said to him, "YOU SHALL LOVE THE LORD YOUR GOD WITH ALL YOUR HEART, AND WITH ALL YOUR SOUL, AND WITH ALL YOUR MIND."
> This is the great and foremost commandment.
> The second is like it, "YOU SHALL LOVE YOUR NEIGHBOR AS YOURSELF."
> (Matt. 22:36–39)

---

[1] Mark 11:17 is unique among these three in mentioning the Gentile nations.

Jesus quoted Deuteronomy 6:5, which concerns loving God with every part of one's being. He also quoted Leviticus 19:18 which commands people to love their neighbor as themselves. Jesus used these two verses to apply the timeless principle that love of God and love of neighbor are the two most important things God expects from man. That principle was true in Moses' day, and it is true in Jesus' day and always.

## Luke 10:27 / Deuteronomy 6:5; Leviticus 19:18

The point in this connection is similar to the previous example. On this occasion, a lawyer asks Jesus what must be done to inherit eternal life. Jesus returns the question to the lawyer, and the lawyer then quotes the love God and love neighbor commands in Deuteronomy 6:5 and Leviticus 19:18. Jesus says the lawyer answered correctly. This is another example where the principles of Deuteronomy 6:5 and Leviticus 19:18 apply to the present.

## Acts 7:48–50 / Isaiah 66:1–2a

While pointing out that Solomon built the temple (see Acts 7:47), Stephen noted that no building made by men could contain God, who is infinite. Quoting Isaiah 66:1–2a, Stephen said:

> However, the Most High does not dwell in houses made by human hands; as the prophet says:
>
> "HEAVEN IS MY THRONE,
> AND EARTH IS THE FOOTSTOOL OF MY FEET;
> WHAT KIND OF HOUSE WILL YOU BUILD FOR ME?" says the Lord,
> "OR WHAT PLACE IS THERE FOR MY REPOSE?
> WAS IT NOT MY HAND WHICH MADE ALL THESE THINGS?" (Acts 7:48–50)

Thus, Stephen quoted Isaiah 66:1–2a to make the theological point that God's presence is vast and cannot be confined to one place.

## Acts 13:41 / Habakkuk 1:5

The context for the book of Habakkuk was the soon-coming Babylonian captivity that started in 605 BC. Israel's wickedness and lack of justice was the problem, leading to God's judgment upon Judah as a corporate entity (see Hab. 1:4). In Habakkuk 1, the prophet Habakkuk warned Judah that God was going to do something astonishing, something the people would not believe even if they were told (Hab. 1:5). God will judge Judah through the Babylonians (i.e. "Chaldeans," v. 6). Incredibly, God will use the wicked and prideful Babylonian empire to judge His chosen people. Such an idea seemed unbelievable, but it was true.

Then, in Acts 13, while speaking to a synagogue in Pisidian Antioch, Paul told his Jewish listeners there that they needed to "take heed" and believe in Jesus as Messiah (Acts 13:40).[2] If they refused, the warning of Habakkuk 1:5 would apply to them (Acts 13:41).

So why does Paul use Habakkuk 1:5? How can a warning of the impending Babylonian captivity hundreds of years earlier apply to a first-century AD Jewish audience? It applies in that Paul warns Israel as a corporate/national entity to avoid the mistake that Israel made in the past. A moral lesson from the past should be learned. As Eckhard Schnabel observes, Paul "implies the warning to make sure that listeners do not fail to learn the lesson of Hab. 1:5, namely, that the consequence of refusing God's gracious offer is a disaster. If they do not come to faith in Jesus…'what the prophets said' will happen to them."[3]

Israel's wickedness resulted in national catastrophe in the sixth-century BC, so Israel of the present day should avoid making the same mistake. They should understand that unbelief leads to national judgment.

Note also that while quoting Habakkuk 1:5, Paul says this warning is what the "prophets" (plural) said: "Therefore take heed, so that the thing spoken of in the *Prophets* may not come upon you" (Acts 13:40, emphasis mine). Passages such as Deuteronomy 30 and Leviticus 26 predicted calamity and dispersion for Israel's unbelief. What Paul warns in Acts 13:40–41 is certainly more than just spiritual consequences for individual unbelief. His warning carried corporate ramifications for Israel, just as it did with the sixth-century Babylonian captivity. It also probably anticipated the coming destruction of Jerusalem in AD 70 by the Romans, which Jesus also predicted in Matthew 23:37–38; Luke 19:41–44; and Luke 21:20–24.[4]

In sum, Paul's use of Habakkuk 1:5 in Acts 13:40–41 is a contextual use of the OT. Here a NT person quotes an OT warning for Israel in the past and applies it to a first-century Jewish audience in Pisidian Antioch. The century is different, but the principle of warning still applies to Israel in the present. A theological principle applies to the various generations of Israel in history.

---

[2] With his quotation of Habakkuk 1:5 Paul uses the LXX understanding of "You scoffers" over the MT understanding of "among the nations." See I. Howard Marshall, "Acts," in *Commentary on the New Testament Use of the Old Testament*, ed. G. K. Beale and D. A. Carson (Grand Rapids: Baker, 2007), 587.

[3] Eckhard J. Schnabel, *Acts*, Exegetical Commentary on the New Testament (Grand Rapids: Zondervan, 2012), 584–85.

[4] We do not have to choose between whether this warning involves spiritual or temporal consequences since both are probably in view just as they were in Habakkuk. Unbelief and wickedness can have both spiritual and temporal ramifications. Also, while Paul is speaking to Jews outside of Jerusalem this does not mean coming national judgment involving Jerusalem has no significance for them.

# Romans 1:17; Galatians 3:11; Hebrews 10:38a / Habakkuk 2:4

Habakkuk 2:4 is quoted three times in the NT—twice by Paul, and once by the writer of Hebrews. The verse reads:

Behold, as for the proud one,
His soul is not right within him;
But the righteous will live by his faith.

Habakkuk 2:4 contrasts the proud person whose soul is not right with the righteous person who lives by faith.

The writer of Hebrews on several occasions urged his readers to persevere in their faith. In Hebrews 10:38, he quoted Habakkuk 2:4 to support the idea that righteousness is linked with a life of faith: "BUT MY RIGHTEOUS ONE SHALL LIVE BY FAITH; AND IF HE SHRINKS BACK, MY SOUL HAS NO PLEASURE IN HIM." This is a contextual use of the OT as the Hebrews' writer quotes the principle of Habakkuk 2:4 that the righteous will live by faith and that God is displeased with those who do not live by faith.

In Romans 1:16, Paul says the gospel is "the power of God for salvation" for every person. Then he says, "For in it the righteousness of God is revealed from faith to faith; as it is written, 'BUT THE RIGHTEOUS man SHALL LIVE BY FAITH.'" Paul quoted Habakkuk 2:4 to support the idea that faith is at the heart of the gospel. Paul wrote Romans 3:20 through Romans 4 to explain that being right with God is based on faith, not works. So Paul used Habakkuk 2:4 to show continuity with the timeless principle that righteousness is linked with faith.

In Galatians 3, Paul made a strong contrast between the faith-based Abrahamic covenant and the works-based Mosaic covenant. Righteousness is linked with the former, not the latter. In Galatians 3:11, Paul quoted Habakkuk 2:4 to show that justification comes through faith not the Law: "Now that no one is justified by the Law before God is evident; for, 'THE RIGHTEOUS MAN SHALL LIVE BY FAITH.'" In sum, Paul quoted Habakkuk 2:4 contextually to show that being in a right relationship with God has always been through faith, not Law. Thus, all three uses of Habakkuk 2:4 in the NT are contextual.

# Romans 2:24 / Isaiah 52:5 (LXX)

In Romans 2:17–29, Paul argued that the Jews are guilty before God because they break the Mosaic Law. The Jews might see themselves as just before God, but in reality they are lawbreakers deserving of God's judgment. In Romans 2:24, Paul quoted the LXX version of Isaiah 52:5: "For 'THE NAME OF GOD IS BLASPHEMED AMONG THE GENTILES

BECAUSE OF YOU,' just as it is written." In Isaiah 52:5, Israel's sin is a reason God's name is blasphemed among the Gentiles, and Paul's use of this verse in Romans 2:24 is consistent with that point. In sum, Paul quoted Isaiah 52:5 to affirm the theological truth that Israel's sin is not only bad in itself, but it brings shame on God's name among the Gentiles.

## Matthew 16:27; Romans 2:6; Revelation 22:12 / Psalm 62:12

Psalm 62 was authored by David. With verse 12, David declared that a man's deeds matter because the Lord will "recompense a man according to his work." This principle that God will judge a person based on his deeds is reaffirmed by both Jesus and Paul. Jesus said that when He comes in glory, He "will reward each person according to what they have done" (Matt. 16:27). In Revelation 22:12, Jesus declared He is coming quickly and will "render to every man according to what he has done."

When speaking of God's judgment in Romans 2:6, Paul stated that God "WILL RENDER TO EACH PERSON ACCORDING TO HIS DEEDS." An allusion to Psalm 62:12 also seems to appear in 1 Corinthians 3:8; Ephesians 6:8; and 2 Timothy 4:14. These are applications of a timeless moral or theological principle from the OT. God will judge people according to what they do.

## Romans 3:4 / Psalm 51:4

In Romans 1:18–3:20, Paul explained that all people stand condemned before God because of their sins. This is true for both Jews and Gentiles. As Paul began Romans 3, he noted that the Jews had the blessing of being entrusted with the Scriptures—"the oracles of God" (Rom. 3:2). In 3:3, Paul pointed out that Israel's unbelief did not nullify God's faithfulness. Even though Israel was disobedient, God remains true to His word. To support the claim of God's faithfulness, Paul quoted Psalm 51:4 in Romans 3:4:

> Rather, let God be found true, though every man be found a liar, as it is written,
> "THAT YOU MAY BE JUSTIFIED IN YOUR WORDS,
> AND PREVAIL WHEN YOU ARE JUDGED."

Psalm 51 concerns David's recognition of his sin in the Bathsheba adultery incident. David openly acknowledged God's righteous verdict on his sin, as Psalm 51:4 reads:

> Against You, You only, I have sinned
> And done what is evil in Your sight,
> So that You are justified when You speak
> And blameless when You judge.

Paul's quotation of Psalm 51:4 in Romans 3:4 is contextual since the context of both passages involves God's rightful authority to speak to and judge human affairs, including their sin. With Psalm 51, God is right in judging David, while in Romans 3:4 God is right in evaluating unbelieving Israel. Even though Romans 3:1–3 is positive concerning the role of the Jews in God's purposes, God is faithful both in His promises to bless and judge for sin. As Moo notes, "The OT insists that God is equally faithful when he judges his people's sin and when he fulfills his promises."[5] Just as David was condemned for his sin, yet could be restored by God, the same is true for Israel. God is in the right as he judges and blesses Israel.

## Romans 3:10–18 / Several Psalms and Isaiah 59:7

From Romans 1:18 through 3:20, Paul explained that all people, Jew and Gentile, are sinners before God—no exceptions. As he brought his argument to a climax, Paul strung together a large cluster of OT citations from Psalm 14:1–3; Psalm 5:9; Psalm 140:3; Psalm 10:7; Isa 59:7; and Psalm 36:1 to establish the foundational theological point that all people are sinners. Romans 3:10–18 reads:

As it is written,
"THERE IS NONE RIGHTEOUS, NOT EVEN ONE;
THERE IS NONE WHO UNDERSTANDS,
THERE IS NONE WHO SEEKS FOR GOD;
ALL HAVE TURNED ASIDE, TOGETHER THEY HAVE BECOME USELESS;
THERE IS NONE WHO DOES GOOD,
THERE IS NOT EVEN ONE."
"THEIR THROAT IS AN OPEN GRAVE,
WITH THEIR TONGUES THEY KEEP DECEIVING,"
"THE POISON OF ASPS IS UNDER THEIR LIPS";
"WHOSE MOUTH IS FULL OF CURSING AND BITTERNESS";
"THEIR FEET ARE SWIFT TO SHED BLOOD,
DESTRUCTION AND MISERY ARE IN THEIR PATHS,
AND THE PATH OF PEACE THEY HAVE NOT KNOWN."
"THERE IS NO FEAR OF GOD BEFORE THEIR EYES."

This is the largest string of OT quotations in the NT, and with it Paul shows the timeless truth that all people—without exception—are sinful before God.

---

[5] Douglas J. Moo, *The Epistle to the Romans*, in *The New International Commentary on the New Testament* (Grand Rapids: Eerdmans, 1996), 188.

# Romans 4:3 (and Romans 4:9) / Genesis 15:6

In Romans 4, Paul presents an explicit case that salvation is through faith alone, not through works of the Mosaic Law. But this is not just a NT truth. Paul quoted Genesis 15:6 in Romans 4:3 to prove his point: "For what does the Scripture say? 'ABRAHAM BELIEVED GOD AND IT WAS CREDITED TO HIM AS RIGHTEOUSNESS.'" Genesis 15:6 reveals that Abraham was considered righteous through his faith. Paul presents Abraham as the paradigm of faith for everyone (see Rom. 4:11–12). Thus, Paul appeals to a timeless principle that salvation has always been through faith apart from Law. Paul will also quote Genesis 15:6 in Romans 4:9 to again emphasize that salvation is through faith alone for both Jews and Gentiles:

> Is this blessing then on the circumcised, or on the uncircumcised also? For we say, "FAITH WAS CREDITED TO ABRAHAM AS RIGHTEOUSNESS."

These two quotations of Genesis 15:6 in Romans 4 emphasize the point that salvation is through faith alone apart from works of the Law. On this matter, both the OT and NT agree.

# Romans 4:6–8 / Psalm 32:1–2

Paul quoted Psalm 32:1–2 in Romans 4:6–8 to show that David also is an example that being right with God is based on faith alone:

> Just as David also speaks of the blessing on the man to whom God credits righteousness apart from works:
> "BLESSED ARE THOSE WHOSE LAWLESS DEEDS HAVE BEEN FORGIVEN, AND WHOSE SINS HAVE BEEN COVERED. BLESSED IS THE MAN WHOSE SIN THE LORD WILL NOT TAKE INTO ACCOUNT."

Paul cited Psalm 32:1–2 to emphasize the timeless theological point that salvation has always been through faith alone.

# Romans 10:13 / Joel 2:32

In Romans 10:13, Paul employs a principle from Joel 2:32 to show that all who call on the name of the Lord will be saved.

# Romans 10:19 / Deuteronomy 32:21

A strategic use of the OT occurs in Paul's use of Deuteronomy 32:21 in Romans 10:19.[6] Within his broader discussion of how God's Word has not failed concerning Israel (Rom. 9:6), Paul argued that God was using Gentile salvation to make Israel jealous. Referencing Deuteronomy 32:21, Paul declared, "I WILL MAKE YOU JEALOUS BY THAT WHICH IS NOT A NATION, BY A NATION WITHOUT UNDERSTANDING WILL I ANGER YOU" (Rom. 10:19). This quotation reveals what Robert Saucy calls a "minor theme of the salvation of the Gentiles when Israel is in disobedience."[7] This is important to Paul's argument in Romans 9–11 and is strategic to the "mystery" concept he refers to in 11:25, namely that Gentiles will be blessed before the salvation of Israel to provoke Israel to jealousy.

The OT often affirms that Israel's future repentance will usher in greater world blessings (Isa. 2:2–4; 27:6). But the idea of Gentiles experiencing blessings while Israel is disobedient as a means to provoke Israel to jealousy is also hinted at in the OT. Saucy notes, "The Old Testament not only contained revelation of Israel's rebellious unbelief issuing in the rejection of their Messiah. It also hinted that the salvation that would come through the life and death of Christ would go out to the Gentiles when Israel as a nation was in disobedience and under the judgment of partial hardening."[8] Also noting Paul's use of Deuteronomy 32:21 concerning Gentile salvation before Israel's salvation, Beale and Gladd state, "Paul identifies present Israel's judgment of hardening and the Gentiles' salvation followed by Israel's redemption with the same prophesied storyline in Deuteronomy."[9]

Paul's use of Deuteronomy 32:21 in Romans 10:19 is contextual since Deuteronomy 32:21 predicted that God would use Gentiles to make Israel jealous. This is literal application of a theological truth found in the OT.

# Romans 9:27 / Isaiah 10:22

While discussing Israel's unbelief in Romans 9–11, Paul noted that God always kept a believing remnant of Israel, even if the mass of Israel was currently in unbelief. To support this, Paul appealed to Isaiah 10:22: "Isaiah cries out concerning Israel,

---

[6] See Michael J. Vlach, "A Non-Typological Future-Mass-Conversion View," in *Three Views on Israel and the Church: Perspectives on Romans 9–11*, ed. Jared Compton and Andrew David Naselli (Grand Rapids: Kregel, 2018), 36.

[7] Robert L. Saucy, "Does the Apostle Paul Reverse the Prophetic Tradition of the Salvation of Israel and the Nations?," in *Building on the Foundations of Evangelical Theology: Essays in Honor of John S. Feinberg*, ed. Gregg R. Allison and Stephen J. Wellum (Wheaton, IL: Crossway, 2015), 71.

[8] Ibid.

[9] G. K. Beale and Benjamin L. Gladd, *Hidden but Now Revealed: A Biblical Theology of Mystery* (Downers Grove, IL: InterVarsity Press, 2014), 90–91.

'THOUGH THE NUMBER OF THE SONS OF ISRAEL BE LIKE THE SAND OF THE SEA, IT IS THE REMNANT THAT WILL BE SAVED.'" This is literal application of a timeless theological point that while the whole of Israel is characterized by unbelief, God keeps a believing remnant within Israel. That was true in Isaiah's day, and it is true in Paul's day. By extension, this is true today and will continue to be true until the time when "all Israel will be saved" (Rom. 11:26).

## Romans 11:3–4 / 1 Kings 19:10, 14, 18

In Romans 11:3–4, Paul quoted three verses from 1 Kings 19 (vv. 10, 14, 18) to highlight that God always maintains a believing remnant of Israel, even when Israel as a nation is disobedient. This shows that even though Israel as a whole was in unbelief, God's commitment to Israel is evident with this remnant, which functions as a guarantee that God will save the nation. This truth from 1 Kings 19 should help Paul's readers understand the role of the current remnant.

## Romans 11:34 / Isaiah 40:13

Paul quoted Isaiah 40:13 in Romans 11:34 to draw upon the principle that God needs no counselor.

## 1 Corinthians 1:31; 2 Corinthians 10:17 / Jeremiah 9:23–24

In Jeremiah 9:23–24, the Lord declared that a wise man should not boast in his own wisdom or power, but he should boast in the Lord. The context of 1 Corinthians 1 is similar. Paul said boasting should be in the Lord and not in human wisdom: "So that, just as it is written, 'LET HIM WHO BOASTS, BOAST IN THE LORD'" (1 Cor. 1:31). Paul's quotation of Jeremiah 9:23–24 is a contextual application of the enduring moral principle that boasting only should be in God.

Paul also appealed to Jeremiah 9:23–24 when addressing boasting rivals in 2 Corinthians 10:17: "But HE WHO BOASTS IS TO BOAST IN THE LORD." This shows that commending one's self means nothing. Only what the Lord thinks ultimately matters (see 2 Cor. 10:18). An allusion to Jeremiah 9:24 also might occur in Galatians 6:14 when Paul said he would not boast in anything except the cross of Christ.

## 1 Corinthians 10:26 / Psalm 24:1

In Psalm 24:1, David declared, "The earth is the LORD'S, and all it contains, the world, and those who dwell in it." The meaning is that everything on earth belongs to God. The LORD is not only God of Israel, He is LORD over the entire earth. While addressing the issue of eating meat from a market, Paul said: "Eat anything that is sold in the meat market without asking questions for conscience' sake; FOR THE EARTH IS THE LORD'S, AND ALL IT CONTAINS" (1 Cor. 10:25–26). The theological point is that Christians are free to eat meat because all food comes from God. As Ciampa and Rosner observe, "Since all food belongs to the Lord and comes from him, it can be received with thankfulness regardless of how it has been used by others."[10]

## 2 Corinthians 4:13 / Psalm 116:10

Psalm 116 describes the psalmist's love for the Lord and thanksgiving to Him because the Lord delivers the psalmist from death. In 2 Corinthians 4, Paul also described his trust in the Lord during treacherous conditions. Paul stated in verse 11, "For we who live are constantly being delivered over to death for Jesus' sake." Paul's experience is like that of the psalmist. With verse 13, Paul quoted Psalm 116:10 (Ps. 115:1 LXX): "But having the same spirit of faith, according to what is written, 'I BELIEVED, THEREFORE I SPOKE,' we also believe, therefore we also speak." Paul used the exact same words of the LXX—*episteusa, dio elalēsa* ("I believed, therefore I spoke").

This is a contextual use of Psalm 116:10 since Paul draws upon the principle of faith in God during trials. Peter Balla rightly notes, "Paul uses a quotation from the OT in order to emphasize his faith shared with the psalmist. His faith is in line with the faith of his ancestors; he stands in continuity with the faith of the OT writers."[11] Certainly, as a NT apostle, Paul's trust would be specifically in Jesus, but Paul's trust is similar to that expressed in Psalm 116.

## 2 Corinthians 9:9 / Psalm 112:9

Psalm 112 describes the person who fears the Lord and delights in His commandments. This person gives freely to the poor, and his righteousness endures forever according to verse 9. In encouraging the Corinthians to be cheerful givers (2 Cor. 9:7), Paul draws upon the principle of Psalm 112:9 to encourage the Corinthians in their giving.

---

[10] Roy E. Ciampa and Brian S. Rosner, "1 Corinthians," in *Commentary on the New Testament Use of the Old Testament*, ed. G. K. Beale and D. A. Carson (Grand Rapids: Baker Academic, 2007), 730.

[11] Peter Balla, "2 Corinthians," in *Commentary on the New Testament Use of the Old Testament*, 765. See Scott Hafemann, "Paul's Use of the Old Testament in 2 Corinthians," *Interpretation-Journal of Bible and Theology* 52, no. 3 (July, 1998): 250–51.

# 2 Corinthians 13:1 (and Matthew 18:16; 1 Timothy 5:19) / Deuteronomy 19:15

Deuteronomy 19:15 revealed that an accusation from one person was not good enough to convict another person of wrongdoing. There needed to be two or three witnesses: "on the evidence of two or three witnesses a matter shall be confirmed." With 2 Corinthians 13:1, Paul linked his third coming to the Corinthians with the Deuteronomy 19:15 principle. Jesus also used the Deuteronomy 19:15 principle of two or three witnesses concerning confronting a sinning brother in Matthew 18:16. Paul said an accusation against an elder should not be considered unless there are two or three witnesses in 1 Timothy 5:19 (see also Heb. 10:28). Thus, the principle from Deuteronomy 19:15 concerning needing more than one person to receive an accusation against someone is still binding.

## Galatians 3:10 / Deuteronomy 27:26

In Galatians 2–4, Paul asserted that being right with God is not based on the Mosaic covenant and its Law. Instead, being right with God is linked with faith in Christ and the blessings of the Abrahamic covenant. The Mosaic Law was a temporary tutor or guardian that led to the era of Jesus the Messiah and faith in Him for righteousness (see Gal. 3:24–25). With Galatians 3:10 Paul declared:

> For as many as are of the works of the Law are under a curse; for it is written, "CURSED IS EVERYONE WHO DOES NOT ABIDE BY ALL THINGS WRITTEN IN THE BOOK OF THE LAW, TO PERFORM THEM."

By "works of the Law," Paul referred to the requirements of the Mosaic Law. The words, "of the works of the Law," refer to being under and obligated to the Mosaic Law. And since the Mosaic Law comes with a curse, it is a curse-based covenant. Thus, those under the Mosaic Law are under a curse.

What does this mean for the Galatians? According to Paul, if one chooses to be under the requirements of the Mosaic covenant, he willingly identifies with a covenant that brings a curse. To support this point, Paul quoted Deuteronomy 27:26 which says, "'Cursed is he who does not confirm the words of this law by doing them.' And all the people shall say, 'Amen.'"[12] This verse culminates a section of 27:15–16 where the word "cursed" is used twelve times to explain that a curse exists

---

[12] The LXX is more specific than the MT by stating "cursed is *every* man" and "*all* the words of this law". Paul's wording is closer to the LXX than the MT.

for those who break God's commandments. The stark message of Deuteronomy 27 is that a curse awaits those who do not abide by what God requires.

Paul's main point in Deuteronomy 27:26 is that all who are under the Mosaic Law are under a curse, since the Mosaic Law comes with a curse. For the Galatians, they can avoid being under the curse-based Mosaic covenant by trusting in Jesus and participating in the faith-based Abrahamic covenant.

## Galatians 5:14 / Leviticus 19:18

In Galatians, Paul implored his readers to avoid placing themselves under circumcision and the Mosaic Law since doing so would put them back into slavery (Gal. 5:1) and would mean a fall from grace (Gal. 5:4). Instead, they should focus on love and serving one another (Gal. 5:13). Paul then quotes Leviticus 19:18: "For the whole Law is fulfilled in one word, in the statement, 'YOU SHALL LOVE YOUR NEIGHBOR AS YOURSELF.'" This quotation of Leviticus 19:18 highlights the theological truth that fulfillment of the Law is found in love of others. Galatians 5:14 is also similar to Romans 13:8 which states, "Owe nothing to anyone except to love one another; for he who loves his neighbor has fulfilled the law."

Paul's statement might seem contradictory at first glance. Moisés Silva notes that for many scholars, "it seems almost unimaginable that Paul, in the very letter where he gives his most sustained argument against the law, should now speak about the need to fulfill the law."[13] So why would Paul argue against returning to the Mosaic Law and then quote a Mosaic command positively? The answer is this: *A statement that love of neighbor is the fulfillment of the Mosaic Law is not a statement that the Mosaic Law enables a person to love as he should. The New covenant of the Messiah is what is needed to do this*. With Romans 8:3–4, Paul explained that the Mosaic Law did not enable people to love as they should. Only Jesus, His death, and the Holy Spirit can do this:

> For what the Law could not do, weak as it was through the flesh, God did: sending His own Son in the likeness of sinful flesh and as an offering for sin, He condemned sin in the flesh, so that the requirement of the Law might be fulfilled in us, who do not walk according to the flesh but according to the Spirit.

This "requirement of the Law," according to Romans 13:8, is loving one another. Paul says the Mosaic Law could not enable anyone under it to love as they should. But Jesus' death and "the Spirit," which is linked with the New covenant, enable a person to fulfill the law of love. The Mosaic Law is good and holy as it calls on people under it to fulfill its requirement of love of neighbor. But the Mosaic covenant

---

[13] Moisés Silva, "Galatians," in *Commentary on the New Testament Use of the Old Testament*, 810.

did not provide enablement for this command. Jesus and the New covenant, though, now enable Christians to love as they should.

## Ephesians 6:2–3 / Exodus 20:12

Starting with Ephesians 5:22, Paul explained how various relationships should function for Christians. With Ephesians 6:2–3, he noted that children should obey their parents and connects this with a quote from Exodus 20:12[14]:

> Children, obey your parents in the Lord, for this is right. HONOR YOUR FATHER AND MOTHER (which is the first commandment with a promise), SO THAT IT MAY BE WELL WITH YOU, AND THAT YOU MAY LIVE LONG ON THE EARTH.

The context of Exodus 20:12 is the initial giving of the Ten Commandments to Israel at Mount Sinai. Certainly obeying parents is a creation ordinance, but this is now codified in the Mosaic covenant. The reference to prosperity and long life in the land is connected with long physical life in the land of promise.

But how does Paul use Exodus 20:12? The church is not Israel, and the church is not linked with actual land. A common view is that Paul turns Exodus 20:12 into a proverbial statement that is spiritual in nature. Since it is not the case that all children in this present age live long lives in the land if they obey their parents, Paul must be speaking generally and spiritually. Thus, it often will go well for children spiritually in this age if they obey their parents. So the promise of Exodus 20:12 becomes a general, proverbial truth.

Perhaps one could retain a contextual connection with Exodus 20:12 in that the principle of matters going well for children if they obey their parents is true for Israelite children under the Mosaic covenant and children of believers in the New covenant era. But two points of discontinuity involve (1) going from a promise to a general proverb, and (2) going from prosperous and long life in a literal land to spiritual wellbeing.

Perhaps an eschatological understanding can help. In Ephesians 5:3–5, Paul says no immoral person or idolater "has an inheritance in the kingdom of Christ and God." So inheriting the future kingdom (or not) is in the context here. If Ephesians 6:2–3 has an eschatological element, Paul could be saying that children who obey their parents will receive the eschatological promise of land or earth[15] in the coming

---

[14] Paul probably quoted the LXX version of the fifth commandment in Exodus 20:12.

[15] Paul uses *gēs* here, a term often translated as "land" and "earth" in the New Testament.

kingdom.[16] This maintains the "promise" element of Exodus 20:12 and would apply to all Christian children who obey their parents. Plus it allows for a literal understanding of land/earth that is found in Exodus 20:12 since believers in Jesus will dwell in the land/earth of Jesus' coming kingdom (see Rev. 5:10).[17]

## Philippians 2:10–11 / Isaiah 45:23

Isaiah 45 announced that only God is God, and all who turn to Him from among the nations will be saved (Isa. 45:22). Also, everyone will submit to the God of Israel as verse 23 states: "That to Me every knee will bow, every tongue will swear allegiance." Paul draws upon this theological truth in Philippians 2:10–11 and applies it to Jesus where he states, "that at the name of Jesus EVERY KNEE WILL BOW" and "every tongue will confess that Jesus Christ is Lord." This is a contextual use of the OT since Paul applies the theological truth that all will acknowledge God to Jesus— the God-man—who because of His humility at the cross, has been exalted above all (Phil. 2:8–9). Such a use of the OT highlights the deity of Jesus, since only God is worthy of such reverence.

It should be noted that neither Isaiah 45:23 nor Philippians 2:10–11 teaches a universal salvation in which all people will be saved. Isaiah 45:24 states that all who oppose God "will be put to shame" (Isa. 45:24), and Philippians 2:10–11 teaches that all will have to acknowledge Jesus as Lord.

## 1 Timothy 5:18 / Deuteronomy 25:4

First Timothy 5:17 says that elders who rule well are worthy of compensation. To make his point, Paul quoted Deuteronomy 25:4: "For the Scripture says, 'YOU SHALL NOT MUZZLE THE OX WHILE HE IS THRESHING'" (1 Tim. 5:18). Paul makes a moral point using a lesser-to-greater argument. Just as one should not muzzle an ox and stop it from eating while it is working, the elder who works hard, especially at teaching, should not be stymied by lack of material resources. The elder is worthy of compensation for his work. This is the same point Paul makes in 1 Corinthians 9:9–10 where he also quoted Deuteronomy 25:4. This is application of a moral principle to a current situation. Workers should receive compensation, and Deuteronomy 25:4 supports this principle.

---

[16] This view is promoted by James Revelino, "Paul's Use of Exodus 20:12 in Ephesians 6:2–3," unpublished paper. March 31, 2020.

[17] Frank S. Thielman seems to take an eschatological understanding when he says, "Paul may be saying that children whose obedience to their parents arises from their commitment to 'the Lord' (6:1) will live eternally not on a particular land…but rather on an earth without boundaries, as God created it to be." *Commentary on the New Testament Use of the Old Testament*, 830.

# Hebrews 1:5 / Psalm 2:7

Psalm 2 is a messianic passage that predicts the coming earthly reign of the Messiah, who is God's "Son," over the nations that currently are in rebellion against God. God will defeat scoffers and establish His Messiah as King over the world. Verse 7 tells of the exalted status of the Messiah from God's standpoint:

> I will surely tell of the decree of the LORD:
> He said to Me, "You are My Son,
> Today I have begotten You."

The Messiah is God's Son with an exalted position. With Hebrews 1, the author offered an extended discussion on the superiority of Jesus over angels. Hebrews 1:5 then quotes Psalm 2:7:

> For to which of the angels did He ever say,
> "YOU ARE MY SON,
> TODAY I HAVE BEGOTTEN YOU?"

The point here is that Jesus alone, not angels, is God's unique Son who receives these lofty words and exaltation from God. The Messiah, as the ideal Davidic King and representative of mankind, will rule the nations. Also, since Psalm 2 is a prophetic passage about the Messiah, Jesus is the literal fulfillment of Psalm 2.

# Hebrews 1:8–9 / Psalm 45:6–7

Hebrews 1 extols the superiority of Jesus in several ways. Particularly striking is verses 8–9 where God the Father refers to Jesus as God:

> But of the Son He says,
> "YOUR THRONE, O GOD, IS FOREVER AND EVER,
> AND THE RIGHTEOUS SCEPTER IS THE SCEPTER OF HIS KINGDOM.
> "YOU HAVE LOVED RIGHTEOUSNESS AND HATED LAWLESSNESS;
> THEREFORE GOD, YOUR GOD, HAS ANOINTED YOU
> WITH THE OIL OF GLADNESS ABOVE YOUR COMPANIONS."

The writer is quoting, Psalm 45:6–7. But does Psalm 45, in its context, support the claim of Hebrews 1:8–9 that Jesus is God?

Psalm 45, a maskil of the sons of Korah, celebrates the marriage of a King: "I address my verses to the King" (v. 2). Some believe the psalm was directed to

Solomon or another king in the Davidic line. The psalm does speak of marriage (vv. 10–15) and the King having sons (v. 16).

Yet the language of this psalm is very exalted, so much so that it seems to go beyond a mere human king. This King is "fairer than the sons of men" (v. 2a). He is one who possesses "splendor" and "majesty" (vv. 3–4a). His "name" will "be remembered in all generations," and "the peoples will give You thanks forever and ever" (v. 17). Most striking is 6a which declares, "Your throne O God, is forever and ever." The Septuagint and most English translations understand this in the vocative sense of the King being called or named, "God." Guthrie observes that "the punctuation and syntax of the MT [Masoretic Text] support the reading 'Your throne, O God'."[18] The term for "God" is *elohim*, which is used over 2,300 times for the God of the Bible. Simon Chi-Chung Cheung notes that "Ps 45 takes pains to show that the Israelite king shares many of the attributes, even the title, of the Israelite God."[19] So the psalm's exalted language and use of *elohim* point to this King being divine.

The best candidate for Psalm 45 is the divine Messiah. The Targum of Psalm 45:2 says, "Your beauty, O King Messiah." A divine understanding of the ultimate Davidic King seems to be the case in Psalm 2 where the nations are called to worship God's King and Son—"Do homage to the Son" (v. 12a; v. 6). With Psalm 110:1, David's "Lord," the Messiah, shares the throne of deity with God the Father. For the King of Psalm 45 to be a divine being is possible. The writer of Hebrews certainly connected Psalm 45:6–7 with Jesus' deity.

So does the writer of Hebrews quote Psalm 45:6–7 contextually? The answer is likely, Yes. A divine Messiah is in view in Psalm 45, and the writer of Hebrews drew upon this truth. This appears to be a case where a NT writer draws upon an OT truth that the coming Messiah is divine.

## Hebrews 3:7b–11; 3:15; 4:3; 4:5; 4:7b / Psalm 95:7b–8a

Psalm 95 is a psalm of praise and warning written by David. Enns observes that "Psalm 95 is an a fortiori argument couched in creation language to warn the people against disbelief."[20]

Concerning praise, Israel should "shout joyfully" (v. 1) to the Lord who made all things (vv. 5–6). But there also is a warning in verses 7b–11. With verses 7b–8 Israel is told, "Today, if you would hear His voice, do not harden your hearts, as at

[18] George H. Guthrie, "Hebrews," in *Commentary on the New Testament Use of the Old Testament*, 937. The RSV takes *elohim* as an adjective and translates 45:6 as "Your divine throne."

[19] Simon Chi-Chung Cheung, "'Forget Your People and Your House,': The Core Theological Message of Psalm 45 and Its Canonical Position in the Hebrew Psalter," *Bulletin for Biblical Research* 26, no. 3 (2016): 330.

[20] Peter E. Enns, "Creation and Re-Creation: Psalm 95 and Its Interpretation in Hebrews 3:1–4:13," *Westminster Theological Journal* 55 (1993): 280.

Meribah, as in the day of Massah in the wilderness." This is a reference to Israel's grumbling for lack of water recorded in Exodus 17:2–7. We are told that Moses "named the place Massah and Meribah" because it was there that Israel "tested the LORD" (Exod. 17:7).

Psalm 95:8–10 retells this negative event in Israel's history, and then verse 11 states the result from God's perspective: "Therefore I swore in My anger, truly they shall not enter into My rest." *In sum, the main warning of Psalm 95 is that Israel should avoid hardness of heart because those characterized by unbelief will not enter God's rest.* Psalm 95:10 states that forty years of wilderness wandering was the result of unbelief.

Psalm 95 was strategic to the writer of Hebrews who references this psalm five times in Hebrews 3–4: 3:7b–11; 3:15; 4:3; 4:5; and 4:7b. Hebrews 3:7b–11 quotes the larger section of Psalm 95:7b–11, retelling Israel's sin followed by God's evaluation that Israel, at that time, did not enter God's rest. Both Hebrews 3:15 and 4:7b quote Psalm 95:7b–8a:

> TODAY IF YOU HEAR HIS VOICE,
> DO NOT HARDEN YOUR HEARTS, AS WHEN THEY PROVOKED ME. (3:15)

> TODAY IF YOU HEAR HIS VOICE,
> DO NOT HARDEN YOUR HEARTS. (4:7b)

Hebrews 4:3 and 4:5 emphasize Psalm 95:11's statement concerning not entering God's rest because of unbelief:

> AS I SWORE IN MY WRATH,
> THEY SHALL NOT ENTER MY REST. (4:3b)

> THEY SHALL NOT ENTER MY REST. (4:5b)

Why do these five references to Psalm 95 occur in Hebrews 3–4? While the majority of the Jewish readers had believed in Jesus as Messiah, the writer was aware some had not. While understanding the realities of Jesus and His New covenant, some were considering returning to Mosaic Law observance, which would be a rejection of Jesus and His perfect New covenant sacrifice. Doing this would be considered unbelief, making them unqualified for God's rest, just like those in Exodus 17. Enns observes, "We see then that both Psalm 95 and Hebrews apply the example of the wilderness rebellion to motivate their communities to obedience."[21] Thus, *Psalm 95 is quoted*

---

[21] Enns, "Creation and Re-Creation: Psalm 95 and Its Interpretation in Hebrews 3:1–4:13," 277. Enns does believe the use of Psalm 95 here has "similarities to *pesher* exegesis" (272).

*five times in Hebrews 3–4 to highlight the theological principle that belief is required for experiencing God's rest.*[22] The time and audience are different, but the theological principle of not hardening one's heart to God's message still applies.

This use of Psalm 95 in Hebrews 3–4 also is the only time that an OT passage is quoted five separate times in the same NT section.

## Hebrews 10:30 / Deuteronomy 32:35a, 36a

In Hebrews 10:30, the writer quoted Deuteronomy 32:35a and 36a: For we know Him who said, "VENGEANCE IS MINE, I WILL REPAY." And again, "THE LORD WILL JUDGE HIS PEOPLE." The context of Deuteronomy 32 is the Song of Moses late in Moses' career. Much of Deuteronomy 32 details Israel's disobedience. Deuteronomy 32:35–36 reveals that vengeance belongs to God and that God will judge His people, Israel. The judgment of Deuteronomy 32:36 appears positive as it speaks of a judgment of vindication—"For the LORD will vindicate His people."

The context of Hebrews 10:30 is more negative since it speaks of God taking vengeance and judgment upon Jews who reject Jesus and His New covenant. Yet the use of Deuteronomy 32:35–36 in Hebrews 10:30 remains contextual since both passages speak of God taking vengeance on His enemies and judging His people. Judgment can take a negative or positive form (vindication), but the truth remains that God will judge His people Israel. Both Deuteronomy 32:36 and Hebrews 10:30 affirm this.

## Hebrews 12:5–6 / Proverbs 3:11–12

Hebrews 12:5–6 describes God's discipline upon those who belong to Him. In doing so, the writer quotes Proverbs 3:11–12 to show the theological principle that God disciplines those whom He loves.

## Hebrews 13:5 / Joshua 1:5

In Hebrews 13, the writer encouraged his readers to love each other and do what is right. Then in 13:5 he says, "Make sure that your character is free from the love of money, being content with what you have; for He Himself has said, 'I WILL NEVER DESERT YOU, NOR WILL I EVER FORSAKE YOU.'" This quotation comes from Joshua 1:5 where God told Joshua that He would be with Joshua and not forsake him.

---

[22] It does not fit our purposes here to cover the nature of "rest" the writer of Hebrews is referring to. Our opinion is that "rest" involves salvation in the present while still involving physical and land rest in the future when Jesus returns. "Rest" involves a spiritual element but is not limited to that idea.

Certainly, Joshua 1:5 did not have the audience of Hebrews in mind, but the principle that God does not forsake His people is transcendent. The writer of Hebrews applied the enduring principle that God does not forsake His own.

## Hebrews 13:6 / Psalm 118:6

In Psalm 118:6, the psalmist offered thanksgiving to the Lord for His goodness. He exclaimed, "The LORD is for me; I will not fear; What can man do to me?" The writer of Hebrews quoted this verse in 13:6 to show that Christians also can draw upon the truth that God's nearness is superior to what man can do.

## 1 Peter 1:16 / Leviticus 11:44 (19:2; 20:7)

Peter called his readers to holiness by appealing to God's holiness. He quoted Leviticus 11:44 (and 19:2; 20:7): "but like the Holy One who called you, be holy yourselves also in all your behavior; because it is written, 'YOU SHALL BE HOLY, FOR I AM HOLY'" (1 Pet. 1:15–16). Peter applied the timeless theological principle from Leviticus that God's holiness is the reason for personal holiness.

## 1 Peter 1:24–25a / Isaiah 40:6–8

In 1 Peter 1:23, Peter said the Word of God is "living and enduring." To support this point he appealed to Isaiah 40:6–8 which states that "all flesh is grass." Even though "the grass withers" and "the flower fades," "the word of our God stands forever." Peter quoted Isaiah 40:6–8 in 1 Peter 1:24–25a to prove that God's Word never fades away. He quoted an OT passage to apply an unchanging theological truth concerning God's Word.

## 1 Peter 3:10–12 / Psalm 34:12–16

In 1 Peter 3:1–8, Peter offered a list of instructions for godly living. Then in verse 9 he stressed the importance of not returning evil for evil. Instead, Christians should give a blessing to receive a blessing. To support this point he offered a lengthy quotation from Psalm 34:12–16 (see 1 Pet. 3:10–12). Psalm 34 states that one who desires life must keep his tongue and deeds from evil and should seek to do good. The Lord is for the righteous and against those who do evil. Thus, Peter used moral instruction from Psalm 34 to instruct his readers.

# 1 Peter 4:18 / Proverbs 11:31

First Peter 4:18 is a literal word-for-word translation of the LXX of Proverbs 11:31. Appealing to the principle of Proverbs 11:31, Peter's point is this: if God's judgment is not relaxed for His people, how much more so do those who disobey God have no chance to escape God's judgment. Peter's readers can know they are trusting their lives to a Creator God who does what is right (see 1 Pet. 4:19).

# 1 Peter 5:5 (and James 4:6) / Psalm 138:6

Psalm 138 is a psalm of David concerning thanksgiving for God's lovingkindness and truth (v. 2). In verse 6, David stated that God "regards the lowly, but the haughty He knows from afar." God kindly recognizes the lowly but is not near the arrogant. Peter picked up this principle in 1 Peter 5:5 when he instructed younger men: "You younger men, likewise, be subject to your elders; and all of you, clothe yourselves with humility toward one another, for GOD IS OPPOSED TO THE PROUD, BUT GIVES GRACE TO THE HUMBLE." The timeless principle of expressing humility and avoiding pride is used by Peter for his audience.

The use of Psalm 138:6 is also found in James 4:6 where James addressed the issues of "quarrels and conflicts among you" (4:1). James exhorted his readers, "But He gives a greater grace. Therefore it says, 'GOD IS OPPOSED TO THE PROUD, BUT GIVES GRACE TO THE HUMBLE.'" James applied the principle that God is opposed to the proud from Psalm 138:6 to his readers.

# 2 Peter 2:22 / Proverbs 26:11

Proverbs 26 is about the way of fools and how they will eventually return to their unwise ways. As Proverbs 26:11 states, "Like a dog that returns to its vomit is a fool who repeats his folly."

Peter notes that false prophets may have "escaped the defilements of the world" for a time (2 Pet. 2:20), but because they are not truly saved, they will become "entangled" and "overcome" by such defilements again. In the end, they will be in a worse state than before (2:21). Peter then quotes Proverbs 26:11a, "It has happened to them according to the true proverb, 'A DOG RETURNS TO ITS OWN VOMIT'" (2 Pet. 2:22). Drawing upon the principle of Proverbs 26:11, Peter shows that false prophets are fools who return to their sinful ways. For a while they might seem appealing, but eventually they will go back to their own sin like a dog returns to its vomit. Thus, Peter quotes Proverbs 26:11 to apply a timeless principle to false prophets.

# CHAPTER FIFTEEN

# LITERAL RELIANCE ON AN OLD TESTAMENT EVENT OR STATEMENT

At times, the NT persons and writers quoted OT passages concerning an event or statement in OT history. We call this category "Literal Reliance on an OT Event or Statement." This often occurs as part of a broader moral or theological point, yet still, the NT sometimes quoted the OT to highlight a historical occurrence or statement.

## Examples

### Matthew 1:3–6 / Ruth 4:18–22

As Matthew presents Jesus' genealogy in Matthew 1:1–17, his wording in verses 3–6 is heavily reliant on Ruth 4:18–22 which documents descendants from Perez to David. So as Matthew compiled the record of Jesus' lineage, he did so drawing upon the actual genealogy of Ruth 4:18–22. This might be the only clear quotation or use of Ruth in the NT, and it is done so in a contextual way.

### Luke 2:23 / Exodus 13:2, 12

Luke 2:21–38 describes the infant Jesus being presented to the Lord in the temple in fulfillment of Mosaic Law requirements. Verse 23 states, "(as it is written in the

Law of the Lord, 'EVERY firstborn MALE THAT OPENS THE WOMB SHALL BE CALLED HOLY TO THE LORD')." The wording here relies on both Exodus 13:2 and 13:12. Exodus 13 described what was necessary for newborn males, and Luke 2:23 quoted this chapter to show that Jesus' parents fulfilled what the Law required concerning their infant Son, Jesus.

## Matthew 19:4; Mark 10:6 / Genesis 1:27

Genesis 1:27 declared that God made man in His image, including both genders—"male and female He created them." When addressing Pharisees who questioned Jesus concerning divorce, Jesus appealed to the creation event of Genesis 1:27: "Have you not read that He who created them from the beginning MADE THEM MALE AND FEMALE" (Matt. 19:4). Jesus' quotation of Genesis 1:27 is also found in the parallel verse of Mark 10:6. This is a case where Jesus appealed to an OT verse concerning God's creation of male and female to support his argument concerning divorce. God's creation of male and female in Genesis 1 is the factual basis for Jesus' point concerning no allowance for divorce in Matthew 19.

## John 6:31 / Exodus 16:4; Psalm 78:24

In John 6, Jesus says He is the bread of life, and eating from Him means a person will no longer hunger (6:35). In 6:31, Jesus references the historical event of God providing manna for Israel in the wilderness. In doing so, He refers to Exodus 16:4 (and Ps. 78:24): "Our fathers ate the manna in the wilderness; as it is written, 'HE GAVE THEM BREAD OUT OF HEAVEN TO EAT.'" This is an example of a NT person (Jesus) quoting a historical event in the OT.

## Luke 18:20 / Exodus 20:12–16

In His encounter with the Rich Young Ruler concerning eternal life, Jesus quoted the commandments found in Exodus 20:12–16:

> You know the commandments, "DO NOT COMMIT ADULTERY, DO NOT MURDER, DO NOT STEAL, DO NOT BEAR FALSE WITNESS, HONOR YOUR FATHER AND MOTHER."

Jesus' words, "You know the commandments," followed by five of the ten commandments from Exodus 20, show that He was pointing to truths already revealed in Scripture. A principle is also explained that eternal life is for those who keep God's commandments.[1] Also, the order of the five commandments mentioned in Luke 18:20 does not match Exodus 20:12–16, but the content certainly does.

## Luke 20:28 / Deuteronomy 25:5

Luke 20:27–41 presents an encounter between the Sadducees and Jesus concerning the resurrection. Luke 20:28 states:

> And they questioned Him, saying, "Teacher, Moses wrote for us that IF A MAN'S BROTHER DIES, having a wife, AND HE IS CHILDLESS, HIS BROTHER SHOULD MARRY THE WIFE AND RAISE UP CHILDREN TO HIS BROTHER."

The Sadducees presented Deuteronomy 25:5, a verse concerning levirate marriage and the circumstance of a married man dying before having children. The Sadducees used this verse to argue against the reality of the resurrection of the dead, but Jesus shows the opposite. A full discussion of this encounter is beyond our purposes here, but Deuteronomy 25:5 is brought up as a "controversy dialogue," or "battle over the Scriptures."[2] Thus, this verse is cited as a factual statement from Moses as part of a debate over the resurrection.

## Luke 20:37 / Exodus 3:6

In the same context as the previous example, Jesus quoted Exodus 3:6 in Luke 20:37:

> But that the dead are raised, even Moses showed, in the passage about the burning bush, where he calls the Lord THE GOD OF ABRAHAM, AND THE GOD OF ISAAC, AND THE GOD OF JACOB.

Jesus referenced Exodus 3:6 to support resurrection from the dead since God currently *is*, not *was*, the God of Abraham, Isaac, and Jacob. This is a case where an OT passage was quoted concerning a real historical event.

---

[1] This is not affirmation that salvation can be merited by good works. But those who know God will obey what He says.

[2] David W. Pao and Eckhard J. Schnabel, "Luke," in *Commentary on the New Testament Use of the Old Testament*, ed. G. K. Beale and D. A. Carson (Grand Rapids: Baker, 2007), 366–67.

# The Old Testament in Stephen's Sermon in Acts 7

Multiple examples of literal reliance on OT events occur in Acts 7. During his encounter with hostile Jewish religious leaders, Stephen referenced several OT sections to trace Israel's history until Jesus. What was occurring with Jesus was consistent with Israel's history. Verses 2–8 concern Abraham. Verses 9–16 concern Joseph and Jacob. Verses 17–44 involve Moses. Verse 45 is about Joshua. And verses 46–47 are about David and Solomon. This led to the culminating point in Acts 7:51–52 where Stephen indicted Israel's leaders for their stubbornness and killing of God's messengers, including Jesus.

While there are many allusions to the OT in Acts 7, our discussion below focuses on actual quotations of the OT. These reveal a literal reliance on OT events.

## Acts 7:3 / Genesis 12:1

In Acts 7:3, Stephen quoted Genesis 12:1 concerning Abraham: "And [the Lord] said to him, 'LEAVE YOUR COUNTRY AND YOUR RELATIVES, AND COME INTO THE LAND THAT I WILL SHOW YOU.'" This documents the historical fact that God called Abraham to leave his home area to travel to the land of promise.

## Acts 7:5 / Genesis 17:8

In Genesis 17:8, God told Abraham He would give Abraham and his descendants the land of promise as an everlasting possession. Stephen referred to this historical event in Acts 7:5: "But He gave him [Abraham] no inheritance in it, not even a foot of ground, and yet, even when he had no child, He promised that HE WOULD GIVE IT TO HIM AS A POSSESSION, AND TO HIS DESCENDANTS AFTER HIM."

## Acts 7:6–7 / Genesis 15:13–14

Acts 7:6–7 refers to Genesis 15:13–14 where God told Abraham that his descendants would be enslaved in Egypt for four hundred years but then would be rescued:

"But God spoke to this effect, that his DESCENDANTS WOULD BE ALIENS IN A FOREIGN LAND, AND THAT THEY WOULD BE ENSLAVED AND MISTREATED FOR FOUR HUNDRED YEARS. 'AND WHATEVER NATION TO WHICH THEY WILL BE IN BONDAGE I MYSELF WILL JUDGE,' said God, 'AND AFTER THAT THEY WILL COME OUT AND SERVE ME IN THIS PLACE.'"

This is a literal reliance on Genesis 15:13–14 concerning the coming Egyptian slavery and Israel's exodus from Egypt.

## Acts 7:18 / Exodus 1:8

In Acts 7:18, Stephen quoted Exodus 1:8 concerning the historical fact that after Joseph a new king of Egypt arose who was not favorable to the Hebrew people: "The people increased and multiplied in Egypt, until THERE AROSE ANOTHER KING OVER EGYPT WHO KNEW NOTHING ABOUT JOSEPH" (Acts 7:17b–18).

## Acts 7:27–29 / Exodus 2:14a, 15b

In Acts 7:27–29, Stephen quoted and paraphrased the historical account of Exodus 2:14a, 15b concerning Moses' flight to Midian after a fellow Hebrew brought up Moses' killing of an Egyptian:

> But the one who was injuring his neighbor pushed him away, saying, "WHO MADE YOU A RULER AND JUDGE OVER US? YOU DO NOT MEAN TO KILL ME AS YOU KILLED THE EGYPTIAN YESTERDAY, DO YOU?" At this remark, MOSES FLED AND BECAME AN ALIEN IN THE LAND OF MIDIAN, where he became the father of two sons.

## Acts 7:40 / Exodus 32:23

In Acts 7:40, Stephen referred to Moses questioning Aaron as to why the idolatrous golden calf was built. Stephen noted what the people of Israel said to Aaron at that time: "SAYING TO AARON, 'MAKE FOR US GODS WHO WILL GO BEFORE US; FOR THIS MOSES WHO LED US OUT OF THE LAND OF EGYPT—WE DO NOT KNOW WHAT HAPPENED TO HIM.'" This is a quotation of Exodus 32:23.

## Acts 7:42–43 / Amos 5:25–27

In Acts 7:42–43, Stephen quoted Amos 5:25–27 to highlight the historical event of Israel committing idolatry in the wilderness during the time of Moses as the basis for rebuking the current generation of Israel. As Gert Steyn notes, the quotation of Amos in Acts 7:42–43 "becomes the turning point in Stephen's speech" since "it forms the transition between the past and the present of God's people."[3] In one sense, the meaning of Stephen's quote of Amos here is clear. Like past generations, the current generation of Israel continued its stubborn opposition to God's activity—this time concerning Jesus. But the meaning of Amos 5:25–27 and Stephen's use of Amos 5:25–27 present the interpreter with several challenges. The Amos text reads:

> "Did you present Me with sacrifices and grain offerings in the wilderness for forty years, O house of Israel? You also carried along Sikkuth your king and Kiyyun, your images, the star of your gods which you made for yourselves. Therefore, I will make you go into exile beyond Damascus," says the LORD, whose name is the God of hosts. (Amos 5:25–27)

Stephen's quotation of Amos reads as follows:

> But God turned away and delivered them up to serve the host of heaven; as it is written in the book of the prophets, "IT WAS NOT TO ME THAT YOU OFFERED VICTIMS AND SACRIFICES FORTY YEARS IN THE WILDERNESS, WAS IT, O HOUSE OF ISRAEL? YOU ALSO TOOK ALONG THE TABERNACLE OF MOLOCH AND THE STAR OF THE GOD ROMPHA, THE IMAGES WHICH YOU MADE TO WORSHIP. I ALSO WILL REMOVE YOU BEYOND BABYLON." (Acts 7:42–43)

The most obvious difference concerns differing names for the deities. Amos 5:26 speaks of Israel worshipping "Sikkuth your king" and "Kiyyun." "Sikkuth" could refer to the Assyrian war god, Adar.[4] Kiyyun or Kaiwan (HCSB) probably refers to an Assyrian star god associated with the planet Saturn. Thus, in this passage worship of Assyrian deities is in view. But does Amos say that Israel worshipped Assyrian deities in the wilderness even though Assyrian deities were not known to Israel at this time?[5]

In Acts 7:43, Stephen quoted the LXX version of Amos 5:26 which used Moloch, not Sikkuth. And Stephen also mentioned Rompha, not Kiyyun: "YOU ALSO TOOK ALONG THE TABERNACLE OF MOLOCH AND THE STAR OF THE GOD ROMPHA." The Mesopotamian god, Moloch (or Molech), was associated with child sacrifice and is mentioned five times in Leviticus (18:21; 20:2, 3, 4, 5). Rompha (or Rephan) seems to refer to an Egyptian deity linked with Saturn and could be related to Kiyyun

---

[3] Gert J. Steyn, "Trajectories of Scripture Transmission: The Case of Amos 5:25–27 in Acts 7:42–43," *HTS Teologiese Studies/Theological Studies* 69, no. 1 (2013): 2. http://dx.doi.org/10.4102/hts.v69i1.2006.

[4] The LXX and NIV do not think Sikkuth is a proper name. The LXX has Moloch for Sikkuth and Rephan, an Egyptian deity linked to the planet Saturn, for Chiun.

[5] According to 2 Kings 17:30, "Babylonian deities were introduced in Canaan by Babylonian settlers immediately after the second deportation in about 720 BC. "Sikkuth Meaning," http://www.abarim-publications.com/Meaning/Sikkuth.html#.XMTzYTBKipo. Accessed April 27, 2019.

mentioned in Amos 5:26. Why Stephen referred to the LXX translation and not that of the Masoretic Text is debated.

Another issue concerns location. Amos 5:27 speaks of an "exile beyond Damascus." But Stephen in Acts 7:43 mentions an exile "beyond Babylon." Certainly, Damascus and Babylon are different, but Stephen focuses on the more significant Babylonian exile which is beyond Damascus. While Stephen quoted Amos 5:25–27, he also said he was referring to "the book of the prophets" (Acts 7:42a), and the prophets at times predicted the Babylonian captivity.

## Acts 7:48–50 / Isaiah 66:1–2a

While pointing out that Solomon built the temple, Stephen said no building made by men could contain the infinite God. Quoting Isaiah 66:1–2a, Stephen said:

> However, the Most High does not dwell in houses made by human hands; as the prophet says:
>
> "HEAVEN IS MY THRONE,
> AND EARTH IS THE FOOTSTOOL OF MY FEET;
> WHAT KIND OF HOUSE WILL YOU BUILD FOR ME?" says the Lord,
> "OR WHAT PLACE IS THERE FOR MY REPOSE?
> "WAS IT NOT MY HAND WHICH MADE ALL THESE THINGS?" (Acts 7:48–50)

Thus, Stephen quoted Isaiah 66:1–2a to highlight the theological point that God's presence is vast and cannot be confined to one place.

## Acts 13:22 / Psalm 89:20; 1 Samuel 13:14

While speaking in a synagogue in Pisidian Antioch during his first missionary journey, Paul explained that Jesus was the fulfillment of the Law and the Prophets. After mentioning the exodus, the conquest of the land, the judges, Samuel, and Saul, Paul then notes that God raised up David to be king. In so doing, Paul combined Psalm 89:20 and 1 Samuel 13:14 in Acts 13:22: "He raised up David to be their king, concerning whom He also testified and said, 'I HAVE FOUND DAVID [Ps. 89:20] the son of Jesse, A MAN AFTER MY HEART [1 Sam. 13:14], who will do all My will.'" Then in the next verse, Paul stated that Jesus is the descendant of David whom God brought to Israel as a Savior (Acts 13:23). In addition to offering several allusions to OT events, Paul quoted Psalm 89:20 and 1 Samuel 13:14 in a contextual way to note the historical fact that God chose David for His purposes. This is a case where a NT person (Paul) quoted OT texts concerning factual events in history.

## Acts 23:5 / Exodus 22:28b

Exodus 22:28 states: "You shall not curse God, nor curse a ruler of your people." The second part of the verse is a clear command to avoid cursing a leader in Israel. This verse is mentioned in Acts 23 when Paul defended himself before the Jews. After stating that he had lived his life with a good conscience (23:1), Ananias the high priest ordered Paul to be struck in the mouth. Paul harshly responded by saying, "God is going to strike you, you whitewashed wall!" (23:2–3). Paul quickly was told that his response was made against a high priest of Israel (23:4), of which Paul did not realize. Paul then acknowledged his error by quoting Exodus 22:28:

> And Paul said, "I was not aware, brethren, that he was high priest; for it is written, 'YOU SHALL NOT SPEAK EVIL OF A RULER OF YOUR PEOPLE.'"

This is a case where Paul relied upon an OT command to avoid cursing a leader of Israel.

## Romans 9:7–13 / Genesis 21:12; 18:10; 25:23; Malachi 1:2–3

In Romans 9:6–13, Paul argued that God's Word had not failed concerning Israel (9:6a) by appealing to several passages in Genesis that show God's sovereign selection of the patriarchs of Israel to be His instrument for worldwide blessing. Paul's quotations in Romans 9:7–12 reveal a straightforward reliance upon Genesis 21:12; 18:10; and 25:23 concerning Abraham, Isaac, and Jacob as the seed line of Israel.

In Romans 9:7, Paul stated, "THROUGH ISAAC YOUR DESCENDANTS WILL BE NAMED." This is a straightforward quotation of Genesis 21:12. In Romans 9:9, Paul quoted Genesis 18:10: "For this is the word of promise: 'AT THIS TIME I WILL COME, AND SARAH SHALL HAVE A SON.'" This showed that the seed line of promise would go through Isaac, not Ishmael.

The next two references involve God's choice of Jacob over Esau in God's purposes. In Romans 9:12, Paul quoted Genesis 25:23: "it was said to her, 'THE OLDER [ESAU] WILL SERVE THE YOUNGER [JACOB].'" The beginning of Genesis 25:23 says this relates to "two nations" and "two peoples," therefore this was a prediction that the descendants of Esau (Edomites) would be servants of Jacob (Israel). During their lives Esau never served Jacob, but later Edom would serve Israel.

Then in Romans 9:13, Paul quoted Malachi 1:2–3 to show that God chose the nation Israel as a corporate vessel for his purposes: "Just as it is written, 'JACOB I LOVED, BUT ESAU I HATED.'" The context of Malachi 1 concerns the people groups of Israel and Edom, so God's choice of Israel over Edom for His purposes is in view here.

These quotations from Genesis and Malachi in Romans 9 reveal that God's sovereignty is related to specific historical events and people. They are also examples of a NT writer relying upon real situations in OT history. God's sovereignty is seen in his choosing a special seed line from Abraham that would result in Israel and the blessing of the nations.

# 1 Corinthians 10:7 / Exodus 32:6

In 1 Corinthians 10, Paul encouraged his readers to make good decisions and avoid the mistakes that Israel made in the past. In 1 Corinthians 10:7, he warned against idolatry by saying, "Do not be idolaters, as some of them were; as it is written, 'THE PEOPLE SAT DOWN TO EAT AND DRINK, AND STOOD UP TO PLAY.'" Paul quotes Exodus 32:6, which describes Israel sitting, eating, and playing during the idolatrous worship of the golden calf:

> So the next day they rose early and offered burnt offerings, and brought peace offerings; and the people sat down to eat and to drink, and rose up to play. (Ex. 32:6)

As part of his argument concerning idolatry, Paul referred to the historical event of Israel's participation in the golden calf incident. This is a case where a NT writer referred to an OT event to make a broad theological argument against idolatry.

# Hebrews 9:20 / Exodus 24:8

Hebrews 8–10 reveals that Jesus and His New covenant are superior to Moses and the Mosaic covenant. In Hebrews 9, the writer explains the details of the Mosaic covenant, including its tabernacle structure. He also says that covenants must be inaugurated with blood. This was true of the Mosaic covenant and is also true for Jesus and the New covenant He inaugurated with His superior sacrifice. In 9:20, the writer then quotes Exodus 24:8 to draw upon the historical incident of the people being sprinkled with blood at Mount Sinai:

> For when every commandment had been spoken by Moses to all the people according to the Law, he took the blood of the calves and the goats, with water and scarlet wool and hyssop, and sprinkled both the book itself and all the people, saying, "THIS IS THE BLOOD OF THE COVENANT WHICH GOD COMMANDED YOU." (Hebrews 9:19–20)

Here a NT writer draws upon an historical event to prove that the shedding of blood is necessary for a covenant to be inaugurated. In this case, blood is connected with the beginning of the Mosaic covenant. As George Guthrie explains, "Very simply, the quotation of Ex. 24:8 at [Heb.] 9:20 serves to reinforce the idea that the covenants are established with blood sacrifice."[6]

## Hebrews 11:5 / Genesis 5:24

Much like Acts 7, Hebrews 11 quotes the OT often. The purpose was to highlight great people of faith. When listing great people of faith in history, the writer of Hebrews referred to Enoch being taken to heaven as mentioned in Genesis 5:24: "By faith Enoch was taken up so that he would not see death; AND HE WAS NOT FOUND BECAUSE GOD TOOK HIM UP." The writer of Hebrews presented the snatching of Enoch to heaven as a real historical event.

## Hebrews 11:12/Genesis 22:17

Hebrews 11:8–12 tells of the great faith of both Abraham and his wife, Sarah. In Hebrews 11:12, the writer quoted Genesis 22:17 in which many descendants were promised to Abraham:

Therefore there was born even of one man, and him as good as dead at that, as many descendants AS THE STARS OF HEAVEN IN NUMBER, AND INNUMERABLE AS THE SAND WHICH IS BY THE SEASHORE.

God's promise of innumerable descendants for Abraham was a real event.

## Hebrews 11:18 / Genesis 21:12

Hebrews 11:17–19 again discusses the great faith of Abraham who was called by God to offer up his firstborn son, Isaac. The writer appealed to Genesis 21:12 in which God affirmed that Isaac, not Ishmael, was the one in whom the seed line of promise will be fulfilled: "It was he to whom it was said, 'IN ISAAC YOUR DESCENDANTS SHALL BE CALLED.'"

---

[6] George H. Guthrie, "Hebrews," in *Commentary on the New Testament Use of the Old Testament*, 974.

# Hebrews 12:20–21 / Exodus 19:12; Deuteronomy 9:19

Hebrews 12:18–24 explains that followers of Jesus are not related to Mount Sinai. Instead, they are connected with the New Jerusalem. In explaining how fearful the events at Mount Sinai were, the writer mentioned Exodus 19:12 and Deuteronomy 9:19: "For they could not bear the command, 'IF EVEN A BEAST TOUCHES THE MOUNTAIN, IT WILL BE STONED.' And so terrible was the sight, that Moses said, 'I AM FULL OF FEAR and trembling.'" This is another case of appealing to an OT text to refer to a past historical event.

As mentioned earlier, references to historical events in OT history usually come within the context of making broader theological or moral points. But the examples in this chapter demonstrate that the NT writers took the events of OT history seriously and used them to connect God's present actions with what He did in the past. Christianity truly is related to actual history.

# CHAPTER SIXTEEN

# DIVINE CORRESPONDENCE BETWEEN ISRAEL AND JESUS

Several uses of the OT in the NT reveal divinely-intended correspondences between Israel and Jesus. These show that Jesus is the ultimate Israelite who can restore Israel and bring blessings to the Gentiles (see Isa. 49:6). So not only are there direct prophecies concerning Jesus the Messiah, there also are events in Jesus' life that correspond with events in Israel's history. This is consistent with the biblical ideas of *corporate representation* and *the one-and-the-many* in which a group is closely related to a special person. So at times in the Bible, events in the lives of the many relate to those of the individual to reveal a connection. This occurs with Jesus and Israel.

Most of the correspondences between Israel and Jesus occur in Matthew 1–2. These involve: (1) Matthew 1:23/Isaiah 7:14; (2) Matthew 2:15/Hosea 11:1; (3) Matthew 2:17–18/Jeremiah 31:15; and (4) Matthew 2:23.[1]

## The Argument in Matthew 1–2

Before we address these passages, some observations need to be made concerning what is happening in the early chapters of Matthew's Gospel and why Matthew uses the OT in the manner he does. I also will comment on Matthew's use of the Greek term, *pleroō* ("fulfill").

---

[1] I have not included the use of Micah 5:2 in Matthew 2:5–6 since this is an example of direct fulfillment of a specific messianic prediction.

In the early chapters of his Gospel, Matthew highlights correspondences between events in Israel's history and events in Jesus' life. In doing so, Matthew intentionally links Jesus with Israel. These correspondences reveal that Jesus is the ultimate Israelite and the corporate head of Israel who represents Israel and brings to pass all God intends for Israel. Note the following:

- A child born in Isaiah's day to a young woman/virgin prefigures or corresponds to the virgin birth of Jesus Christ. (Matt. 1:23/Isa. 7:14)
- Israel's calling and exodus from Egypt as God's son prefigures/corresponds to Jesus' calling and return from Egypt as God's Son. (Matt. 2:15/Hos. 11:1)
- The mourning over the men in Jerusalem deported to Babylon via Ramah prefigures/corresponds to the mourning that took place in Bethlehem as a result of the slaughter of infants under Herod. (Matt. 2:17–18/Jer. 31:15)
- Israel's forty-year wandering in the wilderness prefigures/corresponds to Jesus' forty-day temptation in the wilderness from Satan. (Matt. 4:1–11)
- Moses' reception of the Mosaic Law on Mount Sinai prefigures/corresponds to Jesus' Sermon on the Mount where He offers New covenant law. (Matt. 5–7)

These examples demonstrate that the connection between the OT and the NT is not limited to fulfillment of verbal predictions and prophecies, such as the prophecy that the Messiah would be born in Bethlehem (see Matt. 2:5–6 with Micah 5:2). God also intends for historical events in the OT to prefigure later events in the NT. These highlight God's workings in history and reveal a divine Author behind salvation history.

This concept of historical events prefiguring later events often goes unnoticed by modern readers who usually expect "fulfillment" terminology to refer solely to direct literal fulfillment of prophecy. But historical correspondences would have been significant to an ancient Jewish audience. As Craig Blomberg notes, "For believing Jews, merely to discern striking parallels between God's actions in history, especially in decisive moments of revelation and redemption, could convince them of divinely intended 'coincidence.'"[2] He also says, "The logic is not identical to the classic 'proof from prophecy' arguments of much of church history, but given the theistic worldview that presupposes, it was every bit as compelling in first century Judaism."[3]

---

[2] Craig L. Blomberg, "Matthew," in *Commentary on the New Testament Use of the Old Testament*, 8.
[3] Ibid.

# A Word about "Fulfill" Language

For modern readers of the Bible, it seems natural to conclude that the word "fulfill" means that an OT prophecy has been literally fulfilled. But "fulfill" language does not always mean direct fulfillment of a prophecy. The key word for "fulfill" in the NT is the Greek term *pleroō*. This word is found ninety times in the NT. Seventeen occur in Matthew's Gospel.

Depending on context, the word has various nuances including, "to fill up," "to make full," "to realize," "to bring to realization," "to complete," "to bring to pass," "to accomplish," "to fill to the top," "to consummate," or "to make complete." The term can refer to the filling up of fishing nets (Matt. 13:48), the completion of a speech (Luke 7:1), complete joy (John 16:24; Acts 2:28; 1 John 1:4; 2 John 1:12), being filled up with knowledge (Col. 1:9), Satan influencing someone to lie (Acts 5:3), a full number of martyrs (Rev. 6:11), among other uses. Context will determine the meaning of "fulfill" (*pleroō*). Its use does not necessarily refer to the direct realization of an OT prophecy or prediction, although that certainly does occur.

Below are cases where we find direct literal completion/realization of an OT prophecy or prediction connected with the word "fulfill" (*pleroō*):

**Matthew 4:14:** The Servant of the Lord bringing the light of salvation to Israel and Gentiles
**Matthew 8:17:** Messiah to take away diseases
**Matthew 12:17:** Messiah will have God's Spirit put upon Him, and He will proclaim hope to the Gentiles and do so with gentleness
**Matthew 21:4 (Zech. 9:9):** The Messiah comes to Israel as Israel's king, lowly on a donkey
**Matthew 27:9–10 (Zech. 11:12–13):** The Messiah valued at thirty pieces of silver

Of the seventeen occurrences of *pleroō* in Matthew, only four to six refer to a direct literal fulfillment of an OT prophecy. Outside of Matthew, the use of *pleroō* for direct fulfillment of OT prophecies and predictions also occurs in:

**Mark 15:28 (Isa. 53):** The Servant will suffer for transgressors.
**Luke 4:21 (Isa. 61:1–2a):** The Servant will proclaim release from captivity, miracles, and salvation.
**Luke 21:22 (Dan. 9:27):** The fulfillment of all things related to Jerusalem (likely Daniel 9).
**John 19:24:** Likely a direct fulfillment of Psalm 22 and Jesus' suffering.

Of the ninety uses of *pleroō*, or a form of it, eight–ten concern a direct literal fulfillment of an OT prophecy or prediction. This is eleven percent of all *pleroō* uses. These eight–nine uses of *pleroō* for direct prophetic fulfillment are significant. Also, there are times when direct fulfillment of a prophecy occurs without the term *pleroō* being used. But it should alert the reader that *pleroō* sometimes has a wider range of meaning than just literal fulfillment of an OT prophecy. Context will determine the meaning of each use of the term. Several instances exist where "fulfill" is used to indicate that what the OT or Jesus stated must come to pass (see Matt. 5:17–18; 26:54, 56; Mark 14:49; Luke 4:21; 24:44; John 17:12; 18:32; Acts 1:16; 3:18; 13:27).

For the purposes of this chapter, we will focus on the occasions when "fulfill" is used to link events in Israel's history with events in Jesus' life to connect Israel with Jesus.

# Matthew 2:15 and Hosea 11:1

One example where Matthew shows a correspondence between Israel and Jesus is Matthew 2:15 and its use of Hosea 11:1. According to Matthew 2:13–14, Mary and Joseph took the child Jesus to Egypt to escape Herod's attempt to kill Him. Matthew 2:15 then relates Jesus' return from Egypt with Israel's journey in the exodus from Egypt centuries earlier: "He [Jesus] remained there until the death of Herod. This was to fulfill what had been spoken by the Lord through the prophet: 'OUT OF EGYPT I CALLED MY SON.'" Jesus' return from Egypt is said to "fulfill" [*pleroō*] the event of Israel's journey from Egypt as referred to in Hosea 11:1. Hosea 11:1 reads: "When Israel was a youth I loved him, And out of Egypt I called My son." But how can Jesus' return from Egypt be a fulfillment of a historical event for Israel that occurred centuries earlier? Hosea was referencing the historical exodus of the Hebrew people from Egypt seven-hundred years earlier. So how can an event that occurred centuries earlier be fulfilled with Jesus' return from Egypt? Can a statement about a past event also be a prophecy about a coming person?

The answer is found in *corporate representation* in which events for the "many" are linked with events of the "One." This involves Israel and Jesus. While Israel has several purposes in God's plans, one is to be the vehicle for the Messiah. Paul made this point in Romans 9:5: "and from them [Israel], by physical descent, came the Messiah" (HCSB). Because Jesus is the ultimate and ideal "Israelite," Matthew wants to show his readers that Jesus is the Messiah of Israel. To do that, Matthew connected events in Israel's history with events in Jesus' life. For Matthew, the fact that both Israel and Jesus came out of Egypt was not an accident or coincidence. God intended this correspondence.

Significantly, the connection between Israel and the Messiah concerning Egypt was not invented by Matthew. This connection is made in Numbers 23 and 24. Compare the following oracles of Balaam in Numbers 23 and 24:

- "God brings them [Israel] out of Egypt, He [God] is for them like the horns of the wild ox." (Num. 23:22)
- "God brings him [Israel's king (see Num. 24:7)] out of Egypt, He is for him like the horns of the wild ox." (Num. 24:8)

In these verses both Israel and Israel's King are said to be brought out of Egypt. Thus, even before Hosea wrote Hosea 11:1, Numbers 23 and 24 connected *Israel* as a whole who came out of Egypt with the *King of Israel* who also would come out of Egypt. Hosea likely knew this when he wrote Hosea 11:1. If so, while he primarily had the historical exodus event in mind, he also may have had the coming King of Israel in mind.

Also, the use of "son" by both Hosea and Matthew is strategic. Terms like "seed" and "son" are strategic in the Bible and often carry both a collective and individual sense in the OT. And when these terms were used collectively, they also could imply a coming "Seed" and "Son". So when Hosea referred to Israel as God's "son" who came out of Egypt, he may also have had a messianic hope in mind. This is not an argument for double meaning, but a realization that certain terms in the OT carried both a corporate and individual sense. Even if one sense is primary, the other could be present as well. This is true in Genesis 3:15 when "seed" is used in both a collective sense of mankind and an individual sense ["he"] of the one who would defeat the serpent.

So to answer the original question—how does Jesus "fulfill" Israel's exodus from Egypt according to Matthew 2:15? The answer is that Jesus is the ultimate Israelite. He is related to Israel, and His return from Egypt is connected to corporate Israel's exodus from Egypt centuries earlier. Jesus is Israel's Messiah who can restore Israel and bring blessings to Gentiles (see Isa. 49:6). As Luke 2:32 states, Jesus is "A LIGHT OF REVELATION TO THE GENTILES, And the glory of Your people Israel."

# Matthew 2:17–18 and Jeremiah 31:15

Matthew 2:17–18 also connects an event in Israel's history with an event in Jesus' life to show a divine correspondence between Israel and Jesus. According to Matthew 2:16, Herod was enraged and massacred all male children in Bethlehem. Matthew then links this event with Jeremiah 31:15:

Then what had been spoken through Jeremiah the prophet was fulfilled:
"A VOICE WAS HEARD IN RAMAH,
WEEPING AND GREAT MOURNING,
RACHEL WEEPING FOR HER CHILDREN;
AND SHE REFUSED TO BE COMFORTED,
BECAUSE THEY WERE NO MORE." (Matt. 2:17–18)

Jeremiah 31 is a chapter of great hope for Israel. It comes in the midst of Jeremiah 30–33, often known as the Book of Consolation, which is a hopeful section describing the salvation and restoration of national Israel. Jeremiah 31 also discusses the New covenant that one day will be given to Israel (see Jer. 31:31–34).

Yet sandwiched in the middle of Jeremiah 31 is verse 15, a sad verse referring to the deportation of the young men of Israel from Jerusalem to Babylon during the Babylonian captivity (586 BC). Ramah, just north of Jerusalem, served as a place where Jewish men were gathered before departing for Babylon. The women of Jerusalem, who were not exiled, wept over the deportation of their young men.

But like his use of Hosea 11:1, Matthew's quotation of Jeremiah 31:15 can seem odd at first glance. Some questions may arise. First, how can a first century AD event be a fulfillment of another event hundreds of years earlier? Second, how can the slaughter of infants be a fulfillment of a deportation of young men? Third, how can an event in Ramah be a fulfillment of an event in Bethlehem?

Certainly Matthew knows these events are separated by centuries of time. He comprehends that a slaughter of infants is not a deportation of young men. He also knows the difference between Ramah and Bethlehem. So what is Matthew doing? As was the case with Hosea 11:1, Matthew highlights a correspondence between an important event in Israel's history and an important event in Jesus' life. He shows the connection between Israel and Jesus. In Jeremiah 31:15, we see a tragic event for Israel in the context of hope. This corresponds to a tragic event in the life of Jesus, the ultimate Israelite, in the context of hope, since Jesus is the Savior of Israel.

In sum, God intended for the deportation of the sons of Israel of Jeremiah's day to "fulfill" or correspond to the slaughter of infants in Jesus' day. What happened in Jesus' day relates to what Israel experienced earlier. Both events involve sorrow in the midst of tragedy. But Jeremiah 31:15 is a lament in the context of future hope. Similarly, Jesus brings hope for Israel. The hope element found in Jeremiah corresponds to the hope that Jesus brings Israel. Thus, we see another example of correspondence between Israel and Jesus.

# Matthew 2:23 and "The Prophets"

Another use of "fulfill" (*pleroō*) in Matthew's Gospel is found in 2:23, a verse describing Jesus' relationship to the town of Nazareth: "And [Jesus] came and lived in a city called Nazareth. This was to fulfill what was spoken through the prophets: 'He shall be called a Nazarene.'" In this verse, Matthew views Jesus' life in Nazareth as a fulfillment of what the prophets spoke. But one puzzling issue is that there is no specific OT text that explicitly states the Messiah would be called a "Nazarene." So what is going on here?

Three options (perhaps four) are possible for how Matthew can link Jesus being from Nazareth with the OT prophets. First, Nazareth was a small town and an unlikely place to spawn anything or anyone significant. Nathanael asked, "Can anything good come out of Nazareth?" (John 1:46). Nazareth did not have a good reputation. It hosted a Roman garrison, and Jews who lived there were at times viewed as traitors for associating with the enemy. Being called a "Nazarene" could be a term of derision, like being labeled a "hillbilly" today. Thus, Matthew could be appealing to an OT truth that the Messiah would have humble origins and a humble ministry (see Isa. 52 and 53). Perhaps being from lowly Nazareth summarizes what the prophets predicted concerning the righteous Servant's lowly origins.

A second option is to link Jesus being a Nazarene with the concept of "branch" discussed in the OT prophets. The OT prophets presented the Messiah as a branch of David. Isaiah stated that the Messiah would come from Jesse's roots—a "branch" (11:1). Jeremiah told of a coming "Branch of David" (Jer. 33:15; see also 23:5). The Hebrew term for "branch" is *neser*, which has consonants similar to those found in "Nazarene." Thus, Matthew, with a wordplay, could be connecting the "branch" prophecies of Isaiah and Jeremiah with Nazareth.

Third, perhaps Matthew links Nazareth with the Nazirite vow (see Num. 6:1–21) to emphasize Jesus' full devotion to God. The Nazirites were to evidence strict devotion to God—something Jesus fulfills perfectly.

A fourth option is that Matthew is purposely ambiguous. Perhaps all or some of the three views mentioned above could be part of the argument—humble beginnings, "branch", and "Nazirite."

Note also that Matthew refers to "prophets" in the plural to indicate that the point he is making is a collective summation of several OT prophets, not just one. Whichever of the four views stated above is correct, Matthew is connecting a principle from the OT to Jesus. Matthew 2:23 could be categorized as "summation of an OT truth or principle."

# Matthew 1:22–23 and Isaiah 7:14

Matthew's use of "fulfill" in Matthew 1:22–23 concerning Isaiah 7:14 is the most difficult example to categorize in Matthew 1–2. In Matthew 1:21, an angel tells Mary she will bear a son who will save His people, Israel, from their sins. Then Matthew 1:22–23 states:

> Now all this took place to fulfill what was spoken by the Lord through the prophet: "BEHOLD, THE VIRGIN SHALL BE WITH CHILD AND SHALL BEAR A SON, AND THEY SHALL CALL HIS NAME IMMANUEL," which translated means, "GOD WITH US."

Matthew explicitly stated that Jesus will be born of a virgin since the term for "virgin" in Greek is *parthenos*, which means a young woman with no sexual relations with a man. Isaiah also speaks of a "virgin" in Isaiah 7:14. But debate exists as to how this term should be understood. The Hebrew term *almah* could be translated "young woman" without emphasizing virginity. Yet it is also true that the six other uses of *almah* in the OT seem to indicate young women who are virgins. There are no uses of *almah* where virginity is ruled out. The Septuagint (Greek translation of the OT) translates *almah* as "virgin" (*parthenos*), giving further weight to the "virgin" understanding of Isaiah 7:14.

So what is the connection between Matthew 1:22–23 and Isaiah 7:14? In what sense is Isaiah 7:14 fulfilled with Jesus' virgin birth? Three views exist: (1) Isaiah's prediction only has Jesus in view; (2) his prediction had multiple fulfillments or referents in view; and (3) there is a divine correspondence in view.

The first view is that Isaiah 7:14 specifically predicts the virgin birth of Jesus. The wording of Isaiah indicates that this is not just "a" virgin, but "the" virgin, perhaps revealing a specific virgin to come (i.e. Mary). In addition, the grand nature of the context indicates something big will happen. The message of 7:13–14 is a "sign" for the "house of David." In addition, God told Ahaz to ask for an incredible sign that could be "as deep as Sheol or high as heaven" (7:11). This shows God was thinking of something astounding. These factors point to a sign from God much bigger than a natural conception of a young woman of Isaiah's day. Also, Isaiah 9:6–7 appears to be a messianic text. It mentions a "son" who will be given who will rule from David's throne. So messianic implications are found in the near context of Isaiah 7. Thus, Isaiah 7:14 could be a prediction of the virgin birth of Jesus the Messiah.

One criticism of this view is that it does not address the immediate historical situation involving the two kingdoms threatening Jerusalem. King Ahaz of Judah faced a real threat from the two predator kingdoms of Aram and Israel. Isaiah 7 seems to address that immediate issue. Also, Isaiah 7:15–17 indicates that before the predicted child is old enough to discern good from evil, the two kingdoms of Aram and Israel that threatened Jerusalem would be removed as a threat. Historically, both of these kingdoms were conquered and removed by the Assyrian empire. Thus, Isaiah 7:14 appears to have some relevance to Ahaz's day. It also is possible to understand 7:14–15 as referring to the coming Messiah, while "the boy" of 7:16 is referring to Isaiah's young son, Shear-jashub, standing in front of Ahaz with the prophet (7:3). In addition, Isaiah 8:3–4 could fulfill Isaiah 7:14 since Isaiah is said to have relations with a woman who conceived and gave birth. And before the child could speak, the two kingdoms were removed as a threat:

> So I approached the prophetess, and she conceived and gave birth to a son. Then the LORD said to me, "Name him Maher-shalal-hash-baz; for before the boy knows how to cry out 'My father' or 'My mother,' the wealth of Damascus and the spoil of Samaria will be carried away before the king of Assyria."

The second view—"multiple fulfillments view"—asserts that there are two referents in the Isaiah 7:14 prophecy. Isaiah's prophecy finds an initial fulfillment with a child born in Isaiah's day (first referent), but the final and full fulfillment takes place with Jesus Christ (second referent). Allegedly, Isaiah's young son mentioned in Isaiah 8:3–4 is the first referent, and the Messiah is the second referent.

A third view—the "divine correspondence view"—asserts that Isaiah prophesied of a child in Isaiah's lifetime who would be a sign to King Ahaz that the two predator kingdoms of Aram and Israel would be removed as threats. So a child of Isaiah's day fulfills the prophecy of Isaiah 7:14. Yet this child born in Isaiah's day prefigures the divine child, Jesus Christ, who also is predicted specifically in Isaiah 9:6–7. In this view, the predicted child of Isaiah 7:14 was a child born in Isaiah's day who functions as a real sign to King Ahaz. But under inspiration, Matthew says the child of Isaiah's day corresponds to God's greater Child, Jesus, who was born of a virgin. Jesus' deliverance of the house of David will be even greater than what occurred in Isaiah's time. This understanding seems to fit the other two occurrences in Matthew—2:15; 2:17–18—where historical events in Israel's history prefigure or correspond to events in the life of Jesus.

So what should we conclude? This is a close call. It is possible that Isaiah 7:14 is a direct prediction of the virgin birth of Jesus. So we could have a literal fulfillment of an explicit prophecy. Also possible is the view that Matthew intends a divine correspondence between the events of Isaiah 7:14 and the birth of Jesus. Thus, Matthew 1:22–23 is like Matthew 2:15 and 2:17–18 in that Matthew connects an event in Israel's history to an event in Jesus' life to show a correspondence between Israel and Jesus. This reveals that Jesus is the ultimate representative of Israel who can restore the nation Israel and bring blessings to the Gentiles.

# Isaiah 8:17–18 in Hebrews 2:13

Isaiah 8 appears within a larger section of 7:1–12:6 with two options for Israel. Israel can either trust God or trust in earthly political powers in the face of the ominous threat of Assyria.[4] In 8:16–18, Isaiah and a small remnant chose the path of trusting in and waiting patiently upon the Lord. Then in 8:17, Isaiah says, "I will wait for the LORD," and "I will even look eagerly for Him." And then he says, "Behold, I and the children whom the LORD has given me." So Isaiah and a believing band of brothers together trusted in the Lord.

In addition, Isaiah 8 is surrounded by a context of messianic hope. As mentioned above, Isaiah 7:14 could be a messianic text. And Isaiah 9:6–7 predicts a coming child who will sit on the throne of David. So there may be messianic overtones in Isaiah 8. The main point of 8:16–18, though, is that Isaiah and a believing remnant are like family as they wait together on the Lord, unlike the unbelieving nation.

In Hebrews 2:13, the writer of Hebrews quoted Isaiah 8:17–18 concerning the solidarity Jesus has with those whom He has saved. Hebrews 2:11 stated that Jesus "is not ashamed to call them brethren." Then, after quoting Psalm 22:22 which speaks of proclaiming God's name "to My brethren," Hebrews 2:13 states:

> And again,
> "I WILL PUT MY TRUST IN HIM."
> And again,
> "BEHOLD, I AND THE CHILDREN WHOM GOD HAS GIVEN ME."

The words of Isaiah 8:17–18 are applied to Jesus to emphasize Jesus' trust in God and His familial solidarity with His people. Guthrie notes that the quotation of Isaiah 8:17–18 in Hebrews 2:13 is messianic and is used "to describe Christ's posture of trust and his solidarity with his followers. The Son and his special group of people constitute the remnant prepared by God for himself."[5]

So this is a case where the words of Isaiah and the principle of trust in God found in Isaiah 8 are used to describe the trust Jesus has in God which Jesus shares with His followers. They are like family as they trust God together.

---

[4] George H. Guthrie, "Hebrews," in *Commentary on the New Testament Use of the Old Testament*, 950.
[5] Ibid., 951.

# Psalm 118:22 / Matthew 21:42; Mark 12:10–11; Luke 20:17; Acts 4:11

Psalm 118 is the last of the *Hallel* or "Praise" psalms comprising Psalms 113–118. These psalms reveal God's goodness and covenant faithfulness to Israel. By NT times, the *Hallel* psalms were a regular part of the Passover, Pentecost, and Tabernacle celebrations.

Psalm 118 may have been written to celebrate the Feast of Booths or the dedication of the rebuilt temple after the Babylonian exile.[6] If written by David, its date would be earlier. This psalm repeatedly praises God for His "lovingkindness," including the first and last verses of the psalm. Psalm 118 is quoted about ten times in the NT, rivaling Psalm 110 as the most quoted chapter/psalm from the OT in the NT. Verse 6 is quoted in Hebrews 13:6 and perhaps alluded to in Romans 8:31. The two most quoted verses from Psalm 118 are verses 22 and 26.

In reference to Israel's relationship to other nations, Psalm 118:22 states, "The stone which the builders rejected has become the chief corner stone." Some think this "stone" is messianic, and thus a reference to a coming Deliverer who will be rejected by the leaders of Israel.[7] Kaiser believes Psalm 118 was written by David, and if so, heightens the possibility that this psalm is messianic in nature.[8] Pao and Schnabel observe that, "Several scholars claim that Ps. 118 and indeed the entire body of Hallel psalms had eschatological and messianic connotations."[9] Hyuk Kown notes that "the Hallel, as a whole, was interpreted eschatologically and/or Messianically in late Judaism."[10] More specifically, "The second section of the Hallel in particular [including Ps. 118] was interpreted Messianically in rabbinic literature."[11]

Some take a different approach. For example, Allen Ross notes: "The stone symbolizes Israel, represented by the Judean prince; and the builders symbolize the empire builders, the great powers of the world."[12] With this view, as powerful Gentile nations swept through the region, they considered Israel and her king of no value. But

---

[6] "Psalms," in *The Moody Bible Commentary*, ed. Michael Rydelnik and Michael Vanlaningham (Chicago: Moody Publishers, 2014), 855.

[7] This is the view of *The Moody Bible Commentary* section on Psalms. Ibid., 856.

[8] Walter C. Kaiser, Jr., *The Messiah in the Old Testament* (Grand Rapids: Zondervan, 1995), 100–103.

[9] David W. Pao and Eckhard J. Schnabel, "Luke," in *Commentary on the New Testament Use of the Old Testament*, 337.

[10] Hyuk J. Kwon, "Psalm 118 (117 lxx) in Luke–Acts: Application of a 'New Exodus Motif,'" *Verbum et Ecclesia* 30, no. 2 Art. 59 (2009): 2.

[11] Ibid. Craig Evans observes, "The rabbis understood Ps 118:26 in reference to the day of redemption." Craig A. Evans, "Prophecy and Polemic: 'Jews in Luke's Scriptural Apologetic,'" in *Luke and Scripture: The Function of Sacred Tradition in Luke–Acts*, ed. Craig A. Evans and James A. Sanders (Minneapolis: Fortress, 1993), 179, n. 33.

[12] Allen P. Ross, *A Commentary on the Psalms, Volume 3 (90–150)* (Grand Rapids: Kregel Academic, 2016), 453.

what they rejected as worthless became valuable and prominent. The next verse then says, "This is the LORD'S doing; It is marvelous in our eyes" (118:23). In sum, the Gentile powers viewed Israel and Israel's king as lowly and valueless, but the Lord made them prominent.

The NT certainly connects Psalm 118:22 (and v. 23) with the Messiah, Jesus, on several occasions. As Jesus confronted the Jewish religious leaders in Matthew 21:42, He used the words of Psalm 118:22–23:

> Jesus said to them, "Did you never read in the Scriptures,
> 'THE STONE WHICH THE BUILDERS REJECTED,
> THIS BECAME THE CHIEF CORNER stone;
> THIS CAME ABOUT FROM THE LORD,
> AND IT IS MARVELOUS IN OUR EYES'?"

A parallel of this account with a quotation from Psalm 118:22 occurs in Mark 12:10–11 and Luke 20:17.[13] These sections connect Jesus with the "stone" that was rejected.

In Acts 4:11, when Peter addressed the Jewish religious leaders while the apostles were under arrest, he quoted Psalm 118:22 in reference to Jesus: "He [Jesus] is the STONE WHICH WAS REJECTED by you, THE BUILDERS, but WHICH BECAME THE CHIEF CORNER stone." All four of these NT quotations of Psalm 118:22 have two things in common: (1) Jesus is viewed as the chief corner stone, and (2) the ones rejecting the stone are the Jewish religious leaders.

So how should we understand the NT use of Psalm 118:22? While a hint of a messianic expectation could exist, there appears to be a typological connection or correspondence between Israel/Israel's king and Jesus. The "stone" of Psalm 118:22 represents Israel and its king, while the "stone" in the NT represents Jesus, the King of Israel. Also, those rejecting the stone in Psalm 118:22 are Gentile powers who correspond to the Jewish religious leaders. The Jewish leaders were like the Gentiles in their opposition to Israel's King. Ross notes this typological connection:

> According to the usage of the passage in the New Testament, Israel represented by its prince, was a type of Christ…What was true of the nation was therefore true of him on the highest level. And so in Matthew Jesus claims to be the 'stone' of the psalm, the true king and representative head of the nation (Matt. 21:42–44). And the 'builders' then are the political and religious leaders, the chief priests and Pharisees (see Matt. 21:45), the kings, and the Romans, most of whom who rejected him and tried to destroy him. In spite of their efforts, this stone became the center of God's new program.[14]

---

[13] Luke 20:17 refers to v. 22 but not v. 23.

[14] Ross, *A Commentary on the Psalms*, 453–54.

Classifying the use of Psalm 118:22 in the NT is challenging. The verse does not seem to be explicitly messianic in its own context, but messianic expectations about Psalm 118:22 are found in both later Judaism and in the NT. This makes me hesitant to deny messianic implications in this verse. Perhaps this is a case where a typological correspondence is primary with a hint of messianic expectation. In sum, a real connection exists between Israel and Israel's king in Psalm 118:22 and Jesus the Messiah.

# Psalm 118:26 / Matthew 21:9; 23:39; Mark 11:9; Luke 13:35; 19:38; John 12:13

Psalm 118:26 is quoted six times in the NT and by all four Gospel writers. Verses 25–27 of this psalm trace the procession of faithful Israelites into the sanctuary. They enter the sanctuary calling on God to save and grant prosperity. Verse 26 describes a blessing, probably by priests, to the whole assembly of workers:

Blessed is the one who comes in the name of the LORD;
We have blessed you from the house of the LORD.

Opting for a messianic understanding of Psalm 118:26, *The Moody Bible Commentary* states, "When Israel beseeches this One to save them and recognizes that He comes in the name of the Lord, the nation will be delivered."[15]

But how is Psalm 118:26 used in the NT? The crowds that welcomed Jesus into Jerusalem attributed Psalm 118:26a to Jesus, as the four Gospel writers mention:

- The crowds going ahead of Him, and those who followed, were shouting, "Hosanna to the Son of David; *BLESSED IS HE WHO COMES IN THE NAME OF THE LORD;* Hosanna in the highest!" (Matt. 21:9)
- Those who went in front and those who followed were shouting: "Hosanna! *BLESSED IS HE WHO COMES IN THE NAME OF THE LORD.*" (Mark 11:9)
- shouting: "*BLESSED IS THE KING WHO COMES IN THE NAME OF THE LORD;* Peace in heaven and glory in the highest!" (Luke 19:38)
- [The large crowd] took the branches of the palm trees and went out to meet Him, and began to shout, "Hosanna! *BLESSED IS HE WHO COMES IN THE NAME OF THE LORD,* even the King of Israel." (John 12:13)
(emphases added above)

---

[15] "Psalms," in *The Moody Bible Commentary*, 856.

The Jewish crowd viewed Psalm 118:26 as messianic, concerning Jesus. Of course, just days later a Jewish crowd, incited by the hostile religious leaders, would cry out, "Crucify Him!" While we cannot assume the two crowds were exactly the same, the tragic irony exists that Israel viewed Jesus as both the blessed one of Psalm 118:26 and one worthy of crucifixion.

The other two references to Psalm 118:26 in Luke 13 and Matthew 23 show that Jesus did not view Israel as genuinely calling Him "Blessed" at His first coming. Instead, the genuine cry awaits the future—after judgment and after Jesus' presence would be hidden for a time:

- O Jerusalem, Jerusalem, the city that kills the prophets and stones those sent to her! How often I wanted to gather your children together, just as a hen gathers her brood under her wings, and you would not have it! Behold, your house is left to you desolate; and I say to you, you shall not see Me until the time comes when you say, "BLESSED IS HE WHO COMES IN THE NAME OF THE LORD!" (Luke 13:34–35)
- Jerusalem, Jerusalem, who kills the prophets and stones those who are sent to her! How often I wanted to gather your children together, the way a hen gathers her chicks under her wings, and you were unwilling. Behold, your house is being left to you desolate! For I say to you, from now on you will not see Me until you say, "BLESSED IS HE WHO COMES IN THE NAME OF THE LORD!" (Matt. 23:37–39)

In Luke 13:34–35 and Matthew 23:37–39, Jesus announced that desolation would come to Jerusalem and its temple because the inhabitants of Jerusalem rejected Him. Jesus also stated that He would remove His presence from the people of Jerusalem until the day they say, "BLESSED IS HE WHO COMES IN THE NAME OF THE LORD!" Thus, Jesus' kingly presence among Israel necessitates Israel genuinely acknowledging Him as its Messiah. The words "until you say" reveal a time period is coming when the present situation would be reversed and Israel would genuinely call out to Jesus as the blessed One in a salvation context.

# Theological Implications of Psalm 118:26 in the NT

Some believe Jesus used Psalm 118:26 in Luke 13 and Matthew 23 to describe a future forced and reluctant recognition of Jesus by the Jews.[16] For example, John Calvin stated, "He [Jesus] will not come to them [the Jews] until they cry out in fear—too late—

[16] See R. T. France, *The Gospel According to Matthew*, TNTC, vol. 1 (Grand Rapids: Eerdmans, 1985; reprint, 1987), 332–33.

at the sight of His Majesty."[17] But this view is too pessimistic. As Graham Stanton points out, "The difficulty with this interpretation is that Ps. 118.26 which is cited in Matt. 23.39 is surely an expression of joyful praise rather than of fear or mourning."[18] Psalm 118:26b states, "We have blessed you from the house of the LORD." So Psalm 118:26 reveals a happy and willing declaration from Israel, not a reluctant admission by Israel on its way to judgment. Bock, too, argues against the forced recognition view: "Still another faulty explanation is that Jews will be forced to recognize him at the second coming...The quotation from Ps. 118 is positive and anticipates a positive recognition, not a forced one."[19]

In addition, the use of Psalm 118:26 in the NT reveals that the removal of national calamity and the ushering in of blessings for national Israel is linked with Israel's willful and genuine acceptance of Jesus as Messiah. As Dale Allison puts it:

> The text then means not, when the Messiah comes, his people will bless him, but rather, when his people bless him, the Messiah will come. In other words, the date of the redemption is contingent upon Israel's acceptance of the person and work of Jesus.[20]

Heart-felt recognition of Jesus by Israel did not occur with Jesus' first coming, but it will with His return (see Zech. 12:10; Rom. 11:26). Concerning Luke 13:35 Kwon rightly says, "They will not see him again before the day he is welcomed into Jerusalem as the end-time Messiah."[21] Concerning Matthew 23:39, Charles H. Talbert observes, "When his [Jesus'] people bless him, the messiah will come (cf. Acts 3:19–21). The date of redemption for the Matthean Jesus, then, is contingent on Israel's acceptance of him."[22]

In sum, the conclusion here is similar to that of Psalm 118:22 mentioned above. The blessed one of Psalm 118:26 is the faithful Israelite who comes to the temple. This corresponds or typologically anticipates the ultimate Israelite—Jesus, the Messiah of Israel. A hint of messianic expectation also is possible, especially if David is the author of Psalm 118.

---

[17] John Calvin, *A Harmony of the Gospels Matthew, and Luke, and James and Jude*, vol. 3, trans. A.W. Morrison (Edinburgh: The Saint Andrews Press, 1972), 71.

[18] Graham Stanton, *A Gospel for a New People: Studies in Matthew* (Edinburgh: T&T Clark, 1992), 249.

[19] Darrell L. Bock, *Luke 9:51–24:53*, BECNT (Grand Rapids: Baker, 1996), 2:1251. Mark Elliott claims the message of Matthew 23:39 and Luke 13:35 "implies the warm reception of the Son of Man by Israel at some future date." Mark Elliott, "Israel," in *Dictionary of Jesus and the Gospels*, ed. Joel B. Green, Scot McKnight, and I. Howard Marshall (Downers Grove, IL: InterVarsity, 1992), 363.

[20] Dale C. Allison Jr., "Matt. 23:39 = Luke 13:35b as a Conditional Prophecy," *Journal for the Study of the New Testament* 18 (1983): 77.

[21] Kwon, "Psalm 118 (117 lxx) in Luke–Acts: Application of a 'New Exodus Motif,'" 4.

[22] Charles H. Talbert, *Matthew*, in *Commentaries on the New Testament* (Grand Rapids: Baker Academic, 2010), 260.

# CHAPTER SEVENTEEN

# DIVINE CORRESPONDENCE BETWEEN DAVID AND JESUS

On several occasions, NT writers connected words and events involving David to Jesus. While these connections are not hard to spot, explaining them can be more difficult. For example, did David predict Jesus? And if so, how much did David know about Jesus? How can we apply statements and actions of David to Jesus? And how can an event in David's life be "fulfilled" with an event in Jesus' life? Before looking at specific correspondences between David and Jesus by the NT writers, I offer some observations on this topic.

## Observations on David and the Psalms

First, the Davidic covenant of 2 Samuel 7 is foundational for understanding the David/Jesus relationship. In God's purposes, David will have a relationship to the ultimate David (Jesus). And Israel's kingdom under David and other Davidic kings will have a relationship to Israel's coming kingdom under Jesus.

Second, David looked beyond his own life to the future. God told David, "When your days are complete and you lie down with your fathers, I will raise up your descendant after you." (2 Sam. 7:12). This "descendant" would involve Solomon, but it would also include other offspring in the Davidic line, leading eventually to the Messiah. Thus, words and events involving David are oriented to the future. Also, 2 Samuel 7 predicted a time when David's "house," "kingdom," and "throne" would be "be established forever" (v. 16). The Davidic covenant involved matters concerning "the distant future" (v. 19). So, what God was accomplishing with David was never just for David or Solomon or the first Davidic kings after them. Chou notes that David "was aware his work would have ramifications upon any Davidic king including the Messiah."[1]

Third, while the concept of a specific messianic hope in the psalms is debated among scholars, Psalms 2 and 110, among others, appear likely to be directly messianic.[2] They show that David himself knew of a coming Messiah. In Psalm 110 in particular, David is privy to a conversation between God the Father (*Yahweh*) and the Messiah (*Adonai*).

Fourth, the NT says David foresaw NT realities. Peter said David was a "prophet" who specifically predicted the Messiah's resurrection (see Acts 2:25–31). So we have inspired revelation from Peter affirming that David had a messianic hope. In Acts 1:16, Peter indicated that David was inspired by the Holy Spirit and predicted matters concerning Judas:

> Brethren, the Scripture had to be fulfilled, which the Holy Spirit foretold by the mouth of David concerning Judas, who became a guide to those who arrested Jesus.

If David had a messianic expectation, it is likely that at times David wrote with the Messiah in mind. In addition, when David spoke of his own experiences of oppression and deliverance, these could have relevance for the coming Messiah.

Fifth, Psalms 1 and 2 serve as an introduction and foundation for the rest of the Psalter, and their trajectory carries throughout the remainder of the book. Psalm 1 describes the importance of delighting in God's law. Psalm 2 then shows that God will establish His King, who is also His Son, upon the earth in the midst of the nations that scoffed at Him. Psalm 2 is a messianic psalm that predicts the coming Messiah we now know as Jesus. This King is one who must be worshipped (see Ps. 2:11–12), revealing that this Son/King is divine. If the rest of the psalms are an expansion on Psalms 1 and 2, then one cannot divorce a messianic hope from the Psalms, both individually and as a whole.[3] Messianic expectation is embedded in the psalms from the start. As Brandon D. Crowe observes, "To ask the question 'what makes a psalm messianic,' then, is not simply to ask an *ex post facto* question, but one that was already intended from the beginning."[4] If this is so, we can expect connections

---

[1] Abner Chou, *The Hermeneutics of the Biblical Writers: Learning to Interpret Scripture from the Prophets and Apostles* (Grand Rapids: Kregel, 2018), 143.

[2] For an outstanding defense of a messianic hope in the Old Testament see Michael Rydelnik, *The Messianic Hope: Is the Hebrew Bible Really Messianic?* (Nashville, TN: B&H Publishing Group, 2010).

[3] This is not to say all psalms express an explicit messianic hope but that there is a messianic trajectory that can be detected in many psalms.

[4] Brandon D. Crowe, "Reading Psalm 40 Messianically," https://journal.rts.edu/article/reading-psalm-40-messianically/. n.d. (accessed December 27, 2018).

between David and Jesus because the first David points to the ultimate David we now know as Jesus. Crowe rightly notes:

> Given the Spirit-inspired eschatology of the OT, as part of God's unified and unfolding work of redemption, all psalms are messianic because they anticipate, in various ways, God's ultimate salvation that comes through his anointed one; we can also say, however, that some psalms have a heightened sense of messianic focus and anticipation.[5]

Sixth, not all connections between David and Jesus are the same. At times David explicitly spoke of the coming Messiah as in Psalm 2 and Psalm 110. At other times David described events in his own life but then drifted forward to events concerning the Messiah. This seems to be the case in Psalm 22:16–18 when discussions of David's suffering seem to move to crucifixion details only true of Jesus. There are also times when events in David's life prefigure similar events in the life of the Messiah. This can involve David's zeal for God or times when David was betrayed by a friend.

# Examples

## John 2:17 / Psalm 69:9

Psalm 69 was written by David concerning his enemies who also were God's opponents. Here David is a zealous, righteous sufferer who bears reproach for the sake of God. He also has a zeal for God's temple: "For zeal for Your house has consumed me" (Ps. 69:9). David's zeal for God is connected with the hope that "God will save Zion and build the cities of Judah" so that God's people can live there (Ps. 69:35–36).

David's zeal is also true for the greater David—Jesus. When Jesus drove out the money changers, John applied Psalm 69:9 to Jesus: "His disciples remembered that it was written, 'ZEAL FOR YOUR HOUSE WILL CONSUME ME'" (John 2:17). Certainly, John knew Jesus was not David, but John notes a point of correspondence between David and the ideal son of David. Köstenberger rightly states, "The function of the quotation of Ps. 69:9a in John's account of the temple clearing is to characterize Jesus' action and to do so in scriptural terms by linking Jesus with the righteous

---

[5] Crowe, "Reading Psalm 40 Messianically."

sufferer of this Davidic psalm."[6] This is application of an imprecatory psalm of David, which concerns zeal for God amidst enemies, to Jesus, who also expresses zeal for God.

## John 13:18 / Psalm 41:9

In John 13, Jesus washed the feet of His disciples just hours before His death. In verse 18, Jesus predicted His betrayal by one of them:

I do not speak of all of you. I know the ones I have chosen; but it is that the Scripture may be fulfilled, "HE WHO EATS MY BREAD HAS LIFTED UP HIS HEEL AGAINST ME."

Jesus viewed his imminent betrayal as fulfillment of Psalm 41:9 and its statement that one eating bread will be a betrayer. Psalm 41 was written by David as a complaint concerning his enemies. In Psalm 41:5, David said, "My enemies speak evil against me." Then in 41:9, David noted that his enemy was a close friend with whom he ate bread:

Even my close friend in whom I trusted,
Who ate my bread,
Has lifted up his heel against me.

This enemy who betrayed David probably is Ahithophel, a counselor for David who betrayed David to support David's son, Absalom (see 2 Samuel 16–17).

But the main issue here concerns how Judas' betrayal of Jesus is a fulfillment of Ahithophel's betrayal of David. After all, Judas was not Ahithophel. This is an example where a betrayer in David's life prefigures a betrayer in Jesus' life. Whoever betrayed David corresponds to Jesus' betrayer—Judas. What happened to David is now filled up with Judas' betrayal of Jesus. This also has implications for the Davidic line. Kaiser aptly notes, "What is unusual here is that this psalm's referents are not restricted to David and his heirs; rather, the psalm refers also to the *enemy* of the promised line, including both David and by extension, the Messiah."[7] Similarly, S. Lewis Johnson states, "It is perfectly natural and justifiable to see [David's enemies]

[6] Andreas J. Köstenberger, "John," in *Commentary on the New Testament Use of the Old Testament*, 433.

[7] Walter C. Kaiser, "Single Meaning, Unified Referents," in *Three Views on the New Testament Use of the Old Testament*, ed. Darrell L. Bock (Grand Rapids: Zondervan, 2007), 63. Emphases in original. Kaiser believes the coming Antichrist is also part of the evil seed line that opposes the Davidic line (ibid.).

as prefiguring the Messiah's enemies."[8] So not only is there correspondence between David and Jesus, there is correspondence between the enemies of David and the opponents of Jesus.

## John 15:25 / Psalm 69:4

John 15:25, like John 2:17, relies upon the righteous sufferer concept of Psalm 69. Psalm 69:4 states: "Those who hate me without a cause are more than the hairs of my head." David, the psalm's author, did not deserve the hate he received from God's enemies, but he experienced this hate nonetheless. In John 15:18–25 Jesus declared that the world will also hate His followers because the world hated Him first (15:18). In John 15:24, Jesus said the world hates both Him and the Father. Then John 15:25 quotes Psalm 69:4: "But they have done this to fulfill the word that is written in their Law, 'THEY HATED ME WITHOUT A CAUSE.'"

Psalm 69 described David's experiences as a righteous sufferer on God's behalf, but how can opposition to Jesus and His followers "fulfill" what David experienced? There is a correspondence between the experiences of David and those of the Son of David—Jesus. The opposition David experienced is "filled up" with the opposition Jesus experienced.

## Mark 15:34 / Psalm 22:1

While on the cross Jesus quoted Psalm 22:1, as revealed in Mark 15:34:
At the ninth hour Jesus cried out with a loud voice, "ELOI, ELOI, LAMA SABACHTHANI?" which is translated, "MY GOD, MY GOD, WHY HAVE YOU FORSAKEN ME?"

Psalm 22, written by David, describes great suffering with the hope of God's deliverance. There is debate whether David wrote about his own sufferings or those of the coming Messiah. Or perhaps he wrote about both. David could be writing about his own experiences, but then shifts into predictions concerning the Messiah's sufferings. Verses 11–18 describe a level of specific suffering that seems truer of Jesus' affliction on the cross than David's own experience.

Jesus quoted David's words in Psalm 22:1 and continues the righteous sufferer theme seen in other passages where the sufferings of David find a greater fulfillment in the sufferings of Jesus. I personally think David predicted the crucifixion in Psalm 22:11–18, but this belief also is consistent with the suffering

---

[8] S. Lewis Johnson, *The Old Testament in the New: An Argument for Biblical Inspiration* (Grand Rapids: Zondervan, 1980), 77.

connection between David and Jesus. This connection also exists in the next example concerning John 19:24 and Psalm 22:18.

## John 19:24 / Psalm 22:18

John 19 describes Jesus' crucifixion. While on the cross, the Roman soldiers divided Jesus' outer garments into four parts (v. 23). But when they came to Jesus' seamless tunic, they were reluctant to tear it. Verse 24 describes what happened next:

> So they said to one another, "Let us not tear it, but cast lots for it, to decide whose it shall be"; this was to fulfill the Scripture: "THEY DIVIDED MY OUTER GARMENTS AMONG THEM, AND FOR MY CLOTHING THEY CAST LOTS."

According to John, the dividing of Jesus' garments and the casting of lots for Jesus' tunic was linked with Psalm 22:18 which states, "They divide my garments among them, and for my clothing they cast lots."

As mentioned in the previous section concerning Mark 15:34/Psalm 22:1, it is difficult to know how much of Psalm 22 is describing David's experiences and how much is predictive of Jesus' experiences on the cross. I believe Psalm 22:11–18 is predictive concerning Jesus, thus Psalm 22:18 was directly fulfilled when the soldiers divided Jesus' outer garments and cast lots for His tunic. Yet there is a close connection between David as a righteous sufferer for God and Jesus being the ultimate Righteous Sufferer. In sum, in Psalm 22:18 the suffering of David prefigures the suffering of the Messiah. But there also could be an element of explicit messianic prediction since Jesus, not David, literally experienced the conditions of Psalm 22:11–18. As Walter Kaiser notes, "While to a lesser degree it is possible to speak of some of these things happening in the life of David, it is only with that climactic descendant of his, the Messiah, that it is possible to see most of these things fulfilled in detail."[9]

## John 19:36 / Psalm 34:20

In Psalm 34:19–20, David celebrated the Lord as a deliverer:
Many are the afflictions of the righteous,
But the LORD delivers him out of them all.
He keeps all his bones,
Not one of them is broken.

---

[9] Walter C. Kaiser, Jr., *The Messiah in the Old Testament* (Grand Rapids: Zondervan, 1995), 118.

In John 19:36, John applied Psalm 34:20 to the soldiers piercing Jesus' side instead of breaking Jesus' legs: "For these things came to pass to fulfill the Scripture, 'NOT A BONE OF HIM SHALL BE BROKEN.'" For John, the words of David were fulfilled with Jesus' bones not being broken while on the cross. A theological truth stated by David is applied to Jesus who is the ultimate example of righteousness.

# Matthew 27:34, 48; Mark 15:36; Luke 23:36; John 19:28–29 / Psalm 69:21

As explained earlier, Psalm 69 is an imprecatory psalm of David that expresses David's zeal for God in the context of enemies. Psalm 69:20–21 states:

> Reproach has broken my heart and I am so sick.
> And I looked for sympathy, but there was none,
> And for comforters, but I found none.
> They also gave me gall for my food
> And for my thirst they gave me vinegar to drink.

Psalm 69:21 and its mention of vinegar being offered is alluded to five times in the NT and is one of the few OT verses referred to by all four Gospel writers. All four used Psalm 69:21 concerning Jesus being offered vinegar on the cross (Matt. 27:34, 48; Mark 15:36; Luke 23:36; John 19:28–29). While it may be too strong to say this verse is "quoted" by the Gospel writers, the offering of "sour wine" or "vinegar" is at least an intentional allusion. John 19:28 links the offering of vinegar to Jesus with the fulfilling of Scripture—"to fulfill the Scripture." The use of Psalm 69:21 in these five Gospel references indicates a connection between David and Jesus, with the latter filling up the meaning of David's words.

# Luke 23:46 / Psalm 31:5

Psalm 31 describes David's trust in God while in distress. While in turmoil, it is the Lord in whom David takes refuge; and it is the Lord who is David's rock and fortress (Ps. 31:1–3). In verse 5, David declared: "Into Your hand I commit my spirit; You have ransomed me, O LORD, God of truth." David trusted the Lord with his life.

Centuries later, while on the cross, Jesus the Messiah quoted David's words of trust in Psalm 31:5:

> And Jesus, crying out with a loud voice, said, "Father, INTO YOUR HANDS I COMMIT MY SPIRIT." Having said this, He breathed His last. (Luke 23:46)

This is no coincidence. The first David trusted God during troubling times, and now the ultimate David, Jesus, trusts His life to God during His darkest moment on the cross. Pao and Schnabel point out that Jesus' quotation of Psalm 31:5 reveals two truths. First, it demonstrates that Jesus' death fulfills God's purposes in the midst of darkness. And second, it reveals "that he [God] will rescue him [Jesus] from his enemies and raise him from the dead."[10] Thus, Jesus' final words are more than interesting famous last words; they were "a gesture of confidence."[11] They were a statement of trust in God to decisively vindicate Jesus and raise Him from the dead.

Psalm 31 expresses David's heartfelt trust that God would deliver him. While Psalm 31:5 probably is not a direct prophecy of what Jesus would say on the cross, Jesus used the words of David concerning trust in the Lord as His earthly life expired. This is a contextual use of the OT. As Pao and Schnabel note: "The appropriation of Ps. 31:5 in v. 46 does not violate the original context and meaning in the psalm."[12] It takes David's trust of God in life and extends it to death, in this case the death of the Messiah.

## Acts 1:20a / Psalm 69:25

In Acts 1:15–21, Peter described the tragic plight of the traitor, Judas, and the necessity of a replacement for Judas among the Twelve. Judas committed suicide in a field purchased with his own blood money, a field appropriately called the "Field of Blood" (Acts 1:18–19). Peter linked Judas' awful fate with Psalm 69:25 in Acts 1:20a: "For it is written in the book of Psalms, 'LET HIS HOMESTEAD BE MADE DESOLATE, AND LET NO ONE DWELL IN IT.'"

Some have struggled with this statement since Psalm 69 does not explicitly mention Judas. Yet the answer to this alleged problem is similar to previous examples. Psalm 69 was written by David. Not only are David's experiences linked to the experiences of Jesus—so too are David's enemies linked to Jesus' enemies. We saw this concerning Jesus' use of Psalm 41:9 in John 13:18 when Jesus linked Judas' betrayal of Himself with Ahithophel's betrayal of David. Thus, an enemy of David is also the enemy of David's line, including the Messiah. A similar thing occurs with Peter's quotation of Psalm 69:25. David's hope that his enemies would become desolate is fulfilled with Jesus' enemy—Judas. Desolation awaits the enemies of the Davidic line and the ultimate David—Jesus the Messiah. According to Acts 1:20, Judas the betrayer is made desolate.

---

[10] David W. Pao and Eckhard J. Schnabel, "Luke," in *Commentary on the New Testament Use of the Old Testament*, ed. G. K. Beale and D. A. Carson (Grand Rapids: Baker, 2007), 399.

[11] Ibid.

[12] Ibid.

# Acts 1:20b / Psalm 109:8

Closely related to the above example is Peter's use of Psalm 109:8 in Acts 1:20b concerning the deceased Judas: "and 'LET ANOTHER MAN TAKE HIS OFFICE.'" Again Peter quoted a psalm where David calls on God to avenge his enemy, perhaps Doeg the Edomite, Ahithophel, or Shimei.[13] On sixteen occasions in 109:6–15, David used "Let" to describe some calamity upon his foe. Two of these are found in 109:8:

> Let his days be few;
> Let another take his office.

While Psalm 109:8 is not a direct prophecy of Judas, it expressed David's hope that his enemy would have his office removed. This is tied to Judas, the enemy of the ultimate David (Jesus). In the spirit of what David expressed, Judas would lose his office as an apostle. Enemies of David are also the enemies of the Messiah—including Judas. Kaiser notes, "The messianic aspect of this psalm [109] is to be found…in the fact that all the enemies of David, his throne, his dynasty, and his kingdom, are finally epitomized in one final hostile adversary upon whom God's judgment must fall. Is it any surprise that Judas became that opponent of the Messiah?"[14]

# Romans 15:3 / Psalm 69:9

As with John 2:17 and John 15:25, we see Psalm 69 quoted, but this time by Paul. Paul applied an imprecatory psalm of David concerning zeal for God amidst enemies to Jesus. Psalm 69:9 states:

> For zeal for Your house has consumed me,
> And the reproaches of those who reproach You have fallen on me.

Because David loved God, he gladly took the attacks of those who reproached God. This selfless attitude was picked up by Paul in Romans 15.

In Romans 15:1–2, Paul explained that the "strong" should bear the weaknesses of those who are weaker, and a believer should seek the edification of his neighbor. Paul then appealed to Christ's example in Romans 15:3 by quoting Psalm 69:9b: "For even Christ did not please Himself; but as it is written, 'THE REPROACHES OF THOSE WHO REPROACHED YOU FELL ON ME.'" Paul's point is evident—Christ did not come to please Himself. Like David, Jesus bore the reproaches of those who reproached God. Psalm 69

---

[13] See Kaiser, *The Messiah in the Old Testament*, 108.
[14] Ibid., 109.

presents David as a righteous sufferer on God's behalf, and Jesus, the ultimate David, is *the* Righteous Sufferer who acted selflessly on behalf of God. Paul points to Jesus' example of selflessness, which also was true of David, as an example of how Christians should be selfless and seek the edification of others. So Paul applies an imprecatory psalm of David concerning zeal for God amidst enemies to Jesus, the ideal David.

## Hebrews 10:5–9 / Psalm 40:6–8

Another connection between David and Jesus is found in the use of Psalm 40:6–8 in Hebrews 10:5–9. Psalm 40 is a lament of David concerning deliverance from trial. Here David offered thanksgiving (vv. 1–10) and then a prayer for deliverance (11–17). In verse 6, David stated that God does not require sacrifice, meal offering, burnt offering, and sin offering. This might seem odd since these were required for Israel under the Mosaic covenant. But the point here is likely similar to Micah 6:6–8 that God is concerned primarily about the heart, not ritualistic acts of sacrifice and offering. This verse might also hint that the Mosaic sacrifices and offerings were imperfect and temporary.

Then in verse 7, David said that he (or the Messiah) was written about in previous Scripture: "Then I said, 'Behold, I come; In the scroll of the book it is written of me.'" If David has himself in view, perhaps he is referring to passages such as Genesis 17:6 and Deuteronomy 17:14–20 that explain the requirements of coming Israelite kings. Or if David is referring to the Messiah, he may have messianic texts like Genesis 3:15; 49:8–10; Numbers 24:17–19; and Deuteronomy 18:15–18 in mind. Significantly, this person of Psalm 40:7 would do God's will: "I delight to do Your will, O my God; Your Law is within my heart" (v. 8). Verse 8 is strategic to the psalm because it presents David (or perhaps the Messiah) as one who delights in doing God's will.

Hebrews 10:5–9 draws upon Psalm 40:6–8 to support the argument that through His body, Jesus and His superior New covenant sacrifice replace the Mosaic covenant and its inferior sacrifices.[15] The writer not only quotes Psalm 40:6–8 in Hebrews 10:5–7, but he also offers commentary on its significance in 10:8–9. After stating that "the blood of bulls and goats" under the Mosaic covenant never did "take away sins" (Heb. 10:4), the writer quoted Psalm 40:6–8:

Therefore, when He comes into the world, He says,
"SACRIFICE AND OFFERING YOU HAVE NOT DESIRED,
BUT A BODY YOU HAVE PREPARED FOR ME;
IN WHOLE BURNT OFFERINGS AND sacrifices FOR SIN

---

[15] Psalm 40:6b says, "My ears" while Hebrews 10:5c says "body." Kaiser notes, "The use of 'body' for 'ear' is…a case of the whole being used for the part." Walter C. Kaiser, Jr., *The Uses of the Old Testament in the New* (Chicago: Moody Press, 1985), 137. "This common figure of speech is known as synecdoche." (ibid., fn. 46).

YOU HAVE TAKEN NO PLEASURE.
"THEN I SAID, 'BEHOLD, I HAVE COME
(IN THE SCROLL OF THE BOOK IT IS WRITTEN OF ME)
TO DO YOUR WILL, O GOD.'" (Heb. 10:5–7)

The writer then comments on the quote he just offered:

After saying above, "SACRIFICES AND OFFERINGS AND WHOLE BURNT OFFERINGS AND sacrifices FOR SIN YOU HAVE NOT DESIRED, NOR HAVE YOU TAKEN PLEASURE in them" (which are offered according to the Law), then He said, "BEHOLD, I HAVE COME TO DO YOUR WILL." He takes away the first in order to establish the second. (Heb. 10:8–9)

With his quotation and explanation of Psalm 40:6–8, the writer of Hebrews claims that Jesus does God's will in His body to bring an end to the Mosaic covenant and its sacrifices. As verse 9 says, Jesus "takes away the first [i.e. Mosaic covenant sacrifices] in order to establish the second [i.e. the superior New covenant sacrifice of Jesus]." The main point is this: *Hebrews 10:5–9 reveals that Jesus is the righteous One of Psalm 40:6–8 who does God's will to transition God's purposes from the Mosaic covenant to the New covenant.*

But is this a contextual use of the OT by the writer of Hebrews? Two issues challenge this idea. First, Psalm 40 describes David's words while Hebrews 10:5 attributes Psalm 40:6–8 as the words of Jesus. But how can the writer rightly take David's words and say they are Jesus' words? And second, Psalm 40:6–8 does not speak of removing Mosaic sacrifices, while in Hebrews 10:5–9 the removal of Mosaic sacrifices is in view. Schreiner asks an important question: "How do we explain the author [of Hebrews] seeing here support for the setting aside of the sacrificial system?...there is no warrant for understanding the psalm to teach that the sacrifices of the OT are no longer necessary."[16]

Concerning the first issue there are three options. First, this could be a non-contextual or *pesher* use of Psalm 40 since Jesus is not David and David's words are not Jesus' words. Perhaps the writer of Hebrews is applying the words of David to Jesus out of context since Jesus has arrived. This view is consistent with the Second Temple Judaism approach discussed earlier in this book.

Or second, this could be a case of *correspondence* or *typology*. David might not have had Jesus in view, but God meant for David's words to typologically point to the coming Jesus. Guthrie takes this view: "This fulfillment, moreover, probably should be seen as a fulfillment of indirect typological prophecy, the experience of

---

[16] Thomas R. Schreiner, *Commentary on Hebrews*, ed. T. Desmond Alexander, Andreas J. Köstenberger, and Thomas R. Schreiner (Nashville, TN: B & H Publishing Group, 2015), 297.

David the king being understood as a pointer to the experience of Christ."[17] Schreiner agrees: "Hence, Psalms about David were read typologically and eschatologically and messianically. What was said about David anticipated the coming of the Christ. Typology also usually includes escalation, so Jesus is the greater David."[18]

Or third, perhaps Psalm 40:6–8 is directly predictive of the Messiah. This view might seem difficult to sustain since David is speaking in the first person ("I"). But the reference to "in the scroll of the book it is written of me" in Psalm 40:7 opens the possibility that the Messiah could be in view since the Messiah, not David, is the focus of several messianic predictions in previous Scripture (see Gen. 3:15; 49:8–10; Num. 24:17–19; and Deut. 18:15–18). Taking this third view, *The Moody Bible Commentary* asserts that Psalm 40:6–8 was originally messianic: "David remembered what was written in the scroll of the book about the future Deliverer (vv. 6–8). Quoting what that Deliverer would say, David used the first person, in the voice of the Deliverer, referring to the book of the Law (Torah)."[19] If this third view is correct the quotation of Psalm 40 in Hebrews 10 is contextual since Jesus literally fulfilled what David predicted Jesus would say in Psalm 40:6–8.

A fourth view is that since all Davidic psalms are directly or indirectly messianic by nature, the application of David's words to Jesus is consistent with the informing theology of the psalms. David wrote about his own experiences, but he also understood that what was true of him would be true of the coming Messiah. This harkens back to our earlier discussion that a messianic hope is embedded into all the psalms because of Psalm 2, which is a foundational psalm. Thus, with this view, Psalm 40:6–8 is not directly prophetic, but neither is it true that David had no idea his words could in some way apply to the Messiah. This seems similar to Crowe's view: "Psalm 40 is messianic as part of the Spirit-inspired eschatological outlook of the Psalms that anticipates a greater Son of David."[20] In evaluating these four views, positions three and four offer the best solutions for understanding Hebrews 10:5–9.

Concerning the second issue, Psalm 40:6–8 does not predict the end of the Mosaic sacrifices, but there is a hint that these sacrifices were not the perfect ideal by the words, "You have not desired" (v. 6). That Hebrews 10:5–9 presents Jesus as the One who accomplishes God's will to "take(s) away" the Mosaic sacrifices and "to establish" the New covenant seems consistent with what the OT predicted concerning the Messiah. Other prophetic passages present the ultimate David as the One who transitions Israel from the Mosaic covenant to the New covenant (see Ezek. 37:24–25; Jer. 33:14–26), just as the writer of Hebrews does. To mention that Jesus

---

[17] George H. Guthrie, "Hebrews," in *Commentary on the New Testament Use of the Old Testament*, ed. G. K. Beale and D. A. Carson (Grand Rapids: Baker Books, 2007), 977.

[18] Schreiner, *Commentary on Hebrews*, 297.

[19] "Psalms," in *The Moody Bible Commentary*, ed. Michael Rydelnik and Michael Vanlaningham (Chicago: Moody Publishers, 2014), 794.

[20] Crowe, "Reading Psalm 40 Messianically."

is the righteous One who brings a transition to the New covenant hardly seems like a non-contextual use of the OT.

While acknowledging the complexity of this example, it is best to view the use of Psalm 40:6–8 in Hebrews 10:5–9 as contextual. As Kaiser says, "Psalm 40:6–8 contains fewer messianic clues and less promise phraseology than other messianic passages (e.g., Psalms 2, 22, 72, 89, or 110), but patient attendance on the text will reveal that the writer to the Hebrews was on strong exegetical grounds."[21]

# Hebrews 1:5b / 2 Samuel 7:14a

The examples in this chapter have focused on connections between David and Jesus. Yet with Hebrews 1:5b, there could be a connection between David's son, Solomon, and Jesus. I say "could be" because there is some debate whether the mention of David's "descendant" or "seed" in 2 Samuel 7:12 is Solomon or the coming Messiah.[22] Perhaps both are in view.

Second Samuel 7 is the foundational chapter explaining the Davidic covenant. In 7:12–16, the prophet Nathan explained how David's coming "descendant" (or "seed") will contribute to God's plans. Verses 12–13 predicted that after David's death, God would raise up David's descendant who would establish David's "kingdom," "house," and "throne" forever. Concerning the coming descendant, verse 14 states: "I will be a father to him and he will be a son to Me; when he commits iniquity, I will correct him with the rod of men and the strokes of the sons of men." Verse 14a emphasizes the familial relationship of God to the coming descendant. God will be a "father" to him, and the coming descendant will be a "son." Sonship is key here. With Hebrews 1:5a, the writer quoted Psalm 2:7 concerning Jesus, emphasizing that Jesus is God's unique Son. Then Hebrews 1:5b used 2 Samuel 7:14a to again emphasize the sonship issue:

> And again,
> "I WILL BE A FATHER TO HIM
> AND HE SHALL BE A SON TO ME"?

The Hebrews' writer did not quote 2 Samuel 7:14b, which predicted the descendant's sin (or possible sin), but he did use 7:14a, which refers to "son." The use of 2 Samuel 7:14a in Hebrews 1:5a emphasizes Jesus as God's unique Son who is superior to

---

[21] Walter C. Kaiser, Jr., *The Uses of the Old Testament in the New*, 141.

[22] For the view that 2 Samuel 7:12ff. is about the Messiah specifically, see Winfred O. Neely, "2 Samuel," in *The Moody Bible Commentary*, 454–55.

angels. But is this a contextual use of 2 Samuel 7:14 since (1) this verse could refer to Solomon, and (2) this verse speaks of "iniquity" that leads to God's correction?

Part of the answer relates to whether 2 Samuel 7:12–16 is directly messianic or whether Solomon is a referent. If this passage is directly messianic, then the quotation of 2 Samuel 7:14a in Hebrews 1:5b is obviously contextual, since the Messiah would be the referent in both sections. Proponents of this messianic view of 2 Samuel 7:12–16 believe the words, "when he commits iniquity," are better translated "*if* he commits iniquity." Thus, this is not a prediction that the descendant *will* sin, but *if* a Davidic descendant does sin then this disqualifies him from being the fulfillment of the offspring who will bring the eternal kingdom predicted in 2 Samuel 7.[23] This view is possible.

Yet it is difficult to conclude that Solomon is not at all in view in 2 Samuel 7:12–16. Solomon does build the temple and he did commit iniquity, so his exclusion as a referent in 2 Samuel 7 is unlikely. Yet this in no way removes a messianic expectation in 2 Samuel 7. The "forever" language of 2 Samuel 7 points beyond the lives of David and Solomon.[24] In addition, later OT passages focus on the futurity of the Davidic covenant and the father-son relationship between God and the Davidic heir. Guthrie notes, "The permanence of God's covenant with David formed the basis for Israel's hope in a future king who would carry on David's line and be the inheritor of covenant promises (Isa. 11:1–5; Jer. 23:5; 33:15; Amos 9:11; Zech. 3:8; 6:12)."[25] This naturally ties in with a messianic expectation linked with 2 Samuel 7: "Thus, it is understandable that 2 Sam. 7 would be appropriated by later generations as a vital messianic text."[26] O'Brien agrees: "God's promise to David was understood by later prophets as extending beyond Solomon to the ideal king of David's line known as the Messiah."[27]

In later OT texts and in non-canonical Jewish expectations, a messianic hope concerning 2 Samuel 7 existed. The linking of 2 Samuel 7:14a with Jesus was natural by the writer of Hebrews. If one understands that from the beginning of the Davidic covenant announcement there was an expectation of a messiah-figure beyond David and Solomon, then such a connection between Solomon and Jesus is to be expected in the NT.

Thus, the answer is not to see 2 Samuel 7:12–16 as *only* applying to Solomon, or *only* to the Messiah. Solomon is part of the Davidic line, thus he can be included in the prophecy. And the Messiah can be in view as well. When the writer of Hebrews relates Jesus with 2 Samuel 7:14a, he is making a contextual connection.

---

[23] Neely says, "Thus the prediction of being the Seed is potentially true of each of the descendants of David. Each one is potentially the fulfillment of the covenant but *if* he commits iniquity, he is disqualified." Neely, "2 Samuel," 455.

[24] Eight times "forever" is mentioned in this chapter—vv. 13, 16 (twice), 24, 25, 26, 29 (twice).

[25] George H. Guthrie, "Hebrews," in *Commentary on the New Testament Use of the Old Testament*, ed. G. K. Beale and D. A. Carson (Grand Rapids: Baker Academic, 2007), 928–29.

[26] Ibid., 929.

[27] Peter O' Brien, *The Letter to the Hebrews*, The Pillar New Testament Commentary (Grand Rapids: Eerdmans, 2010), 68.

# CHAPTER EIGHTEEN

# GENERATIONAL FULFILLMENT

## Isaiah 6:9–10

Every quotation of the OT in the NT is significant. Yet when a particular OT passage is cited multiple times, we do well to study why the NT authors understood this text to be so important. Such is the case in Isaiah 6:9–10—a text quoted five times in the NT. As will be shown, Isaiah 6:9–10 has important implications for Israel's unbelief.

The context of Isaiah 6:9–10 is Isaiah's commission to disobedient Israel around 740 BC. Isaiah's message to Israel would not result in the nation's repentance, but in further hardening:

> He [the Lord] said, "Go, and tell this people:
> 'Keep on listening, but do not perceive;
> Keep on looking, but do not understand.'
> 'Render the hearts of this people insensitive,
> Their ears dull,
> And their eyes dim,
> Otherwise they might see with their eyes,
> Hear with their ears,
> Understand with their hearts,
> And return and be healed.'"

# Isaiah 6:9–10 in the NT

Isaiah 6:9–10 is quoted by each of the Gospel writers (Matt. 13:14–15; Mark 4:11–12; Luke 8:10; John 12:40) and once by Paul (Acts 28:26–27). Why is this text so important?

Significantly, all quotations of Isaiah 6:9–10 in the NT occur in the context of national Israel's unbelief in Jesus as Messiah. This passage is applied to Israel as a corporate entity even though some individual Jews did believe in Jesus. In Matthew 13:14–15, Jesus applied Isaiah 6:9–10 to unbelieving Israel:

In their case the prophecy of Isaiah is being fulfilled, which says,
"YOU WILL KEEP ON HEARING, BUT WILL NOT UNDERSTAND;
YOU WILL KEEP ON SEEING, BUT WILL NOT PERCEIVE;
FOR THE HEART OF THIS PEOPLE HAS BECOME DULL,
WITH THEIR EARS THEY SCARCELY HEAR,
AND THEY HAVE CLOSED THEIR EYES,
OTHERWISE THEY WOULD SEE WITH THEIR EYES,
HEAR WITH THEIR EARS,
AND UNDERSTAND WITH THEIR HEART AND RETURN,
AND I WOULD HEAL THEM."

The context of this statement is important. According to Matthew 3:2; 4:17; and 10:5–7, the kingdom was presented as "near" to Israel. Matthew 10:5–7 reveals that the kingdom message at this time was only for the lost sheep of the house of Israel. So the cities of Israel were in focus here. Yet according to Matthew 11:20–24, Jesus rebuked the cities of Israel for their unbelief: "Then He began to denounce the cities in which most of His miracles were done, because they did not repent" (Matt. 11:20). Thus, the kingdom presented to the cities of Israel was rejected by these cities.

Then in Matthew 12, the religious leaders of Israel expressed their rejection of Jesus when they attributed His miracles to Satan and thus committed blasphemy against the Holy Spirit (Matt. 12:25–32). Matthew 11 and 12 reveal that both the people and leaders of Israel rejected Jesus as the Messiah. There are national implications for this.

So when Jesus quoted Isaiah 6 in Matthew 13 saying, "the prophecy of Isaiah is being fulfilled," He connected Israel's unbelief in Isaiah's day with the unbelief of Israel during His earthly ministry. One might ask, How can a prophecy concerning Isaiah centuries earlier be fulfilled during Jesus' day? The answer is this: Israel is a corporate national entity with trans-generational implications. Israel's unbelief in Isaiah's day can be heightened or fulfilled by the unbelief of Israel during the time of Jesus. Both in Isaiah's day and in Jesus' day, national Israel evidenced a hardened unbelief.

Jesus' quotation of Isaiah 6:9–10, in connection with national Israel's unbelief and Jesus' giving of parables, is found also in Mark and Luke.

### Mark 4:11–12
And He was saying to them, "To you has been given the mystery of the kingdom of God, but those who are outside get everything in parables, so that WHILE SEEING, THEY MAY SEE AND NOT PERCEIVE, AND WHILE HEARING, THEY MAY HEAR AND NOT UNDERSTAND, OTHERWISE THEY MIGHT RETURN AND BE FORGIVEN."

### Luke 8:9–10
His disciples began questioning Him as to what this parable meant. And He said, "To you it has been granted to know the mysteries of the kingdom of God, but to the rest it is in parables, so that SEEING THEY MAY NOT SEE, AND HEARING THEY MAY NOT UNDERSTAND."

In John 12 the apostle John also quoted Isaiah 6:10 with some commentary.

### John 12:39–42
For this reason they could not believe, for Isaiah said again, "HE HAS BLINDED THEIR EYES AND HE HARDENED THEIR HEART, SO THAT THEY WOULD NOT SEE WITH THEIR EYES AND PERCEIVE WITH THEIR HEART, AND BE CONVERTED AND I HEAL THEM." These things Isaiah said because he saw His glory, and he spoke of Him. Nevertheless many even of the rulers believed in Him, but because of the Pharisees they were not confessing Him, for fear that they would be put out of the synagogue.

Three factors are noteworthy here. First, Jesus applied Isaiah 6 to Israel's unbelief. Second, John says Isaiah understood his words in connection with Jesus: "These things Isaiah said because he saw His glory, and he spoke of Him." This shows Isaiah had a specific messianic hope. And third, we are told that "many" of "the rulers" of Israel "believed in Him [Jesus]." Thus, some of Israel's rulers did believe.

Putting it all together, Isaiah's words apply to Israel as a corporate entity. Even though many rulers in Israel believed in Jesus, the leadership as a whole did not, even to the point of intimidating other Jewish leaders who had believed. Thus, Israel's national rejection of Jesus, even in spite of the belief of "many...rulers" of Israel, is a cause for applying Isaiah 6:10 to Israel as a whole. Israel as a national entity is expected to believe in its Messiah.

# Acts 28:17–29

The last chapter of Acts describes a significant encounter between Paul and "leading men of the Jews" in Rome (Acts 28:17). This gathering of Jewish leaders reveals the formal tone of this encounter; this is more than just a chance gathering of individual Jews. There are corporate implications here.

As Paul addresses these Jewish leaders, he calls them "Brethren," and he identifies with them by referring to "our people" and "our fathers" (28:17). He also told them, "I am wearing this chain for the sake of the hope of Israel" (28:20). There is a heavy Israelite context to this meeting, and Paul takes seriously the Jewish element of this encounter.

Then these Jewish leaders came to Paul at his lodging place "in large numbers" (28:23). Here Paul testified about the kingdom of God and tried to persuade them concerning Jesus from the Law and the Prophets (i.e. Hebrew Scriptures) from morning until evening.

The result of this all-day encounter is described in verse 24: "Some were being persuaded by the things spoken, but others would not believe." Some Jewish leaders were persuaded by Paul and believed, while others refused. We are not told which of these groups was larger, but there seems to be a significant number who had believed. This should not be overlooked. *Some Jewish leaders believed in Jesus the Messiah.* But what is the significance of this?

Certainly, Paul must have been pleased with the individual Jews who believed. They would be part of the remnant of Israel he discusses in Romans 11:1–6. But his strong words reveal that he hoped for more. Verse 25 reveals that the two groups could not agree, and this hindered a unified belief in Jesus as Messiah by Israel as a corporate entity. This led to a stinging rebuke of corporate Israel by Paul as he used Isaiah 6:9–10 in Acts 28:25–27:

> And when they did not agree with one another, they began leaving after Paul had spoken one parting word, "The Holy Spirit rightly spoke through Isaiah the prophet to your fathers, saying,
> 'GO TO THIS PEOPLE AND SAY,
> 'YOU WILL KEEP ON HEARING, BUT WILL NOT UNDERSTAND;
> AND YOU WILL KEEP ON SEEING, BUT WILL NOT PERCEIVE;
> FOR THE HEART OF THIS PEOPLE HAS BECOME DULL,
> AND WITH THEIR EARS THEY SCARCELY HEAR,
> AND THEY HAVE CLOSED THEIR EYES;
> OTHERWISE THEY MIGHT SEE WITH THEIR EYES,
> AND HEAR WITH THEIR EARS,
> AND UNDERSTAND WITH THEIR HEART AND RETURN,
> AND I WOULD HEAL THEM.'"

The disagreement between the believing and unbelieving Jews led Paul to quote Isaiah 6:9–10 with its message of judgment for unbelieving Israel. But why would Paul do this when some Jewish leaders believed in Jesus? Should this not be considered a successful encounter since "some" Jewish leaders believed? Kinzer asks an appropriate question:

> Why does Paul respond so negatively to what Christians today might consider a rather successful evangelistic encounter? His fierce reaction appears disproportionate to the mixed attitudes of his audience.[1]

But for Paul, this was not a successful encounter. While likely encouraged by the Jewish men who did believe, this meeting did not result in a corporate acceptance of Jesus as Messiah by the Jewish leadership. That was what Paul was seeking: belief in Jesus as Messiah by the leaders of Israel.

Concerning the encounter in Acts 28, Kinzer notes, "This scene makes little sense if we view Paul's audience as a collection of Jewish individuals and Paul's aim in addressing them as the 'salvation' of as many of them as possible."[2] Instead, Paul was seeking a communal belief in Jesus as the Messiah. As Tannehill writes:

> The presence of disagreement among the Jews is enough to show that Paul has not achieved what he sought. He was seeking a communal decision, a recognition by the Jewish community as a whole that Jesus is the fulfillment of the Jewish hope. The presence of significant opposition shows that this is not going to happen.[3]

This encounter in Acts 28 parallels John 12 where Jesus quoted Isaiah 6:9–10 against Israel, even though "many" of the Jewish leadership had believed. But in both John 12 and Acts 28 the leadership of Israel as a whole did not believe. Thus, the condemnation of Isaiah 6:9–10 again applies.

# Significance of Isaiah 6:9–10 in the New Testament

The five references to Isaiah 6:9–10 in the NT concern national Israel's unbelief concerning Jesus the Messiah and a rejection of the kingdom of God. Even though some Israelites believed in Jesus, thus comprising the remnant of

---

[1] Mark S. Kinzer, "Zionism is Luke–Acts," in *The New Christian Zionism: Fresh Perspectives on Israel & the Land* (Downers Grove, IL: InterVarsity Press, 2016), 159.

[2] Ibid., 160.

[3] Robert C. Tannehill, *The Narrative Unity of Luke–Acts, vol. 2, The Acts of the Apostles* (Minneapolis: Fortress, 1990), 347.

Israel (see Rom. 11:1–6) and the "Israel of God" (Gal. 6:16), the lack of corporate belief by Israel merited a stinging rebuke from both Jesus and Paul. Both men used the words of Isaiah 6:9–10 against their current Jewish audiences. This situation will be reversed one day when national Israel believes in Jesus as Messiah, as passages like Zechariah 12:10 and Romans 11:26 indicate.

# Luke 23:30 / Hosea 10:8

Hosea 10 has words of rebuke against Israel for her idolatry. Verse 1 states that Israel was a "luxuriant vine" (or "degenerate vine"), yet Israel trampled on God's goodness and made altars and pillars for idolatry. Verse 2 then states that Israel will "bear their guilt" and God "will break down their altars and destroy their sacred pillars." God will use Assyria to judge Israel (v. 6). Verse 8b describes what the people will say on the day of judgment: "Then they will say to the mountains, 'Cover us!' And to the hills, 'Fall on us!'" The immediate referent for this event was the coming Assyrian invasion of 722 BC.

Fast forward approximately 750 years. As Jesus carried His cross, a number of women "were mourning and lamenting Him" (Luke 23:27). Jesus then told the women to weep not for Him but for themselves, since a severe time of trial was coming when those with no children would be better off than those who did have children. In Luke 23:30, Jesus then quoted Hosea 10:8: "Then they will begin TO SAY TO THE MOUNTAINS, 'FALL ON US,' AND TO THE HILLS, 'COVER US.'" With these words, Jesus predicted the coming destruction of Jerusalem in AD 70 by the Romans.

This quotation of Hosea 10:8 by Jesus is a case of generational fulfillment in which an eighth-century message of judgment for Israel is picked up and applied to the current generation of Israel who rejected Jesus and missed its time of visitation (see Luke 19:44). Both generations of Israel have something in common—disobedience leads to national calamity in which the people of Israel will want the mountains and hills to cover them. A similar use of Hosea 10:8 also occurs in Revelation 6:15–16 when the people on earth call on the mountains to hide them from the wrath of God and the Lamb.

# PART THREE

## CASE STUDIES

# CHAPTER NINETEEN

# THE MESSIAH AND THE RIGHT HAND OF GOD

## PSALM 110 IN THE NEW TESTAMENT

Psalm 110:1 is the most quoted and alluded to OT verse in the NT. Written by David,[1] this verse is strategic to the theology of the NT persons and writers. It reads:

> The LORD says to my Lord:
> "Sit at My right hand
> Until I make Your enemies a footstool for Your feet."

## The Context of Psalm 110

In Psalm 110, David is given a glimpse into an encounter between the LORD (*Yahweh*) and David's Lord (*Adonai*). The LORD summons David's Lord, the Messiah, to a session at the LORD's right hand in heaven.[2] This session is to occur

---

[1] Other options posited for authorship of this psalm include Zadok, David, and an unnamed poet-prophet. Several NT references to David as the author appear to settle the issue—Matthew 22:43–44; Mark 12:36; Luke 20:42–44; and Acts 2:34–35.

[2] Rydelnik observes, "Psalm 110 has long been understood as a direct prediction of the Messiah. Even Franz Delitzsch, who generally viewed the messianic character of the Psalms to be merely typical, recognized Psalm 110 as a direct messianic prophecy." Michael Rydelnik, *The Messianic Hope*, in *New American Commentary Studies in Bible & Theology* (Nashville, TN: B & H Publishing Group), 2010. Kindle Locations 4511–4512.

for a time "until" the LORD makes the enemies of David's Lord (the Messiah) a footstool for His (the Messiah's) feet. This involves a reign from Zion (i.e. Jerusalem) on earth as verse 2 indicates: "The LORD will stretch forth Your strong scepter from Zion, saying, 'Rule in the midst of Your enemies.'" According to verse 4, this King is also a priest according to the order of Melchizedek. In sum, David's Lord (the Messiah) will have a session at the right hand of Yahweh in heaven for a time until David's Lord reigns from Jerusalem on earth.

Scholars have debated whether the LORD is speaking to David, Solomon, the Davidic kingship line, or the Messiah. The best understanding is that David's Lord here is the coming Messiah. This seems natural from the context since David is presented as viewing an interaction between the LORD and another kingly and priestly figure who is destined to reign on the earth (v. 2). Only Jesus fits this dual status of king and priest. And in Matthew 22:42–45, Jesus explicitly said David is the author of Psalm 110, and that the "my Lord" David referred to in Psalm 110:1 is the Messiah. This was used by Jesus to confound the unbelieving religious leaders of Israel. Jesus' words should settle the issue of whether Psalm 110 is messianic, because Jesus explicitly says it is. This account is restated in Mark 12:35–37 and Luke 20:41–44, demonstrating the importance of this event for the three Gospel writers.

The quotation of Psalm 110:1 in Matthew 22:44; Mark 12:36; and Luke 20:42–43 indicates direct literal prophetic fulfillment of Psalm 110:1. Psalm 110:1 predicted that the coming Messiah would sit at Yahweh's right hand, and Jesus is the fulfillment of this Messiah figure. So Jesus is the referent of David's Lord in Psalm 110:1.

Next, with his speech in Jerusalem, Peter quoted Psalm 110:1 to show his Jewish audience that Jesus is the resurrected Messiah now at the right hand of God. Acts 2:32–33a reads: "This Jesus God raised up again, to which we are all witnesses. Therefore having been exalted to the right hand of God." Like the above references in Matthew 22, Mark 12, and Luke 20, Peter's use of Psalm 110:1 in Acts 2 indicates that Jesus is the referent of Psalm 110:1. So Peter's use of Psalm 110:1 also indicates a case of direct literal prophetic fulfillment.

Then there are the three quotations of Psalm 110:1 in Hebrews. In Hebrews 1, the writer extols the superiority of Jesus over everything. Hebrews 1:3 says that when Jesus "made purification of sins, He sat down at the right hand of the Majesty on high." Jesus is the direct fulfillment of the one who would sit at God's right hand.

The writer then quotes Psalm 110:1 in Hebrews 1:13 to show that God never promised that angels would sit at His right hand. But God did promise this privilege to Jesus. This seems to be a case of *application of a theological point*, namely that a special man (i.e. Jesus), not angels, will sit at God's right hand. The quotation of Psalm 110:1 in Hebrews 10:12 proves that Jesus is the High Priest who sat down at the right hand of God, "waiting" until His enemies are made a footstool for His feet.

Thus, Jesus is at the right hand of God currently waiting for His kingdom reign to begin. Hebrews 10:12 also is a case of direct literal fulfillment of Psalm 110:1.

Psalm 110:1 also is alluded to in other NT verses. First Corinthians 15:25 says Jesus "must reign until He has put all His enemies under His feet." Ephesians 1:20 and Colossians 3:1 state that Jesus is currently at God's right hand. Ephesians 1:22 says God has "put all things in subjection under His feet." Hebrews 1:3; 8:1; and 12:2 state that Jesus is our high priest who, after the cross, sat down at the right hand of God.

Psalm 110 is important to the NT writers and persons. Jesus is the direct fulfillment of the one who was destined to have a session at the right hand of God for a time until God establishes Jesus' kingdom reign upon the earth. As a result of His death, resurrection, and ascension, Jesus is currently at the right hand of God in heaven.

# CHAPTER TWENTY

# MAN'S RIGHT TO RULE

## PSALM 8 IN THE NEW TESTAMENT

Written by David, Psalm 8 extols the majesty of the Lord and reaffirms that mankind is expected to rule over God's creation. Both the first and last verses of the psalm declare the greatness of God—"O LORD, our Lord, How majestic is Your name in all the earth!" (Ps. 8:1, 9). So God's glory is at the forefront of this psalm. But this psalm also declares the exalted position of man in God's purposes concerning the earth. Psalm 8:4–8 states:

> What is man that You take thought of him,
> And the son of man that You care for him?
> Yet You have made him a little lower than God [or "the heavenly beings (ESV)],
> And You crown him with glory and majesty!
> You make him to rule over the works of Your hands;
> You have put all things under his feet,
> All sheep and oxen,
> And also the beasts of the field,
> The birds of the heavens and the fish of the sea,
> Whatever passes through the paths of the seas.

Psalm 8 draws upon the truth of Genesis 1:26–28 that God created man to "rule" and "subdue" the world. In fact, Psalm 8 functions much like a commentary on Genesis 1:26–28. Even in a fallen world, man's right to rule over creation has not been revoked, even though in his sinful state man is not able to fulfill it as he should (see Gen. 3).

Psalm 8 is explicitly quoted four times in the NT—Matthew 21:16; Hebrews 2:5–8; 1 Corinthians 15:27; and Ephesians 1:22.

# Matthew 21:16

The first reference to Psalm 8 occurs in Matthew 21:16. After Jesus' entry into Jerusalem just days before His death, the Pharisees were upset that children in the temple were proclaiming, "Hosanna to the Son of David" (Matt. 21:15). Verse 16 then says:

> And [the chief priests and the scribes] said to Him, "Do You hear what these children are saying?" And Jesus said to them, "Yes; have you never read, 'OUT OF THE MOUTH OF INFANTS AND NURSING BABIES YOU HAVE PREPARED PRAISE FOR YOURSELF'?"

Jesus quoted Psalm 8:2 to show that God will use the words of babies to speak truth and confound those who think they are wise. In Matthew 21, young children speak wisely in contrast to the skepticism of the religious leaders. So the use of Psalm 8 in Matthew 21:16 is contextual since Matthew 21:16 reaffirms a principle evident in Psalm 8:2.

# Hebrews 2:5–8

The three other quotations of Psalm 8 in the NT focus upon Psalm 8:6. We begin with Hebrews 2 since this chapter involves the most significant quotation of Psalm 8. The writer of Hebrews quoted three verses of Psalm 8 (vv. 4–6) and offered commentary on when the conditions of Hebrews 8 would be fulfilled. Hebrews 2:5–8a reads:

> For He did not subject to angels the world to come, concerning which we are speaking. But one has testified somewhere, saying,
> "WHAT IS MAN, THAT YOU REMEMBER HIM?
> OR THE SON OF MAN, THAT YOU ARE CONCERNED ABOUT HIM?
> "YOU HAVE MADE HIM FOR A LITTLE WHILE LOWER THAN THE ANGELS;
> YOU HAVE CROWNED HIM WITH GLORY AND HONOR,
> AND HAVE APPOINTED HIM OVER THE WORKS OF YOUR HANDS;
> YOU HAVE PUT ALL THINGS IN SUBJECTION UNDER HIS FEET."

This Hebrews passage is consistent with the message of Psalm 8, namely that man possesses an exalted position that involves ruling over the creation. Yet the writer of Hebrews also offers inspired commentary concerning when Psalm 8 will be fulfilled. Man's rule over the world will occur in the future. It is not happening now. This is evident by the words "world to come" (Heb. 2:5), and by the fact that at the end of verse 8 he says, "We do not yet see all things subjected to him." Even though man still possesses the right to rule creation, we do not yet see his successful rule—it awaits the future.

Hebrews 2:9 then brings up Jesus who suffered and is now exalted: "But we do see Him who was made for a little while lower than the angels, namely, Jesus, because of the suffering of death crowned with glory and honor, so that by the grace of God He might taste death for everyone." Man's successful reign over the earth cannot occur while man is estranged from God. But Jesus, the representative of mankind, suffered and "taste[d] death for everyone" so that the successful reign of man over the earth can occur. This shows that the cross is related to the coming kingdom. Without the cross,there would be no kingdom.

In sum, the message of Hebrews 2:5–8 and its quotation of Psalm 8:4–6 is that mankind is still destined to rule the earth, but this has yet to occur. This rule awaits the "world to come." This fulfillment is tied to Jesus who tasted death for everyone so that man can one day successfully fulfill his mandate to rule the earth. The following two verses show further how this relates to Jesus.

# 1 Corinthians 15:27

In 1 Corinthians 15:20–28, Paul explained a three-stage resurrection program and how this relates to the kingdom of God: (1) Jesus' resurrection; (2) a resurrection of believers with Jesus' second coming; then, (3) a resurrection associated with "the end" which comes after Jesus has reigned and defeated all His enemies (see Rev. 20:5). In verses 27–28, Paul focused on the issue of "subjection." He quoted Psalm 8:6:

> For HE HAS PUT ALL THINGS IN SUBJECTION UNDER HIS FEET. But when He says, "All things are put in subjection," it is evident that He is excepted who put all things in subjection to Him. When all things are subjected to Him, then the Son Himself also will be subjected to the One who subjected all things to Him, so that God may be all in all.

Paul points out that Psalm 8:6 teaches that God "put all things in subjection" to man. The only exception to this "subjection" is God the Father. The Father is not subject to the Son, but the Son to the Father. And when the Son has ruled successfully, He will hand His kingdom over to the Father "so that God may be all in all" (1 Cor. 15:24, 28).

But there is an interesting development in verses 27–28. Whereas Psalm 8 and Hebrews 2:5–8 focus on mankind's right to rule, in this passage Paul ties Psalm 8:6 specifically to Jesus. So why does Paul quote a passage about mankind in general and say it will be fulfilled with Jesus? Did Paul misinterpret Psalm 8?

No, Paul is not using Psalm 8 in a non-contextual manner. The key here is understanding the biblical concept of "corporate headship," or "corporate representation," in which a single representative can act on behalf of the many. In this case, Jesus is the ultimate Man (the one) who acts on behalf of mankind (the many). In Genesis 3:15 when the first man sinned, God said a battle would ensue between the seed of the woman (righteous mankind) and the seed of the evil power behind the serpent (unrighteous mankind). Yet from the seed of the woman would come a "He" who would reverse the curse and defeat the power behind the serpent (Satan). So Genesis 3:15 involves both mankind in general *and* a coming single deliverer from mankind. This deliverer is Jesus, the Last Adam (see 1 Cor. 15:45).

Since Jesus is the sinless and perfect representative of man who is able to restore mankind, Paul views Jesus as the one who will fulfill the Psalm 8 (and Gen. 1:26–28) expectation of a successful rule of man on and over the earth. Yet this does not leave out mankind. Other verses indicate that saved people in Jesus will also participate in Jesus' rule upon the earth. For example, Revelation 5:10 states: "You have made them [believers in Jesus] to be a kingdom and they will reign upon the earth." Revelation 2:26–27 and 3:21 also teach that believers in Jesus will share in a coming kingdom reign on the earth.

So does the fulfillment of Psalm 8 apply to mankind in general or Jesus? *The answer is both.* Jesus—as the Last Adam and federal head of mankind—will fulfill Psalm 8 and Genesis 1:26–28 and share His reign with people in union with Him. Both Jesus and all people in union with Him will rule the earth.

## Ephesians 1:22

In Ephesians 1:19, Paul explained that Christians have the power of God working in their lives, the very power that raised Jesus from the dead. He then said Jesus is now at the right hand of God "far above all rule and authority and power and dominion" (1:21). Then in verse 22, Paul writes, "And He [God] put all things in subjection under His feet, and gave Him as head over all things to the church." This draws upon Psalm 8:6.

Paul, in Ephesians 1:22, links Psalm 8:6 to Jesus. Jesus is the ultimate man who has been granted all authority at the right hand of the Father and will one day exercise this authority over the world (see Rev. 19:15; Matt. 19:28; 25:31). This does not mean He is exercising this authority fully in the present, but He does possess it. So like

Paul in 1 Corinthians 15:27 and the writer of Hebrews in Hebrews 2:5–9, Jesus is linked with the fulfillment of the Psalm 8 expectation, even though the fulfillment of Psalm 8 awaits the future.

# Summary

Psalm 8 is quoted four times in the NT, showing its importance for understanding the Bible's storyline. All uses of Psalm 8 in the NT are contextual and consistent with the meaning of this psalm. In Matthew 21:16, Jesus drew upon the Psalm 8:2 principle that God will use babies to speak the truth and confound the wise. The other three uses focus on Psalm 8:6. Hebrews 2:5–8; 1 Corinthians 15:27; and Ephesians 1:22 quote Psalm 8:6 contextually to affirm that mankind is destined for a successful reign upon the earth. Hebrews 2:5–8 declares that Psalm 8 will be fulfilled in "the world to come." In 1 Corinthians 15:27 and Ephesians 1:22, Paul connects Psalm 8 with Jesus, and in doing so reveals that the Psalm 8 expectation will occur through Jesus. Because of sin and the fall, man cannot fulfill the Psalm 8 expectation on his own. But mankind's rule over creation will occur because of the ultimate man, the Last Adam—Jesus. He will rule the world and share His rule with those in union with Him (see Rev. 2:26–27; 3:21).

# CHAPTER TWENTY-ONE

# BETRAYAL AND THIRTY PIECES OF SILVER

## MATTHEW 27:9–10 AND ZECHARIAH 11:12–13

Matthew 27:3–9 describes an encounter between Jesus' betrayer, Judas, and the Jewish religious leaders who pursued Jesus' death. After receiving blood money to betray Jesus, a remorseful Judas realized the grave nature of his traitorous deed and sought to return the thirty pieces of silver he had received from the religious leaders. The Jewish leaders refused, and Judas then threw the silver pieces into the temple sanctuary. Knowing that blood money was not fit to be in the temple, the Jewish leaders took the silver and bought the "Potter's Field" as a burial place for strangers. Matthew notes that this was a fulfillment (*pleroō*) of what was written in the OT:

> Then that which was spoken through Jeremiah the prophet was fulfilled: "AND THEY TOOK THE THIRTY PIECES OF SILVER, THE PRICE OF THE ONE WHOSE PRICE HAD BEEN SET by the sons of Israel; AND THEY GAVE THEM FOR THE POTTER'S FIELD, AS THE LORD DIRECTED ME." (Matt. 27:9–10)

This quotation has baffled interpreters for two main reasons. First, the quotation most aligns with Zechariah 11:12–13, not Jeremiah. And second, some think Zechariah describes an event involving the prophet Zechariah's life, not the Messiah. So how can Matthew 27:9–10 be a fulfillment of Zechariah 11 if that text refers to the prophet Zechariah and not Jesus?

Concerning the first issue, it could be that Matthew appeals to Jeremiah as a representative of the prophets, of which Zechariah is one. A better view, though, is that while Zechariah 11:12–13 is prominent, the quotation does involve Jeremiah, and Matthew mentioned Jeremiah as the more significant prophet. The phrase, "AS THE LORD DIRECTED ME" is found in Jeremiah 13:5, not Zechariah. In addition, the potter concept is significant in Jeremiah 18 and 19. God is presented as the potter of the nations in Jeremiah 18. And in Jeremiah 19, the Lord tells Jeremiah to buy a clay jar from a potter and then break it to represent God breaking the people and city "even as one breaks a potter's vessel" (Jer. 19:11). Jeremiah 18–19 is the most prominent "potter" section in the OT. In addition, the specific phrase, "the potter," only occurs in Jeremiah and Zechariah.[1] So Matthew could be conflating Jeremiah and Zechariah, while only mentioning Jeremiah. Or as Chou states, "Matthew's statement about Jeremiah is to alert his readers of how he reads Zechariah with Jeremiah."[2] This conflation tactic was not unusual for ancient Jewish writers. Concerning Matthew's use of both Zechariah and Jeremiah, Kaiser notes:

> While the logic of this type of exegesis is strange to the modern Western way of thinking, it would have been viewed as quite normal in Matthew's time...Thus judged by first-century standards, Matthew is quite accurate and acceptable in what he does.[3]

Concerning the second issue of what is being fulfilled, there are two possible options. First, Matthew could be applying a correspondence or typological connection between the events of Zechariah 11:12–13 involving the prophet Zechariah and the events of Matthew 27:3–10 involving Judas. As the chart below indicates, there are at least five points of similarity between the two passages. Blomberg asserts, "Clearly, Matthew is employing typology here."[4] According to this view, Zechariah represents a shepherd who is rejected and devalued by the people of Israel. Correspondingly, Jesus is the True Shepherd who was rejected and devalued by Israel. Both Zechariah and Jesus pasture the flock of Israel, while the Jewish leaders think they (Zechariah and Jesus) are only worth the price of a gored slave, which is thirty pieces of silver (see Ex. 21:32). In both Zechariah and Matthew, the throwing of thirty pieces of silver concerns a potter. So this could be another case where an event in Israel's history corresponds to an event in Jesus' life. This view is possible, although I think more is going on here.

---

[1] See Abner Chou, *The Hermeneutics of the Biblical Writers: Learning to Interpret Scripture from the Prophets and Apostles* (Grand Rapids: Kregel, 2018), 140.

[2] Ibid.

[3] Walter C. Kaiser, Jr., Peter H. Davids, F. F. Bruce, Manfred T. Brauch, *Hard Sayings of the Bible* (Downers Grove, IL: InterVarsity Press, 1996), 400.

[4] Craig L. Blomberg, "Matthew," in *Commentary on the New Testament Use of the Old Testament*, ed. G. K. Beale and D. A. Carson (Grand Rapids: Baker Books, 2007), 96.

More likely, the connection between Zechariah 11:12–13 and Matthew 27:9–10 is that of *literal direct prophetic fulfillment*. While not a verbal prophecy, Zechariah 11 comes in the form of a prophetic sign-act, picturing and predicting the rejection of the Messiah by Israel. With Zechariah 11, the prophet Zechariah represented Israel's devaluing of the Messiah, and that occurred when Judas betrayed Jesus for thirty pieces of silver. Thus, Zechariah role-played the Messiah and events associated with Him, and Matthew perceived this to be fulfilled in the events of Matthew 27.

Zechariah 11 is both prophetic and messianic.[5] Mark J. Boda has observed that Zechariah 11:4–16 "is structured according to a prophetic form typical of the earlier prophets, especially Jeremiah and Ezekiel."[6] This form involves a prophetic sign-act. *A prophetic sign-act occurs when a prophet engages in theater or non-verbal displays to communicate the outcome of a prophecy.* Zechariah 11:4–16 offers two "prophetic sign-acts." Zechariah plays the role of a good shepherd (11:4–14) and then an evil shepherd (11:15–16). As Boda observes, these two prophetic sign-acts "draw heavily" from Ezekiel's prophetic sections in Ezekiel 34:1–31 and 37:15–28 where shepherd and flock language are used and the unification of Israel is in mind.[7]

Also significant to both prophetic sign-acts in Ezekiel 34 and 37 is the presence of "David my Servant" who is mentioned as both "shepherd" (34:23) and "king" (37:24). This heavily implies that "the good shepherd in Zechariah 11:4–16 is a Davidic descendant."[8] And it is likely that this "Davidic descendant" is the Messiah, for only He can bring the conditions explained in Ezekiel 34 and 37. Therefore, the close parallels in form and content with Ezekiel 34 and 37 argue for a prophetic-messianic understanding of Zechariah 11:4–16. Zechariah is role playing the Messiah and then the role of an evil shepherd. Some speculate this evil shepherd could be an antichrist figure. In addition to Ezekiel, there is precedent for this type of activity in other sections of Zechariah. Rydelnik points out that "role plays are common in the book of Zechariah. Previously, in hinge passages, Joshua and his fellow priests represented Israel (3:1–10), and Joshua played the role of the Priestly Messiah (6:9–15)."[9]

Also, the location of Zechariah 11 in the book of Zechariah tilts towards a messianic understanding of this chapter. Zechariah 11 is a hinge chapter connecting the two burdens of Zechariah 9–10 and Zechariah 12–14. The former describes the

---

[5] Chou notes, "Although the issues are complex, a good argument can be made that Zechariah intended chapter 11 to portray future realities," 139.

[6] Mark J. Boda, *The Book of Zechariah*, The New International Commentary on the Old Testament (Grand Rapids: Eerdmans, 2016), 648.

[7] Ibid, 650–51.

[8] Ibid., 652.

[9] Michael Rydelnik, "Zechariah," in *The Moody Bible Commentary*, ed. Michael Rydelnik and Michael Vanlaningham (Chicago: Moody Publishers, 2014), 1430.

coming of Israel's true King (Zech. 9–10). The latter describes end-time events describing the salvation and rescue of national Israel coinciding with the Messiah's return and His earthly kingdom (Zech. 12–14). Both burdens involve the Messiah. So Zechariah 11 most likely involves the Messiah as well.

Zechariah 11:11–14 describes a sinful devaluing of God's Shepherd at thirty pieces of silver by the Jewish religious leaders. And that reality is what Matthew draws upon. When the Jewish leaders paid Judas thirty pieces of silver, the price at which they actually valued the Messiah, this was a literal fulfillment of Zechariah 11:11–14.

There are some aspects of Zechariah 11 that could be more in the realm of correspondence with Matthew 27. In Zechariah 11:13, Zechariah himself is told to "Throw it [the silver] to the potter" in the temple. With Matthew 27:3–10, Judas throws the thirty pieces of silver into the temple. In both cases, the thirty pieces of silver are thrown into the temple, but in Zechariah 11 the prophet throws the silver, while in Matthew 27 it is Judas. In Zechariah 11, the prophet throws the pieces of silver at the potter in the temple, while in Matthew 27 the thrown pieces of silver are used to purchase a Potter's Field. These details are not a coincidence, for they reveal that a fulfillment of Zechariah 11 has occurred. A comparison of the two passages is seen below.

| Comparison of Zechariah 11:12–13 and Matthew 27:3–10 | | |
|---|---|---|
| | **Zech. 11:12–13** | **Matt. 27:3–10** |
| Shepherd | Zechariah is a shepherd to Israel | Jesus is the Shepherd to Israel |
| Shepherd devalued | Zechariah valued at a measly thirty pieces of silver (price of a slave) | Jesus valued at a measly thirty pieces of silver (price of a slave) |
| Religious leaders give thirty pieces of silver | Religious leaders give Zechariah thirty shekels | Religious leaders give Judas thirty pieces of silver |
| Thirty pieces of silver thrown into temple | Zechariah threw thirty shekels of silver in the temple | Judas threw thirty pieces of silver into the temple |
| Relationship to the potter | Zechariah threw thirty shekels of silver to the potter | Religious leaders took the thirty pieces of silver to buy the Potter's field |

# CHAPTER TWENTY-TWO

# RESURRECTION OF THE MESSIAH

## PSALM 16:8–11 IN ACTS 2:25–28, 31
## AND ACTS 13:35–37

Peter's use of Psalm 16:8–11 in Acts 2:25–28 is challenging to understand. While Psalm 16 seems to refer to David's experiences, Peter used it to argue that David foresaw the resurrection of Jesus. But did David actually foresee the resurrection of Jesus, and did Peter quote Psalm 16 contextually or not?

Psalm 16 was written by David and expresses David's trust in the Lord in both life and death. David spoke of God as his "portion" in life (v. 5) and as the One who counsels him (v. 7). Particularly significant is David's statement concerning death in verse 10:

> For You will not abandon my soul to Sheol;
> Nor will You allow Your Holy One to undergo decay.

In 10a, David said the Lord will not abandon his soul to *Sheol*. The word, "soul" is the Hebrew word *nephesh*, and in this context refers to David in his entirety (see Ex. 4:19), not just his spirit. So David said that God would not abandon him as a person to *Sheol*, which means the grave. David might die, but the Lord will not allow David to remain in the grave forever.

But in Psalm 16:10b, David shifted pronouns from "my" to "Your." He refers to "Your Holy One" (*hasid*) who will not "undergo decay." This may indicate a change in person in the psalm. Also, 16:10b involves even more than what was declared in 16:10a. It is one thing not to be abandoned to the grave; it is another to say that decay will not even happen. That this "Holy One" will not "undergo decay" means the complete avoidance of bodily decay.

The meaning of Psalm 16 is debated. Some believe the whole psalm is messianic, with David speaking entirely on behalf of the coming Messiah.[1] Most, however, understand David to be describing his own experiences. Another view is that David wrote the majority of this psalm about himself, but in 16:10, or even just 10b, he specifically referred to the Messiah. According to this third view, David had in mind both himself and the coming Messiah. Peter's words in Acts 2 will help solve this issue.

# Psalm 16 in Acts 2

In Acts 2, Peter proclaimed to the Israelites in Jerusalem that Jesus is the resurrected Lord and Messiah (see Acts 2:22, 36). In Acts 2:24, Peter stated that God raised Jesus from the grave to put an end to the agony of death. It was impossible for death to keep Jesus in its power. Then with 2:25–28, Peter quoted Psalm 16:8–11 to claim that David spoke of Jesus' resurrection:

> For David says of Him,
> "I SAW THE LORD ALWAYS IN MY PRESENCE;
> FOR HE IS AT MY RIGHT HAND, SO THAT I WILL NOT BE SHAKEN.
> "THEREFORE MY HEART WAS GLAD AND MY TONGUE EXULTED;
> MOREOVER MY FLESH ALSO WILL LIVE IN HOPE;
> BECAUSE YOU WILL NOT ABANDON MY SOUL TO HADES,
> NOR ALLOW YOUR HOLY ONE TO UNDERGO DECAY.
> "YOU HAVE MADE KNOWN TO ME THE WAYS OF LIFE;
> YOU WILL MAKE ME FULL OF GLADNESS WITH YOUR PRESENCE."

Peter then again declared that David, the author of Psalm 16, explicitly wrote of the Messiah's resurrection in Acts 2:29–32. Peter first quoted Psalm 132:11 and then he referenced Psalm 16:10:

> Brethren, I may confidently say to you regarding the patriarch David that he both
> died and was buried, and his tomb is with us to this day. And so, because he was
> a prophet and knew that GOD HAD SWORN TO HIM WITH AN OATH TO SEAT one OF
> HIS DESCENDANTS ON HIS THRONE, he looked ahead and spoke of the resurrection

---

[1] William Pettingill says, "The speaker throughout the Psalm is Christ. Written a thousand years beforehand, the Psalm yet describes the meditations of the Holy One as He trod the path toward the cross of Calvary." William L. Pettingill, *Christ in the Psalms* (Findlay, OH: Fundamental Truth Publishers, 1937), 39. Matt Boettner calls this the "Messianic Speech" view. "NT Use of the OT Case Study: Acts 2:25–28 and Psalm 16:8–11," unpublished M.Div. paper, The Master's Seminary, April 2019, 14.

of the Christ, that HE WAS NEITHER ABANDONED TO HADES, NOR DID His flesh SUFFER DECAY. This Jesus God raised up again, to which we are all witnesses. (Acts 2:29–32)

Note that Peter said David "was a prophet" and that David explicitly knew about the Messiah and His resurrection. Thus, on two occasions Peter said David wrote about Jesus. *This is inspired commentary from Peter concerning what David understood.* Also, in Acts 1:16, Peter said David was inspired by the Holy Spirit when David wrote about Judas who betrayed Jesus:

> Brethren, the Scripture had to be fulfilled, which the Holy Spirit foretold by the mouth of David concerning Judas, who became a guide to those who arrested Jesus.

This is another text where Peter claims that David knew something about the days of Jesus. But many believe that David wrote only about himself in Psalm 16. David's use of "I," "me," and "my" throughout the psalm allegedly supports this position.

How should we understand Peter's statement that David wrote about the resurrection of the Messiah? There are five major views. First, some believe Peter used a *sensus plenior* approach. Longenecker, for example, said the use of Psalm 16:8–11 in Acts 2:25–28 is an "obvious" example of *sensus plenior*.[2] It is also linked to both midrash and pesher approaches:

> The application of Pss 16:8–11 and 110:1 to the resurrection and ascension of Jesus in Acts 2:25–36. While a midrashic understanding has brought these two passages together, it is a pesher understanding that evokes such an introduction as "David said concerning him."[3]

Second, others understand Psalm 16 to have two referents—David first and then later, Jesus. Roy Zuck says, "Though David had himself in mind, Peter and Paul pointed out that from the New Testament perspective the psalm refers to Christ."[4] Zuck also says Psalm 16 has one meaning but "two referents"—"namely, David and ultimately, in the fullest sense, Christ."[5] Zuck does not believe David intentionally referred to Jesus in Psalm 16; instead, Jesus is later added as a referent.

Third, some believe typology best explains the connection. Darrell Bock holds that David was referring to himself in Psalm 16, although there are hints that his words

---

[2] Richard N. Longenecker, *Biblical Exegesis in the Apostolic Period* (Grand Rapids: Eerdmans, 1975, 1999), xxxiii.

[3] Ibid., 84.

[4] Roy B. Zuck, *Basic Bible Interpretation* (Colorado Springs, CO: ChariotVictor Publishing, 1991), 276.

[5] Ibid.

go beyond himself to the Messiah. Bock writes, "The first person references throughout this psalm make a more natural reading to refer to the psalmist himself, who is the subject throughout."[6] Bock also says, "A better way to read Psalm 16 is as a typological text" which later "can ultimately be about Jesus."[7] So for Bock, Psalm 16 is a case of "TYPOLOGICAL-prophetic" hermeneutics in which "the pattern is not anticipated by the language, but is seen once the decisive pattern (or fulfillment pattern) occurs."[8]

A fourth view is that David penned Psalm 16 as if the Messiah were the author of the psalm. David specifically referred to the Messiah throughout the psalm even though David used first person pronouns such as "I," "me," and "mine." Thus, Peter used Psalm 16 in Acts 2 contextually since he knew David was explicitly writing about the Messiah.

A fifth and preferred view is that David consciously referred to both himself and the Messiah in Psalm 16, but at different points. While most of Psalm 16 is about David as evidenced by the "me" and "my" statements, in at least verse 10b, David refers specifically to the Messiah.[9] Here David shifts to the second person, "your"—"Nor will You allow *Your* Holy One to undergo decay" (emphasis mine). The second person plural ("Your") and the reference to "Holy One" signals that someone other than David is in view, namely the Messiah.

Another factor for this view concerns David's actual experience. While David possessed a resurrection hope, he did not avoid decay. In the Davidic covenant of 2 Samuel 7, God told David that he would "lie down with your fathers" (2 Sam. 7:12a). Thus, David knew he would enter the grave, and David's death is a historical fact. As Peter makes clear in Acts 2, David did die and his body did experience decay. In fact, Peter said one could visit David's tomb to verify this fact (see Acts 2:29).

---

[6] Darrell L. Bock, "Response to Kaiser," in *Three Views on the New Testament Use of the Old Testament*, ed. Kenneth Berding and Jonathan Lunde (Grand Rapids: Zondervan, 2007), 95.

[7] Ibid., 95.

[8] Darrell L. Bock, "Single Meaning, Multiple Contexts and Referents," in *Three Views on the New Testament Use of the Old Testament*, 119–20. The emphasis is in the original.

[9] Trull notes how Lenski explained this view: "Lenski divides the referent of verse 10 between David and Christ. Neither David nor Christ would be abandoned to hell (v. 10a), but only Christ would not experience decay (v. 10b). Lenski makes this separation because of the contrast between 'my soul' in verse 10a and 'thy Holy One' in verse 10b. 'The former ("my soul") refers to David and to Christ, the latter ("Holy One") only to Christ.' Peter's explanation about the decay of David's body also demands the separation of referents. In this way David prophesied of Messiah's resurrection. Much of Lenski's explanation of Peter's interpretation of Psalm 16 could be classified as 'reference plenior,' except that he understands David to shift referents in verse 10b. This shift indicates a single line of direct prophecy concerning Messiah. In this line David spoke 'as a prophet…by revelation and by inspiration.' This prophecy was then literally fulfilled by Jesus. Therefore the original sense of verse 10b was the resurrection of Messiah. Lenski says David was the original referent for all of the psalm except for verse 10. In verse 10 the reference is first to David and Messiah and then Messiah alone. The psalm, then, speaks of David's future hope based on the resurrection of Messiah, and Peter proclaimed this same sense." Gregory V. Trull, "Views on Peter's Use of Psalm 16:8–11 in Acts 2:25–32," *Bibliotheca Sacra* 161 (April–June, 2004): 213. See R. C. H. Lenski, *The Interpretation of the Acts of the Apostles* (Minneapolis: Augsburg, 1934), 85–93.

But Psalm 16:10b speaks of a person who does not decay. David is not saying that decay will one day be reversed, *but decay will not happen at all*. Thus, the nature of this specific promise points to a very special person—the Messiah. Peter makes this point in Acts 2:29–31:

> Brethren, I may confidently say to you regarding the patriarch David that he both died and was buried, and his tomb is with us to this day. And so, because he was a prophet and knew that GOD HAD SWORN TO HIM WITH AN OATH TO SEAT one OF HIS DESCENDANTS ON HIS THRONE, he looked ahead and spoke of the resurrection of the Christ, that HE WAS NEITHER ABANDONED TO HADES, NOR DID His flesh SUFFER DECAY.

While David could hope for resurrection from the grave (Ps. 16:10a), David could not be the fulfillment of Psalm 16:10b because David died, was buried, and was currently in his tomb.

Also, since David was an inspired prophet who had a messianic hope, he could predict the resurrection of the Messiah. This should remove doubt concerning what David meant in Psalm 16:10. Peter tells us David explicitly predicted the resurrection of the Messiah. Peter does not use typology or correspondence language concerning Psalm 16:10. He explicitly says David predicted the resurrection of the Messiah.

Thus, the reason David could be confident of his future resurrection from the grave in Psalm 16:10a is because of his relationship to the coming "Holy One" who would be resurrected and avoid decay (10b). In other words, David will live because the Messiah lives. So even before one examines Peter's words in Acts 2, the concept of a messianic hope appears in Psalm 16:10b. When Peter says David was a prophet who spoke of the resurrection of the Messiah, he meant it. He was quoting Psalm 16 contextually.

One final issue here. We established that Psalm 16:10b is messianic in its own context, and Peter used Psalm 16:10b contextually. "Your Holy One" is the Messiah, and David knew that. But what about Psalm 16:10a concerning David's statement that his [David's] soul would not be abandoned to the grave? Peter also said that this referred to Jesus in Acts 2:31? How can Psalm 16:10a refer to David in Psalm 16:10a and Jesus in Acts 2:31? Answering this is more difficult. Our estimation is that David consciously referred to both himself and the Messiah in 16:10a. Thus, this would be another case where David knew that an experience of his would also be experienced by the Messiah. If this is accurate, David knew that both himself and the Messiah would not be abandoned to the grave. In sum, when Psalm 16:10 is evaluated as a whole, David did two things—he knew that his experience of rescue from the grave would also be the experience of the Messiah (16:10a), and he wrote specifically of the Messiah not experiencing decay (16:10b).

# Psalm 16 in Acts 13

In Acts 13:35–37, Paul mentioned Psalm 16:10b and the fact that David underwent decay while Jesus did not. Acts 13:35 states: "Therefore He also says in another Psalm, 'YOU WILL NOT ALLOW YOUR HOLY ONE TO UNDERGO DECAY.'" Then more explanation is given in 13:36–37:

> For David, after he had served the purpose of God in his own generation, fell asleep, and was laid among his fathers and underwent decay; but He whom God raised did not undergo decay.

So again we are told that Psalm 16:10b was not about David since David experienced bodily decay. Jesus, however, did not experience decay—He was resurrected. This is further evidence that Psalm 16:10b was messianic in its own context. Both Peter and Paul interpreted it this way.

# Conclusion

In sum, God provided for David in life and will not abandon David's soul to the grave. But the avoidance of "decay" in Psalm 16:10b does not fit David. Both Acts 2:29 and 13:35 state that David's body underwent decay, but not so with the Messiah who was raised three days after His death. The shift to the second person "Your" and the specific prediction of not undergoing decay in Psalm 16:10b reveal a referent other than David. When Peter said David was a prophet who intentionally looked ahead and spoke of the resurrection of the Messiah, this reveals that Peter was using Psalm 16:10 contextually. *This is a case of direct literal fulfillment of an OT prophecy.*

There is also another reason why Psalm 16:10b could be directly messianic. The mention of "Holy One" [*Hasid*] could be a messianic title in this context. Kaiser noted that when David used "Holy One," David had the Messiah in mind: "The identity of God's 'Holy One' (*Hasid*) is a technical term like the terms 'Seed,' 'Servant of the Lord,' and 'Messiah' in the OT."[10] So while not used exclusively of the Messiah, technical terms like "Holy One" could have a 'one and the many' aspect to them, with the one having implications for the Messiah.

Kaiser applies "Holy One" (*Hasid*) to the concept of corporate solidarity "in which the One (the Messiah) and the many (the Davidic line and those who believe

---

[10] Walter C. Kaiser, Jr., "Single Meaning, Unified Referents," in *Three Views on the New Testament Use of the Old Testament*, 75, 77–78.

in the Messiah) are embraced in a single meaning usually indicated by a collective singular, instead of it being either a simple singular or plural noun."[11] Thus, for Kaiser, Psalm 16:10b refers to the coming Messiah with implications for David: "If Messiah could be resurrected, then David's hope of being raised from the dead was just as good and just as sure."[12] Chou makes a similar point concerning God's "Holy One" being used of the Messiah:

> While "holy one" is relatively frequent, God's holy one (e.g., "Your holy one" or "His holy one"), seems to be a more unique title. It *never refers* to David but does explicitly refer to the Messiah. (1 Sam. 2:9–10)[13]

If accurate, this understanding of "Holy One" is further evidence that David expressed a messianic hope in Psalm 16:10b, and that Peter understood David literally and contextually.

---

[11] Kaiser, "Single Meaning, Unified Referents," 78–79.

[12] Ibid., 79.

[13] Abner Chou, *The Hermeneutics of the Biblical Writers* (Grand Rapids: Kregel, 2018), 144–45.

# CHAPTER TWENTY-THREE

# THE SERVANT, JESUS, AND PAUL

## ISAIAH 49:6 IN ACTS 13:47

Acts 13:14–52 describes Paul's encounters with a Jewish audience in Pisidian Antioch. Upon being asked to speak in a synagogue, Paul recounted key events in Israel's history and then concluded that forgiveness of sins and freedom from the Mosaic Law are found in Jesus (see Acts 13:28–39). But the next Sabbath when Paul spoke, the Jews thwarted him. This sparked a sharp rebuke from Paul. Paul declared that he and Barnabas would shift to proclaiming Jesus to the Gentiles (Acts 13:46). In so doing, he quoted Isaiah 49:6 (and perhaps Isaiah 42:6):

> For so the Lord has commanded us,
> "I HAVE PLACED YOU AS A LIGHT FOR THE GENTILES,
> THAT YOU MAY BRING SALVATION TO THE END OF THE EARTH." (Acts 13:47)

Isaiah 49 (and Isaiah 42) explain the ministry of the Servant of the Lord who will restore Israel and bring blessings to the Gentiles. Isaiah 49:6 is also used in reference to Jesus in Luke 2:32 and Acts 26:23.

What is debated, though, is why Paul and Barnabas say Isaiah 49:6 referenced "us" (Paul and Barnabas) and not Jesus. After all, Paul and Barnabas are not the Servant that Isaiah spoke of in Isaiah 49. Some, like Robert Thomas, claim this is a non-contextual use of the OT since Paul applies to himself and Barnabas a mission that was promised specifically to the Servant we now know as Jesus. Thomas says, "He [Paul] applies the words to his own ministry among the Gentiles during the present age, not to that of the LORD's Servant during the future age of the kingdom. Here again is clearly a nonliteral application of the prophet's words."[1]

So is this a non-contextual use of an OT passage? It is not. Paul certainly knew Isaiah 49 was about Jesus and His mission, not about himself. In fact, in Acts 26:23 Paul argued that the prophets and Moses declared that "the Christ was to suffer, and that by reason of His resurrection from the dead He would be the first to proclaim light both to the Jewish people and to the Gentiles." Paul probably had Isaiah 49:6 in mind when he stated this. Thus, Paul viewed Isaiah 49:6 as being fulfilled in Jesus.

So what is happening here? When Paul was converted, Jesus commissioned Paul to represent Him to the Gentiles: "He [Paul] is a chosen instrument of Mine, to bear My name before the Gentiles and kings and the sons of Israel" (Acts 9:15). While Paul himself is not the Servant of Isaiah 49, when Jesus saved and appointed him as an apostle to the Gentiles, the mission of the Servant (Jesus) became Paul's mission too. And by extension, this was also Barnabas's mission. Beale rightly notes that this is a case of corporate representation where the mission of the Servant Jesus becomes the mission of His followers:

> And it is this same idea of corporate representation which allows Paul in his own mind to understand how the very context of the Isaiah 49 servant could apply to himself without distorting the way in which he thought it may have been intended originally. Furthermore, in that he was continuing the mission of Jesus, the Servant, he could easily apply this Servant prophecy to himself.[2]

Klyne Snodgrass also affirms this idea:

> Often words that find their climax in Jesus find further correspondence in his followers. If Jesus is the fulfillment of Isaiah 49:6 as the light to the Gentiles (Luke 2:32), the words can still be applied to Paul (Acts 13:47).[3]

Since Jesus' mission as the Servant is carried out by His followers, a proper understanding of corporate representation reveals that Acts 13:47 is a contextual use of the OT. Isaiah 49 predicted that the coming Servant would minister both to Israel and the Gentiles, and that is what Paul (and Barnabas) were doing as they represented Jesus.

---

[1] Robert L. Thomas, "The New Testament Use of the Old Testament," *The Master's Seminary Journal* 13, no. 1 (Spring: 2002): 85.

[2] G. K. Beale, "The Old Testament Background of Reconciliation in 2 Corinthians 5–7," in *The Right Doctrine from the Wrong Texts? Essays on the Use of the Old Testament in the New*, ed. G. K. Beale (Grand Rapids: Baker, 1994), 230–31.

[3] Klyne Snodgrass, "The Use of the Old Testament in the New," in *The Right Doctrine from the Wrong Texts?*, 38.

# CHAPTER TWENTY-FOUR

# THE SALVATION OF ISRAEL

## ISAIAH 59:20–21 IN ROMANS 11:26–27

One example where a NT writer understood an OT prophetic passage as needing to be fulfilled literally in the future is Paul's use of Isaiah 59:20–21 in Romans 11:26–27:

> and so all Israel will be saved; just as it is written,
> "THE DELIVERER WILL COME FROM ZION,
> HE WILL REMOVE UNGODLINESS FROM JACOB."
> "THIS IS MY COVENANT WITH THEM,
> WHEN I TAKE AWAY THEIR SINS."

This statement concerning Israel's salvation comes in the context of Paul's discussion concerning why God's Word has not failed concerning Israel in Romans 9–11 (see Rom. 9:6a). In showing how Paul used this passage, we begin with discussing the context of Isaiah 59:20–21.

## Isaiah 59:20–21 in Context

Isaiah 59:20–21 reads:

> "A Redeemer will come to Zion,
> And to those who turn from transgression in Jacob," declares the Lord.

"As for Me, this is My covenant with them," says the Lord: "My Spirit which is upon you, and My words which I have put in your mouth shall not depart from your mouth, nor from the mouth of your offspring, nor from the mouth of your offspring's offspring," says the Lord, "from now and forever."

The last two major sections of Isaiah are chapters 49–57 and 58–66. Isaiah 49–57 focuses on the coming Suffering Servant who will atone for the sins of His people. We now know that Jesus is this Suffering Servant. Isaiah 58–66 then emphasizes glorious kingdom blessings that will come upon Israel and the world. Israel will be restored and the nations of the earth will then bless Israel.

Together, these two sections focus on salvation and kingdom. So when Isaiah 59:20–21 foretells the Lord's salvation of Israel, the backdrop for this truth is the work of the Suffering Servant. Without Him, there would be no blessings.

Isaiah 59 addresses: (1) Israel's sin (vv. 1–8); (2) Israel's national confession of guilt (vv. 9–15a); (3) the Lord's rescue of Israel (vv. 15b–19); and (4) the salvation of Israel and Israel's inclusion into the New covenant (vv. 20–21). Beginning in Isaiah 59:15b, the Lord is presented as Israel's interceder who is displeased because there was "no justice" and "no one to intercede" for Israel. So He decides to act alone on Israel's behalf against the nations. This interceding on Israel's behalf will include Israel's deliverance from enemies and spiritual salvation from her sins.

Isaiah 59:16–19 emphasizes the coming wrath of God against the nations, even distant nations—"Wrath to His adversaries, recompense to His enemies; to the coastlands He will make recompense" (59:18). This is clearly a physical deliverance from oppression. This also is the message of Zechariah 14 and Isaiah 63:3–6 which speak of the Lord's physical deliverance of Israel from her enemies. Also, in the NT, Zacharias declared that the coming Messiah (Jesus) would bring "Salvation from our enemies" (Luke 1:71). He also said that with fulfillment of the Abrahamic covenant, God will grant rescue "from the hand of our enemies" (Luke 1:74).

Yet in addition to national deliverance from enemies, the "Redeemer" of Isaiah 59:20 is also a Savior from sin. Much of Isaiah 58–66 concerns Israel's sinfulness and Israel's national confession of sin. Isaiah 59 began with, "Behold, the Lord's hand is not so short that it cannot save" (v. 1). That this includes salvation from sin is supported by the fact that Isaiah 59:1–15a concerns Israel's sin and confession of sin. So the "Redeemer" of verse 20 is more than a deliverer from oppressing nations, He also is a Savior from sin. This Redeemer is also the Suffering Servant of Isaiah 52–53 who "bore the sin of many and interceded for the transgressors" (53:12). Also, this "Redeemer" comes "to those who turn from transgression in Jacob" (59:20). So the Redeemer's coming to Zion is linked with forgiveness of sins in Israel.

This salvation that the Redeemer brings is linked with Israel's inclusion and participation in the New covenant—"'As for Me, this is My covenant with them,' says the LORD: 'My Spirit which is upon you'" (21a). Jeremiah 31:31, 34 explicitly links the New covenant with Israel's forgiveness of sins. Ezekiel 36 also links the Holy Spirit with the New covenant: "I will put My Spirit within you" (Ezek. 36:27a). This inclusion of Israel into the New covenant is also tied with Abrahamic covenant blessings since the New covenant is an extension of the Abrahamic covenant.

In sum, Isaiah 59 reveals that Israel one day will recognize her sin. When this occurs, the Lord will act alone on Israel's behalf to rescue Israel from her enemies. He also comes to Israel with salvation, a salvation based on the work of the Suffering Servant of Isaiah 52–53. This salvation means inclusion into the New covenant.

# Romans 11:26–27

So how does Isaiah 59:20–21 connect with Romans 11:26–27? In Romans 9–11, Paul addressed Israel's unbelief and whether or not God's Word had failed (see Rom. 9:1–6). Israel missed God's righteousness since the nation pursued righteousness through works of the Mosaic Law, not through faith in Jesus who is the end of the Law (see Rom. 9:30–10:4).

Paul explained that God's Word had not failed. In doing so, he appeals to past, present, and future truths. Concerning the past, Israel is still related to adoption, the covenants, the promises, temple service, the patriarchs, and the Messiah (see Rom. 9:4–5). Concerning the present, God has kept a remnant of believing ethnic Israelites (Rom. 11:1–6). This remnant is a guarantee that God has not permanently rejected the nation Israel. In the present, God is also saving many Gentiles. In fact, the salvation of Gentiles is being used by God to make Israel jealous (11:11).

Concerning the future, God will save and reinstall national Israel to Abrahamic covenant blessings after the "fullness of the Gentiles" (Rom. 11:17–25; see Lev. 26:40–42). This "fullness of the Gentiles" relates to God's purposes for Gentiles in this age, including their salvation and provocation of Israel to jealousy. This leads to the salvation of Israel as Paul states in 11:25–26a:

> For I do not want you, brethren, to be uninformed of this mystery—so that you will not be wise in your own estimation—that a partial hardening has happened to Israel until the fullness of the Gentiles has come in; and so all Israel will be saved.

"All Israel" in Scripture refers to the nation Israel as a whole at any given point in time. Since the context in this verse is future-oriented, the "all Israel" refers to Israel as a whole at some point in the future.

To support the assertion that "all Israel will be saved," Paul draws upon Isaiah 59:20–21a in Romans 11:26–27:

And so all Israel will be saved; just as it is written,
"THE DELIVERER WILL COME FROM ZION,
HE WILL REMOVE UNGODLINESS FROM JACOB."
"THIS IS MY COVENANT WITH THEM,
WHEN I TAKE AWAY THEIR SINS."

In this verse, Paul contextually relies upon Isaiah 59:20–21. The Isaiah passage predicts a future salvation of Israel as a corporate entity that reverses the nation's unbelief. This, too, is Paul's point. The coming of the Redeemer, Jesus the Messiah, will be linked with the salvation of national Israel and Israel's inclusion in the New covenant. This is the message of both Isaiah and Paul. To compare:

**Isaiah 59:20–21:** Predicts a coming salvation of national Israel and the inclusion of Israel into the New covenant.

**Romans 11:26–27:** Predicts a coming salvation of national Israel and the inclusion of Israel into the New covenant.

# "To" or "From" Zion

Another issue concerns Paul's use of "Zion." Isaiah 59:20 says the Deliverer will come "to Zion," but Paul says the Deliverer will come "from [*ek*] Zion." Zion is consistently used to refer to an earthly mountain in Jerusalem. But some think that since Paul says the Deliverer is returning "from Zion," that "Zion" in Romans 11:26 must refer to heaven. If this is the case, the normal, earthly sense of "Zion" would not exist in 11:26.

But to understand "Zion" in a heavenly manner is likely inaccurate. Paul's use of "Zion" in Romans 9:33 concerns earthly Zion, and it is unlikely that Paul is changing the meaning of "Zion" in 11:26. But why does Paul say "from" and not "to" concerning Zion? Is Paul being creative in his interpretation?

Probably not. Paul could be drawing upon Psalm 14:7, which states that Israel's salvation will "come from Zion." But even if he is not, the different prepositions ("to" and "from"), while acknowledged, should not be given too much significance. The OT prophets spoke of both a coming "to Zion" and "from Zion" almost indistinguishably, with no major distinction between the two.

Paul's use of "from Zion" may emphasize Jesus' rule from earthly Zion (i.e. Jerusalem) as a result of Jesus' return "to Zion." In Psalm 110:1–2, the Messiah is said to rule "from Zion" in Jerusalem after a session in heaven at God's right hand. But for this rule "from Zion" to occur, a return "to Zion" (i.e. Jerusalem) had to occur. Isaiah himself declared both concepts. In addition to saying the Deliverer comes "*to*

Zion" (Isa. 59:20), Isaiah also says, "For the law will go forth *from* Zion" (Isa. 2:3, emphasis added). So the prepositions "to" and "from" are closely related.

In sum, the statements that the Deliverer is coming "to Zion" (Isa. 59:20) and "from Zion" (Rom. 11:26) are closely linked and can be harmonized. Paul could refer to Jesus' rule "from Zion" (earthly Jerusalem) that is connected with Jesus' second coming "to" Jerusalem as stated in Isaiah 59:20.

# Conclusion

Paul's use of Isaiah 59:20–21a in Romans 11:26b–27 is contextual as he relies upon Isaiah's intent. This is an example of a NT writer expecting a literal fulfillment of an OT prophetic text that has yet to be fulfilled.

# CHAPTER TWENTY-FIVE

# THE COMING PROPHET

## DEUTERONOMY 18:15 IN THE
## NEW TESTAMENT

Did Moses predict the coming of Jesus? This chapter examines the use of Deuteronomy 18:15 in the NT, particularly in Acts 3:22 and 7:37. The context of Deuteronomy 18:15 is Moses' instructions concerning a coming prophet like him as explained in Deuteronomy 18:15–19:

> The LORD your God will raise up for you a prophet like me from among you, from your countrymen, you shall listen to him. This is according to all that you asked of the LORD your God in Horeb on the day of the assembly, saying, "Let me not hear again the voice of the LORD my God, let me not see this great fire anymore, or I will die." The LORD said to me, "They have spoken well. I will raise up a prophet from among their countrymen like you, and I will put My words in his mouth, and he shall speak to them all that I command him. It shall come about that whoever will not listen to My words which he shall speak in My name, I Myself will require it of him."

In verse 15, Moses stated, "The LORD your God will raise up for you a prophet like me from among you, from your countrymen, you shall listen to him." Many take the coming "prophet like me" to refer to the prophetic office that would include multiple prophets from the time of Moses. Allegedly, verse 15 does not predict a coming specific prophet, but the prophetic office as a whole. Jesus eventually will be the ultimate prophet from this line of prophets, but Moses did not have an individual prophet in view.

I do not think this view is accurate. Moses' intent in Deuteronomy 18:15–19 is to give a specific Messianic/Prophetic hope concerning a unique person who, in every way, will be equal to and greater than Moses. This prophet has arrived and is identified as Jesus the Messiah in the NT (see Acts 3:22). More than just the prophetic office was intended in Deuteronomy 18.

# The Context of Deuteronomy 18:15–19

According to Deuteronomy 18:15–19 the coming prophet like Moses will be defined by the following:

- God will raise him up (vv. 15, 18).
- God will raise him up from "your countrymen," i.e. the people of Israel (v. 15).
- This coming prophet will be like Moses ("like me") (v. 15).
- The people of Israel are commanded to listen to this coming prophet (v. 15).
- God will put His words in this prophet's mouth and he will speak what God has commanded him (v. 18).
- The people will be held accountable for listening to this coming prophet (v. 19).

There are several reasons why the coming "prophet" whom the Lord will raise up will be an individual prophet like Moses. First, the singular "prophet" corresponds to the singular person of Moses—"a prophet like me." Moses is a specific prophet, so too will be the coming prophet.

Second, to be a prophet like Moses is a high standard that is left unfulfilled by the prophets who followed Moses prior to Jesus. Two other sections in the Pentateuch support this understanding—Numbers 12:6–8 and Deuteronomy 34. Numbers 11 and 12 list a number of prophets, including Moses. This involved seventy elders, Miriam, and Aaron. God's words to Miriam and Aaron in Numbers 12:6–8 show a clear contrast between the prophet Moses and all other prophets:

He [the Lord] said,
"Hear now My words:
If there is a prophet among you,
I, the LORD, shall make Myself known to him in a vision.
I shall speak with him in a dream.
"Not so, with My servant Moses,
He is faithful in all My household;

With him I speak mouth to mouth,
Even openly, and not in dark sayings,
And he beholds the form of the LORD.
Why then were you not afraid
To speak against My servant, against Moses?"

As this passage reveals, unlike the other prophets, God speaks with Moses "mouth to mouth" (or "face to face"). This shows a qualitative difference between Moses and the other prophets. Those others are not "like" Moses.

Also, Deuteronomy 34:10–12 explicitly states that the prophets after Moses were not like Moses:

> Since that time no prophet has risen in Israel like Moses, whom the LORD knew face to face, for all the signs and wonders which the LORD sent him to perform in the land of Egypt against Pharaoh, all his servants, and all his land, and for all the mighty power and for all the great terror which Moses performed in the sight of all Israel.

God's Spirit would come upon others, but the prophets after Moses were not like Moses. Moses was unique.

Thus, Numbers 12:6–8 and Deuteronomy 34:10–12 reveal what being a prophet *like* Moses meant, and make clear that no prophet in Israel's history before Jesus met that criteria. This is a case where the canon of the Pentateuch helps us conclude that the prophets after Moses were not like him and could not fulfill the conditions of the coming prophet of which Moses spoke.

Third, there is a strong, specific Messianic/Prophetic hope in the NT. Four verses in John's Gospel reveal an expectation concerning a coming specific "prophet":

**John 1:21**
They asked him [John the Baptist], "What then? Are you Elijah?" And he said, "I am not." "Are you the Prophet?" And he answered, "No."

**John 1:25**
They asked him, and said to him, "Why then are you baptizing, if you are not the Christ, nor Elijah, nor the Prophet?"

**John 6:14**
Therefore when the people saw the sign which He [Jesus] had performed, they said, "This is truly the Prophet who is to come into the world."

**John 7:40**
Some of the people therefore, when they heard these words, were saying, "This certainly is the Prophet."

While these verses do not explicitly mention Deuteronomy 18, they are consistent with a specific prophetic expectation. Deuteronomy 18:15–19 may be the source of this expectation.

Fourth, NT persons explicitly state that Jesus fulfilled the Deuteronomy 18 prophecy concerning a coming prophet like Moses. This occurs in Acts 3 when Peter declared to the "men of Israel" (3:12) that Jesus was the resurrected Lord and Messiah who could bring forgiveness of sins and the restoration of all things (3:18–21). In Acts 3:20, Peter says Jesus is the Messiah appointed for Israel. Then Peter mentions Deuteronomy 18:15 and Moses' prediction of a coming prophet in reference to Jesus:

> [Jesus] whom heaven must receive until the period of restoration of all things about which God spoke by the mouth of His holy prophets from ancient time. Moses said, "THE LORD GOD WILL RAISE UP FOR YOU A PROPHET LIKE ME FROM YOUR BRETHREN; TO HIM YOU SHALL GIVE HEED to everything He says to you. And it will be that every soul that does not heed that prophet shall be utterly destroyed from among the people." (Acts 3:21–23)

Peter explicitly stated that Jesus is that prophet whom Moses predicted would come. Jesus is not merely the culmination of the prophetic line from the time of Moses; He is the individual, specific prophet Moses predicted. Peter offered inspired commentary concerning what Moses understood. The prophet that Moses said would come is Jesus.

A quotation of Deuteronomy 18:15 occurs again in Acts 7:37. In a section where Stephen relayed the role of Moses in God's purposes (7:20–41), Stephen quoted Moses' expectation of a coming prophet— "This is the Moses who said to the sons of Israel, 'GOD WILL RAISE UP FOR YOU A PROPHET LIKE ME FROM YOUR BRETHREN.'" While Stephen did not explicitly connect this coming prophet with Jesus, the clear reference to Jesus in Acts 3:22 heavily implies that Stephen viewed Jesus as the fulfillment of this prophet.

The NT use of Deuteronomy 18:15, especially in Acts 3:22, reveals another case of direct literal prophetic fulfillment of an OT prophecy. Moses predicted a coming single prophet like him for the people of Israel, and Jesus fulfills this expectation.

# CHAPTER TWENTY-SIX

# RESURRECTION AND DAVID'S THRONE

## PSALM 132:11 IN ACTS 2:30

This chapter examines Peter's use of Psalm 132:11 in Acts 2:30 with an intention to grasp Peter's understanding of the concept of the throne of David. This is a case where understanding a NT use of the OT has significant theological implications. Does Acts 2:30 indicate Jesus is currently reigning from David's throne?

Acts 2 describes the baptizing and filling ministry of the Holy Spirit after Jesus' ascension. This is all related to Jesus, the resurrected Messiah, who currently is at the right hand of the Father. Jesus is the One who has poured forth the Holy Spirit (Acts 2:33). The culmination of Peter's argument in Acts 2 is found in his declaration that God has made the resurrected Jesus "both Lord and Christ" (Acts 2:36).

Three quotations from the Psalms are found in Acts 2:29–36— Psalms 16, 132, and 110. The focus of this chapter, though, is on Peter's use of Psalm 132:11 in Acts 2:30 and how it relates to the throne of David. Peter declared:

And so, because he [David] was a prophet and knew that GOD HAD SWORN TO HIM WITH AN OATH TO SEAT one OF HIS DESCENDANTS ON HIS THRONE. (Acts 2:30)

Much debate exists concerning the implications of this verse, mostly involving whether it implies that Jesus currently is sitting upon David's throne today in heaven. Does Peter's quotation of Psalm 132:11 indicate a change or advancement from an earthly reality to a spiritual one concerning the concept of David's throne? This topic involves both how Peter uses Psalm 132:11 and what this use means for understanding the throne of David.

To understand Peter's uses of Psalm 132:11, I will present both the context of Psalm 132 and the NT situation in which Psalm 132:11 is quoted in Acts 2. I believe Peter quotes Psalm 132:11 contextually, and that he is not transcending or changing the meaning of the throne of David from its normal meaning of an earthly throne as expressed in the OT. *Thus, Acts 2:30 is an example of a NT person quoting an OT prophetic text contextually with the expectation that this OT text will be fulfilled literally in the future.*

# Psalm 132

Psalm 132 is a psalm of ascents where the psalmist pleads with God to remember David and the Davidic covenant (see 2 Sam. 7). As *The Moody Bible Commentary* states, "This psalm is the climax of the Psalms of Ascents. In it, the psalmist emphasizes that all of Israel's future hopes are dependent upon the fulfillment of the Davidic covenant."[1] After noting the humility of David (vv. 1–9), the author of Psalm 132 states:

> For the sake of David Your servant,
> Do not turn away the face of Your anointed.
> The Lord has sworn to David
> A truth from which He will not turn back:
> "Of the fruit of your body I will set upon your throne.
> "If your sons will keep My covenant
> And My testimony which I will teach them,
> Their sons also shall sit upon your throne forever." (vv. 10–12)

In Acts 2, Peter focuses mostly on Psalm 132:11 and its statement that God will set a descendant(s) upon David's throne. The context of the Davidic covenant and Davidic throne is 2 Samuel 7 (cf. 1 Chron. 17). Second Samuel 7:16 states, "Your [David's] house and your kingdom shall endure before Me forever; your throne shall be established forever." Thus, Psalm 132:10–12 is reaffirming key aspects of the Davidic covenant first given in 2 Samuel 7.

An inductive study of various Bible passages reveals that the throne of David is related to both *function* and *location*. Functionally, it involves kingly authority and rule. Concerning location, it involves an earthly geographical realm. The one who

---

[1] *The Moody Bible Commentary*, ed. Michael Rydelnik and Michael Vanlaningham (Chicago: The Moody Bible Institute of Chicago, 2014), 866.

functionally rules from David's throne will do so from and over the land of Israel. These two aspects are found in Luke 1:32b–33 when the angel Gabriel told Mary:

> The Lord God will give Him [Jesus] the throne of His father David; and *He will reign over the house of Jacob forever,* and His kingdom will have no end." (Luke 1:32b–33, emphasis mine)

Thus:

**Function:** "He will reign"
**Location:** "over the house of Jacob"

On multiple occasions, the throne of David is linked geographically with Jerusalem and Israel. Second Samuel 3:10 speaks of "the throne of David over Israel and over Judah, from Dan even to Beersheba." In 1 Kings 9:5, God told Solomon, "Then I will establish the throne of your kingdom over Israel forever, just as I promised to your father David, saying, 'You shall not lack a man on the throne of Israel.'" Jeremiah 17:25 links the throne of David with "Judah" and "Jerusalem." On nine occasions, David's throne is called the "throne of Israel" (1 Kings 2:4; 8:20, 25; 9:5; 10:9; 2 Kings 10:30; 15:12; 2 Chron. 6:10, 16), emphasizing that this throne is earthly in location, involving Israel. It should also be noted that this throne in Israel will eventually impact the whole world. Psalm 72:8 indicates that the reign of the Messiah will extend throughout the whole earth:

> May he also rule from sea to sea
> And from the River to the ends of the earth.

This locational emphasis concerning David's throne is important as it demonstrates that this throne involves *location,* not function alone. Both function and location are important.

Also, since the Davidic throne is established by God, it is called "the throne of the Lord" in 1 Chronicles 29:23. This indicates the throne of David has as its source the Lord. It is the Davidic throne that the Lord has established on earth. First Chronicles 29:23 is not a statement that the Lord's throne in heaven is blurred into the Davidic throne so that there is no distinction between them.

# Acts 2:30–36

In Acts 2, Peter argued that Jesus is the resurrected Messiah and Lord who has poured out the Holy Spirit upon His people. Just prior to Acts 2:30, Peter quoted Psalm 16 to show that David consciously predicted the resurrection of Jesus (Acts 2:22–28). Then in Acts 2:29–32 Peter stated:

Brethren, I may confidently say to you regarding the patriarch David that he both died and was buried, and his tomb is with us to this day. And so, because he was a prophet and knew that God had sworn to him with an oath to seat one of his descendants on his throne, he looked ahead and spoke of the resurrection of the Christ, that He was neither abandoned to Hades, nor did His flesh suffer decay. This Jesus God raised up again, to which we are all witnesses.

Peter said David was a "prophet" who consciously predicted the resurrection of Jesus. Some doubt that David predicted the resurrection of the Messiah in Psalm 16, but in this verse we have inspired commentary from Peter as to what David believed. David possessed a specific messianic hope and predicted the resurrection of the Messiah we now know as Jesus.

In Acts 2:30–31, Peter quoted both Psalm 132:11 and Psalm 16:10. The former is a verse concerning the Davidic covenant, and the latter emphasizes God's "Holy One" who will not undergo decay.

Concerning Psalm 132:11, Peter draws upon the truth that God swore to David that one of David's descendants would sit upon David's throne in Jerusalem. So when Peter combines Psalm 132:11 with Psalm 16:10, the message is this: *Since David knew the Messiah is destined to sit upon and reign from David's throne forever, the Messiah must be raised from the dead. A dead Messiah cannot sit upon David's throne forever, so the Messiah must be resurrected.* Peter is not saying Jesus currently sits upon David's throne, but the resurrection means God's promise to seat a descendant of David upon David's throne forever is alive and well.

Peter's understanding of the Davidic throne in Acts 2 is consistent with the meaning of Psalm 132:10–12 and 2 Samuel 7. Nothing in Acts 2 indicates a change or addition has occurred concerning the concept of the Davidic throne.

# Addressing the Heavenly Davidic Throne View

Some believe Peter's quotations of Psalm 132:11 (in Acts 2:30) and Psalm 110:1 (in Acts 2:34–35a) indicate a reinterpretation of the Davidic throne from an earthly to a heavenly reality. For example, concerning Peter's understanding of Jesus' ascension in Acts 2, George Ladd writes: "This involves a rather *radical reinterpretation* of the Old Testament prophecies, but no more so than the entire *reinterpretation* of God's redemptive plan by the early church"[2] (emphases mine).

The argument that Peter is reinterpreting David's throne to be a heavenly reality in Acts 2:30–36 is sometimes linked with the fact that Jesus' session in heaven coincides with Peter's reference to David's throne in Acts 2:30. This understanding seems to rely on the following logic:

---

[2] George Eldon Ladd, *A Theology of the New Testament* (1974; rev. ed., Grand Rapids: Eerdmans, 1994), 373.

The resurrected and ascended Jesus is now in heaven.
Peter quotes a passage involving the Davidic throne.
Therefore, Jesus must be sitting upon David's throne in heaven.

This logic, though, does not accurately represent what Peter is saying. Peter is most likely making a cause-and-effect argument. Jesus' ascension to heaven is a step in the process to Jesus reigning from David's throne in the future, which is what Psalm 110:1–2 actually predicts. Thus, the correct link between Jesus, heaven, and David's throne is this: the resurrected *Jesus* who currently is in *heaven* at the right hand of God is destined to reign upon *David's throne*.

Notice that Peter does not say Jesus has been exalted to the throne of David in Acts 2:33. Instead, Peter says Jesus has been "exalted to the right of hand of God." The Scripture consistently presents God's throne as existing in heaven. Isaiah 66:1a states, "Heaven is my throne." Psalm 11:4 declares, "the Lord's throne is in heaven." Yet, as mentioned earlier, David's throne is consistently presented as an earthly reality involving Israel and the nations upon the earth (2 Sam. 3:10; 1 Kings 2:12; Jer. 17:25; Luke 1:32–33; Matt. 25:31).

Also, Peter is not emphasizing Jesus reigning in Acts 2:33b. Instead, Jesus is receiving and pouring forth the Holy Spirit. One would expect a statement about Jesus reigning if Peter connected the right hand of God with the Davidic throne. In addition, after Acts 2:30–36 there are thirteen statements that Jesus is at the "right hand" of God, but none say He is sitting upon the throne of David. The NT writers seem intentional about identifying Jesus as being at the right hand of God, but not on the throne of David.

# Thrones and Sitting

Another argument for the heavenly Davidic throne view concerns the issue of *sitting*, which Peter mentions concerning both David's throne and the right hand of God:

**David's throne:** "to **seat** one of his descendants on his throne." (Acts 2:30)
**God's throne:** "**Sit** at My right hand." (Acts 2:34, emphases mine)

Since both Psalm 132:11 and Psalm 110:1 speak of the Messiah sitting in these contexts, some think the Davidic throne of Psalm 132:11 and the right hand of the father of Psalm 110:1 must be the same. Or to put another way:

Psalm 132:11 speaks of a descendant of David *sitting* on David's throne.
Psalm 110:1 speaks of the Messiah *sitting* at the right hand of God.

214 | *The Old in the New*

Therefore, since both texts mention sitting, David's throne and the right hand of the Father are the same.

But the act of sitting alone does not imply the two thrones are the same. The act of sitting can apply to the Father's throne in heaven (Psalm 110:1) and David's throne in Jerusalem (Psalm 132:11). In fact, Jesus makes such a distinction between these thrones in Revelation 3:21:

> He who overcomes, I will grant to him to *sit down with Me on My throne* [David's throne], as I also overcame and *sat down with My Father on His throne* [Father's throne]. (emphases mine)

So the two thrones are distinguished. Also, it appears that the act of sitting applies to two different thrones at two different times. Jesus is *currently* seated at the right hand of the Father ("I also overcame") and will in the *future* grant to overcomers the right to sit upon the throne of David ("I will grant to him").

Another point to consider is that Jesus himself placed His Davidic throne assumption in the future in Matthew 25:31: "But when the Son of Man comes in His glory, and all the angels with Him, then He will sit on His glorious throne." In this verse, Jesus' sitting upon His glorious throne must be future since it is linked with His coming in glory with His angels. Matthew 25:32 then links this throne with the judgment of the nations, which is a future event on earth.

Matthew 19:28 also teaches that Jesus' Davidic-throne reign is future and connected with other future events such as the coming "regeneration" or renewal of the earth (*palingenesia*) and the rule of the apostles over the twelve tribes of Israel:

> And Jesus said to them, "Truly I say to you, that you who have followed Me, in the regeneration when the Son of Man *will sit on His glorious throne*, you also shall sit upon twelve thrones, judging the twelve tribes of Israel."
> (emphasis mine)

Finally, Psalm 110:1–2 explicitly teaches that the Messiah would have a session at God's right hand in heaven "until" the Messiah begins His earthly reign from Jerusalem. So why would a quotation of Psalm 110 by Peter be taken to mean that Jesus is upon David's throne in heaven now? Psalm 110 predicted that a session of the Messiah at God's right hand (v. 1) will eventually lead to a reign from Jerusalem (v. 2). Also, Hebrews 10:12–13 states that Jesus is at the right hand of God "waiting" to reign:

> But He, having offered one sacrifice for sins for all time, sat down at the right hand of God, *waiting* from that time onward until His enemies be made a footstool for His feet. (emphasis mine)

The right hand of God is linked with God's throne in heaven. It is not simply a place of authority without location. In Acts 7:49, Stephen quoted Isaiah 66:1 saying, "Heaven is My [God's] throne." Then while being stoned, we are told that Stephen saw "Jesus standing at the right hand of God" (Acts 7:55), and then he said, "'Behold, I see the heavens opened up and the Son of Man standing at the right hand of God" (Acts 7:56). Stephen saw Jesus standing at the right hand of God at God's heavenly throne. So just as David's throne has a locale in Jerusalem, the right hand of God has a locale at God's throne in heaven. These thrones are not the same—one is heavenly and the other is on earth.

# Conclusion

The purpose of Acts 2:30–36 (and all of Acts 2) is to show Israel that the resurrected Jesus is both Lord and Messiah. Jesus is at the right hand of God, and He has poured His Holy Spirit upon His followers. Peter is not stating that Jesus has assumed a heavenly Davidic throne to rule over a spiritual kingdom.

Peter's quotation of Psalm 132:11 in Acts 2:30 is contextual and relies upon the literal meaning of Psalm 132:11 which speaks of a descendant of David sitting upon the Davidic throne in Israel. Peter argues that Jesus is the One destined to reign upon the Davidic throne on earth. Because of this, Jesus could not remain dead after His crucifixion. He must be resurrected. *So Peter's use of Psalm 132:11 is an example of a NT person (Peter) relying upon the literal meaning of an OT text (Psalm 132:11), and seeing the fulfillment of this passage as needing to occur in the future.*

# CHAPTER TWENTY-SEVEN

# MESSIAH'S COMING REIGN

## THE OLD TESTAMENT IN REVELATION 19:15

Studying the OT in the book of Revelation is rewarding yet challenging. No NT book is saturated with as much OT content as Revelation, yet there may be no formal quotations of the OT in it.[1] As Moyise notes, "It is the only book to incorporate allusions in almost every verse, while never explicitly quoting scripture."[2] This makes the book an enigma in certain ways. The focus of this chapter is the presence of the OT in Revelation 19:15, but first some thoughts on the OT in Revelation are necessary.

## The OT in Revelation

The book of Revelation stems from a vision of events from Jesus while the apostle John was on the island of Patmos in the 90s AD. As 1:1a states: "The Revelation of Jesus Christ, which God gave Him to show to His bond-servants, the things which must soon take place." Also, on three occasions we are told the genre of this book—prophecy:

---

[1] "It is generally recognized that Revelation contains more OT references than does any other NT book." G. K. Beale and Sean M. McDonough, "Revelation," in *Commentary on the New Testament Use of the Old Testament*, ed. G. K. Beale and D. A. Carson (Grand Rapids: Baker, 2007), 1082. "No other book of the NT is as permeated by the OT as is Revelation. Although its author seldom quotes the OT directly, allusions and echoes are found in almost every verse of the book" (1081).

[2] Steve Moyise, *The Old Testament in the New* (Continuum: New York and London, 2001), 126.

- Blessed is he who reads and those who hear the words of the *prophecy.* (Rev. 1:3a)
- Blessed is he who heeds the words of the *prophecy* of this book. (Rev. 22:7b)
- And he said to me, "Do not seal up the words of the *prophecy* of this book." (Rev. 22:10a, emphases mine)

This prophetic element puts John's writing in a similar genre to that of the OT prophets like Ezekiel, Isaiah, and Daniel.

Thus, key to understanding Revelation and the OT in Revelation is knowing that John is recording what he actually saw. This vision includes numerous symbols, many of which are explained. The descriptions of his vision also involve much OT language. Isaiah is alluded to most in Revelation, followed by Ezekiel,[3] Daniel, and Psalms.[4]

So how do we combine the two realities that John recorded a vision he actually saw and that he is using OT language to describe what he saw? The best understanding is that John's deep knowledge of the OT influenced his descriptions. John was aware of the prophecies of Daniel, Ezekiel, and the other prophets. So to use the language of the previous prophets to describe what he saw seems plausible. Addressing how John could see real visions that coincided with OT wording, Beale and McDonough state, "Perhaps one of the reasons for the high degree of OT influence in Revelation is that John could think of no better way to describe some of his visions, which were difficult to explain, than with the language already used by the OT prophets to describe similar visions."[5]

For example, the heavenly throne room scene of Revelation 4–5 is similar to Daniel 7:9–14. The mention of forty-two months and 1,260 days (Rev. 11:2, 3; 13:5) is parallel to the 3.5-year period predicted in Daniel 9:27. What is described in Revelation 6–20 is similar to Isaiah's Little Apocalypse of Isaiah 24–27. The symbol of the woman clothed with the sun and the moon with a crown of twelve stars in Revelation 12 parallels Joseph's dream in Genesis 37:9–11. Not only is the language similar between these OT passages and Revelation, the messages of these OT texts are similar to those presented in Revelation.

# Revelation 19:15 and the OT

This section now focuses on the presence of the OT in Revelation 19:15. This verse comes in the context of Revelation 19:11–21:8, a section within Revelation that is prophetic/apocalyptic narrative. The series of nine *kai eidon* formulas translated

---

[3] Moyise notes there are 138 allusions to Ezekiel in Revelation and eighty-four come from Revelation, 117.

[4] Beale and McDonough, "Revelation," 1082.

[5] Ibid., 1087.

"and I saw" or "then I saw" reveal a progression of chronological events describing the return of Jesus from heaven to earth, the binding of Satan, the reign of the saints, the great white throne of judgment, and the new heaven and new earth.

Revelation 19:15 describes the impact of Jesus' second coming to earth:
From His mouth comes a sharp sword, so that with it He may strike down the nations; and He will rule them with a rod of iron; and He treads the wine press of the fierce wrath of God, the Almighty.

## Four Messianic Passages and Revelation 19:15

While there are no formal quotations in this verse, Revelation 19:15 is closely connected to four OT messianic passages:

**Isaiah 49:2a:** And He [God] has made My [the Servant's] mouth like a sharp sword.

**Isaiah 11:4b:** And He [Messiah] will strike the earth with the rod of His mouth, And with the breath of His lips He will slay the wicked.

**Psalm 2:9a:** You [Messiah] shall break them with a rod of iron.

**Isaiah 63:2–3:** Why is Your [the Lord's] apparel red, And Your garments like the one who treads in the wine press? "I have trodden the wine trough alone, And from the peoples there was no man with Me. I also trod them in My anger, And trampled them in My wrath; And their lifeblood is sprinkled on My garments, And I stained all My raiment."

Together, the connection of these OT verses to Revelation 19:15 can be seen with the following:

From His mouth comes a sharp sword (Isa. 49:2), so that with it He may strike down the nations (Isa. 11:4b); and He will rule them with a rod of iron (Ps. 2:9); and He treads the wine press of the fierce wrath of God, the Almighty (Isa. 63:2–3).

Revelation 19:15 describes a devastating show of force by Jesus as He comes from heaven to earth to defeat His enemies and rule the nations. This is a violent and dramatic event evidenced by the verbs "strike," "rule," "tread," and the words "the fierce wrath of God." Jesus' first coming primarily involved His role as a Lamb and

Suffering Servant (see Acts 3:18). But the second coming emphasizes Jesus' role as the conquering Warrior-King and Judge. The Lamb is also the Lion from the Tribe of Judah (see Rev. 5:5–6).

## The Sharp Sword from Jesus' Mouth

Revelation 19:15a presents the returning Jesus as having a sharp sword coming from His mouth—"From His mouth comes a sharp sword, so that with it He may strike down the nations" (19:15a). Few think that a literal sword will extend from Jesus' mouth at His second coming, but a literal truth is represented by this symbolism. As mentioned, this language was found in the messianic passages of Isaiah 49:2 and Isaiah 11:4 where the Messiah speaks with such authority and power that His mouth can be likened to a sword. Since a literal and grammatical-historical hermeneutic allows for metaphors, similes, and figures of speech, there is no problem with understanding Revelation 19:15a (and 19:21) in a way similar to Isaiah 49:2 and Isaiah 11:4. The dramatic metaphor of a sword coming from Jesus' mouth indicates the authority and power of Jesus' words to defeat His enemies. A similar idea is found in 2 Thessalonians 2:8 which says Jesus will slay the man of lawlessness (i.e. Antichrist) with His words: "Then that lawless one will be revealed whom the Lord will slay with the breath of His mouth and bring to an end by the appearance of His coming."

# Conclusion

How should we understand the presence of the four OT texts in Revelation 19:15? John is not "quoting" the OT in Revelation 19:15. As stated earlier, John saw a vision, so he wrote down what he saw (see Rev. 1:11). But as John sees a vision of the returning Jesus, he describes this event in the language of Isaiah 49:2a; 11:4b; Psalm 2:9a; and Isaiah 63:2–3. John, therefore, used OT language to describe events he saw.

# CHAPTER TWENTY-EIGHT

# CHRISTIAN MINISTERS AND OX MUZZLING

## PAUL'S USE OF DEUTERONOMY 25:4 IN 1 CORINTHIANS 9:9–10

Another challenging example of NT use the OT is 1 Corinthians 9:9–10 and its reference to Deuteronomy 25:4. Some believe this is a non-contextual use of the OT. Some even think Paul allegorizes the OT in this verse. The text from 1 Corinthians 9:8–11 reads:

> I am not speaking these things according to human judgment, am I? Or does not the Law also say these things? For it is written in the Law of Moses, "You shall not muzzle the ox while he is threshing." God is not concerned about oxen, is He? Or is He speaking altogether for our sake? Yes, for our sake it was written, because the plowman ought to plow in hope, and the thresher to thresh in hope of sharing the crops. If we sowed spiritual things in you, is it too much if we reap material things from you?

In these verses, Paul asserts his rights and those of other gospel workers to be paid for their efforts. Just as soldiers have a right to be supported and vineyard planters have a right to eat from vineyards (see 1 Cor. 9:7), so too do those who "sowed spiritual things" have a right to "reap material things" (9:11).

# Is Paul Using Allegory?

What has puzzled interpreters is how Paul supports his point from the OT. He makes an appeal to the OT by saying, "For it is written in the Law of Moses." He then quotes Deuteronomy 25:4: "You shall not muzzle the ox while he is threshing." What makes some conclude Paul is speaking allegorically is his statement "God is not concerned about oxen, is He [implied answer, "No"]? Or is He speaking altogether for our sake? Yes, for our sake it was written" (1 Cor. 9:9b–10a). The issue is that Deuteronomy 25:4 speaks about literal oxen, but Paul appears to be saying that God is not concerned about oxen and is only ("altogether" or "entirely") speaking about human workers. Is Paul using allegory? Richard Longenecker asserts that Paul "seems to leave the primary meaning of the injunction in Deut 25:4" and "interprets the Old Testament allegorically."[1]

*So here is the question: Is Paul interpreting Deuteronomy 25:4 non-contextually, or even allegorically?* To answer this, several areas need to be looked at: NT context, OT context, textual issues, and grammatical issues.

# New Testament Context

The first area involves the context of Paul's statement. Paul establishes the rights of apostles and gospel workers to be supported for their efforts. In 9:4 he said, "Do we not have the right to eat and drink?" He then says, "Do we not have a right to take along a believing wife?" (9:5). Then in 9:11 he established that those who sowed spiritual things have a right to reap material things, including financial support (9:11). Then in 9:9, Paul says that what is true of oxen in Deuteronomy 25:4 should be true of those who proclaim the gospel.

# Old Testament Context

Deuteronomy 25 concerns justice and laws that govern relationships between human beings. There are laws about crime and punishment (25:1–3); men who die without offspring (5–10); appropriate behavior (11–12); and weights (13–16). Thus, justice between people is emphasized. The previous chapter (Deuteronomy 24) addressed the necessity of humane treatment for the poor and marginalized, including their need to

---

[1] Richard N. Longenecker, *Biblical Exegesis in the Apostolic Period* (Grand Rapids: Eerdmans, 1975, 1999), 126.

eat. Compassion for the needy and the marginalized also is present. So Paul quotes a section of Deuteronomy about treating other people well.

The command not to muzzle an ox while threshing is important since oxen naturally like to eat the grain they are threshing. It keeps them content, and it is right that a threshing animal should benefit from the food before him. Just like a chef sampling some of his food, oxen should partake of their labor. A muzzle would stop the ox from eating, which would lead to negative results. If muzzled for long, the ox could become hungry, weakened, or harmed.

There also is an issue of whether the command regarding muzzling is directed at the owner of the ox or someone renting the ox. Many assume the command is given to the owner of the ox, but others think such a command would not be needed for the owner. Why would an owner need such a command? Naturally he would want to take care of his own valuable property. So some think the command is given to one borrowing an ox. If a borrower is in mind, then the command to take care of someone else's property is needed. For this person, the ox would be a means to an end, and concern for the animal would not be as great.

This owner versus borrower issue could carry relevance. If the command is directed towards an owner, then the main issue is *compassion*. In this case, compassion is called for a beast that is working. On the other hand, if the command is directed at a renter, then the main issue is *justice* since a renter is obligated to care for another's property. Both issues of compassion for the needy and justice toward others are found in Deuteronomy 24 and 25.

# Grammatical Issues

Are there any significant grammatical issues in this discussion? Yes. The Greek term *pantos* in 1 Corinthians 9:10 is sometimes translated "altogether" or "entirely." If this translation is correct, then the proper understanding would be that Deuteronomy 25:4 is *only* about human beings, and not at all about oxen. In this case, Paul would not be using Deuteronomy 25:4 contextually, since Deuteronomy 25:4 clearly refers to oxen.

But other satisfactory understandings of *pantos* exist. Kaiser says a better rendering of the term would be "mainly" or "especially."[2] Beale says *pantos* could be admirably understood in this context as "surely," "above all," or "doubtless."[3] If these understandings of *pantos* are accurate, Paul is not denying that Deuteronomy 25:4 is about

---

[2] Walter C. Kaiser, Jr., "Single Meaning, Unified Referents," in *Three Views on the New Testament Use of the Old Testament*, ed. Jonathan Lunde and Kenneth Berding (Grand Rapids: Zondervan, 2007), 81–88.

[3] G. K. Beale, *Handbook on the New Testament Use of the Old Testament: Exegesis and Interpretation* (Grand Rapids: Baker, 2012), 67–68.

animals, but he is claiming that what God says has implications beyond animals. The language could point to what is called a "lesser to the greater" argument—what is true of the lesser (oxen) is also true of the greater (gospel workers).

# The Solution

Paul is not allegorizing Deuteronomy 25:4. Nor is he denying that Deuteronomy 25:4 refers to oxen. Instead, his point is that what was true of oxen also applies to people, in this case, workers for the gospel. Thus, there is an *application of a moral principle* here. Just as it is compassionate and just to take care of an ox that is threshing, so too it is compassionate and just for Paul and ministers of the gospel to benefit materially from their efforts. As Leon Morris states, "There is a principle; the worker shares in the fruit of his work, a principle that applies to oxen. And to apostles."[4] Beale notes, "If such a latter rendering [of *pantos* as discussed above] is viable, then Paul is saying that while this text of Deuteronomy has meaning for animals, how much more so does it have application to human laborers."[5]

Paul worked hard to establish the church at Corinth, and he had a right to benefit from his efforts. Whether he chose to accept these benefits was another matter, but his right to such compensation existed. Deuteronomy 25:4 expressed this principle. John Calvin points out this connection between oxen and men and notes the folly of taking an allegorical approach:

> We must not make the mistake of thinking that Paul means to explain that commandment allegorically; for some empty-headed creatures make this excuse...But what Paul actually means is quite simple: though the Lord commands consideration for the oxen, He does so, not for the sake of the oxen, but rather out of regard for men, for whose benefit even the oxen were created. Therefore that humane treatment of oxen ought to be an incentive, moving us to treat each other with consideration and fairness.[6]

So to answer the question posed earlier about whether Paul uses Deuteronomy 25:4 non-contextually, our answer is, no. He is applying a transcendent principle that can apply to both animals and humans based on a contextual understanding of the OT passage.

---

[4] Leon Morris, *The First Epistle of Paul to the Corinthians: An Introduction and Commentary*, The Tyndale New Testament Commentaries (Grand Rapids: Intervarsity Press, 1985), 132.

[5] Beale, 68.

[6] John Calvin, *The First Epistle of Paul the Apostle to the Corinthians*, trans. J. W. Fraser (Grand Rapids: Eerdmans, 1960), 187–88.

# CHAPTER TWENTY-NINE

# "STONE" IN THE NEW TESTAMENT

On several occasions, the NT identifies Jesus as a "stone." Some key NT passages where this occurs are: Matthew 21:42; Mark 12:10–11; Luke 20:17; Acts 4:11; Romans 9:32–33; and 1 Peter 2:4–8. And in 1 Corinthians 10:4, Paul said Jesus was the rock from which the Israelites drank in the wilderness. What is going on with these references, and why is the stone concept so linked with Jesus?

The most quoted of the OT "stone" passages is Psalm 118:22 which states: "The stone which the builders rejected has become the chief corner stone." Psalm 118 is the last of the *Hallel* (i.e. "Praise") psalms and is one of the most quoted psalms in the NT. In Matthew 21:42; Mark 12:10–11; and Luke 20:17, Jesus quoted Psalm 118:22 to the unbelieving chief priests and Pharisees who planned to kill Him. Jesus viewed himself as the "stone" of Psalm 118:22 who experienced rejection by Israel's religious leaders. The Luke account states:

> But Jesus looked at them and said, "What then is this that is written:
> THE STONE WHICH THE BUILDERS REJECTED,
> THIS BECAME THE CHIEF CORNER stone'?
> Everyone who falls on that stone will be broken to pieces; but on whomever it falls, it will scatter him like dust." (Luke 20:17–18)[1]

In Acts 4, Peter spoke to the religious leaders of Israel, including Annas the high priest, along with Caiaphas, John, and Alexander who also were of high-priestly descent (Acts 4:6). Concerning the resurrected Jesus, Peter told these religious leaders: "He

---

[1] Luke 20:18 could also be an allusion to Daniel 2:34–35 which describes a stone cut without hands crushing a statue with the result that the elements of the statue "became like chaff…and the wind carried them away." Thus Jesus could be relying on two "stone" passages—Psalm 118:22 and Daniel 2:34–35, 44–45.

[Jesus] is the STONE WHICH WAS REJECTED by you, THE BUILDERS, but WHICH BECAME THE CHIEF CORNER stone" (Acts 4:11). So again, the message of Jesus as the chief cornerstone who was rejected is directed at the religious leaders of Israel.

In Romans 9:32b–33, Paul mentioned the "stone" concept concerning unbelieving Israel's rejection of Jesus and attempts to establish righteousness by works of the Law:

> They stumbled over the stumbling stone, just as it is written, "BEHOLD, I LAY IN ZION A STONE OF STUMBLING AND A ROCK OF OFFENSE, AND HE WHO BELIEVES IN HIM WILL NOT BE DISAPPOINTED."

Here Paul combined two "stone" passages—Isaiah 28:16 and Isaiah 8:14. Isaiah 28:16a states, "Behold, I am laying in Zion a stone, a tested stone." This is emphasized in the first part of Paul's statement. Then Paul quoted Isaiah 8:14 which refers to "a stone to strike and a rock to stumble over, And a snare and a trap." This is emphasized in the middle of Paul's quotation. Then for the last part of his statement, Paul goes back to Isaiah 28:16 which states: "He who believes in it will not be disturbed."

The most extended discussion on the "stone" idea in the NT is found in 1 Peter 2:4–8. Here Peter says believers should come to Jesus "as to a living stone which has been rejected by men" (v. 4). This alludes to the "stone" statements in Psalm 118:22 and Isaiah 8:14. As a result, Christians are to be like "living stones" who are built up as a spiritual house for spiritual sacrifices (1 Pet. 2:5). Then in verse 6, he quotes Isaiah 28:16: "BEHOLD, I LAY IN ZION A CHOICE STONE, A PRECIOUS CORNER stone, AND HE WHO BELIEVES IN HIM WILL NOT BE DISAPPOINTED." Peter then follows this in verse 7 with a quotation from Psalm 118:22: "THE STONE WHICH THE BUILDERS REJECTED, THIS BECAME THE VERY CORNER stone." Finally, Peter brings up Isaiah 8:14 in verse 8: "A STONE OF STUMBLING AND A ROCK OF OFFENSE."

The main point of the "stone" statements in 1 Peter 2:4–8 is that Jesus is the "stone" from God referred to in the Psalms and Isaiah. Believers in Jesus find salvation with the "stone," while unbelievers stumble over the "stone" and face doom (see 1 Pet. 2:8b).

In 1 Corinthians 10:4, Paul refers to the event of the rock following Israel and applies it to Jesus: "And all drank the same spiritual drink, for they were drinking from a spiritual rock which followed them; and the rock was Christ." As these examples show, the linking of "stone" and "rock" with Jesus was important to Jesus and the NT writers.

# Rock/Stone in the OT

In the OT there are approximately thirteen terms connected with the idea of stone or rock. The three most significant are—*eben*, *sela*, and *tsur*. All three are used figuratively of both situations and people. Hardy observes that, "One of the most striking features of Old Testament rock symbolism is that it is used to describe, and even address,

God. All three of the most common words meaning 'rock' or 'stone' are used in poetry to make symbolic reference to God."[2] For example:

> **Gen 49:24:** But his bow remained firm,
> And his arms were agile,
> From the hands of the Mighty One of Jacob
> (From there is the Shepherd, the **Stone** [*eben*] of Israel).

> **Deut 32:4a:** The **Rock** [*tsur*]! His work is perfect,
> For all His ways are just.

> **Psalm 18:2:** The LORD is my **rock** [*sela*] and my fortress and my deliverer, My God, my **rock** [*tsuri*], in whom I take refuge; My shield and the horn of my salvation, my stronghold.

> **Psalm 118:22:** The **stone** [*eben*] which the builders rejected Has become the chief corner stone. (emphases mine)

Hardy notes that there are least forty-six cases in OT poetry where *eben*, *sela*, and *tsur* "refer to God in a direct and obvious way."[3] Yet the "stone" or "rock" language used in the NT does not focus on God as a source of help or protection.[4] Instead, the stone language in the NT focuses on the consequences for accepting or rejecting God/Jesus. As Jesus said in Luke 20:18: "Everyone who falls on that stone will be broken to pieces; but on whomever it falls, it will scatter him like dust."

# Understanding "Stone" Language in the New Testament

So how should these OT stone passages concerning Jesus be understood and categorized? First, it is important to grasp what is not happening. It is not the case that Jesus and the NT writers are taking passages about actual stones and rocks and then arbitrarily saying they are about Jesus. They are not offering reinterpretations of OT stone passages that are divorced from the OT contexts.

---

[2] See Frank W. Hardy, "The Old Testament Basis for New Testament Rock Symbolism," 3, http://www.historicism.org/Documents/Jrnl/Rock.pdf. 2006.

[3] Ibid., 8.

[4] Ibid., 9.

At least two of the OT stone passages are linked with messianic contexts. Psalm 118:26 states: "Blessed is the one who comes in the name of the LORD." Jesus linked this verse to himself in Matthew 23:39. The Isaiah 8:14 stone reference is sandwiched between Isaiah 7:14 and Isaiah 9:1–7, which many believe are specific messianic sections. Also, D. A. Carson notes that "Targum Jonathan on Isa. 28:16 understands the stone to refer to a Davidic king. This is part of an extensive tradition in which various texts referring to a 'stone' were applied to the Messiah and to the eschatological age."[5]

Messianic overtones are connected with these stone verses. So in the OT, the Messiah is mentioned in the context of stone statements. When the NT links Jesus and His followers with the stone idea, this is not far removed from what was spoken of in the OT.

# 1 Corinthians 10:1–4

One of the more intriguing uses of "rock" language is found in 1 Corinthians 10:1–4. Here Paul refers Israel's time in the wilderness under Moses when God provided water for Israel from a rock as described in Exodus 17:1–7. Preceding this was God's deliverance of Israel from the Egyptians with the Red Sea event (Exodus 14), and His provision of food for the people in Exodus 16. Particularly interesting is Paul's statement in 10:4: "For they were drinking from a spiritual rock which followed them; and the rock was Christ." As he alludes to Exodus 17:1–7, Paul says that Jesus was the rock the Israelites drank from. Is Paul playing fast and loose with the OT account by linking the "rock" in the wilderness with Jesus? We think not. Exodus 3 mentions "the angel of the LORD [Yahweh]," which many Christian scholars think was the pre-incarnate Christ. Then in Exodus 14:19, "the angel of God" is presented as moving among the camp of Israel:

> The angel of God, who had been going before the camp of Israel, moved and went behind them; and the pillar of cloud moved from before them and stood behind them.

Exodus 23:20–23 also mentions an angel of God moving with the people to protect them. If this "angel of God" moving among Israel was the pre-incarnate Jesus, then one can rightly conclude that Paul was right when he stated that Jesus was among Israel at this time.

---

[5] D. A. Carson, "1 Peter," in *Commentary on the New Testament Use of the Old Testament*, ed. G. K. Beale and D. A. Carson (Grand Rapids: Baker Academic, 2007), 1025. Carson also says, "Almost certainly the LXX presupposes a messianic reading."

Moses explicitly calls God "The Rock" in Deuteronomy 32:4. Also, since the LORD was providing the water from the rock, it is feasible to connect this rock with Jesus, the second person of the Godhead. Concerning Paul's use of Exodus 17 in 1 Corinthians 10:4, Greg Beale states:

> Thus, in light of the fact that Exod. 17:6 very closely associates God with the "rock" (as does Psalm 78), it does not take much ingenuity to see how Paul could posit that Christ was a "following rock" in his pre-incarnate divine existence as the "angel of the Lord."[6]

Chou also observes, "Paul's statement Christ was the Rock who accompanied and provided for Israel is reasonable" (1 Cor. 10:4).[7]

In sum, when one connects verses such as Exodus 3:2; 14:19; 17:1–7; and 23:20–23, it is no stretch to connect Jesus with the rock that provided for Israel in the wilderness.

---

[6] Greg Beale, "Did Paul Teach That a Rock Followed the Israelites in the Wilderness?" in *The Aquila Report*, (August 2014), https://www.theaquilareport.com/did-paul-teach-that-a-rock-followed-the-israelites-in-the-wilderness/. Cited January 23, 2019.

[7] Abner Chou, *The Hermeneutics of the Biblical Writers: Learning to Interpret Scripture from the Prophets and Apostles* (Grand Rapids: Kregel, 2018), 136.

# CHAPTER THIRTY

# PAUL'S USE OF "SEED" IN GALATIANS 3:16

Near the top of the list of alleged non-contextual uses of the OT is Galatians 3:16 where Paul states:

> Now the promises were spoken to Abraham and to his seed. He does not say, "And to seeds," as referring to many, but rather to one, "And to your seed," that is, Christ.

At first glance it seems Paul's hermeneutic is non-contextual. It appears that he takes the usual collective or multiple sense of "seed" in Genesis and turns it into a single reference to Jesus. But most Genesis references to "seed" or "offspring" refer to Abraham's descendants collectively. Does Paul reinterpret the plural and collective meaning of "seed" in Genesis to make it fit with the single person of Jesus? Is Paul using the OT non-contextually? Using David Daube as support for this idea, Richard Longenecker says Paul is using "a midrashic mode of interpretation" that goes beyond normal historical-grammatical hermeneutics.[1]

## What Is Paul Doing?

Our view is that Paul does not quote the OT non-contextually in Galatians 3:16. This is based on two factors. *First, the concept of "seed," going back to Genesis 3, involves both a collective and individual sense.* This idea is found in Genesis 3:15:

---

[1] Richard Longenecker, "Can We Produce the Exegesis of the New Testament," *Tyndale Bulletin* 21 (1970): 37.

232 | *The Old in the New*

Between you and the woman,
And between your *seed* and her *seed*;
*He* shall bruise *you* on the head,
And *you* shall bruise *him* on the heel." (emphases mine)

Just like the English term "seed," the Hebrew word *zera* ("seed") can involve a collective singular (many) and/or a unitary singular (one). In Genesis 3:15, a collective sense of "seed" is found in the statement "between your seed and her seed." This predicts an ongoing battle between the collective, plural seed of the woman and the collective, plural seed of the serpent. This involves multiple descendants on both sides. Yet a singular sense is found with, "*He* shall bruise you on the head, and *you* shall bruise him on the heel" (emphases mine). So in Genesis 3:15, the collective sense of "seed" culminates in an individual battle between the ultimate seed of the woman (whom we now know as Jesus) and the power behind the serpent (probably Satan). This indicates a specific messianic hope stemming from the "seed" concept in Genesis 3:15. A coming specific deliverer from the collective seed of the woman will be the one who defeats the power behind the serpent. An individual sense of "seed" (*zera*) also is found in Genesis 4:25:

Adam had relations with his wife again; and she gave birth to a son, and named him Seth, for, she said, "God has appointed me another *offspring* [*zera*] in place of Abel, for Cain killed him." (emphases mine).

In this verse the "seed" or "offspring" is the individual, Seth. Of course, there are many collective senses of "seed" in Genesis referring to multiple descendants of Abraham (Gen. 13:15; 15:5; 17:8). But since there is a specific messianic hope stemming from Genesis 3:15, the individual sense of "seed" is never lost or disconnected from the plural sense. From the collective seed, an individual seed will arrive who will accomplish God's purposes. Thus, for Paul to see Jesus as the ultimate referent of the "seed" concept from Genesis in Galatians 3:16 is not allegorical or typological hermeneutics. A specific messianic hope already was connected with the "seed" concept in Genesis 3:15.

*Second, Paul could be relying literally on the grammar of the Genesis verse he is referring to in Galatians 3:16.* Unanimity is lacking concerning which passage Paul quotes in Galatians 3:16. Some believe Paul refers either to Genesis 13:15, 17:8, or 22:18. Paul's use of "and" leads Schreiner to believe that either Genesis 13:15 or

17:8 is in view.[2] But in his extensive study of what verse Paul was referring to, Collins opts for Genesis 22:18:

> Genesis 22:18 seems to be the best candidate for Paul's source here, because, of the Genesis "blessing" texts that might lie behind the composite quotation of Galatians 3:8, it is the one that has the dative of σπέρμα. This, then, allows us to make sense of Paul's argument in Galatians 3:16.[3]

If Paul quotes Genesis 22:18, he could be relying on a straightforward understanding of this verse in Galatians 3:16. When researching all references to *zera* ("offspring"/"seed") in the Hebrew Bible, Collins concluded that a unitary single sense of *zera* ("seed") concerning one person can be discerned when the term is connected with singular verb inflections, adjectives, and pronouns. This applies to Genesis 3:15. Building upon the work of Collins, T. Desmond Alexander applies this criteria for a singular understanding of *zera* to Genesis 22:17–18a and 24:60.[4]

If this is accurate, the last reference to "seed" [*zera*] in Genesis 22:17 and the reference to "seed" in 22:18 could be understood in a singular way. The English Standard Version translates Genesis 22:17 as singular, "And your offspring shall possess the gate of *his* enemies" (emphasis mine). This contrasts with other versions that opt for "their enemies." But if the singular sense is true in 22:17, it is likely that the "offspring" reference in 22:18 (which Paul could be quoting in Galatians 3:16) also refers to a single individual. Alexander explains:

> If the immediately preceding reference to 'seed' in 22:17 denotes an individual, this must also be the case in 22:18a, for there is nothing here to indicate a change in number. The blessing of 'all the nations of the earth' is thus associated with a particular descendant of Abraham, rather than all those descended from him.[5]

This individual understanding of "seed" is bolstered by the allusion to Genesis 22:17b–18a in Psalm 72:17: "And may all nations be blessed in *him*" (emphasis mine). Psalm 72 is likely a messianic passage that speaks of Messiah's coming kingdom. It connects the Messiah, an individual, with the fulfillment of the "seed" described in Genesis 22:17–18.

---

[2] Thomas R. Schreiner, *Galatians*, Exegetical Commentary on the New Testament (Grand Rapids: Zondervan, 2010), 230.

[3] C. John Collins, "Galatians 3:16: What Kind of Exegete Was Paul?," *Tyndale Bulletin* 54, no. 1 (2003): 86.

[4] T. Desmond Alexander, "Further Observations of the Term 'Seed' in Genesis," *Tyndale Bulletin* 48, no. 1 (1997): 363.

[5] Ibid., 365.

What does this all mean? *If Paul's use of "seed" in Galatians 3:16 is a reference to Genesis 22:18, then Paul could be quite literal with his singular sense of seed.* Applying the seed concept to a singular person (Jesus) is consistent with the literal meaning of Genesis 22:18. Concerning Galatians 3:16 Peter Gentry argues, "So Paul's argument in Galatians 3:16 that the text speaks of 'seed' and not 'seeds' appears to be based upon solid exegesis of the Hebrew Scriptures."[6]

---

[6] Peter J. Gentry and Stephen J. Wellum, *Kingdom through Covenant: A Biblical-Theological Understanding of the Covenants* (Wheaton, IL: Crossway, 2012), 289.

# CHAPTER THIRTY-ONE

# WHAT LAW ARE CHRISTIANS UNDER?

## PAUL'S USE OF DEUTERONOMY 30:11–14 IN ROMANS 10:6–8

One of the most challenging uses of the OT in the NT involves Paul's quotation of Deuteronomy 30:11–14 in Romans 10:6–8. Here Paul connects Jesus with an OT passage that does not mention Jesus directly, and Paul seems to make Moses a witness to Christ. Some think a transformation of meaning occurs here. For example, Richard Hays asserts that, "Paul takes possession of Moses' exhortation and transforms its sense so that Moses is made to bear witness to the gospel."[1] But is this what is happening?

Paul's quotation of Deuteronomy 30:11–14 comes in the context of explaining how Israel missed righteousness in Jesus by trying to establish its own righteousness through works of the Mosaic Law (Rom. 9:30–10:3). Israel did not grasp that Jesus is the end/goal (*telos*) of the Law (Rom. 10:4). So trying to establish righteousness through the Mosaic Law was misguided. Ironically, the Gentiles who were not looking for salvation found righteousness through faith in Jesus (Rom. 9:30–31) while Israel did not.

In Romans 10:5, Paul explains the implications of Jesus being the end/goal of the Mosaic Law. He says, "For Moses writes that the man who practices the righteousness which is based on law shall live by that righteousness." Paul's meaning

---

[1] Richard B. Hays, *Echoes of Scripture in the Letters of Paul* (New Haven: Yale University Press, 1989), 1.

here, which seems reliant on Leviticus 18:5, is heavily debated. Some think Paul is stating that righteousness before God is ultimately based on perfect law-keeping, but that is not the point here. Instead, Paul makes an epochal or dispensational distinction concerning what God required in differing eras—the Mosaic era (Rom. 10:5) versus the New covenant era (Rom. 10:6–8). Paul's point in 10:5 is that Israelites who lived during the era of the Mosaic covenant were expected to live by the requirements of that covenant. There was no other option at that time.

But in Romans 10:6, Paul introduces a different situation and era because of Jesus. Moo notes that Paul's use of *de* ("but") early in verse 6 carries "an adversative meaning."[2] So a contrast occurs. The new situation Paul addresses in 10:6–8 is different than what verse 5 described concerning keeping the Mosaic Law for righteousness. Whereas righteousness was linked with the Law of Moses in 10:5, Paul now speaks of a new situation linked with a "righteousness based on faith." As he explains:

> But the righteousness based on faith speaks as follows: "Do NOT SAY IN YOUR HEART, 'WHO WILL ASCEND INTO HEAVEN?' (that is, to bring Christ down), or 'WHO WILL DESCEND INTO THE ABYSS?' (that is, to bring Christ up from the dead)." But what does it say? "THE WORD IS NEAR YOU, IN YOUR MOUTH AND IN YOUR HEART"—that is, the word of faith which we are preaching. (Rom. 10:6–8)

Paul personifies this "righteousness based on faith," making it speak like a human person.[3] He appeals to Moses' wording from Deuteronomy 30:11–14. Significantly, though, Paul is not explaining or interpreting the meaning of Deuteronomy 30:11–14. Understanding this is crucial for a correct interpretation. Instead, Paul quotes this passage to contrast what Moses said needed to be done during the Mosaic covenant era with what must now be done in the New covenant era. Thus, the quotation is not given to exegete Deuteronomy 30:11–14 but to contrast a new situation in Christ.

So what is the context of Deuteronomy 30:11–14? Deuteronomy 30 detailed both blessings and curses for keeping and breaking the Mosaic covenant to the second generation of Israelites after the Exodus (see Deut. 28–30). Moses offered a big-picture, trans-generational presentation of Israel's future in Deuteronomy 30. Israel will experience both blessings and curses, including eventual removal from the promised land because of covenant disobedience. This prediction was particularly remarkable since Israel had not yet started the conquest of Canaan, but the people were told that Israel would be removed from the land into captivity. But after this

---

[2] Douglas Moo, *The Epistle to the Romans* (Grand Rapids: Eerdmans, 1996), 650.

[3] Moo notes that "Paul follows the biblical pattern of personifying activities and concepts that are closely related to God." Ibid., 650.

expulsion and captivity by the nations, the Lord will save and restore Israel and bring Israel back into the land of promise with many blessings (Deut. 30:1–10). In sum, Israel would be judged and dispersed for disobedience to the Mosaic covenant, but at a future time God would "circumcise" the "heart" of Israel in what appears to be a reference to the New covenant (see Jer. 31:31–34).

After offering this big-picture prediction of Israel's future, Moses encouraged the current generation of Israel to obey the Mosaic covenant because it is straightforward in meaning and accessible. He told Israel, "this commandment...is not too difficult for you" (Deut. 30:11). Thus, God's law is not mysterious or shrouded in mystery. Also, this commandment is accessible. The people of Israel do not have to travel to heaven to get it (Deut. 30:12). Nor is the commandment beyond the sea, so they don't have to get on a ship and cross the sea to find and observe it (Deut. 30:13). Then Moses' message concerning the nearness of God's commandment is summed up in Deuteronomy 30:14: "But the word is very near you, in your mouth and in your heart, that you may observe it."

Thus, the message of Deuteronomy 30:11–14 is this: the Mosaic Law is understandable and accessible. Israel should keep it with no excuses. This is what God expected during that time in history. This message is not hard to understand. It describes the *nearness* and *accessibility* of the Mosaic Law. But what is challenging is how Paul appeals to Deuteronomy 30:11–14 in Romans 10:6–8. For example, how can the ascending that Moses mentioned be linked with bringing Christ down? And how can descending into the abyss be tied to bringing Jesus up from the dead? And why does Paul refer to the "abyss" when Moses mentioned the "sea"? Also, how can the message to keep the Mosaic Law in Deuteronomy 30:14 be tied with Paul's "word of faith" which is tied to Jesus and the New covenant? After all, isn't Paul's point to convince Israel to stop trying to establish their righteousness through the Mosaic Law?

So what is Paul doing? Could he be using a second temple "pesher" hermeneutic by applying an OT passage to a new situation concerning Christ without regard for the original OT context? Is this a christocentric reinterpretation of an OT passage in light of Christ? Or maybe Paul is using language from Deuteronomy 30 to make an impressive rhetorical point without much concern for the original context. Perhaps Paul sees Jesus as the bridge between the Mosaic covenant and the New covenant. Paul did say that Jesus is the "end" or "goal" (*telos*) of the law in Romans 10:4, so maybe Paul is saying Jesus is ultimately the fulfillment of what Moses discussed in Deuteronomy 30:11–14. This latter alternative seems better than the other views mentioned, but still there is a better solution.

The best understanding is that *Paul is taking the language and formula used of the Mosaic covenant in Deuteronomy 30:11–14 and using this formula to explain New covenant realities in Christ.* Paul uses the words and formula once used of the

Mosaic covenant to make a point about conditions with the New covenant. An epochal transition from the Mosaic covenant era to the New covenant era has occurred, and this affects how righteousness should be sought.

Paul is not saying that his words in Romans 10:6–8 are a fulfillment of Deuteronomy 30:11–14 or that his words are the real meaning of Deuteronomy 30. But he uses Moses' words in Deuteronomy 30:11–14 to contrast the nearness in Moses' day of the Mosaic covenant to the nearness of Jesus and the New covenant in the present. In sum, Paul contrasts Moses and seeking righteousness in the era of Moses with Jesus and seeking righteousness in the New covenant period. The point is that it is futile to seek righteousness through the Mosaic Law now that Jesus and the New covenant era have arrived. Note the points of comparison and how Paul substitutes Jesus for the Mosaic Law in the following paraphrases:

> **Moses:** You do not need to travel to heaven to bring the Mosaic covenant down (because it is already near you). (Deut. 30:12)
>
> **Paul:** You do not need to travel to heaven to bring Jesus down (because His incarnation and message are already near you). (Rom. 10:6)
>
> **Moses:** You do not have to cross the sea to get the Mosaic covenant because it is near you. (Deut. 30:13)
>
> **Paul:** You do not have to descend into the abyss to bring up Jesus from the dead (because He and His message are near you). (Rom. 10:7)
>
> **Moses:** The Mosaic covenant is near you. (Deut. 30:14)
>
> **Paul:** The "word of faith" connected with Jesus and the New covenant is near you. (Rom. 10:8)

So Paul is not explaining the meaning of Deuteronomy 30:11–14. He assumes its meaning at face value—namely that the Mosaic covenant was both understandable and accessible. Instead, he uses Moses' formula concerning the Mosaic covenant from Deuteronomy 30:11–14 and replaces the command to keep the Law of Moses with Jesus and the New covenant. This is how "the righteousness based on faith speaks." It is all about Jesus now. What Moses said about the Mosaic covenant was true and operative for a time. But the righteousness based on faith is not about the Mosaic Law anymore; the righteousness based on faith is about Jesus. This addresses Israel's error that Paul explained in 9:30–10:4, namely that Israel was pursuing righteousness through the Mosaic Law after Jesus arrived. As Paul revealed in Galatians 3, the Mosaic Law functioned as a tutor leading to Christ, but now that Christ has arrived that tutor (i.e. the Law) is no longer the way to express righteousness (see Gal. 3:24–25). Now Paul is imploring all people to find God's righteousness in Jesus which is both understandable and near.

What the statements from Moses and Paul have in common are the concepts of easy-to-understand and accessible. Just as the Mosaic covenant was not complicated and readily accessible to Israel during the era of the Mosaic covenant, so too Jesus and His word of faith are not complicated and are readily accessible in the New covenant era.

So how should the use of Deuteronomy 30:11–14 in Romans 10:6–8 be categorized? *This is a case where a NT writer used language concerning the Mosaic covenant and applied it to new conditions associated with Jesus and the New covenant.*

# CHAPTER THIRTY-TWO

# JESUS AS NEW COVENANT LAWGIVER IN MATTHEW 5:21–48

In Matthew 5:21–48, Jesus quoted the OT seven times. Six of these involved an OT command from the Law of Moses followed by the statement, "But I say to you." A seventh concerned a statement that Jerusalem is "the city of the great King," a reference to Psalm 48:2 in Matthew 5:35. This latter example, from Psalm 48:2, is a contextual affirmation of the significance of Jerusalem. Our attention, though, focuses on the other six uses of the OT. These reveal how Jesus viewed himself in relation to the Law of Moses. They are:

- You have heard…"'YOU SHALL NOT COMMIT MURDER' and 'Whoever commits murder shall be liable to the court'…But I say to you…" (Matt. 5:21–22; quotation of Exod. 20:13)
- You have heard that it was said, "'YOU SHALL NOT COMMIT ADULTERY'; but I say to you…" (Matt. 5:27–28; quotation of Exod. 20:14)
- It was said, "'WHOEVER SENDS HIS WIFE AWAY, LET HIM GIVE HER A CERTIFICATE OF DIVORCE'; but I say to you…" (Matt. 5:31–32; quotation of Deut. 24:1)
- Again, you have heard…"'YOU SHALL NOT MAKE FALSE VOWS, BUT SHALL FULFILL YOUR VOWS TO THE LORD.' But I say to you…" (Matt. 5:33–34; allusion to Lev. 19:12; Deut. 23:21)
- You have heard that it was said, "'AN EYE FOR AN EYE, AND A TOOTH FOR A TOOTH.' But I say to you…" (Matt. 5:38–39; quotation of Exod. 21:24; Lev. 24:20; Deut. 19:21)

- You have heard that it was said, "'YOU SHALL LOVE YOUR NEIGHBOR and hate your enemy.' But I say to you…" (Matt. 5:43–44; quotation of Lev. 19:18)

Note the recurring formula, "You have heard" or "It was said," followed by "But I say to you." This repetition links these six uses of the OT with a broader argument.

But how is Jesus using these OT texts from the Law of Moses? Before commenting on this question, observe that the meaning of Matthew 5:21–48 is heavily debated, as is Matthew 5:17–20. These two sections reveal how Jesus viewed the Law of Moses and whether the Mosaic Law is binding on Christians today. Much debate concerns what Jesus meant in these sections.

One view is that Jesus explains the true meaning of the Mosaic Law in Matthew 5:21–48. Thus, Jesus quotes the Mosaic Law to explain it and validate its continued relevance as a binding law.

A second perspective is that Jesus is not quoting the Mosaic Law. Instead, He corrects distortions and additions that the Jewish religious leaders made to the Mosaic Law. Allegedly, Jesus removes rabbinic-tradition clutter from the Law of Moses so the Law can be correctly understood. If this is accurate, Jesus is not really "quoting" Mosaic commands, but He is correcting rabbinic misunderstandings of the Law. Charles Quarles seems to affirm this position: "The formula ["But I say to you"] contrasts Jesus's interpretation of the Scriptures with popular rabbinic interpretations."[1]

A third position is that Jesus actually quotes Mosaic Law instructions to contrast these with His own instructions for the new era He brings. With this view, Jesus is the better Moses and King who offers New covenant instructions that supersede the Mosaic commands. Jesus quotes the Mosaic commands to make a contrast with His teaching.

A fourth and mediating view is that Jesus maintained the Mosaic Law as a rule for life, but He made some modifications to it—namely, He internalized and individualized the Mosaic Law. Turner seems to affirm a version of this perspective: "On the one hand, Jesus does not contradict the law, but on the other hand, he does not preserve it unchanged."[2]

So is Jesus exegeting and confirming the Mosaic Law as a rule of life or is He is giving New covenant instructions for a new era? Or is He doing both, perhaps merging the Mosaic Law with His new commands? Which view one holds affects how the six quotations in Matthew 5:21–48 will be understood.

---

[1] Charles L. Quarles, *Matthew*, Exegetical Guide to the Greek New Testament (Nashville, TN: B & H Publishing, 2017), 55. By "formula" Quarles means the "You have heard it said," and "But I say to you" statements by Jesus.

[2] David L. Turner, *Matthew*, in Baker Exegetical Commentary on the New Testament (Grand Rapids: Baker Academic, 2008), 167.

The third view mentioned above seems best: Jesus was quoting the Mosaic commands to contrast these with His New covenant instruction. This is based on two beliefs. First, Jesus quoted actual Mosaic instructions; He was not addressing rabbinic additions to the Law. All six statements by Jesus are linked with actual Mosaic commands. And second, Jesus emphasized His new words as the Messiah; He was not explaining Moses' words. In His Sermon on the Mount in Matthew 5–7, Jesus offered at least forty-six explicit commands. Note Jesus' emphasis on *His words* at the end of the Sermon:

- Therefore everyone who hears *these words of Mine* and acts on them (Matt. 7:24)
- Everyone who hears *these words of Mine* and does not act on them (Matt. 7:26)
- for He was teaching them *as one having authority* (Matt. 7:29, emphases mine)

The stress in these statements is on Jesus' authoritative words, not those of Moses.

In Matthew 5:17–19, Jesus declared that He did not come to abolish the Hebrew Scriptures (i.e. "the Law or the Prophets"). He came to "fulfill" them. Matthew 5:18 reveals that fulfillment means that everything in the Hebrew Scriptures (i.e. the OT) must come to pass. And one of these predictions from the OT was that there would be a coming New covenant that would supersede the previous Mosaic covenant. Jeremiah 31:31–32 predicted this:

"Behold, days are coming," declares the LORD, "when *I will make a new covenant* with the house of Israel and with the house of Judah, *not like the covenant which I made with their fathers in the day I took them by the hand to bring them out of the land of Egypt*, My covenant which they broke, although I was a husband to them," declares the LORD. (emphases mine)

So fulfillment of the Law and the Prophets includes the prediction that the New covenant would replace the Mosaic covenant.

This does not mean Jesus' New covenant instruction is contrary to what Moses said. This is not an issue of going from wrong to right, but from good to better. As Hebrews 8:6 states concerning the transition from the Mosaic covenant to the New covenant: "He [Jesus] is also the mediator of a better covenant, which has been enacted on better promises." *In sum, with Matthew 5:21–48, Jesus is the ultimate Prophet and Lawgiver who now brings a transition from Moses and the Mosaic covenant to Himself and the New covenant.*

An epochal transition has occurred (see 2 Cor. 3:6–11). Hebrews 8:13 states: "When He said, 'A new covenant,' He has made the first [Mosaic] obsolete." In Galatians 3, Paul said the Law was a "tutor" that leads us to Christ, but now that Christ has come the tutor is no longer needed (see Gal. 3:24–25). This development

244 | The Old in the New

was not unforeseen. Moses himself predicted a coming Prophet to whom the people would listen (see Deut. 18:15, 18), and that prophet arrived with Jesus (see Acts 3:22–23).

Important in Matthew 5:21–48 are the six transitions from "You have heard it said" to "But I say to you." The "but" (*de*) is adversative and indicates a contrast. The "I say" (*egō legō*) highlights the authority of Jesus. To paraphrase, "Moses said...*but I say to you...*" This is more than Jesus explaining Moses; Jesus is the authority as one greater than Moses. John Reisinger rightly notes that Jesus' words, "But I say to you," indicate "redemptive-historical movement."[3]

What does this mean for NT use of the OT? *Jesus' six quotations from the Mosaic Law are contextual and offered for the point of contrast with the new era in Jesus.* There are no explanations of the Mosaic commands mentioned because Jesus takes them at face value in order to transition to His new requirements. And there are no hidden meanings or reinterpretations being offered. Jesus is saying, "Moses said this, but now I'm telling you what I expect."

This understanding is bolstered by the fact that Jesus' six "But I say to you" statements reveal *differing requirements and consequences* than Moses spoke of. Jesus quoted Exodus 20:13 in Matthew 5:21 to show that whoever committed murder during the Mosaic era would be liable to a judicial court. But with the new era Jesus brings, hatred is considered murder, and the consequences of hatred lead to the "fiery hell" (5:22). While the Mosaic Law also addressed heart issues such as coveting (e.g. coveting in Exodus 20:17), Jesus goes beyond the physical act of murder to address hatred. He also points out more severe consequences for hatred—eternal fiery judgment.

Next, in Matthew 5:27 Jesus quoted Exodus 20:14 concerning adultery, and He stated that lust is adultery of the heart (Matt. 5:28). Jesus then declared that radical removal of tempting influences is necessary to avoid adultery, which can lead to hell (Matt. 5:29–30). Jesus requires purity of heart for His followers with implications for eternity.

In Matthew 5:31, Jesus quoted Deuteronomy 24:1, a section of the Mosaic Law that allowed for divorce. But in Matthew 5:32, Jesus declared that divorce should never happen except for sexual immorality. What Jesus said is not much different from what Deuteronomy 24:1–4 stated, but the Mosaic Law temporarily allowed for divorce because of the hardness of men's hearts (see Matt. 19:8). Jesus, though, reestablished the principle from creation that God made man and woman to be joined for life (see Matt. 19:3–9). No divorces were allowed except for sexual immorality. The temporary allowance for divorce under the Mosaic era is removed.

In Matthew 5:33, Jesus alluded to Leviticus 19:12 and Deuteronomy 23:21. Under the Mosaic Law era, oaths to the Lord were not mandated but were allowed.

---

[3] John G. Reisinger, *In Defense of Jesus, the New Lawgiver* (Frederick, MD: New Covenant Media, 2008), 157.

But in the New covenant era, oaths should not be made at all. This is not a statement that oaths in a court of law were not allowed. But for Jesus' followers, their words should be so sure that no oaths are needed (see Matt. 5:34–37).

In Matthew 5:38, Jesus stated that the Mosaic Law command concerning retaliation in Exodus 21:24 should not be enforced for His followers as they serve Him. Instead of seeking retaliation, the followers of Jesus should show radical kindness to those who afflict them (see Matt. 5:39–42) in the cause of Jesus. This is not a statement that governments cannot seek justice for wrongs done, but retributive justice should not be sought for those who persecute Jesus' followers.

Lastly, in 5:43–48 Jesus called for loving both friends and enemies. The command to love your neighbor is an obvious reference to Leviticus 19:18, although the words "as yourself" are missing. The following command in Matthew 5:43b to "hate your enemy" is more difficult to understand. Since there is no explicit command to hate your enemy in the Mosaic Law, some think Jesus is correcting misguided Jewish oral tradition here. A better understanding, though, is that Jesus paraphrased Mosaic instructions concerning enemies of Israel. Deuteronomy 23:3–6 forbade entrance to the assembly for Ammonites and Moabites since they denied food and water to Israel when Israel came out of Egypt. Likewise, Deuteronomy 25:17–19 commanded harsh treatment of the Amalekites for how they mistreated Israel after the exodus from Egypt. According to the Law of Moses, Ammonites, Moabites, and Amalekites were to be treated as enemies for a time.[4] While acknowledging that Jesus could be correcting Jewish oral tradition, Blomberg notes, "It is equally possible that Jesus is summarizing in the second clause of his 'quotation' a very natural inference that could be drawn from the original meaning of various OT passages (e.g. Deut. 23:3–6; 25:17–19…)."[5] Jesus' reference to avoiding hating enemies probably refers to the Mosaic commands concerning Israel's enemies.

In sum, with six of the OT quotations in Matthew 5:21–48, Jesus offered commands for a new era. *He quoted the OT contextually in order to make a contrast.* He did not change the meaning or reinterpret the Mosaic commands. Jesus quoted these to emphasize His role as the New covenant Lawgiver.

---

[4] This will change with New covenant conditions (see Amos 9:11–15).

[5] Craig L. Blomberg, "Matthew," in *Commentary on the New Testament Use of the Old Testament*, ed. G. K. Beale and D. A. Carson (Grand Rapids: Baker, 2007), 27.

# CHAPTER THIRTY-THREE

# GIVING GIFTS TO MEN

## PSALM 68:18 IN EPHESIANS 4:8

Paul's use of Psalm 68:18 in Ephesians 4:8 is one of the most difficult cases to grasp. Psalm 68 itself is challenging to interpret. Referencing Dahood, Harold W. Hoehner noted that "Ps 68 is reckoned 'as textually and exegetically the most difficult and obscure of all the psalms,' and various attempted interpretations have been proposed."[1] In addition, Paul's use of Psalm 68 varies at points from the wording in this psalm.

Psalm 68 is a psalm of triumph written by David. The setting "is probably one of David's victorious returns from battle."[2] The first six verses picture the greatness of God in victory. When He arises His enemies must flee and melt before Him like wax before a fire (vv. 1–2). But the righteous are those who praise Him (vv. 3–4). Verses 7–17 tell of God's great victories. He brought Israel out of Egypt (v. 7), encountered Israel at Sinai (v. 8), brought victory in the land of Canaan (vv. 9–14), and triumphed over Mount Bashan (vv. 15–17). Bashan, as Michael Heiser points out, "carries a lot of theological baggage."[3] It "was the Old Testament version of the gates of hell, the gateway to the underworld realm of the dead."[4] While Sinai was God's mountain, Bashan was viewed as a mount belonging to dark spiritual forces.

---

[1] Harold W. Hoehner, *Ephesians: An Exegetical Commentary* (Grand Rapids: Baker Academic, 2002), 525; Mitchell J. Dahood, *Psalms (51–100)* Anchor Bible, (Garden City, NY: Doubleday, 1966), 133.

[2] Walter C. Kaiser, Jr., *The Messiah in the Old Testament* (Grand Rapids: Zondervan, 1995), 130. Kaiser believes the immediate setting was David's defeat of the Syro-Ammonite coalition (see 2 Sam. 10).

[3] Michael S. Heiser, *The Unseen Realm: Recovering the Supernatural Worldview of the Bible* (Bellingham, WA: Lexham Press, 2015), 289.

[4] Ibid.

Kaiser notes, "The heart of this psalm is verse 18, which depicts the theophanic person ascending into heaven."[5] Psalm 68:18 declares that the Lord (*Adonai*) has: (1) "ascended on high"; (2) "led captive" his "captives"; and (3) "received gifts among men." Some think that the "captives" taken into captivity refer to Israel's opponents defeated in the conquest of the land of Canaan.[6] Kaiser, however, understands the "captives" positively and views them as the Levites who were set apart for service according to Exodus 32 and Numbers 8.[7] Heiser, on the other hand, asserts that the victory is spiritual and involves an assault on evil spiritual forces at Bashan by Yahweh and His holy army. Heiser says, "Yahweh, the divine warrior, will one day tear down the strongholds of Bashan. He will lead a train of captives down from the mountain (v. 18)."[8]

The receiving of gifts among men refers to the spoils of war received from God's vanquished opponents. The truths of the first eighteen verses are an encouragement to Israel for both the present and future (vv. 19–31).

Arnold notes that Psalm 68 "is a prayer that the Divine Warrior will manifest his power, strengthen his people, and defeat the enemies of Israel."[9] In sum, the ascended and triumphant Lord who acted on Israel's behalf in the past is able to do so in the present and in the future. Kaiser understands Psalm 68 as a messianic psalm about the coming Messiah we now know as Jesus. He views verse 18, which Paul will quote in Ephesians 4:8, as "both the pivotal and climactic verse" and "the grand messianic verse of the psalm."[10]

So how does Paul use Psalm 68? In Ephesians, Paul presents Jesus as a victorious and ascended Warrior who is raised from the dead and seated at the right hand of God (see Eph. 1:20–22). This involves Jesus' victory over the spiritual forces of darkness since Jesus is "far above all rule and authority and power and dominion, and every name that is named" (Eph. 1:21; cf. Col. 2:15). In Ephesians 4, Jesus is the triumphant Warrior who gives gifts to His church as a result of His ascension to heaven. To support this, Paul quotes Psalm 68:18 in Ephesians 4:8:

---

[5] Kaiser, *The Messiah in the Old Testament*, 131.

[6] See *The Moody Bible Commentary*, ed. Michael Rydelnik and Michael Vanlaningham (Chicago: Moody Press, 2017), 816.

[7] Kaiser, *The Messiah in the Old Testament*, 132.

[8] Heiser, *The Unseen Realm*, 292. Heiser believes that God (*Elohim*) in 68:15 should be translated "the gods" and refers to evil spiritual forces. Thus, Mount Bashan is ruled by evil forces who look upon God's mountain, Mount Sinai, with envy (see 68:16).

[9] Clinton E. Arnold, *Ephesians: Exegetical Commentary on the New Testament* (Grand Rapids: Zondervan, 2010), 247.

[10] Kaiser, 130.

Therefore it says,
"WHEN HE ASCENDED ON HIGH,
HE LED CAPTIVE A HOST OF CAPTIVES,
AND HE GAVE GIFTS TO MEN."

Paul links Psalm 68:18 with Jesus in three ways: (1) ascension to heaven; (2) victory over enemies; and (3) giving gifts to men. The first point relates to Jesus' ascension to heaven after His earthly ministry including His death, burial, and resurrection. Second, based on Ephesians 1:20–23, the vanquished captives probably refer to evil spiritual forces that Jesus conquered. Third, the giving of gifts refers to the giving of gifted men to the church (i.e. apostles, prophets, evangelists, pastors, teachers).

But how do these truths relate to Psalm 68? After all, Psalm 68 does not appear to predict Jesus and His ascension. Nor does Psalm 68 speak of Jesus giving gifts to the church. And how do we deal with the reality that Psalm 68:18 refers to *receiving* gifts from men, while Ephesians 4:8 tells of Jesus *giving* gifts to men? Receiving gifts from men is not the same as giving gifts to men.[11]

Some believe Paul introduces a startling discontinuity between Psalm 68 and Ephesians 4. Concerning Paul's use of Psalm 68:18, Lunde and Dunne state, "The result is a jarring departure from the meaning of the psalmist and an apparent abandonment of the psalmic context."[12] Referencing Longenecker, Beale notes that some believe the use of Psalm 68:18 in Ephesians 4:8 is a case of "Noncontextual midrashic treatments."[13]

So is Paul being creative and using a non-contextual hermeneutic when he quotes Psalm 68:18 concerning Jesus? Psalm 68 is a description of the ascended and

---

[11] An Aramaic Targum does state "you have given it [i.e. Torah] as gifts to my people." Richard B. Hays and Joel B. Green, "The Use of the Old Testament by New Testament Writers," in *Hearing the New Testament: Strategies for Interpretation* (Grand Rapids: Eerdmans, 1995), 225. Thus, the Targum emphasizes giving gifts like Paul does in Ephesians 4:8. Gleason Archer thought this was significant when he wrote, "Paul also follows the Targum in this—which constitutes significant evidence, by the way, of the antiquity of the interpretative oral tradition that preceded the written form of the Targum (in the third century A.D.). As one trained in the graduate school of Gamaliel, Paul would have been familiar with this Targumic rendition of Psalm 68:18." Gleason L Archer, *Encyclopedia of Bible Difficulties* (Grand Rapids: Zondervan, 1982), 404. Most believe this tradition was too late to be used by Paul and therefore is not a probable solution to this issue.

[12] Jonathan M. Lunde and John Anthony Dunne, "Paul's Creative and Contextual Use of Psalm 68 in Ephesians 4:8," *Westminster Theological Journal* 74 (2012): 101.

[13] G. K. Beale, *Handbook on the New Testament Use of the Old Testament* (Grand Rapids: Baker Academic, 2012), 2. See Richard N. Longenecker, "Can We Reproduce the Exegesis of the New Testament?" *Tyndale Bulletin* 21 (1970): 3–38. Beale is not saying this actually is a case of "noncontextual" use of the OT, but it is "alleged." Lincoln believes this is a case of *midrash pesher*: "The tradition has been taken over by this writer and incorporated into a midrash pesher rendering of the text in which he integrates his exposition of its meaning in the light of fulfillment in Christ into the actual quotation, a procedure which is, of course, not unusual in the contemporary Jewish exegetical techniques or elsewhere in the use of the OT in the NT." Andrew T. Lincoln, "Ephesians," *Word Biblical Commentary* (Dallas, TX: Word Books, 1990), 243.

triumphant Lord who received gifts from men. This encourages God's people both in the present and in the future. While not a prophecy *per se*, it does have a forward element anticipating that the Lord will be triumphant in the future as well. Kaiser even sees this psalm as "a harbinger of the final day of the Lord in the end times."[14]

While a dogmatic conclusion on this issue should be avoided, our estimation is that Paul draws a *correspondence* between the triumphant and ascended Warrior of Psalm 68 and Jesus' ascension, victory over evil forces, and giving of gifts to His church. As Arnold states, "By analogy to God as the triumphant Divine Warrior who, after he ascended his throne, received gifts of homage from his captives, Paul 'depicts Christ as the triumphant Divine Warrior who, after he ascended to his throne, blesses his people with gifts.'"[15] Also, since David expressed a specific messianic hope in other psalms (see Pss. 2, 16, 110), it is not unreasonable to see a hint of messianic expectation in Psalm 68:18.

Altogether, we can say that God has done it again. The ascended and triumphant Divine Warrior of Psalm 68 has shown Himself victorious again in Jesus who has ascended to heaven triumphant over the powers of darkness. He also gives gifts to His people as a result of His victory. Lunde and Dunne observe, "Seen in this light, it is quite plausible that Paul employs this verse because it summarizes the historical parallel between God's actions in the psalm and those accomplished by Jesus."[16]

The difference between receiving gifts (Ps. 68:18) and giving gifts (Eph. 4:8) can be harmonized. The One who receives gifts is also positioned to give gifts as He shares the spoils of victory with His people. In this case, Jesus shares gifted men such as apostle, prophets, evangelists, pastors, and teachers with His church.

While the use of Psalm 68 in Ephesians 4 remains difficult to understand, there are points of continuity between the two passages that indicate a contextual understanding is possible.

---

[14] Kaiser, *The Messiah in the Old Testament*, 131.

[15] Clinton E. Arnold, *Ephesians: Exegetical Commentary on the New Testament* (Grand Rapids: Zondervan, 2010), 252. Arnold quotes Timothy Gombis, "Cosmic Lordship and Divine Gift-Giving: Psalm 68 in Ephesians 4:8," *Novum Testamentum* 47 (October, 2005): 373.

[16] Lunde and Dunne, 107.

# CHAPTER THIRTY-FOUR

# ISRAEL, GENTILES, AND THE PEOPLE OF GOD

## AMOS 9:11–12 IN ACTS 15:16–18

One case that has received much attention is James' quotation of Amos 9:11–12 in Acts 15:16–18. Several exegetical, theological, and textual issues make this a challenging example to interpret. James quotes an OT text that predicted a restored Davidic dynasty and applies this to the current salvation of Gentiles in Acts 15. In doing so, some believe James transcends Amos' original message concerning a restored kingdom for national Israel and makes this about spiritual salvation in the church. Others think James is quoting Amos contextually and that the message of Acts 15 is consistent with the original message of Amos 9. Who is right? To address this issue, this chapter will explain the context of Amos 9:11–15 and then discuss how James quotes this passage in Acts 15:16–18.

## Context of Amos 9:11–15

Amos was from Tekoa in the southern kingdom (Amos 1:1) approximately eleven miles from Jerusalem. He directed his message to the northern kingdom of Israel in the eighth century BC. Even though Israel was prospering, Amos foretold Israel's coming judgment because of covenant disobedience. While conditions seemed normal, calamity was coming for Israel. But while mostly negative in tone, the book ends with a strong message of hope and future blessings in 9:11–15.

Judgment must occur, but ultimately God's promises to David will be fulfilled and the dynasty of David will be restored with blessings both for Israel and the nations on a restored earth. Amos 9:11 reads:

> In that day I will raise up the fallen booth of David,
> And wall up its breaches;
> I will also raise up its ruins
> And rebuild it as in the days of old.

Amos' use of "In that day" points to the indefinite future after a period of judgment also described earlier in his book. On a coming day, God will raise up the "fallen booth" (or "hut"/"tent") of David. This "booth" (*sukkah*) likely refers to the dynasty and house of David (see 2 Sam. 7:11), with implications for a restored Davidic kingdom. The "booth" of David fell on hard times after the days of David and Solomon with division and dispersion for Israel. As Smith states, the dynasty is like "a dilapidated little hut."[1] But God will "raise up" this "fallen booth of David." And, as the last part of verse 11 states, God will "rebuild it as in the days of old." Thus, the Davidic dynasty/kingdom that started with David, but underwent decay because of covenant disobedience, will be rebuilt. Raising up and rebuilding are acts of restoration.

Some believe the words, "I will also raise up its ruins," in Amos 9:11b is best translated, "I will raise up *his* ruins"[2] since the suffix is masculine singular. If so, this emphasizes the kingdom of David and could point to the future David—the Messiah. Kaiser states, "The masculine singular suffix on 'his ruins' . . . referred to David himself and not to the 'hut,' which is feminine."[3] The implications of this are personal and could be messianic: "Thus, under a new, coming David (the Messiah himself), the destroyed house of that promised line of David would rise from the ashes."[4] Amos 9:11 was understood in a messianic way in the intertestamental period. According to 4Q174 1 I, 10–13, there will be a "Branch of David" who "will raise up the tent of David that has fallen, who will arrive to save Israel."[5] This shows a connection between the expectation of the Messiah and Amos 9:11. Sanhedrin 96–97a also interprets Amos 9:11 in a messianic manner.[6] So both contextually and historically,

---

[1] Gary V. Smith, *Amos*, A Mentor Commentary (Ross-shire: Great Britain: Christian Focus Publications, 1998), 379.

[2] "His ruins" is the translation of the King James Bible, English Revised Version, and JPS *Tanakh* 1917.

[3] Walter C. Kaiser, Jr., *The Promise-Plan of God: A Biblical Theology of the Old and New Testaments* (Grand Rapids: Zondervan, 2008), 166.

[4] Ibid.

[5] Geza Vermes, *The Complete Dead Sea Scrolls in English* (New York: Penguin Books, 1998), 494.

[6] It reads, "'Have you heard when Ben Nafle (son of the fallen) will come?' 'Who is Bar Nafle?' he asked. 'Messiah,' he replied. 'Do you call Messiah Bar Nafle?' Yes, for it is written, 'In that day will I raise up the tabernacle of David ha-nofeleth' (that is fallen)." http://www.come-and-hear.com/sanhedrin/sanhedrin_96.html.

there are good reasons to hold that Amos 9:11–12 includes the idea of a personal Messiah. Verse 12a then reveals how a rebuilt dynasty of David will affect the Gentiles:

> That they may possess the remnant of Edom
> And all the nations who are called by My name.

A rebuilt Davidic dynasty means a possession of Edom and other nations who will be called by God's name at this time.

The "that" offers what will happen as a result of the restored Davidic dynasty. Edom, a traditional enemy of Israel, will be possessed by Israel. More specifically, the text speaks of the "remnant of Edom." Glenny believes the remnant "is most likely whatever remains after the judgment of the cities of Edom described in 1:11–12."[7]

Being possessed by a restored Israel could at first glance seem oppressive for Edom. Yet in this context, the "nations" possessed by Israel will be called by God's name. In other words, Edom and the nations will become the people of God—hardly a negative happening. The possession seems related to blessings.

This idea of Amos 9:12 is not unique. Isaiah 19 predicts that Israel on a coming day (v. 16) will "become a terror to Egypt" (v. 17) at the same time Egypt also is called "My [God's] people" (v. 25). Egypt will even build a monument to God in the land of Egypt (see Isa. 19:19). Egypt's coming fear of Israel will coincide with Egypt's blessings and inclusion in the people of God alongside Israel and other nations.

Because of a prevailing conquest-ethic throughout history, being possessed by another nation often meant calamity for the possessed nation. But that will not be the case when Israel is restored under the Messiah in a righteous kingdom. The foundational Abrahamic covenant indicated that God's choice of Israel would mean the blessings of the nations (see Gen. 12:2–3; 18:18; 22:18). Psalm 67:7 states: "God blesses us [Israel], that all the ends of the earth may fear Him." When Israel is restored, the nations of the world will be blessed too.

Verses 13–15 then describe the prosperity of kingdom conditions at this time. The ruined cities of Israel will be rebuilt and great prosperity will occur, including agricultural abundance. Also, Israel will never be removed from her land again.

In sum, the message of Amos 9:11–15 is this: *After severe judgment for covenant disobedience, God will restore the fallen dynasty of David from its decayed*

---

Accessed May 11, 2018. See Davis Prickett, "Acts 15:13–18 and the Use of Amos 9:11–12," unpublished paper (The Master's Seminary, 2008), 20.

[7] W. Edward Glenny, "Gentiles and the People of God: A Study of Apostolic Hermeneutics and Theology in Acts 15," unpublished paper presented at National Evangelical Theological Society meeting (2006), 5.

condition. *This includes a restored Israel in which Israel's cities will be rebuilt and will prosper in abundance. These conditions will be permanent. This restored Davidic dynasty and kingdom also results in blessings for the nations who will be called by God's name.* Thus, a book focused much on the judgment of Israel ends with a stunning and glorious picture of hope for Israel and the nations.

# The Informing Theology of Amos 9:11–15

In addition to the context of Amos, there is a deeper theological backdrop for Amos 9:11–15 that involves four major areas. The first is the Abrahamic covenant and the Davidic covenant. These covenants predicted that Israel and Israel's land would be the basis for blessing Gentile nations. Genesis 12:2–3 foretold that through Abraham and Israel "all the families of the earth will be blessed." In 2 Samuel 7, God said David's dynasty would be linked with permanent blessings for Israel (see 2 Sam. 7:10). This Davidic covenant was also a "charter for mankind" that would bless all people groups beyond Israel (2 Sam. 7:19).[8] As Robert Saucy explains:

> The Davidic promise has universal dimensions. It was not limited to a narrow nationalism that concerned only the kingdom of Israel. Rather, the blessing of the righteous rule of the promised Davidic seed was to extend to all nations.[9]

A second backdrop of Amos 9:11–15 is the Israel-Edom relationship stemming from the trajectories of the twin sons of Isaac—Jacob and Esau, as explained in Genesis 25:22–23. There it was predicted that "two nations are in your womb [Israel and Edom]," and "the older [Esau] shall serve the younger [Jacob]" (cf. Mal. 1:2–3). Esau's descendants, which became Edom, became a nemesis for the people of Israel stemming from Jacob. Edom even blocked the people of Israel from moving through their land as Israel proceeded to the promised land (see Num. 20:18–21). So the historical enmity between Edom and Israel is an important backdrop for Amos 9:11–12.

Third, Numbers 24:17–18 is also important for Amos 9:11–15 since this is a messianic text with implications for Israel and Edom. When the people of Israel were on their journey to the Promised Land, Balak, king of Moab, wanted the prophet

---

[8] Paul Williamson translates this as "this is the instruction of/for humanity" and "relates to David's exalted status in the larger scheme of things." Paul R. Williamson, *Sealed with an Oath: Covenant in God's Unfolding Purpose* (Downers Grove, IL: InterVarsity Press, 2007), 129.

[9] Robert L. Saucy, *The Case for Progressive Dispensationalism: The Interface between Dispensational and Non-Dispensational Theology* (Grand Rapids: Zondervan, 1993), 62.

Balaam to curse God's people. But not only did Balaam not curse Israel, he offered a messianic prophecy:

> I see him, but not now;
> I behold him, but not near;
> A star shall come forth from Jacob,
> A scepter shall rise from Israel. (Num. 24:17a)

Then Numbers 24:18a connects the predicted Messiah of 24:17a to the possession of Edom: "Edom shall be a possession." Together, these two verses reveal that the coming Messiah is linked with the possession of Israel's enemy, Edom, something also predicted in Amos 9:11–12.

Fourth, Edom is often presented as representative of other nations. With Psalm 137; Isaiah 34; Isaiah 63; Lamentations 4; and Obadiah 1, Edom is presented as an archetype for all nations opposed to Israel. However, if Edom can be the archetype of Israel's enemies, then it can also be the archetype of the nations who will be blessed by God when Israel is restored. This is probably the case in Amos 9:12 when Amos mentions Edom and other nations who will be called by God's name.

# Acts 15:14–18

According to James, Amos 9:11–12 intersects with the situation described in Acts 15. Acts 15 recounts the famous Jerusalem Council which offered a decision from the apostles and elders in Jerusalem concerning Gentile believers. Some from the "sect of the Pharisees" wanted to circumcise believing Gentiles and force them to observe the Law of Moses (Acts 15:1, 5). This would mean putting Gentiles under the umbrella of Israel and the Mosaic covenant. Understanding the main issue in Acts 15 is crucial for understanding how James uses Amos 9. *The issue before the Jerusalem Council was not kingdom promises to Israel in the OT. Instead, it concerned how believing Gentiles should be viewed and what was required of them.*

After Peter explained that God had saved the Gentiles through faith and gave them the Holy Spirit (Acts 15:6–11), Barnabas and Paul also related how God was doing great things among the Gentiles (15:12). James then quoted Amos 9:11–12 in making his argument:

> Simeon has related how God first concerned Himself about taking from among the Gentiles a people for His name. With this the words of the Prophets agree, just as it is written,

"AFTER THESE THINGS I will return,
AND I WILL REBUILD THE TABERNACLE OF DAVID WHICH HAS FALLEN,
AND I WILL REBUILD ITS RUINS,
AND I WILL RESTORE IT,
SO THAT THE REST OF MANKIND MAY SEEK THE LORD,
AND ALL THE GENTILES WHO ARE CALLED BY MY NAME,"
SAYS THE LORD, WHO MAKES THESE THINGS KNOWN FROM LONG AGO.
(Acts 15:14–18)

James asserted that God is taking the Gentiles to be "a people for His [God's] name" (v. 14). Believing Gentiles were becoming the people of God. While once limited to Israel, the "people of God" concept has been expanded beyond Israel to include non-Israelites. This point was not yet fully grasped. Yet this truth was not unforeseen. James says the "Prophets agree" with this reality (v. 15), showing that multiple OT prophets predicted this development. Although he will only quote Amos, the message of Amos is detected in other prophets too.

The word "agree" (*sumphoneō*) has caused some debate. Some think "agree" is synonymous with "fulfill" (*pleroō*), so what Amos predicted was being fulfilled. Others, though, believe James' use of "agree" does not mean fulfillment is occurring. Some think a *principle* from Amos is being drawn upon without a fulfillment occurring.

James then quotes Amos 9:11–12. But his quotation, at times, differs from both the Masoretic Text (MT) and the Septuagint (LXX). For example:

| | |
|---|---|
| MT | Amos 9:11a: "In that day" |
| LXX | Amos 9:11a: "In that day" |
| NT | Acts 15:16a: "After these things" |

James' use of "After these things" probably indicates a paraphrase of "In that day" and does not indicate an intentional change of Amos' meaning.[10] Both Amos and James refer to the time period when God restores the booth of David in a way connected with Gentile blessings. Another difference between the MT and LXX concerns Acts 15:16b and the rebuilding of the booth/tent of David:

| | |
|---|---|
| MT: | Amos 9:11b: "I will raise up the booth of David which is fallen." |
| LXX: | Amos 9:11b: "I will raise up the tent of David that has fallen." |
| NT: | Acts 15:16b: "I will return and I will rebuild the tabernacle [i.e. tent] of David which has fallen." |

---

[10] O. Palmer Robertson, "Hermeneutics of Continuity," in *Continuity and Discontinuity*, 97, 101.

Differing from the MT and LXX, James adds, "I will return." Some think James adds "I will return" to refer to the second coming of Jesus. Others believe the additional wording relies on Jeremiah 12:15 which tells of the Lord restoring Israel after uprooting them from the land. That James could rely on ideas and wording from other OT passages is possible since he already stated that his message is connected with the "prophets" in a plural sense. So to add words from elsewhere is not inconceivable. "I will return" probably refers to the time when the Lord begins to restore the Davidic dynasty after a period of judgment.

Amos also spoke of the "booth" or "hut" (*sukkah*) of David being raised up again. A booth is often depicted as a temporary dwelling place (see Lev. 23:42–43). In this context, "booth" probably refers to the dynasty and house of David that declined since the time of David and Solomon. James' use of *skene* is best translated "tent" and is consistent with the *sukkah* ("booth") that Amos mentioned.

In Acts 15:16c, James quoted Amos 9:11b: "AND I WILL REBUILD ITS RUINS, AND I WILL RESTORE IT." This shows that James believed the Davidic dynasty had been rebuilt and restored in some way. But how? Does this mean the promised Davidic kingdom in all its dimensions was currently being fulfilled? If so, this would mean a considerable spiritualizing or reinterpreting of Amos 9 and the OT prophets since they predicted a restored national Israel with the Messiah reigning from Jerusalem over the nations on a prosperous earth (see Isaiah 11). If a spiritualization occurs, some say this could mean the church is the new Israel and that the Davidic kingdom is no longer an earthly kingdom involving geo-political entities on earth. It also would mean the restored Davidic kingdom is primarily about individual salvation and the church. This indeed would mean a major change in the Bible's storyline. Anthony Hoekema argues that the Amos passage "is being fulfilled right now, as Gentiles are being gathered into the community of God's people."[11] To him, this is "a clear example in the Bible itself of a figurative, nonliteral interpretation of an Old Testament passage dealing with the restoration of Israel."[12]

But such a dramatic change concerning the kingdom is not justified. In Acts 1:6 the apostles asked Jesus, "Lord, is it at this time You are restoring the kingdom to Israel?" Jesus' answer in 1:7 was not that the kingdom was currently restored to Israel, but instead that they were not to know when this would occur. Also, in Acts 3:20–21 Peter explicitly linked the "restoration of all things" with the future, second coming of Jesus. The word for "restoration" (*apokatastasis*) in Acts 3:21 is the same word for "restore" (*apokathistēmi*) in Acts 1:6. This shows that the restoration of the kingdom to Israel is a literal, future reality, not a spiritual present one. In addition, at the end of Acts Paul preached Jesus and the kingdom to the leaders

---

[11] Anthony A. Hoekema, *The Bible and the Future* (Grand Rapids: Eerdmans, 1979), 210.

[12] Ibid.

of Israel with no hint that a dramatic change in the nature of the kingdom had occurred (see Acts 28:17–31). If James revealed a radical change in the nature of the kingdom in Acts 15, this idea does not show up before or after this section in Acts. In short, to claim that the prophesied kingdom concerning Israel in the OT has undergone a major transformation or reinterpretation because of Acts 15:16 seems too much to rightly conclude.

So what does James mean? There is some fulfillment occurring. While the restoration of the kingdom to national Israel with physical blessings awaits the future, *what has been fulfilled is the arrival of Jesus who fulfills the Davidic dynasty expectation. He is the Messiah—the very centerpiece of the Davidic covenant.* Peter's speech in Acts 2:22–36 proved that Jesus is the Messiah, the Son of David, who is now seated at God's right hand. And because of the resurrected and ascended Jesus, both Jews and Gentiles in Him are now part of the people of God. The arrival of Jesus means messianic salvation is now extended to Gentiles. This is explained in Acts 15:17:

> **MT Amos 9:12:** That they may possess the remnant of Edom and all the nations who are called by my name.

> **LXX Amos 9:12:** That the remnant of men, and all the Gentiles upon whom my name is called, may earnestly seek [me].

> **NT Acts 15:17:** SO THAT THE REST OF MANKIND MAY SEEK THE LORD, AND ALL THE GENTILES WHO ARE CALLED BY MY NAME.

The purpose of Acts 15:17 and its use of Amos 9:12 is to show that the rebuilt Davidic dynasty in Jesus is linked with Gentile inclusion in the people of God, which is now happening. So Gentiles becoming the people of God is linked with Jesus the Messiah who has brought this to reality.

Note that Acts 15:17 aligns more with the LXX than the MT by referring to mankind in general. James does not mention "Edom." While the MT mentions "Edom" specifically and then more generally the "nations," James, like the LXX, focuses on mankind in general and not Edom. But why did James not mention "Edom"? It seems that James summarized a truth of the "prophets," more so than exegeting every word of Amos 9. Perhaps James viewed Edom as representative of mankind, and then went directly to implications for the nations in this age. Even the Hebrew spelling of "Edom" and "man" are very similar,[13] which certainly was known by James. Also, it was not the case that Edom was being possessed by national Israel

---

[13] Compare *edom* and *adam*.

at the time of Acts 15. That aspect of Amos 9:12 probably points to conditions associated with Jesus' second coming and kingdom.

Therefore, the point of Acts 15:16–17 is that *the rebuilt Davidic dynasty in Jesus is linked with the Gentiles seeking the Lord and being called by His name.* This culminates in James' point in 15:14. The implication of this truth is stated by James in Acts 15:19: "Therefore it is my judgment that we do not trouble those who are turning to God from among the Gentiles." The verdict was that Gentiles did not need to come under the umbrella of Israel to be saved.

Thus, what the sect of the Pharisees sought was denied. *The Gentiles will not be required to be circumcised and keep the Mosaic Law. They will not be required to become proselytes to Israel. They are being saved as Gentiles with no requirement of being incorporated into Israel.* James' use of Amos 9:11–12 reveals that this idea was predicted in the OT prophets.

So a real partial fulfillment of Amos 9:11–12 is occurring with Gentile inclusion in the people of God as a result of Jesus. But the meaning of Amos 9:11–12 and the broader section of 9:11–15 is not exhausted and looks to the future. The restoration of national Israel along with physical blessings in the land await future fulfillment. Fulfillment comes in stages. As O. Palmer Robertson stated concerning Amos 9:11–12, "The present fulfillment of Amos' prophecy may be seen as only the 'first stage' of God's consummation activity."[14] More is still to come and will occur with Jesus' second coming to earth.

# Categorizing How James Used Amos in Acts 15:16–18

James' quotation of Amos 9:11–12 in Acts 15:16–18 should be categorized as "Direct Literal Prophetic Fulfillment." Amos predicted that a rebuilt Davidic dynasty would result in Gentiles becoming the people of God as Gentiles, and this was occurring with events in the book of Acts. Jesus, the ultimate David, is the fulfillment of the Davidic dynasty, and He brings messianic salvation to Gentiles as Gentiles.

This does not mean everything predicted in Amos 9:11–15 was fulfilled yet or that Israel's kingdom was fully restored in the present. Amos 9:13–15 is not quoted in Acts 15, and no indication exists that agricultural prosperity and rebuilt cities of Israel were fulfilled. But Jesus the Messiah, who is the centerpiece of the Davidic dynasty, has arrived bringing New covenant salvation to Gentiles as the people of God. Isaiah 52:15 predicted that the Servant of the Lord would "sprinkle many

---

[14] Robertson, "Hermeneutics of Continuity," 108.

nations" with His atoning sacrifice, and the benefits of this were now occurring for believing Gentiles.

In sum, James' use of Amos 9:11–12 is contextual. Amos 9 predicted that Gentiles would become the people of God because of the restored Davidic dynasty. Jesus—the ultimate David—has appeared bringing messianic salvation to Gentiles. This part of Amos 9:11–12 is being fulfilled presently.

# CHAPTER THIRTY-FIVE

# "DO THIS AND LIVE"

## LEVITICUS 18:5 IN ROMANS 10:5 AND GALATIANS 3:12

Another strategic use of the OT in the NT concerns Paul's uses of Leviticus 18:5 concerning the Mosaic Law in Romans 10:5 and Galatians 3:12. A debated issue concerns whether Paul takes a statement about long life in the land and uses it to refer to eternal life. If so, is this a non-contextual use of the OT? We start with a discussion of the context of Leviticus 18:5 as a starting point for understanding how Paul uses this verse.

Leviticus 18:5 stresses the need for Israel to keep God's Law during the Mosaic era as the basis for living prosperously in the land of promise. The verse reads: "So you shall keep My statutes and My judgments, by which a man may live if he does them; I am the Lord." The meaning of Leviticus 18:5 is this: *As God's covenant people, Israel is in relationship with God. So Israel is mandated to obey God by keeping all His commandments. Obeying God's commandments will result in Israel remaining in and living abundantly in the land of promise associated with the Abrahamic covenant.* Note the following from Leviticus 18:5.

## Israel Belongs to God

The first seventeen chapters of Leviticus focus on God's holiness and the significance of offerings and sacrifices. God's presence among His people means His people are to be holy (see Lev. 11:44–45). Leviticus 18:1–5 then functions as a preamble to what follows concerning God's expectations for His people, Israel. Three times God declared the foundational truth that He is Israel's God:

**18:2:** Speak to the sons of Israel and say to them, "I am the Lord your God."

**18:4:** I am the Lord your God.

**18:5:** I am the LORD.

Just before giving the Mosaic covenant in Exodus 20, God claimed the people of Israel as His own when he declared, "I am the LORD Your God" (Ex. 20:2).

Israel, too, had committed themselves to the Lord. Exodus 14:31 states that the people of Israel already had "believed in the Lord," which is similar language to Genesis 15:6 where Abram "believed in the LORD." At Mount Sinai, the people of Israel declared, "All that the Lord has spoken we will do!" (Exod. 19:8; cf. 24:3, 7). So Israel had believed in God, and Israel belonged to Him. As Thomas Schreiner observes, Leviticus 18 "is addressed to those who belong to the Lord." This is because "Israel has been redeemed from Egypt and liberated by God's grace."[1]

Significantly, the command for Israel to obey God's commandments in Leviticus 18:5 comes within a covenantal relationship between God and Israel. Expected obedience is not presented as a means or requirement for a relationship with God (i.e. salvation), but rather the proper response of a people already belonging to God. As Daniel Block states, the Law of Moses was not given as a means of salvation, but "as the grateful response of those who had already been saved."[2] Put another way, in Leviticus 18:5:

It is not:

Obey to *become* My people.

It is:

*Because* you are My people—obey!

## God Commands and Rewards

Leviticus 18:5 begins with, "So you shall keep My statutes and My judgments." The "statutes" and "judgments" refer to the laws of the Mosaic covenant, including the commands in the legal sections of the Pentateuch. These are in contrast to the "abominable customs" of Egypt where Israel previously was enslaved (18:30). Israel was in bondage to Egypt and under its laws, but now Israel belonged to God and was expected to obey God's commandments.

Next, obeying God will result in life—"by which a man may live if he does them" (Lev. 18:5). The "may live" here refers to living a long and abundant life in the land of promise and remaining in the blessings of the Abrahamic covenant. It contrasts with death

---

[1] Thomas R. Schreiner, *40 Questions about Christians and Biblical Law* (Grand Rapids: Kregel, 2010), 59.

[2] Daniel Block, "Law, Ten Commandments, Torah," in *Holman Illustrated Bible Dictionary*, ed. Chad Brand, Charles Draper, and Archie England (Nashville, TN: Holman Bible Publishers, 2003), 1016.

and being cut off and removed from the land of promise. Other passages in Leviticus and Deuteronomy show that obedience is linked with living a long and prosperous life in the land:

> **Lev. 25:18:** You shall thus observe My statutes and keep My judgments, so as to carry them out, that *you may live securely on the land.*

> **Deut. 4:40:** So you shall keep His statutes and His commandments which I am giving you today, that it may go well with you and with your children after you, and that *you may live long on the land* which the Lord your God is giving you for all time.

> **Deut. 5:33:** You shall walk in all the way which the Lord your God has commanded you, that you may live and that it may be well with you, and that *you may prolong your days in the land* which you will possess.

> **Deut. 30:16:** in that I command you today to love the Lord your God, to walk in His ways and to keep His commandments and His statutes and His judgments, that you may live and multiply, and that the Lord your *God may bless you in the land where* you are entering to possess it. (emphases above mine)

In addition, what immediately follows Leviticus 18:5 supports this understanding of life in the land. In Leviticus 18:6–23, God warned Israel to avoid a long list of sexual sins that characterized both the Egyptians and the Canaanites. Then in 18:24–25, God said other nations were being removed from their lands because of sinful actions. Disobedience is linked with removal from the land:

> Do not defile yourselves by any of these things; for by all these the nations which I am casting out before you have become defiled. *For the land has become defiled, therefore I have brought its punishment upon it, so the land has spewed out its inhabitants.* (emphasis mine)

So the nations were being "spewed out" from their lands because of sinful activities. What is significant here is that Leviticus 18 reveals that sinful activity leads to expulsion from the land.

Leviticus 18:26–29 then explicitly states that keeping God's commandments is necessary for Israel to avoid being removed from the land:

> *But as for you, you are to keep My statutes and My judgments* and shall not do any of these abominations, neither the native, nor the alien who sojourns among you

(for the men of the land who have been before you have done all these abominations, and the land has become defiled); *so that the land will not spew you out,* should you defile it, as it has spewed out the nation which has been before you. *For whoever does any of these abominations, those persons who do so shall be cut off from among their people.* (emphases mine)

For Israel, the consequences for disobeying God's commands in Leviticus 18 involved being spewed from the land and "cut off" from the people. Obedience, however, meant remaining in continued blessings in the land.

Leviticus 26 will detail what obedience means. Walking in "My statutes" and keeping "My commandments" (26:3) will lead to rains, agricultural abundance, successful harvests, satisfaction with food, security in the land, lack of harmful beasts, success over enemies, and God's presence (26:3–12). However, disobeying God's commands leads to a reversal of these blessings and dispersion from the land (26:14–45). Leviticus 26, therefore, is a commentary on what living means. Thus, in Leviticus 18:5, "may live" refers to abundant living in the land of promise.

# Leviticus 18:5 in the Old Testament

Inner-biblical connections with Leviticus 18:5 are found in Ezekiel and Nehemiah. The references below reveal that Israel did not heed the instruction of Leviticus 18:5. Israel did not obey God's commands and thus would experience God's cursing in judgment, including expulsion from the land of promise.

**Ezekiel 20:11:** I gave them My statutes and informed them of My ordinances, by which, if a man observes them, he will live.

**Ezekiel 20:13a:** But the house of Israel rebelled against Me in the wilderness. They did not walk in My statutes and they rejected My ordinances, by which, if a man observes them, he will live.

**Ezekiel 20:21a:** But the children rebelled against Me; they did not walk in My statutes, nor were they careful to observe My ordinances, by which, if a man observes them, he will live.

**Nehemiah 9:29:** And admonished them in order to turn them back to Your law. Yet they acted arrogantly and did not listen to Your commandments but sinned against Your ordinances, by which if a man observes them he shall live. And they turned a stubborn shoulder and stiffened their neck, and would not listen.

# Implications of Leviticus 18:5 in the OT

What are some theological implications from Leviticus 18:5 in the OT? First, "may live" in Leviticus 18:5 refers to life in the land of promise for Israel. It does not teach that observance of the Mosaic Law was the requirement for personal salvation or eternal life. As Schreiner notes, "Therefore, in context the verse should not be construed as legalistic or as offering salvation on the basis of works."[3] Some later Jewish tradition will use this verse to claim eternal life is based on law-keeping. But in its context, Leviticus 18:5 and its uses in Ezekiel and Nehemiah were about abundant life in the land.

Second, law-keeping in Leviticus 18:5 concerns those already in a relationship with God. Because Israel belonged to God, Israel was commanded to obey. Thus, keeping the Mosaic Law concerned sanctification, not justification. Adhering to the Mosaic Law was required for all within Israel as a way to express obedience to God. Abraham, the chief example of justification through faith alone (Gen. 15:6), established that justification occurs through faith before and apart from the Mosaic Law (see Gal. 3:17).

Third, law-keeping for Israel is both a corporate and individual matter. Israel as a whole was to keep God's laws and would be held accountable for doing so. Passages such as Leviticus 26 and Deuteronomy 30 predicted that Israel as a corporate entity would be held accountable for covenant disobedience. These chapters predicted a coming dispersion and removal from the land for disobeying God's commands. Hundreds of years later, Ezekiel 20, with its three connections to Leviticus 18:5 (Ezek. 20:11, 13, 21), indicted Israel as a whole for Mosaic covenant disobedience. So too did Nehemiah 9:29. Individuals within Israel also were required to keep the Mosaic covenant (see Deut. 27:15–26). Individuals within Israel could be cut off from Israel for flagrant violations of the Law.

# Leviticus 18:5 in the New Testament

## Romans 10:5

Paul quoted Leviticus 18:5 in Romans 10:5 and Galatians 3:12.[4] Great debate exists concerning how Paul used Leviticus 18:5 in these verses. We begin with Romans 10:5.

In Romans 9:30–10:12, Paul addressed why Gentiles found righteousness while Israel missed it. The reason is that Gentiles discovered faith in Jesus, while Israel tried to establish its righteousness by the Mosaic Law apart from Jesus. In Romans 10:4 Paul

---

[3] Schreiner, *40 Questions about Christians and Biblical Law*, 59.

[4] Some believe Luke 10:28 also references Leviticus 18:5.

asserted that "Christ is the end [*telos*] of the law for righteousness to everyone who believes." He then used Leviticus 18:5 in Romans 10:5: "For Moses writes that the man who practices the righteousness which is based on law shall live by that righteousness."

How Paul used Leviticus 18:5 is heavily debated.[5] Some believe Paul referenced Leviticus 18:5 typologically or non-contextually to argue that eternal life is based on perfect law-keeping, even though no sinful human being actually could obey God's law perfectly. If this is the case, Paul uses Leviticus 18:5 non-contextually, since eternal life was not the issue in Leviticus 18:5. A better view, though, is that Paul is making an epochal or historical contrast between what was required during the era of the Mosaic Law (Rom. 10:5) and what was required with the new era of "faith" in Jesus (Rom. 10:6–8).

Romans 10:6 begins with a contrast from verse 5, "*But* the righteousness based on faith speaks as follows..." (emphasis mine). In sum, Paul contrasts pursuing righteousness during the Mosaic covenant era (Rom. 10:5) with pursuing righteousness in the era of Jesus the Messiah (see Rom. 10:6–8). During the Mosaic covenant era, a person was expected and obligated to live by the commands of the Mosaic covenant as Leviticus 18:5 reveals, but with the coming of Jesus one should follow "the righteousness based on faith" linked with Jesus (Rom. 10:6). If this understanding is accurate, then Paul used Leviticus 18:5 contextually since he simply pointed out that before Christ the people of Israel were expected to obey the Mosaic commands. The primary issue is not whether the phrase "shall live" refers to eternal life or not. The issue concerns adherence to the Mosaic Law commands during the era of Moses. That changes with the New covenant era in Jesus.

## Galatians 3:12

Another Pauline use of Leviticus 18:5 is found in Galatians 3:12, which reads: "However, the Law is not of faith; on the contrary, 'HE WHO PRACTICES THEM SHALL LIVE BY THEM.'" Is Paul's words, "HE WHO PRACTICES THEM SHALL LIVE BY THEM" a declaration that the Mosaic Law demanded perfect law-keeping for salvation? Or, is Paul making an epochal or historical comparison between the Mosaic covenant and Abrahamic covenant realization in Jesus? In a way similar to Romans 10:5, the answer appears to be the latter.

Galatians 3:12 is given in the context of Paul's explanation that the Galatians should not put themselves under the Mosaic Law after having received the Holy Spirit through faith (see Gal. 3:1–5). Paul argued that Christians are now connected with the Abrahamic

---

[5] Commenting on Paul's use of Leviticus 18:5 in Galatians 3:12 Willitts declares, "The function of Leviticus 18:5 in the argument of [Galatians] chapter 3 is hotly debated as is the entire section in which it appears." Joel Willitts, "Context Matters: Paul's Use of Leviticus 18:5 in Galatians 3:12," *Tyndale Bulletin* (January 2003): 105.

covenant as realized in Christ, not the Mosaic covenant (see Gal. 3:6–29). The contrast between the Mosaic and Abrahamic covenants is key to a proper understanding here. God had His purposes for the Mosaic Law, but salvation in this law was not one of them.

With 3:10, Paul asserted that everyone under the Mosaic Law is under a curse. Then with verse 11, he states that "no one is justified by the Law." When he says, "The Law is not of faith; on the contrary, 'HE WHO PRACTICES THEM SHALL LIVE BY THEM'" in Galatians 3:12, Paul again declared an epochal or historical transition from the Mosaic era to the New covenant era in Jesus, an era of Abrahamic covenant realization (see Gal. 3:16). Those under the Mosaic Law were required to live by the mandates of the Mosaic Law—a law that comes with a curse and is not characterized by faith. But now that Jesus arrived, the situation has changed. With Galatians 3:24–25, Paul says the Mosaic Law functioned as a "guardian" or "tutor" until Christ, but now that Christ has come, the tutor (i.e. the Law) is no longer needed. This is an epochal transition statement showing a contrast in eras. Thus, two eras are in view. "Law" represents the Mosaic Law era, and "faith" represents Abrahamic covenant realization in Jesus. As Joel Willetts rightly notes:

> Read this way, the contrast between 'faith' and 'law' implied in 3:11b and 12 is not between two mutually exclusive bases for righteousness (law/gospel antithesis), or two contradictory statements in the scripture (apocalyptic fulfilment), but between historical periods in salvation history: the period of unrealised covenant potential (3:12) and the period of realised covenant potential (3:11b). In other words, to be related to the Sinai covenant is to be related to the age (or historical period) of unfaithfulness and judgment (covenantal curse). On the other hand, being related to the new eschaton signified in the term πίστις (3:23) means being related to the age of faithfulness and blessing (covenantal promise) through Christ's redemption.[6]

This use of Leviticus 18:5 in Galatians 3:12 supports Paul's argument from 3:1–5 that Christians should not place themselves under the Mosaic covenant. Receiving the Holy Spirit is the result of Abrahamic covenant realization in Jesus, not returning to the Mosaic covenant.

In sum, Paul's two uses of Leviticus 18:5 in Romans 10:5 and Galatians 3:12 are contextual. He quotes Leviticus 18:5 in both to show that living by the Mosaic covenant was required for an earlier era, but not for the new era in Jesus.

---

[6] Willetts, "Context Matters," 119.

# CHAPTER THIRTY-SIX

# "ALLEGORICALLY SPEAKING" IN GALATIANS 4:21–31

Do the NT writers ever use the OT allegorically? To answer this question we must look at the curious case of Galatians 4:21–31 where allegory wording is mentioned.

In Galatians 4:21–31, Paul refers to Genesis concerning the mother-son relationships of Hagar/Ishmael and Sarah/Isaac.[1] He also quotes the OT twice— Isaiah 54:1 (in Gal. 4:27) and Genesis 21:10 (in Gal. 4:30). Of particular interest though is Paul's mention of allegory language in Galatians 4:24; Paul writes concerning Hagar and Sarah: "This is allegorically speaking, for these women are two covenants." Does Paul's mention of allegory here (*allēgoreō*) sanction the use of allegorical interpretation for understanding the OT? Or is there another option?

The context is key to understanding what Paul is doing here. Paul's main point in Galatians is to warn his readers against placing themselves under the Mosaic Law, since being under the Law cuts them off from grace in Christ (see Gal. 5:4). Galatians 3–4 is a polemic concerning the superiority of the faith and promise-based Abrahamic covenant and the works and curse-based Mosaic covenant. Paul's overall argument is stated explicitly in Galatians 3:17–18:

> What I am saying is this: the [Mosaic] Law, which came four hundred and thirty years later, does not invalidate a [Abrahamic] covenant previously ratified by God, so as to nullify the promise. For if the inheritance is based on law, it is no

---

[1] Sarah's name is not explicitly mentioned, but Sarah is strongly implied.

269

longer based on a promise; but God has granted it to Abraham by means of a promise.

Paul will then say that the Mosaic Law functioned as a temporary tutor until Christ (see Gal. 3:23–25), and all believers belong to Christ as descendants of Abraham (see Gal. 3:28). Paul continues his explicit discussion of these issues in Galatians 4:1–20.

After his didactic explanation concerning why Christians are under the Abrahamic covenant, not the Mosaic covenant, Paul then offers his "allegorically-speaking" discussion of Hagar and Sarah (4:21–31). Thus, Paul appeals to the accounts of Hagar and Sarah, as found in Genesis, to further support his argument previously made in Galatians 3:1–4:20.

In 4:21 Paul asked, "Tell me, you who want to be under law, do you not listen to the law?" This again shows that the Galatian problem was their desire to be under the Mosaic Law. Also, Paul's message comes from "the law" of which they should be listening:

> For it is written that Abraham had two sons, one by the bondwoman and one by the free woman. But the son by the bondwoman was born according to the flesh, and the son by the free woman through the promise. (Gal. 4:22–23)

As Paul notes, Genesis presents Sarah's son, Isaac, as a child of promise, while Hagar's son, Ishmael, was a child of the flesh—not a son of promise. Isaac, not Ishmael, would be the descendant of Abraham through whom the special seed line of Israel would come. Interesting, though, is how these characters of Sarah/Isaac and Hagar/Ishmael relate to Paul's argument that his readers should not place themselves under the Mosaic covenant.

In 4:24b Paul stated: "These women are two covenants: one proceeding from Mount Sinai bearing children who are to be slaves; she is Hagar." Particularly significant is Paul's statement that Hagar and Sarah "are two covenants." The two women are likened to two covenants. Hagar represents the Mosaic covenant linked with Mount Sinai. And Sarah represents the Abrahamic covenant associated with the Jerusalem from above (4:26).[2] According to Paul, the historical event of the casting out of Hagar represents the superiority of the Abrahamic covenant over the Mosaic covenant in the present age. Quoting Genesis 21:10, Paul declared:

---

[2] The strong presence of Abraham and the Abrahamic covenant in Galatians, particularly chapter 3, makes this understanding highly likely. This is not to say that the New covenant is not also in view by Paul since the New covenant is an extension and outworking of the Abrahamic covenant.

But what does the Scripture say?
"CAST OUT THE BONDWOMAN AND HER SON,
FOR THE SON OF THE BONDWOMAN SHALL NOT BE AN HEIR WITH THE SON OF THE
FREE WOMAN."
So then, brethren, we are not children of a bondwoman, but of the free woman.
(Gal. 4:30–31)

What are the implications from Paul's hermeneutics here? In Genesis, the accounts of Hagar and Sarah together do not appear to represent a contrast between the Mosaic and Abrahamic covenants, although Sarah is the mother of Isaac who is related to the Abrahamic covenant. Hagar and Ishmael are not related to the Mosaic covenant. Hagar was an Egyptian, and her son, Ishmael was not part of the promised seed line (see Rom. 9:7). In addition, they lived hundreds of years before the Mosaic covenant began. So when Paul linked Hagar with the Mosaic covenant, this seems beyond the context of Genesis.

Key to our question is Paul's statement in Galatians 4:24a—"This is allegorically speaking." Allegory wording often is linked with a meaning unconnected with the context of a text. Schreiner offers a helpful definition: "Allegory may be defined as assigning a meaning to the biblical text that does not fit with its historical context."[3] The mention of allegory often brings to mind allegorists like Philo and Origen who were known for strong allegorical interpretations of Scripture that were divorced from context. But what does Paul mean by "allegorically speaking"?

Four options exist for understanding Paul's use of allegory language. First, Paul could be using "allegory" like Philo did—to convey a meaning totally unconnected with the context of Genesis. If so, Paul abandoned a contextual understanding of Genesis for a non-contextual, allegorical meaning. Some believe this is the case. Moisés Silva observes that "many…are convinced that the apostle is treating us here to a full-blown allegorical interpretation."[4] Thus, one view is that Paul used allegorical interpretation in the traditional sense of meaning unconnected with context.

A second view is that Paul makes a *typological* connection between (1) Hagar/Ishmael and the Mosaic covenant and (2) Sarah/Isaac and the Abrahamic covenant. In this view, Paul understands the Genesis narrative contextually, but he uses Hagar and Sarah to make correspondences with the Mosaic and Abrahamic covenants. In 4:25a, Paul uses the Greek term *sustoicheō* which means

---

[3] Thomas Schreiner, *Galatians*, in Exegetical Commentary on the New Testament, ed. Clinton E. Arnold (Grand Rapids: Zondervan, 2010), 300.

[4] Moisés Silva, "Galatians," in *Commentary on the New Testament Use of the Old Testament*, ed. G. K. Beale and D. A. Carson (Grand Rapids: Baker, 2007), 808. Silva himself does not hold this view.

"corresponds": "Now this Hagar is Mount Sinai in Arabia and *corresponds* to the present Jerusalem."[5] Silva argues for this typological view: "We must not simply assume, however, that his [Paul's] use of the verb *allēgoreō*...corresponds to what modern scholars mean when they speak of 'allegorical interpretation.'"[6] He then says, "Thus, if it turns out that Paul is pointing out a correspondence between two historical realities, we may with good reason regard his reading of Genesis as 'typological' rather than 'allegorical.'"[7]

A third view is that Paul combines both typology and allegory in Galatians 4:21–31. Schreiner takes this view when he says Isaac and Ishmael are used typologically, while Hagar is cited allegorically:

> Probably the best solution is to see a combination of typology and allegory. Paul argues typologically with reference to Isaac and Ishmael, especially in 4:21–23 and 4:28–30...There are clearly, however, allegorical elements in the argument, particularly in 4:24–27. The fundamental reason for seeing the text as having an allegorical component is the identification of Hagar with the Sinai covenant.[8]

Fourth, Paul could be using allegory language as an *illustrative* or *teaching tool* to make his point vivid to his readers. Thus "allegorically speaking" could be understood as "illustratively speaking." After stating explicitly his views concerning the Mosaic and Abrahamic covenants in Galatians 3:1–4:20, Paul utilizes the Hagar and Sarah accounts to culminate his point in a picturesque way. This is not an exegesis of Genesis, but the using of Genesis in an illustrative way. Much like Jesus used parables to connect real life situations with spiritual truths, perhaps Paul uses the persons of Hagar/Ishmael and Sarah/Isaac to illustrate truths concerning the covenants. *The Holman Christian Standard Bible* offers a translation of Galatians 4:24 consistent with this view: "These things are *illustrations*."[9] If this is accurate, Paul is not introducing allegory as an interpretive principle, but as a tool for illustration. Much like the use of metaphors and similes—illustration can be used within a contextual approach for picturing certain truths.

Of the four views mentioned above, the first view is the least plausible. Paul does not show a wanton disregard for history and context like Philo or Origen did. His points are rooted in historical events. Next, the third view that Paul used both typology and allegory seems too complicated, particularly when better and simpler views exist. This leads us to the better options.

---

[5] Emphasis mine.

[6] Silva, "Galatians," 808.

[7] Ibid. Silva makes the main contrast between "Spirit and flesh."

[8] Schreiner, *Galatians*, 300.

[9] Emphasis mine.

The second view, with its typological understanding, is possible. In Galatians 4:25, Paul says "corresponding to" which could indicate a typological connection. To connect Sarah and Isaac with the Abrahamic covenant seems reasonable. On the other hand, it is difficult to see how Hagar could be a type of the coming Mosaic covenant when there is so little to connect these two.

The fourth view is the best option—the illustration view. Paul's mention of "allegorically speaking" does not mean allegorical or typological *interpretation*, but illustration. After explicitly making a case in plain words, Paul then uses Hagar/Ishmael and Sarah/Isaac as illustrations to show the superiority of the Abrahamic covenant over the Mosaic covenant.

The order of Paul's argument also is significant. Paul's assertion is not based solely on the Hagar-Sarah comparison. First comes his argument in explicit teaching language in Galatians 3:1–4:20. In fact, if Paul never offered the Hagar/Sarah analogy, we would still know his main point. But then he uses the illustration from Genesis to support his argument. Paul lets the readers know he is shifting teaching tactics by saying "this is allegorically speaking." He cues the reader that he is using a different tactic to supplement his main point. Paul does not say he is interpreting allegorically. He says the Genesis account is "allegorically speaking." He uses a story from Genesis to make an illustrative point.

It should also be noted that Paul's "allegorically speaking" statement does not concern a particular passage of Scripture—it involves a story from Genesis involving two mothers and their sons. This makes it even more unlikely that he is claiming certain passages have a hidden allegorical meaning or that he believes in an occasional use of allegorical interpretation.

In sum, Paul's use of allegory language in Galatians 4 is challenging. Yet, a reasonable and likely argument can be made for a contextual use of the OT here.

# CHAPTER THIRTY-SEVEN

# LOOKING ON THE PIERCED ONE

## ZECHARIAH 12:10 IN THE NEW TESTAMENT

Zechariah 12:10 is strategic to the theology and message of the NT writers. This verse is referenced in Matthew 24:30; John 19:37; and Revelation 1:7. Also, Zechariah 12:10 has implications for both the first and second comings of Jesus. We begin with the context of Zechariah 12:10 before examining its use in the NT.

## Context of Zechariah 12:10

The book of Zechariah was written around 500 BC. Zechariah 12–14 is the second "burden" offered by the prophet Zechariah to Israel. It is an eschatological section that predicts a coming siege of Jerusalem by the nations. This siege would result in a rescue of the house of David and the inhabitants of Jerusalem with implications for the land of Judah. Yahweh goes forth on Jerusalem's behalf to rescue His people. He delivers, saves, and restores Israel. He also sets up His kingdom upon the earth over the nations (see Zech. 14:9).

In Zechariah 12:1–9, Yahweh is presented as the sovereign Creator of heaven, earth, and men who strategically uses Jerusalem to confuse and punish the nations opposed to His holy city and people. In 12:10, Zechariah makes three points: (1) the Lord (Yahweh) will pour out His Spirit on the house of David (10a); (2) the people of Jerusalem will look on the One they pierced (10b); and (3) Israel will repent—mourning and weeping bitterly for the One they pierced (10c). This verse states:

I [Yahweh] will pour out on the house of David and on the inhabitants of Jerusalem, the Spirit of grace and of supplication, so that they will look on Me whom they have pierced; and they will mourn for Him, as one mourns for an only son, and they will weep bitterly over Him like the bitter weeping over a firstborn.

The pouring out of the "Spirit of grace" probably refers to God bringing Israel into the New covenant and giving Israel His Holy Spirit (see Isa. 59:20–21; Ezek. 36:27). Also significant is Yahweh's statement that the people of Jerusalem will "look on Me whom they have pierced; and they will mourn for Him." The "look on Me" appears to be unto salvation with repentance.[1] Israel will look to Yahweh, upon the One they previously "pierced."

That Yahweh is "pierced" is stunning, particularly since "pierced" is likely literal[2] and involves death. The term *dāqar* is found eleven times in the OT and consistently refers to a stabbing or piercing through with a spear. In Numbers 25:8 Phineas "pierced [*dāqar*]…through" an Israelite man and a Midianite woman who acted wickedly.

But how can Yahweh be pierced resulting in death? Since God is spirit and cannot die, some understand this to be a figurative piercing. But the answer is found in the Messiah, who represents Yahweh and was mentioned in Zechariah 9:9–10 and probably 11:4–14. Piercing the Messiah is piercing Yahweh.[3] This may hint at the divinity of this representative of Yahweh who we now know as Jesus. Isaiah 53 also speaks of a piercing of the Servant of the Lord who dies on behalf of Israel (see Isa. 53:5).

Also significant is that Israel is the agent that "pierced" Yahweh. And with the predicted events of Zechariah 12, Israel repents with a deep mourning, a mourning that affects Israel as a corporate entity and the families and individuals within Israel (see Zech. 12:11–14). The One Israel killed is the One over whom Israel will weep and look to for salvation.

# Zechariah 12:10 in the NT

## Matthew 24:30

The first use of Zechariah 12:10 in the NT occurs in Matthew 24:30 during Jesus' Olivet Discourse concerning the sign of His coming and the end of the age (see Matt. 24:3):

---

[1] In Numbers 21:9 Israel "looked to" the bronze serpent in faith to receive healing.

[2] Rydelnik notes, "Since all other uses of the verb 'pierce' refer to literal piercing (Nm 25:8; Jdg 9:54; 1 Sm 31:4; Is 13:15; Jr 37:10; 51:4; Zch 13:3), it is better to take this verse literally as well." Michael Rydelnik, "Zechariah," in *The Moody Bible Commentary*, ed. Michael Rydelnik and Michael Vanlaningham (Chicago, IL: Moody Publishers, 2014), 1433.

[3] Rydelnik says, "It refers to the piercing of a representative of God, namely the incarnate Messiah." Ibid., 1433.

> And then the sign of the Son of Man will appear in the sky, and then *all the tribes of the earth will mourn,* and they will see the SON OF MAN COMING ON THE CLOUDS OF THE SKY with power and great glory.[4]

In this verse, Jesus refers to His bodily return to earth, or what is often called the Second Coming.[5] But there is debate concerning what Jesus meant by "all the tribes of the earth will mourn." The word for "earth" is *gēs* and could be translated "earth" in a global sense, or "land" more narrowly concerning the land of Israel. Both understandings of *gēs* are found in Matthew, and both meanings are possible here.[6] Context must be the determining factor. Is Jesus referring to all the people groups of earth, or is He referring specifically to the tribes of ethnic Israel in the land of Israel?

Most translations opt for the broader understanding of "earth," and hold that Jesus refers to all people groups on earth who mourn in despair at Jesus' return. Few Christians would dispute that the return of Jesus will be a time of great distress for all people groups on the earth. The global calamities of the seal, trumpet, and bowl judgments that come upon the unrepentant "dwellers of the earth" in Revelation 6–19[7] bolster this understanding. If this broader view is correct, the mourning Jesus speaks of is that of despair, not repentance, by the people groups on earth. If accurate, this would mean there is some discontinuity with the original meaning of Zechariah 12:10, since the mourning in Zechariah 12 concerns repentance by a rescued Israel.

On the other hand, the narrower understanding—"tribes of the land"—in reference to the tribes of ethnic Israel in the land of Israel makes sense contextually. From Matthew 24:15 onward Jesus spoke of events related specifically to Jerusalem, the temple, and the land of Judah. This includes the "abomination of desolation," a very Jewish event (see Dan. 9:27) that causes the Jewish people to flee for their lives (Matt. 24:16–22). That Jesus could refer to a rescue of the tribes of Israel in the land of Israel fits with the Jewish nature of Matthew 24. It also fits symmetrically, since the persecution of Israel (Matt. 24:15–22) will be reversed by the Messiah's rescue of Israel in Matthew 24:30–31. If this understanding is correct, compare how Matthew 24 corresponds with the scenario of events in Zechariah 12:

---

[4] Emphases mine.

[5] We acknowledge that those who hold to a preterist view would put the events of Matthew 24:30 at the time of the destruction of Jerusalem in AD 70.

[6] The broader sense is found in but not limited to Matthew 5:13; 6:10, 19; 9:6; 11:25; 28:18. A more narrow sense for a form of this word exists in Matthew 2:6 ("land of Judah"), 2:20 ("land of Israel"), 2:21 ("land of Israel"); 9:26, 31.

[7] See Revelation 3:10; 6:10; 8:13; 11:10; 12:12; 13:8, 14; 17:2, 8. The earth dwellers are presented as unrepentant.

| Zechariah 12:1–14 | Matthew 24:15–31 |
|---|---|
| Persecution of Jews in Israel (Zech. 12:1–2) | Persecution of Jews in Israel (Matt. 24:15–22) |
| The LORD comes on behalf of Israel (Zech. 12:8–9) | Return of Jesus to rescue Israel (Matt. 24:29–30) |
| Mourning (repentance) of families of Israel (Zech. 12:10–14) | Mourning of tribes of Israel (Matt. 24:30) |

If Matthew 24:30 refers to Israelite tribes in the land of Israel, then the mourning would be comparable to the mourning described in Zechariah 12:10—a mourning of national repentance in Israel, not a mourning of despair as posited by the entire earth view. A similar use of Zechariah 12:10 occurs in Revelation 1:7, but first, we must look at the next use of Zechariah 12:10 in the NT—John 19:37.

## John 19:37

John the apostle quoted Zechariah 12:10 when describing Jesus' crucifixion. John 19:31 says the Jews wanted Jesus' body removed from the cross because of the Sabbath. When the Roman soldiers approached Jesus and perceived He was dead, one of them pierced Jesus' side with a spear (see John 19:33–34). Then in 19:37, John quoted Zechariah 12:10b: "And again another Scripture says, 'THEY SHALL LOOK ON HIM WHOM THEY PIERCED.'" Identifying the "they" who pierced Jesus is not immediately evident. The Jews were responsible for Jesus' crucifixion, but the Romans actually crucified Jesus and pierced His side with a spear (see John 19:34).[8] So is it the Jews, Romans, or both who look upon the pierced Jesus? John probably is not making a distinction here. Both the Jews and the Roman soldiers are probably in view. And eventually, salvation will be for both Jews and Gentiles who look unto the pierced Jesus with faith. But we know that the piercing of Jesus is a fulfillment of the piercing predicted in Zechariah 12:10. That is the main point of correspondence between Zechariah 12:10 and John 19:37.

So Zechariah 12:10b was literally fulfilled, not entirely, but partially with the crucifixion and the viewing of the pierced Jesus as described in John 19:37. Significantly, John does not say the Holy Spirit was poured out on Israel (Zech. 12:10a) or that at that time Israel wept and mourned in repentance (12:10c). Those events await

---

[8] Köstenberger observes, "Later messianic interpretation developed the notion of one pierced into the belief that the Messiah ben Joseph, the precursor of the true Messiah, the Messiah ben David (the 'royal messiah'), would be pierced by Israel's enemies, and people would look to Yahweh." Andreas J. Köstenberger, "John," in *Commentary on the New Testament Use of the Old Testament*, 505.

the second coming of Jesus. Thus, it is best to see the use of Zechariah 12:10b in John 19:37 as a case of *literal, partial fulfillment of an OT prophecy*.

# Revelation 1:7

The third use of Zechariah 12:10 in the NT is found in Revelation 1:7. This example has much in common with Matthew 24:30. Writing from the island of Patmos in the 90s AD, John the apostle wrote the following: "BEHOLD, HE IS COMING WITH THE CLOUDS, and every eye will see Him, even those who pierced Him; and all the tribes of the earth will mourn over Him. So it is to be. Amen."

At the time of John's writing, the return of Jesus had not occurred. But John believed it would happen in the future. The first part of Revelation 1:7 is a quotation of Daniel 7:13, a messianic passage about the "Son of Man" who appears with clouds before the Ancient of Days. Jesus also combined Daniel 7:13 and Zechariah 12:10 in Matthew 24:30.

There are three points of correspondence between Zechariah 12:10 and Revelation 1:7 as noted on the chart below. These involve seeing, piercing, and mourning.

|  | **Zechariah 12:10** | **Revelation 1:7** |
|---|---|---|
| **Seeing** | "they will look on Me" | "every eye will see Him" |
| **Piercing** | "whom they have pierced" | "even those who pierced Him" |
| **Mourning** | "and they will mourn for Him" | "and all the tribes of the earth will mourn over Him" |

As in Matthew 24:30, there is debate about Revelation 1:7 concerning who will see Jesus. Is it every people group and person at the time of Jesus' second coming? If so, this would mean every person on earth. Or does it refer specifically to the Jewish people? The best answer is both. "Every eye" most likely refers to all people globally, but "even those who pierced Him" is a reference to a narrower group—the Jews. The Greek word for "even" is *kai*, which usually means "and." Thus, a good translation is "every eye [all people] will see Him *and* those who pierced Him [i.e. the Jews]."[9] Yet, if the *kai* means "even," as many translations have chosen, the Jews are still in mind as those who pierced Jesus [i.e. the Jews] would be a subset of the broader group of "every eye." The HCSB translation interprets this verse as follows: "every eye will see Him, *including* those who pierced Him."[10]

---

[9] Emphasis mine.

[10] Emphasis mine.

And similar to Matthew 24:30, there is debate concerning the identity of "all the tribes of the earth" who will "mourn over Him [Jesus]." Does this refer to all people groups, or does it point to the tribes of ethnic Israel? A case can be made for both views. The earth dwellers from the nations certainly resist the judgments of Jesus during this coming period of tribulation and will be in despair at His return to earth. Yet Zechariah 12 indicates that the families of Israel are the ones who mourn with repentance in connection with the Messiah's return. If Revelation 1:7 is reliant on Zechariah 12:10, which seems to be the case, the tribes of Israel are probably in view. It is best to see Revelation 1:7 as similar to Matthew 24:30, which also has the tribes of ethnic Israel in view. Yet as stated, this does not deny that all people from around the globe will see Jesus at His return to earth (i.e. "every eye"). Thus, Matthew 24:30 and Revelation 1:7 quote an OT prophetic passage whose fulfillment awaits the future.

# Conclusion

What can we conclude about the three uses of Zechariah 12:10 in the NT? Zechariah 12:10 is used contextually in all three. Zechariah 12:10 predicts that the Messiah, as Yahweh's representative, will be pierced. Yet a day will come when a repentant nation of Israel will look upon the Messiah with a mourning of repentance. John 19:37 draws attention to the actual piercing of Yahweh's Messiah on the cross and the reality that the Jews and Romans looked upon Him, although not unto salvation at this point. So there is a partial fulfillment of Zechariah 12:10 with the events of Jesus' crucifixion as described in John 19. But both Matthew 24:30 and Revelation 1:7 use Zechariah 12:10 with expectation of future fulfillment. In connection with the return of Jesus the Messiah, the tribes of Israel will mourn with repentance in the context of their salvation.

Thus, Zechariah 12:10b was partially fulfilled at the cross while 12:10a and 12:10c will be fulfilled in the future with Jesus' second coming, as shown below.

**12:10a: The Lord pours out the Holy Spirit upon Israel**
Second Coming fulfillment

**12:10b: Israel looks upon the Messiah they have pierced**
First Coming fulfillment as Jews and Romans look upon the pierced Jesus at the cross; and Second Coming fulfillment as Israel (and maybe Gentiles, too) look upon Jesus for salvation

**12:10c: Israel mourns deeply over the Messiah they pierced**
Second Coming fulfillment

# CHAPTER THIRTY-EIGHT

# THE COMING MAN OF LAWLESSNESS

## DANIEL 9:27 IN THE NEW TESTAMENT

Daniel 9:27 is part of Daniel 9:24–27 which discusses events associated with a period often known as Daniel's seventy weeks. Few passages are debated as much as Daniel 9:24–27. We cannot discuss all the issues concerning this section, but we will highlight the significance of Daniel 9:27 in the NT. The main point is that several NT persons and writers viewed elements of Daniel 9:27 as needing to be fulfilled in the future. This includes the actions of a coming evil person and the time frame in which he will execute his nefarious plans.

Daniel 9:27 describes the activities of a coming evil prince (see Daniel 9:26) who will commit an awful act in the Jewish temple at the middle of a seven-year period. The verse states:

> And he will make a firm covenant with the many for one week, but in the middle of the week he will put a stop to sacrifice and grain offering; and on the wing of abominations will come one who makes desolate, even until a complete destruction, one that is decreed, is poured out on the one who makes desolate.

While much of this verse is debated, most scholars agree that there is a coming prince (see Dan. 9:26) who will commit an abomination that desolates the Jewish temple and halts its worship system. Also, the "week" here is a seven-year period of time. The Hebrew word *shabua* literally means "seven," and in this context refers to seven years. So this evil prince makes a covenant with "the many" (i.e. Israel) for seven years. But Daniel says this evil person stops the worship system "in the middle of the week." If a "week" is seven years, then the "middle of the week" would be three-and-a-half years. Thus, the middle of the week refers to a three-and-a-half-year point. This is significant, because, as we will see later in this chapter, Revelation refers to a three-and-a-half-year time period on several occasions. Also, according to Daniel 9:27, the one who halts the Jewish worship system will be destroyed. Paul will bring this point up in 2 Thessalonians 2:8. We now turn to how Daniel 9:27 is used by Jesus, Paul, and John the apostle.

## Matthew 24:15

In Matthew 24:15, Jesus refers to the "abomination of desolation" event of Daniel 9:27 and 12:11:

Therefore when you see the ABOMINATION OF DESOLATION which was spoken of through Daniel the prophet, standing in the holy place (let the reader understand).

Significantly, Jesus explicitly stated that the "abomination of desolation" is linked with Daniel and that Daniel should be sought for understanding this event—"let the reader understand." Thus, Jesus explicitly mentioned the OT prophet Daniel to discuss a prophetic matter that still must happen.

According to Matthew 24:16–22, persecution follows this abomination of desolation event. Jesus warned that Jews in Judea should not return to their homes and seek any personal possessions. Instead, they should flee immediately to avoid the worst persecution in history. So not only does Jesus draw attention to what Daniel said and meant in Daniel 9:27, Jesus expected in the future a literal fulfillment of the Daniel 9:27 event. He also expected His followers to understand what Daniel the prophet stated on this matter. This shows great continuity between OT expectation and future fulfillment.

## 2 Thessalonians 2

According to 2 Thessalonians 2:1–2, Paul noted that the Thessalonians were deceived into thinking they presently were in the Day of the Lord. But Paul assured them they were not in the Day of the Lord because two events associated with that Day had not occurred yet—the apostasy and the revealing of the man of lawlessness.

Paul then combined Daniel 11:36[1] and Daniel 9:27 to describe what a coming evil person will do:

> Let no one in any way deceive you, for it will not come unless the apostasy comes first, and the man of lawlessness is revealed, the son of destruction, who opposes and exalts himself above every so-called god or object of worship, so that he takes his seat in the temple of God, displaying himself as being God. (2 Thess. 2:3–4)

This "man of lawlessness" of 2:3, who appears in connection with the Day of the Lord, seems to be the same evil prince of Daniel 9:27. This evil person "takes his seat in the temple of God, displaying himself as being God" (2:4). This act is consistent with the abomination of desolation event described in Daniel 9:27 (and Matt. 24:15). Paul also used Daniel 11:36 to explain the arrogance of this person. Daniel 11:36a stated that a coming king "will exalt and magnify himself above every god and will speak monstrous things against the God of gods." Paul repeats this truth in 2 Thessalonians 2:4.

Then in 2 Thessalonians 2:8, Paul stated that this "man of lawlessness" will be destroyed: "Then that lawless one will be revealed whom the Lord will slay with the breath of His mouth and bring to an end by the appearance of His coming." This matches what Daniel said in 9:27 about the evil prince being destroyed.

In sum, Daniel 9:27 tells of a coming evil person who will exalt himself and commit a terrible atrocity in God's temple. Yet this wicked one will be destroyed. Like Jesus did, Paul drew upon Daniel 9:27 in 2 Thessalonians 2:3–4, 8 to make these points. Again, continuity with an OT prophetic message occurs.

# Revelation 11:2, 3; 12:6; 13:5

As mentioned above, the "weeks" of Daniel 7 refer to years, and the seventieth week of Daniel refers to a seven-year period. Daniel 9:27 says that an abomination that brings desolation will occur in "the middle of the week." So something happens at the three-and-a-half-year mark with implications for the final three-and-a-half years of this seven-year period. Significantly, Revelation refers to a three-and-a-half-year period four times by mentioning "forty-two months," "twelve hundred and sixty days," and "one thousand two hundred and sixty days":

---

[1] Daniel 11:36 states: "Then the king will do as he pleases, and he will exalt and magnify himself above every god and will speak monstrous things against the God of gods; and he will prosper until the indignation is finished, for that which is decreed will be done."

### Revelation 11:2
Leave out the court which is outside the temple and do not measure it, for it has been given to the nations; and they will tread under foot the holy city for *forty-two months*.

### Revelation 11:3
And I will grant authority to my two witnesses, and they will prophesy for *twelve hundred and sixty days*, clothed in sackcloth.

### Revelation 12:6
Then the woman fled into the wilderness where she had a place prepared by God, so that there she would be nourished for *one thousand two hundred and sixty days*.

### Revelation 13:5
There was given to him a mouth speaking arrogant words and blasphemies, and authority to act for *forty-two months* was given to him.

(emphases in these quotations above are mine)

Thus, a three-and-a-half-year period is significant to the message of Revelation and reveals a connection with the three-and-a-half-year timeframe of Daniel 9:27. John pens the prophecy of Revelation in the 90s AD and holds that the three-and-a-half-years of Daniel 9:27 has relevance for a future time period. This is strong evidence that the seventieth week of Daniel, or at least the last three-and-a-half years of this period, still awaits future fulfillment. Also, Revelation 13:5 is particularly important since it ties an evil "beast" with the three-and-a-half-year period. So both Daniel 9:27 and Revelation 13:5 link an evil person with a three-and-a-half-year timeframe.

Together, Matthew 24:15; 2 Thessalonians 2:3, 4, 8; and Revelation 11:2, 3; 12:6; 13:5 affirm what Daniel 9:27 predicted:

1. A coming abomination of desolation in Jerusalem will occur (Matt. 24:15)
2. A coming evil person will invade the temple of God in Jerusalem (2 Thess. 2:3–4)
3. This coming evil person will be destroyed (2 Thess. 2:8)
4. The last three-and-a-half years of Daniel's seventieth week is still future (Rev. 11:2, 3; 12:6; 13:5)

# CHAPTER THIRTY-NINE

# THE DAY OF THE LORD IN THE NEW TESTAMENT

In Genesis 3, man rebelled against his Creator. But God in His mercy did not extinguish man from the face of the earth. Instead, He instituted a promise plan in which a coming seed of the woman would defeat the power behind the serpent and reverse the curse (see Gen. 3:15; 5:29). While many have been saved throughout history, mankind as a whole continues its rebellion against God. But at various times God has expressed His judgment and wrath against unbelieving people. The global flood of Genesis 6–8 and the fiery judgment of Sodom and Gomorrah described in Genesis 18–19 are two such examples.

Significant to the Bible's storyline is the "Day of the Lord" concept.[1] Known as *yōm Yahweh* in Hebrew and *hē hēmera tou Kuriou* in Greek, the "Day of the Lord" refers to God's intervention in human history, to bring judgment and wrath *en route* to establishing His kingdom on earth.[2] While passages like Joel 1:15 can refer to a past Day of the Lord event,[3] most references to the Day of the Lord in the OT refer to a coming catastrophic judgment upon the entire world. For example, Ezekiel 30:2b–3 declares what this period will mean for the nations:

> Wail, "Alas for the day!"
> "For the day is near,
> Even the day of the LORD is near;

---

[1] There are about thirty explicit references to the Day of the Lord in the Bible, with many other references with slightly different wording.

[2] Joel 3 indicates there is a blessing phase that follows the judgment phase of the Day of the Lord.

[3] In Joel 1:15 a locust plague functions as a harbinger of a much more severe and global Day of the Lord involving Israel and the nations, as explained in Joel 2 and 3.

It will be a day of clouds,
A time of doom for the nations."[4]

The purpose of the Day of the Lord is to punish sinners as Isaiah 13:9 declares: "Behold, the day of the LORD is coming, Cruel, with fury and burning anger, to make the land a desolation; And He will exterminate its sinners from it." Zephaniah 1:14–15 describes the terrifying nature of this period:

Near is the great day of the LORD,
Near and coming very quickly;
Listen, the day of the LORD!
In it the warrior cries out bitterly.
A day of wrath is that day,
A day of trouble and distress,
A day of destruction and desolation,
A day of darkness and gloom,
A day of clouds and thick darkness.

Many other OT passages explicitly mention and describe this Day of the Lord, including Joel 2:1, 11, 30, 31; 3:14; Amos 5:18, 20; Obadiah 1:15; Zephaniah 1:7, 8, 18; 2:2, 3; Malachi 4:5. Carson notes that, "The expression 'day of the Lord' appears about twenty times in the OT."[5] Passages like Isaiah 24 describe the Day of the Lord in great detail without mentioning the exact phrase. Thus, the Day of the Lord is an important theme in Scripture.

The overwhelming emphasis of OT Day of the Lord passages is on judgment and God's divine wrath upon an unbelieving world.[6] The Day of the Lord is also related to a time of tribulation and rescue of Israel (Mal. 4:5; Isa. 24; Zech. 14). When the Day of the Lord has run its course, God's kingdom on earth will follow (see Isa. 24–25; Zech. 14; Matt. 24–25; Rev. 19–20).

# New Testament Mentions of "Day of the Lord"

The "Day of the Lord" is explicitly mentioned four times in the NT—Acts 2:20; 1 Thessalonians 5:2; 2 Thessalonians 2:2; and 2 Peter 3:10. The surrounding contexts of

---

[4] The term for "nations" is *goyim*, which refers to the Gentile nations.

[5] D. A. Carson, "2 Peter," in *Commentary on the New Testament Use of the Old Testament*, 1059.

[6] "The 'day of the Lord' concept has its roots in the OT, where it refers to a future time when God will come to punish the wicked and vindicate his people, though the notion of judgment is more commonly stressed than that of deliverance." Jeffrey A. D. Weima, "1–2 Thessalonians," in *Commentary on the New Testament Use of the Old Testament*, 881.

these passages also offer information on the Day of the Lord. John may refer to the Day of the Lord in Revelation 1:10 when he says, "I was in the Spirit on the *Lord's day*" (emphasis mine). While some believe John is saying he had his revelatory experience on a Sunday, this understanding seems trivial considering that Revelation 6–19 describes Day of the Lord-like conditions. Thus, the Day of the Lord probably is mentioned in Revelation 1:10. It is also likely that the conditions of the Day of the Lord are described in Matthew 24 where Jesus described signs of His coming and the end of the age (see Matt. 24:3).

There is great continuity between the OT and NT understandings of the Day of the Lord. The OT presents the Day of the Lord as an imminent cataclysmic global event of judgment that would overtake an unbelieving world. It also involves God's plans to bring Israel to Himself. The NT affirms these matters and brings the knowledge that the coming of Yahweh is tied to the second coming of Jesus.[7] In fact, it is probable that the Day of the Lord in its entirety is connected with the future coming of Jesus. While not repeating all the details of the OT, the NT highlights many of the same ideas found in the OT concept of the Day of the Lord. These similarities can be seen below.

First, *both testaments present the Day of the Lord as a future event*. This is true for Isaiah 13; 24; Zephaniah 1; Joel 2–3, etc. And this is Paul's explicit point in 2 Thessalonians 1–2. The Thessalonians were deceived into wrongly thinking the Day of the Lord was present (2 Thess. 2:2—"to the effect that the day of the Lord has come"), but Paul told them the Day of the Lord had not yet begun. He started 2 Thessalonians 2:3 by stating, "Let no one in any way deceive you, for it [the Day of the Lord] will not come unless…" Paul then mentions two events that must be present for the Day of the Lord to exist—(1) the apostasy and (2) the revealing of the man of lawlessness (2 Thess. 2:3b–4). Since those two events had not yet occurred, the Thessalonians could know the Day of the Lord had not yet arrived. In 2 Peter 3, Peter also presented the Day of the Lord as a future event. Scoffers mocked the idea of Jesus' return, but Peter said, "the day of the Lord will come." The future tense here ("will come") indicates the Day of the Lord is a coming event.

Second, *both testaments present the Day of the Lord's coming as imminent and surprising*. Isaiah 13:6 declares: "Wail, for the day of the LORD is near!" Zephaniah said, "Near is the great day of the LORD, Near and coming very quickly; Listen, the day of the LORD!" The references to "near" and "quickly" indicate imminence—that it could break forth at any time. We find this imminence idea in the NT as well. Using

---

[7] In Revelation 6:1 Jesus, the Lamb, is the one who opens the first seal which sets in motion a sequence of seals, trumpets, and bowl judgments that comprise the Day of the Lord that culminates in His return to earth as explained in Revelation 6–19. We understand that not all scholars view the seals, trumpets, and bowls sequentially. Nor do all scholars agree that all the seals involve the Day of the Lord.

the analogies of a thief and labor pains, Paul, in 1 Thessalonians 5:2–3, shows that the Day of the Lord is imminent:

> For you yourselves know full well that the day of the Lord will come just like a *thief in the night*. While they are saying, "Peace and safety!" then destruction will come upon them suddenly like *labor pains upon a woman with child*, and they will not escape. (emphases mine)

Isaiah 13:8 also mentions the woman in labor analogy: "Pains and anguish will take hold of them; They will writhe like a woman in labor." In Matthew 24:8 Jesus also referred to coming terrible events as "the beginning of birth pangs." Using the "thief" analogy to indicate imminence and surprise, Peter said "the day of the Lord will come like a thief" (2 Pet. 3:10a). Jesus also used the "thief" analogy in Matthew 24:42–43:

> Therefore be on the alert, for you do not know which day your Lord is coming. But be sure of this, that if the head of the house had known at what time of the night the *thief was coming*, he would have been on the alert and would not have allowed his house to be broken into. (emphases mine)

Concerning the outbreak of the Day of the Lord, Jesus said, "But of that day and hour no one knows, not even the angels of heaven, nor the Son, but the Father alone. For the coming of the Son of Man will be just like the days of Noah" (Matt. 24:36–37). So when it comes to the imminent and surprising outbreak of the Day of the Lord, both testaments agree.

Third, both testaments affirm *that the coming Day of the Lord is a time of terrifying judgment for unbelievers on the earth*. Isaiah 13:11a says, "Thus I will punish the world for its evil and the wicked for their iniquity." Zephaniah 1:18b also states, "For He will make a complete end, indeed a terrifying one, of all the inhabitants of the earth." Likewise, in the NT Peter began his discussion of the Day of the Lord by mentioning "scoffers" who mock the idea of Jesus' return (2 Pet. 3:3–4). In 2 Peter 3:7, Peter says the Day of the Lord will overtake the ungodly: "But by His word the present heavens and earth are being reserved for fire, kept for the day of judgment and destruction of ungodly men." In reference to unbelievers Paul stated, "While they are saying, 'Peace and safety!' then destruction will come upon them suddenly" (1 Thess. 5:3).

Fourth, *the Day of the Lord involves Israel*. Joel 2:1 declares, "Blow a trumpet in Zion, and sound an alarm on My holy mountain! Let all the inhabitants of the land tremble, For the day of the LORD is coming; Surely it is near." Joel 2 and 3 detail how the Day of the Lord affects Israel. It results in blessings in the land (2:18–19, 21–27; 3:18–21); the defeat and judgment of Israel's enemies (2:20; 3:1–8); and the pouring out of God's Holy Spirit upon Israel (2:28–29). Jeremiah 30:7 summarizes Israel's experience with the Day of the Lord well: "Alas! for that day is great, there is none like it; and it is the time of Jacob's distress, but he will be saved from it."

Likewise, in the NT Paul links the coming of the Day of the Lord with future events concerning national Israel, including the revealing of the man of lawlessness and this evil person going into the Jewish temple declaring himself to be God:

> Let no one in any way deceive you, for it [Day of the Lord] will not come unless the apostasy comes first, and the man of lawlessness is revealed, the son of destruction, who opposes and exalts himself above every so-called god or object of worship, so that he takes his seat in the temple of God, displaying himself as being God. (2 Thess. 2:3–4)

As mentioned in an earlier chapter, Paul relies on Daniel 9:27 and Daniel 11:36 which involve an antichrist figure who commits an abomination in the Jewish temple. Matthew's discussion of the Day of the Lord is Jewish as well. Jesus speaks of a coming "abomination of desolation" (Matt. 24:15) that results in extreme persecution of Israelites in the land of Israel (Matt. 24:16–22) . While the meaning of Matthew 24:29–31 is debated, these verses probably describe the salvation and rescue of Israel after the events of the Day of the Lord.

Fifth, *both testaments affirm that the Day of the Lord encompasses the heavens and earth*. Isaiah 24:19–20a states concerning the earth:

> The earth is broken asunder,
> The earth is split through,
> The earth is shaken violently.
> The earth reels to and fro like a drunkard
> And it totters like a shack.

Isaiah 13:10 states concerning the cosmic bodies:

> For the stars of heaven and their constellations
> Will not flash forth their light;
> The sun will be dark when it rises
> And the moon will not shed its light.

The Day of the Lord's impact on the heavens and earth is affirmed in the NT. Second Peter 3:10 and 3:12 state:

> But the day of the Lord will come like a thief, in which the heavens will pass away with a roar and the elements will be destroyed with intense heat, and the

earth and its works will be burned up...looking for and hastening the coming of the day of God, because of which the heavens will be destroyed by burning, and the elements will melt with intense heat! (3:10, 12)

Jesus also quotes Isaiah's mention of cosmic signs in Matthew 24:29, where he alludes to Isaiah 13:10 and perhaps Joel 2:30–31.

## Day of the Lord in the OT and NT

|  | OT | NT |
|---|---|---|
| Future Event | Isa. 13; 24; Joel 2; Zephaniah 1 | Matt. 24; 1 Thess. 5; 2 Thess. 2; 2 Peter 3 |
| Imminent and Surprising | Isa. 13:6, 8; Zeph. 1:14 | Matt. 24:8, 36–37; 1 Thess. 5:2–3; 2 Pet. 3:10 |
| Judgment for Unbelievers | Isa. 13:11; Zeph. 1:18 | 1 Thess. 5:3; 2 Pet. 3:7 |
| Involves Israel | Jeremiah 30:7; Joel 2–3 | Matt. 24:15–22, 30–31; 2 Thess. 2:3–4 |
| Encompasses the Heavens and Earth | Isa. 13:10; 24 | Matt. 24:29; 2 Pet. 3:10, 12 |

In conclusion, the NT concept of the Day of the Lord is continuous with the Day of the Lord presented in the OT. Thus, NT uses of the Day of the Lord idea are contextual and consistent with the OT understanding. This shows great continuity between the messages of the OT and the NT on this issue.

# CHAPTER FORTY

# "YOU ARE GODS"

## PSALM 82:6 IN JOHN 10:34

One of the more difficult uses of the OT to understand involves Jesus' quotation of Psalm 82:6a in John 10:34. The issue here is not whether a contextual or non-contextual use of the OT is occurring, but what Jesus meant when He quoted Psalm 82:6a.

In a book known for its high Christology, John 10 describes an encounter between Jesus and the Jews that offers explicit evidence for Jesus' deity. In John 10:30, Jesus declared "I and the Father are one." Then in 10:38 Jesus stated, "The Father is in Me, and I in the Father." Jesus' claims of equality with God were so clear the Jews said they had reason to stone Jesus for blasphemy "because You, being a man, make Yourself out to be God" (John 10:33). The Jewish leaders understood that Jesus claimed to be God.

Jesus responded to the charge of blasphemy with a quotation and explanation of Psalm 82:6a:

> Jesus answered them, "Has it not been written in your Law, 'I SAID, YOU ARE GODS'? If he called them gods, to whom the word of God came (and the Scripture cannot be broken), do you say of Him, whom the Father sanctified and sent into the world, 'You are blaspheming,' because I said, 'I am the Son of God'?" (John 10:34–36)

Jesus contrasted what God said in Psalm 82:6—"I SAID, YOU ARE GODS," with the claim of the Jews that Jesus was blaspheming—"You are blaspheming." Jesus did this to highlight some point of inconsistency or hypocrisy from the Jewish leaders who opposed Him. Jesus' quote of Psalm 82:6 rebuts the claim of blasphemy.

291

But what specific point was Jesus making with this quotation? Who are the "gods" of Psalm 82:6? Part of the reason Jesus' quotation of Psalm 82:6 in John 10:34 is difficult to understand is because the meaning of Psalm 82 is also challenging and highly debated. Who are these "gods" in Psalm 82? Various views of the "gods" include angels, human judges, Israel at Sinai, and Melchizedek.[1] We will focus on the first two of these.

The term for "gods" in Psalm 82:6 (and 82:1) is *elohim*. *Elohim* is often translated "God," referring to the God of the Bible over 2,300 times. But the term also is used of divine spiritual beings (see Ps. 8:5). In addition, some believe *elohim* is used of human rulers in sections like Exodus 4:16; 21:6; 22:7–8; Judges 5:8; and Psalm 138:1. The Exodus references arguably speak of designated human rulers in Israel, so some believe human rulers are in view in Psalm 82:6. But some challenge the idea that these verses refer to human rulers. For example, concerning the belief that Exodus 22:7–8 refers to human rulers, John Goldingay states, "That understanding of the Exodus passage is itself questionable. Indeed, it is doubtful whether the OT ever uses the word Elohim to mean human authorities, whereas it certainly uses it to mean lesser heavenly beings (e.g., Pss. 86:8; 95:3; 96:4; 97:7, 9)."[2] And likewise, some doubt whether human rulers are in view in Psalm 82:6.

There is debate concerning whether the *elohim* ("gods") in Psalm 82:6 refers to human rulers or divine beings. And this debate will carry over to what Jesus meant by "gods" in John 10:34 when He quoted Psalm 82:6.

# The Views of John 10:34

Those who interpret Psalm 82:6 as referring to human rulers (probably the Jewish religious leadership) often think Jesus is making a lesser to greater argument. If the Scripture can call sinful human rulers "gods," how much more can the divinely sent Jesus apply such language to himself. John Hart in *The Moody Bible Commentary* states:

> Jesus' argument is as follows. In Ps 82:6, even sinful Israelite leaders were given the title *gods* since they had the divine responsibility to speak the word of God and carry out justice under God...Therefore, how much more should the Christ, *sanctified and sent into the world* (v. 36) on a divine mission to speak

---

[1] See Jerome H. Neyrey, "'I Said You Are Gods': Psalm 82:6 and John 10," in *Journal of Biblical Literature* (January, 1989): 647–49. The author here believes in the "Israel at Sinai" view.

[2] John Goldingay, *Psalms, Volume 2: Psalms 42–89*, in Baker Commentary on the Old Testament Wisdom and Psalms, ed. Tremper Longman III (Grand Rapids: Baker, Academic, 2007), 561.

the word of God as the incarnate Word of God (1:1, 14) and to carry out justice (5:22, 27, 30), be rightly called the divine (sinless) "Son of God?"[3]

Walter Kaiser makes a similar claim:

Jesus was demonstrating that the title could be attached to certain men…and therefore there could not be any prima facie objections lodged against his claim to be divine. There was a legitimate attachment of the word *elōhîm* to those people who had been specially prepared by God to administer his law and word to the people.[4]

In this view, if Jewish leaders who ended up failing in their God-given function could be called "gods," then the greater One, Jesus, can rightfully have "god" language applied to Him. Thus, Jesus answers the charge of blasphemy by stating that Israelite leaders also were called "gods" in Psalm 82:6. So how much more should this concept apply to Jesus who speaks for God and proves it by His works? Jesus' works reveal His deity.

Critics of this view say the 'human rulers' understanding does not make sense since it is unrelated to the issue of Jesus' deity. Why would Jesus defend His deity by appealing to a verse about human rulers who are not deity? Why would Jesus say, "You can know I am God and equal to the Father because Psalm 82:6 refers to human rulers as gods?" Not only could this be a *non sequitur* argument (i.e. "it does not follow"), but perhaps the fallacy of equivocation is happening since "gods" is being used inconsistently. It seems like the issue with John 10:34/Psalm 82:6 is Jesus' deity and co-equality with God the Father. So why would Jesus use "gods" to refer to human beings, which shifts the issue away from the deity issue? The lesser to the greater argument is questionable, since an appeal to beings who are lower than God (human rulers) cannot prove that Jesus is God, which is the issue in John 10.

So, does this mean the divine beings in the heavenly council view is correct? Not necessarily. The 'divine beings' view of John 10:34 (and Ps. 82:6) also has its problems. Its major flaw could be similar to that of the human rulers view. Would Jesus appeal to His deity and co-equality with the Father by likening Himself to created, divine beings who were not equal with God? If there is a heavenly council in Psalm 82:6, these beings would not be God since they were created and would be lesser than the God of the Bible. Would Jesus say, "You can know I am co-equal with

---

[3] John F. Hart, "John," in *The Moody Bible Commentary*, ed. Michael Rydelnik and Michael Vanlaningham (Chicago, IL: Moody Publishers, 2014), 1638. Emphases are in the original.

[4] Walter C. Kaiser, Jr., "82:1 God Presides Among the Gods?" in *Hard Sayings of the Bible* (Downers Grove, IL: InterVarsity Press, 1996), 279.

God because there are lesser divine beings in heaven called 'gods'?" Doesn't this view also undercut Jesus' argument that He is equal with God?

A third view has been offered by Michael Heiser who believes Psalm 82 refers to a divine heavenly council, and Jesus refers to this divine council in John 10:34. Heiser believes Jesus quotes Psalm 82:6 to show that *He is the co-regent with God the Father over the divine council*:

> Juxtaposed as its quotation is in John 10, between two statements that identify Jesus with the Father [John 10:30, 38], the point of the theology produced by the quotation in context is that Jesus is not only a divine son of God, but superior to all divine sons of God in his identification with the Father, the Lord of the divine council.[5]

In Heiser's understanding, the deity of Jesus is affirmed in John 10 because Jesus is more than a member of the divine council of heavenly beings—He is *the* co-ruler of this council with God the Father. So Heiser's view removes the problem of comparing Jesus' deity with humans or created heavenly beings. If Jesus is the co-ruler with the Father over a divine council of heavenly beings, that establishes Jesus' deity. The problem with this view, however, concerns the idea of Jesus being co-regent over a heavenly council that is not mentioned in John 10. Jesus does not say He is the co-ruler of a divine council. So Heiser's view could be assuming something not found in John 10.

The use of Psalm 82:6 in John 10:34 is one of the most difficult uses of the OT in the NT to grasp. Scholarship heavily sides with the view that Jesus is speaking of human rulers when He quotes Psalm 82:6. Yet for reasons mentioned above, this view has major problems, particularly as to why Jesus would refer to humans as gods to establish His deity. It is difficult to say which view is best. The difficulty with understanding the right view here though is not evidence for a non-contextual use of the OT in the NT. It simply is a hard case to understand.

---

[5] Heiser, *The Unseen Realm*, 268 n.3.

# CHAPTER FORTY-ONE

# MARRIAGE AND JESUS

## GENESIS 2:24 IN EPHESIANS 5:31–32

In Ephesians 5:22–33, Paul linked the man-woman marriage relationship with Jesus' relationship to His church. Husbands are to love their wives just as Christ loved the church (5:25). And they are to love their wives like they love their own bodies (5:28). This self-sacrificing love characterizes Jesus' love for His church (5:29). Paul then quoted Genesis 2:24 to make a point concerning human marriage with Jesus and the church:

> …because we are members of His body. FOR THIS REASON A MAN SHALL LEAVE HIS FATHER AND MOTHER AND SHALL BE JOINED TO HIS WIFE, AND THE TWO SHALL BECOME ONE FLESH. This mystery is great; but I am speaking with reference to Christ and the church. (Eph. 5:30–32)

For our purposes, the main issue is *how* Paul compares human marriage with Jesus and His church. And how does "mystery" (*musterion*) apply to Paul's point. Four views are possible—analogy, allegory, *sensus plenior* (i.e. hidden meaning), and typology. First, Paul could be making an analogy or illustration between human marriage and Christ's relationship to the church. Since Jesus acts perfectly toward the church, those in a human marriage can learn from His perfect example. For husbands, this involves sacrificial love and care for the wife's needs.

Second, concerning an allegorical approach, Frank Thielman says, "Paul employs an allegorical method" here.[1] And, "God revealed to him [Paul] an allegorical application of the statement in Genesis..."[2] If allegory is in play here, then Paul ignores the contextual meaning of Genesis 2:24 to provide an unrelated meaning.

A third view is that Paul drew upon a *sensus plenior* meaning of Genesis 2:24. With this approach, Genesis 2:24 addresses human marriage, but God also embedded a hidden meaning of Genesis 2:24 that Paul is now revealing—namely the Christ-church relationship. This hidden meaning does not contradict the literal meaning of Genesis 2:24 concerning human marriage, but it is an additional meaning, not grasped until Paul revealed it with his "mystery."

Fourth, Paul could be utilizing a typological connection between human marriage and Jesus' relationship with the church. Thus, there is a divinely intended correspondence between marriage and Jesus' relationship to His church.

So what is the solution? The first view, the analogy/illustration view, has some truth to it since Paul certainly uses the Christ-church relationship to illustrate how men should love their wives. But the fact that Paul says "This mystery is great" indicates that more than an analogy is in view here. Something about human marriage corresponds to Jesus and the church. The other five uses of "mystery" in Ephesians (1:9; 3:3, 4, 9; 6:19) indicate hidden or partially-hidden realities that God brought to fruition in Jesus.

The allegorical interpretation position is not accurate. True allegory is on a different plane than the meaning of a passage quoted, but that is not the case here. Real points of continuity exist between Genesis 2:24 and Ephesians 5:31–32. Relationship and intimate union characterize both relationships, and what Christ does for the church is to be a model for how husbands are to love their wives. Also, Clinton Arnold notes that the allegory is not in mind with Paul's five other uses of "mystery" in Ephesians, so it probably is not here either.[3]

Next, the *sensus plenior* option is possible, but it does not appear that Paul is drawing upon a hidden meaning of Genesis 2:24. So the typological connection seems best. The man-woman relationship pictures the greater relationship between Jesus and the church. This is a mystery that could only be known once Jesus arrived and the church began. Yet even with this typological relationship, the literal truth of the one-flesh relationship of men and women in marriage remains. In 5:33, Paul

---

[1] Frank S. Thielman, "Ephesians," in *Commentary on the New Testament Use of the Old Testament*, ed. G. K. Beale and D. A. Carson (Grand Rapids: Baker Books, 2007), 828.

[2] Ibid.

[3] "It is doubtful that Paul would use the same term that he has used repeatedly with reference to Christ and his people and now shift the meaning to something different, such as the 'hidden' or 'deeper' meaning or 'the allegorical sense' of a passage of Scripture, which in this case is Gen. 2:24." Clinton E. Arnold, *Zondervan Exegetical Commentary on the New Testament: Ephesians* (Grand Rapids: Zondervan, 2010), 394.

returns to human marriage to declare that a husband should love his wife and the wife should respect her husband. So if marriage is a type of the Jesus/church relationship, this does not remove the significance of marriage in this age.

There is debate concerning the role of marriage in the future. The new earth passage of Isaiah 65:17–25 speaks of childbirth which implies marriage, but in Matthew 22:30 Jesus says in the resurrection there will be no marriage. But at least for this present age, Jesus' relationship to the church has a connection to marriage. And those in a human marriage can learn from the example of Jesus.

In sum, Paul's quotation of Genesis 2:24 in Ephesians 5:31 could be a typological use of the OT, but it is one strongly connected with the contextual meaning of Genesis 2:24.

CHAPTER FORTY-TWO

# APPLYING ISRAELITE TITLES TO NEW TESTAMENT BELIEVERS

## THE USE OF THE OLD TESTAMENT IN 1 PETER 2:9–10

First Peter 2:9–10 involves a significant use of the OT as Peter applied a cluster of descriptions used for Israel in the OT to his readers living in the New covenant era. The OT language comes from Exodus 19:5–6; Isaiah 43:20–21; and Hosea 2:23.[1] First Peter 2:9–10 reads:

> But you are A CHOSEN RACE, A royal PRIESTHOOD, A HOLY NATION, A PEOPLE FOR God's OWN POSSESSION, so that you may proclaim the excellencies of Him who has called you out of darkness into His marvelous light; for you once were NOT A PEOPLE, but now you are THE PEOPLE OF GOD; you had NOT RECEIVED MERCY, but now you have RECEIVED MERCY.

Peter's statement involves five descriptions concerning his audience. First, his readers are a "chosen race" (*genos eklekton*). The Greek word for "race," *genos*, can be translated as "offspring," "family," "kind," or "race." Peter's point is that his

---

[1] D. A. Carson notes, "Scholars disagree on how much is quotation and how much is allusion, but even those who insist on some direct quotations cannot find more than two words at a time that apparently spring from specific texts." D. A. Carson, "1 Peter," in *Commentary on the New Testament Use of the Old Testament*, 1030.

299

readers are a chosen people or family of God. Isaiah 43:20 is probably the OT reference here—"My chosen people"[2] (see also Deut. 7:6; 14:2).

Second, the reference to "A royal PRIESTHOOD," is taken verbatim from the LXX of Exodus 19:6 and emphasizes Peter's audience as mediators and representatives of the King to the world.[3]

Third, "a holy nation" (*ethnos hagion*) also comes exactly from the LXX of Exodus 19:6 and shows that Peter's readers are a set-apart people with a common history and purpose.

Fourth, "God's OWN POSSESSION" (*laos eis peripoiēsin*) is closely related to Exodus 19:5 and demonstrates that Peter's readers belong to God.

The fifth designation, concerning a people receiving mercy, comes from Hosea 2:23: "For you once were NOT A PEOPLE, but now you are THE PEOPLE OF GOD; you had NOT RECEIVED MERCY, but now you have RECEIVED MERCY." This shows that Peter's audience went from not being the people of God to being God's people, all by God's mercy.

All five of these descriptions—"race," "priesthood," "nation," "possession," "people of God"—were used of Israel in the OT. The significance of this has been greatly debated. Some believe Peter indicated that the church superseded Israel's identity as the people of God. For example, Paul J. Achtemeier states, "The twofold description of the new community (2:5; 2:9–10) shows by its language that the church has now taken over the role of Israel."[4] In a similar manner, I. Howard Marshall writes, "It is impossible to avoid the impression that Peter deliberately says that the contemporary people of Israel are no longer God's people, standing in community with his people in Old Testament times, but rather that the church is the true heir of Israel."[5] This view is reliant on the belief that Peter's readers included Gentiles and that they are part of a new Israel.

A second view is that Peter applied Israelite language specifically to ethnic Israelites, not to Gentiles. This view has strong historical support. D. Edmond Hiebert notes that many in church history believed that 1 Peter was written to a specific Jewish audience: "Origen and many others, saw them [Peter's audience] as Jewish Christians."[6] These "many others" include John Calvin, John Albert Bengel, Bernard

---

[2] Carson notes, "the linguistic links with 1 Pet. 2:9–10 are at this point much closer to Isa. 43 than to Exod. 19." 1030.

[3] See Greg W. Forbes, *1 Peter*, in Exegetical Guide to the Greek New Testament, eds. Andreas J. Köstenberger and Robert W. Yarbrough (Nashville, TN: B & H Academic, 2014), 68. Forbes says the idea here is mediating God's presence to the world, not the priesthood of all believers.

[4] Paul J. Achtemeier, *1 Peter* (Minneapolis: Fortress, 1996), 152.

[5] I. Howard Marshall, *1 Peter*, IVPNTCS (Downers Grove, IL: InterVarsity, 1991), 72–73.

[6] D. Edmond Hiebert, *1 Peter* (Chicago: Moody, 1992), 24. Hiebert himself believes that 1 Peter was written to both Jews and Gentiles. The points in this paragraph are also noted in my book, *Has the Church Replaced Israel: A Theological Evaluation* (Nashville, TN: B & H Publishing Group, 2010).

Weiss, Henry Alford, E. Schuyler English, and Kenneth Wuest.[7] With its introductory comments on 1 Peter, the *Ancient Christian Commentary on Scripture* states, "With few exceptions, the Fathers believed that this letter [1 Peter] was written by the apostle Peter and sent to Jewish Christians in the Diaspora."[8] This book then lists Eusebius of Caesarea, Didymus, Andreas, and Oecumenius as those holding to a Jewish-audience-only view for 1 Peter.[9]

Internal support within 1 Peter for a Jewish audience includes: (1) Peter's many quotations of the OT; (2) the letter's recipients described as "sojourners" or "aliens" of a dispersion (*diasporas*), a title that best fits ethnic Jews living outside of Israel; and (3) Peter's identity as an apostle to the circumcision (i.e. Jews) by Paul (see Gal. 2:7–8). With these factors in mind, it seems possible that the apostle to the Jews wrote a letter to a Jewish audience. If this view is correct, then Peter's use of Israelite imagery from the OT is contextual, since he is using Israelite language from the OT for ethnic Israelites in his audience. Arnold Fruchtenbaum explains the implications of this understanding:

> First Peter 2:9 does speak of a *holy nation*, but the first two verses of this epistle make it clear that Peter was addressing Jewish believers specifically and not the Church as a whole. This makes sense since Peter was the apostle to the circumcision. The Jewish believers constituted the present Remnant of Israel or the *Israel of God*. The point Peter makes is that while the nation as a whole has failed to fulfill its calling of Exodus 19:5–6, the Jewish believing remnant has not.[10]

As the above discussion reveals, identifying Peter's audience is important for grasping how he used the OT designations from Exodus 19:5–6; Isaiah 43:20–21; and Hosea 2:23. The Jewish audience view has much historical support, although the position that Peter's readers included Gentiles is popular today. If Peter's readers included Gentiles, this does not mean Peter used the OT noncontextually or indicated that the church superseded Israel's place as the people of God.[11] The OT itself explicitly states that language used of Israel would one day also be applied to Gentiles. For example, Isaiah 19:24–25 states:

---

[7] Hiebert, *1 Peter*, 31 n. 79.

[8] Gerald Bray, ed., "James, 1–2 Peter, 1–3 John, Jude," in *Ancient Christian Commentary on Scripture: New Testament* (Downers Grove, IL: InterVarsity, 2000), 11:65.

[9] Ibid.

[10] Arnold G. Fruchtenbaum, *Israelology: The Missing Link in Systematic Theology* (Tustin, CA: Ariel Ministries Press, 1992), 161–62.

[11] J. Ramsey Michaels says, "Nowhere in 1 Peter are the readers addressed as a *new* Israel or a *new* people of God, as if to displace the Jewish community." J. Ramsey Michaels, *1 Peter*, WBC (Waco, TX: Word Books, 1988), 49:107.

> In that day Israel will be the third party with Egypt and Assyria, a blessing in the midst of the earth, whom the LORD of hosts has blessed, saying, "Blessed is Egypt My people, and Assyria the work of My hands, and Israel My inheritance."

Note that the Gentile nation, "Egypt," one day will be called "My people" and Assyria will be designated, "the work of My hands." Both descriptions were used of Israel, but with a coming day they will also apply to Gentiles. Yet as this occurs these Gentiles remain Gentiles, and Israel is still Israel. In this context, Israel is still called God's inheritance—"Israel my inheritance."

So, the OT itself predicted that non-Israelites someday would carry titles first linked with Israel. They too would become the people of God. As Saucy writes, "Although the term 'people of God' begins with the nation of Israel and has the predominant meaning throughout the Old Testament, there is already in the prophets the anticipation that some outside of Israel will come under its purview."[12] This indicates an expansion of the people of God to include Gentiles. Understanding the Bible's storyline and the sweep of biblical history must account for the fact that Gentiles would one day become the people of God alongside believing Israel. Perhaps Peter was drawing upon this concept.

*Thus, a third view of 1 Peter 2:9–10 is that Peter applied descriptions first used of Israel in the OT for believing Jews and Gentiles in the NT.* Since Gentiles joining the people of God was predicted in the OT, Peter's application of such language to Gentiles in the church is consistent with the message of the OT prophets. A similar situation occurs when James quoted Amos 9:11–12 in Acts 15:14–17 concerning Gentiles becoming the people of God.

The second and third views above are both viable options for understanding the Israelite language in 1 Peter 2:9–10, and with either option, the uses of the OT in this section would be contextual.

---

[12] Robert L. Saucy, *The Case for Progressive Dispensationalism; The Interface between Dispensational & Non-Dispensational Theology* (Grand Rapids: Zondervan, 1993), 188.

# CONCLUSION

As this book has shown, NT use of the OT is a complex topic. There are many examples and views to work through. Studying it involves understanding the contexts of both the OT and the NT. When both are sufficiently studied, we have concluded that a connecting link in meaning between the testaments often becomes evident.

If there is a takeaway from this project it is this: *Contextual uses of the OT in the NT occur in the vast majority of cases. This reveals continuity in meaning between the testaments.* Of the approximately 350 quotations of the OT in the NT, most can be explained in ways consistent with the meanings of the OT authors. Of these 350 cases, only a handful possibly could be exceptions to the contextual-use norm. And even these few could be explained adequately in a contextual manner. If a few non-contextual uses of the OT do exist, these are exceptions to the norm, not the rule. The NT writers did not often quote the OT non-contextually. Contextual use is the norm.

This work also concluded that the NT writers viewed the new era in Jesus to be a continuation of the storyline presented in the OT, not a reinterpretation of the story. Jesus is the center of the story and the means for the fulfillment of all things. But there is no reinterpretation, transcending, or transforming of the OT narrative. The NT builds upon the message of the OT, sometimes offering new information, but not offering reinterpretations.

In sum, the relationship between the OT and NT is primarily that of continuity, not discontinuity. The student of Scripture can be confident that the two testaments are joined together in a continuous way. Paul's words in Acts 26:22 summarize this truth well and are a fitting place to end our discussion:

> So, having obtained help from God, I stand to this day testifying both to small and great, *stating nothing but what the Prophets and Moses said was going to take place.*[1]

---

[1] Emphases mine.

# GLOSSARY

**Allusion.** An intentional but less direct reference to the Old Testament in comparison with quotations. Does not have an introductory formula as often seen with quotations.

**Author.** The writer of a text.

**Application.** The putting to use or implementing of a text based on the text's meaning.

**Canonical Interpretation Approach.** Belief that the Bible canon as a whole is the starting point for understanding the parts of the canon. Particularly, the completed New Testament is viewed as the lens for interpreting the Old Testament.

**Contextual.** In accord with the context of a passage. A point of connection exists between the meaning of an Old Testament text and its use by a New Testament writer or person.

**Corporate Solidarity / Federal Representation.** A relationship between a federal or representative head of a group and the many who comprise the group. Also known as "the one and the many" concept. The representative head acts on behalf of the many, and the actions of the one are imputed or credited to the many.

**Dual Authorship.** The reality that the Bible was written by both human authors and God. God inspired the human authors of the Bible to write what they did without overriding their personalities or writing styles.

**Echo.** A reference to the Old Testament that is so slight that an intentional quotation or allusion is improbable.

**Historical-Exegetical and Theological-Canonical Approach.** An eclectic approach to interpretation that attempts to combine historical-grammatical hermeneutics with a canonical perspective that understands later revelation as informing the meaning of earlier revelation.

**Grammatical-Historical Interpretation.** Belief that the meaning of a text can be determined by studying the grammar, history, and context associated with that text. This approach is often linked with the idea of "literal" interpretation.

**Implication.** A conclusion or principle drawn from a text that is not explicitly stated. Something suggested that rightly can be inferred. A likely consequence of something. Implications are connected to the meaning of an author.

**Inspired *Sensus Plenior* Application.** A view of New Testament use of the Old Testament promoted by Robert Thomas that asserts that the New Testament writers often went beyond the grammatical-historical sense of an Old Testament passage. This meaning, not found in the Old Testament, is revealed by God to His apostles but is not a pattern for other Christians to follow. This "ISPA" approach allegedly occurs because of Israel's rejection of Jesus and a new door of blessing being opened to the Gentiles.

**LXX (Septuagint).** The Greek translation of the Old Testament, quoted often by the New Testament writers.

**Masoretic Text (MT).** The authoritative Hebrew text of the Christian Old Testament, copied and edited by Masoretes between the seventh and tenth centuries AD.

**Meaning.** What an author meant or intended in a text.

**Messianic Hope.** An expectation, found in certain Old Testament texts, concerning a specific coming Deliverer and/or Messiah who would save and restore humanity and creation.

**New Testament Priority.** Linked with the idea that the New Testament is the interpretive lens for understanding the meaning of Old Testament passages. The original meaning of Old Testament passages allegedly can be reinterpreted or transcended by the New Testament.

**New Testament Reinterpretation of the Old Testament Approach.** A view that New Testament revelation sometimes reinterprets Old Testament passages.

**Non-contextual Use of the Old Testament.** A meaning offered by a New Testament person or writer concerning an Old Testament text that is not in accord with the context or meaning of an Old Testament passage. No direct connection exists between how a New Testament author used an Old Testament text and the meaning of the Old Testament text in its context.

**Quotation.** An intentional and direct citation of an Old Testament verse or passage by a New Testament person or writer that is recognizable. Sometimes has an introductory formula.

**Reader.** A person who reads and interacts with a text.

**Reinterpretation.** The belief that the New Testament writers, at times, reinterpreted or changed the meaning of Old Testament passages. This concept is often connected with the idea of New Testament priority over the Old Testament.

**Second Temple Judaism Approach.** Belief that the New Testament writers often used non-literal interpretation principles such as midrash, pesher, and allegory that were associated with the era of Second Temple Judaism.

***Sensus Plenior.*** Belief that there are fuller or hidden meanings in an Old Testament passage, usually meaning embedded by God that the Old Testament human authors did not understand. These fuller meanings cannot be discerned by studying the immediate context of a passage. Later revelation is needed to discover this meaning.

**Significance.** The importance or consequence of a text that stems from an author's meaning in a text.

**Single Meaning.** Belief that a text or passage has only one meaning, not multiple meanings. This is often linked with the authorial intent of a human author who wrote a passage.

**Single Meaning / Multiple Implications Approach.** Or "consistent contextual" view. Asserts that the New Testament writers relied upon the original meanings of the Old Testament writers and did not use Old Testament texts out of context. The meaning of a Bible text is one, yet there can be multiple implications or significances that are consistent with this one meaning. This approach is closely connected with grammatical-historical hermeneutics and is resistant to the idea of *sensus plenior* or fuller/hidden meanings in Bible texts.

**Text.** A written work that conveys the meaning of an author through the use of sign symbols.

**Type.** A divinely intended correspondence between a person, place, thing, or institution in the Old Testament and something greater in the New Testament. For example, Adam is a type of Jesus (see Rom. 5:14).

**Typology.** The study of types and correspondences in Scripture. This often involves the belief that the Old Testament contains types and shadows that are superseded by greater New Testament realities. Typology is often connected with the idea that the New Testament brings a change or transformation of the Bible storyline begun in the Old Testament.

**Willed Pattern of Meaning.** Involves the implications of a text that are consistent with the meaning of a text's author even if the author did not explicitly comprehend these implications. The implications are consistent with the spirit of what an author meant.

# GENERAL INDEX

# SCRIPTURE INDEX

318